always up to date

The law changes, but Nolo is always on top of it! We offer several ways to make sure you and your Nolo products are always up to date:

1   **Nolo's Legal Updater**

We'll send you an email whenever a new edition of your book is published! Sign up at **www.nolo.com/legalupdater**.

2   **Updates @ Nolo.com**

Check **www.nolo.com/update** to find recent changes in the law that affect the current edition of your book.

3   **Nolo Customer Service**

To make sure that this edition of the book is the most recent one, call us at **800-728-3555** and ask one of our friendly customer service representatives. Or find out at **www.nolo.com**.

please note

We believe accurate and current legal information should help you solve many of your own legal problems on a cost-efficient basis. But this text is not a substitute for personalized advice from a knowledgeable lawyer. If you want the help of a trained professional, consult an attorney licensed to practice in your state.

Parent Savvy

Straight answers to your family's financial,
legal & practical questions

by Nihara K. Choudhri, Esq.

edited by Amy DelPo

With parenting advice from **BabyCenter·**

5 0503 010832113

FIRST EDITION	NOVEMBER 2005
Editors	AMY DELPO
	MARCIA STEWART
Cover Design	CLEARY & PARTNERS
Book Design	SHERRI TAKAHARA
Index	THÉRÈSE SHERE
Proofreading	ROBERT WELLS
Printing	DELTA PRINTING SOLUTIONS, INC.

Choudhri, Nihara K.
   Parent savvy : straight answers to your family's financial, legal & practical questions / by Nihara Choudhri.-- 1st ed.
      p. cm.
   Includes bibliographical references.
   ISBN 1-4133-0368-4 (alk. paper)
    1. Child care--United States--Handbooks, manuals, etc. 2. Parents--United States--Finance, Personal--Handbooks, manuals, etc. 3. Parent and child (Law)--United States--Popular works. I. Title.

HQ778.63.C564 2005
649'.1'0242--dc22

                                                                              2005051815

Quantity sales: For information on bulk purchases or corporate premium sales, please contact the Special Sales Department. For academic sales or textbook adoptions, ask for Academic Sales. Call 800-955-4775 or write to Nolo, 950 Parker Street, Berkeley, CA 94710.

Acknowledgments

I would like to thank the following people:

My amazing editor at Nolo, Amy DelPo. A devoted mother of two children, Amy developed the idea for *Parent Savvy* and then worked tirelessly to make it readable and accessible. She took the wordy, lawyerly drafts I sent her and edited them with a fine hand, giving the book just the right voice, tone, and balance of information. Amy—You are now more a friend than a colleague, and I am truly indebted to you for your work on this book. It is just as much yours as it is mine.

Nolo Acquisitions Editor Marcia Stewart, who gave me the opportunity to work on *Parent Savvy* and become part of the Nolo family. Not only did Marcia make *Parent Savvy* a high-profile project at Nolo, she helped edit and organize the book with skill and finesse. Marcia—Thank you for your enthusiasm, hard work, and support.

BabyCenter.com Editor in Chief and Vice President for Editorial Jim Scott, for seeing the potential in this project and for having the creativity and vision to lend BabyCenter's support to the book.

Nolo editor and adoption attorney Emily Doskow, for reviewing the guardianship chapter.

Estate planning attorney Liza Hanks and Nolo Senior Vice President for Editorial Mary Randolph, for reviewing the estate planning part of this book.

Nolo editor and employment law expert Stephanie Bornstein, for reviewing the part of this book devoted to balancing work and family.

Nolo Managing Editor Janet Portman, for reviewing the sections of the book covering lead-based paint hazards.

Nolo Group Marketing Director Pat Jenkins, for overseeing the marketing and design efforts. Thanks also to Clark Miller, Brent Johnson, Lindsay Morton, and Sarah Grant for their help on the publicity and marketing front. And special thanks to Nolo Vice President of Sales and Marketing Tom Cosgrove, whose enthusiasm for this book is unflappable.

Sigrid Metson, Group Director, Nolo's Business Division, and Kelly Perri, Nolo's Business Development Manager, for introducing Nolo to BabyCenter.com, and for helping to bring *Parent Savvy* to so many different markets.

Everyone else at Nolo who worked on this book, including Joe Warner, for compiling the appendix; Jaleh Doane, for overseeing the book's production; Sherri Takahara and Susan Putney for designing and laying out the book; Robert Wells for proofreading the book; and Thérèse Shere for a very helpful index.

David Spitzkoff, of Spitzkoff and Associates in Roslyn Heights, New York, for checking every fact and figure in the tax section of this book without charging me a penny.

Jeff Herman, my talented agent, for helping launch my writing career, and for his hard work and his support.

My obstetricians, Shari Brasner and Isabel Blumberg, the best baby doctors in the world. Thank you for caring for me during my pregnancy and delivery, with so much gentleness and kindness. I will always be grateful to you both.

Aman's pediatrician, Ramon Murphy, who has been with us on trips to the emergency room and who has always taken our concerns seriously. Thank you for putting up with Aman's loud screaming during office appointments and with my many phone calls during Aman's first few months of life.

The many amazing Mommies who have provided me with their invaluable wisdom, advice, support, and companionship as I've navigated my way through the challenging journey of Mommy-dom: Barbie (and Jessica), Christine (and Isabella), Jeannie (and Sophie), Jen (and Lauren and Ryan), Lori (and Nicole), Melissa (and Aaron), Nadia (and Zan and Isa and Aadam), Shawna (and Trevor), Suroor (and Farah and Mariyam), and Yasmeen (and Ihsaam and Zareena).

My husband's family, for supporting me in all of my writing endeavors and for being wonderful grandparents, uncles, and aunts to Aman.

My family, for so very many reasons: Dad—for having faith in me and for assuring me that one of my books would one day hit the bestseller list. Sabu-dabu—for having such a big heart and for telling your friends that your big sister is a cool author. Naju-ju—for reading the first draft of my first book and sharing my life's ups and downs with me as if they were your own. Mom—for just about everything, but especially for giving up your Thursdays to care for Aman so that I could write. You are the best mother a kid could have, and I hope that someday I'll be even half as good.

My son, Aman, who is nothing less than a gift from God. I have been privileged to spend these two years almost inseparable from you, watching you grow from a round-faced baby with dimples in your elbows to a little boy who chases pigeons, collects rocks, and loves trains. My little Amu, you will never know just how precious you are. I would not trade these days with you for all the riches in the world.

Finally, and most importantly, my husband, Trin, who believed in this book from the beginning. Trin—my best friend, my life partner—Thank you for always supporting me. You are my rock and the love of my life. I would not be able to breathe (let alone write) without you.

Nihara Choudhri
October, 2005

Table of Contents

Parent Savvy, by Nihara Choudhri

Part 2
Mother's Milk
(And Your Right to Supply It)

Part 3
Balancing Work and Family

Part 4
Who's Minding the Baby?
Choosing and Managing Child Care

Part 7
Guardians, Wills, and Other Things to Do Just in Case

Part 8
Keeping Your Child Safe—At Home, On the Road, and in the Air

Appendix

Introduction by BabyCenter

Having a baby is a life-changing event, one that brings with it a universe of joys and challenges. That's why BabyCenter created its website and magazine—to help you find the information and support you need to raise healthy, happy children.

When the people at Nolo, a company committed to empowering consumers, came to us with an idea for a book that answers parents' legal, financial, and practical questions, we were intrigued. And when they told us the book would specifically tackle family leave, workplace rights, health insurance, taxes, saving for education, wills and guardians, child care, safety, and other pressing matters, we were sold. Parents need and want this information, but it's never before been available in one convenient place. We were thrilled to be asked to contribute to such an important resource. It's a perfect fit with the health, behavior, and hands-on care-giving information we already provide to parents.

If love and milk were enough to ensure your child's safety and well being, there wouldn't be a need for a book like *Parent Savvy*. But our world is complicated, and it's our job as parents to make decisions and take actions that are in the best interests of our children and families. *Parent Savvy* makes that job easier; it's a must-have resource that will help you parent more confidently in these challenging times.

Parent Savvy gives you the detailed, trustworthy legal, financial, and practical information you need, freeing your time for more important things, such as cuddling your newborn, playing hide-and-seek, and exploring your backyard or the world with your children. Here, you'll find time-saving tools, such as checklists and tips, that will help you answer tough questions and solve problems quickly. You'll also find tons of other useful resources, including many from BabyCenter.

We couldn't be happier to introduce you to *Parent Savvy*. We believe it will make your most important job—being a mom or dad—a lot easier and a lot more fun.

Linda Murray
Executive Editor, BabyCenter
October 2005

Introduction by the Author

When I was pregnant, the very first thing my husband and I purchased for our baby-on-the-way was not a crib or a changing table, but a rocking horse. We imagined our little boy giggling with delight as he rocked to and fro. And we thought about how nice it would look in his room, marking the change from a barely used den to a true nursery for our precious new addition. Thus we began our journey into parenthood, blissfully ignoring the practical realities and focusing instead on something whimsical and wonderful.

Then our son, Aman, arrived with tremendous fanfare. Life as we knew it was turned upside down. No more time for whimsical. My days became a blur of feeding, changing, nursing, and cuddling. It is not surprising, then, that we always put the bigger tasks—writing a will, for example, or setting up a college savings plan—on the back burner, postponing them for that imaginary day when we would have enough time and energy to focus on them. And then there were the practical tasks that couldn't be put off—such as making sure the baby products we purchased were safe and finding good child care once I returned to work. Squeezing in time to deal with those issues was a headache.

I looked for an all-in-one resource that would tell me what I needed to know—and only what I needed to know—to accomplish the practical tasks on my to do list. As it turned out, that resource did not exist . . .

until now. I wrote *Parent Savvy* for parents like me and you: Parents who are busy and overwhelmed sometimes, yet who want to make the best possible choices for their family. *Parent Savvy* fills a hole in the information available to parents. Bookstores have literally hundreds of books on everything from sleep to discipline to making healthy baby food—but no all-in-one resource providing answers to the practical questions that arise in the complicated life of every parent, answers to questions such as:

- How do I select a good doctor or midwife for myself? A good pediatrician for my child?
- How much maternity/paternity leave can I take, and how much of it will be paid?
- Are there any restrictions on where I can nurse in public?
- What are my rights at work as a parent? How can I protect myself against unfair treatment?
- Should I buy life insurance? And—if so—how much?
- How can I arrange for health insurance for my new baby?
- What is the best way to save for my child's education?
- Whom should I name to be my child's guardian in case the unthinkable happens?
- Do I need to write a will, and—if so—what are the most important things to cover?

- Should I hire a nanny or use a day care center? How do I make sure I get the best care possible?
- How can I best take advantage of the tax breaks available to parents?
- How can I make sure the baby products I buy are safe?

Parent Savvy answers these questions—and many many more. I have spent the past year writing *Parent Savvy*, and I have never learned as much (not even in law school!). Each chapter has provided me with invaluable information that I've been able to put to use immediately in my own life. After I completed Part 5 *(Saving for the High Cost of Learning)*, for example, I knew enough about our college savings options to feel comfortable opening a New York 529 college savings plan for Aman. My husband and I saved several hundred dollars in taxes in our first year alone, and we feel proud that we've set aside a little money to pay for college one day.

And when I was working on Part 6 *(The Dependent Exemption, Child Care Tax Breaks, and Other Baby Gifts From the IRS)*, I realized that we weren't taking full advantage of the money-saving tools available to us through my husband's employer. So we set up a dependent care account and a flexible health spending account—and this year we're paying for preschool and children's Tylenol with pretax dollars.

I could give you example after example of the ways in which the information in *Parent Savvy* has helped me make smart decisions for my own family. And I know that *Parent Savvy* will do the same for you. Whether you

are expecting your first child or are a parenting veteran with several children, you'll find answers to your questions here.

Parent Savvy is for all types of parents—those in traditional families and those in families that are more complicated. No matter what kind of parent you are—mother or father, birth or adoptive, straight or gay, married or single—*Parent Savvy* has information for you.

So without further ado, I am proud to announce the arrival of *Parent Savvy* (born in October 2005; approximately 2 pounds, 3 ounces, 9" long). May it be a useful new addition to your parenting bookshelf.

With my very warmest wishes for many wonderful years of parenting ahead,

Nihara Choudhri
October 2005

P.S. My son, Aman, is now two years old. The rocking horse is finally getting plenty of use, as Aman (and his little friends) delight in rocking to on fro on the "horsie" in the afternoons.

How to Use *Parent Savvy*

Welcome to *Parent Savvy,* your all-in-one reference for information about the practical side of parenting. Although you can read this book cover to cover, you certainly don't have to. This book was written so that you can open it and read what you need to know—and only what you need to know—about your particular question or problem of the moment. Once you've got your answer or solved your problem, put *Parent Savvy* back on your parenting bookshelf until the next issue or task arises.

In each part of the book, you'll find checklists designed for busy parents who need information quickly and efficiently. These lists condense the information in the chapter in a quick, action-oriented format. If you ever want more information than what is provided in the list, simply read the chapter itself. You'll find everything you need right there.

And for information that is snappy and useful, but beyond the main discussion, look for the following symbols:

ADDITIONAL RESOURCES tells you where you can go for more information about a particular subject. These resources include websites, books, organizations, and government agencies that have useful information and tools for parents.

TIPS gives you the inside scoop on an issue. Usually, it's a tip or a piece of practical advice that only people-in-the-know had—until now.

CAUTION alerts you to potential problems or pitfalls that less savvy parents sometimes fall prey to.

CROSS REFERENCE tells you that another section, chapter, or part of this book has information on a related subject that might interest you.

PROFESSIONAL tells you when it might be a good idea to get help or information from a professional—say, a lawyer or an accountant.

FAST FACTS gives you an interesting statistic or fact about the subject at hand.

BABYCENTER RESOURCES tells you about information and tools on Baby-Center.com that can help you. Usually, but not always, you can find this information on the *Parent Savvy* page at www.babycenter.com/parentsavvy.

BABYCENTER POLL tells you about the results of a BabyCenter.com poll relating to the subject matter at hand.

Each chapter in this book contains references to websites and organizations that are great resources for parents. In the appendix, you can find the all of these resources organized by topic.

Raising a child is one of the most rewarding experiences in any parent's life—but it can also be the stuff of nerves and headaches when you don't have the right tools and resources. *Parent Savvy* is one resource that will help you deal with everyday issues and problems so that you can spend your time and energy enjoying your children. Because that's what it's all about.

I. Before Baby (And Just After)

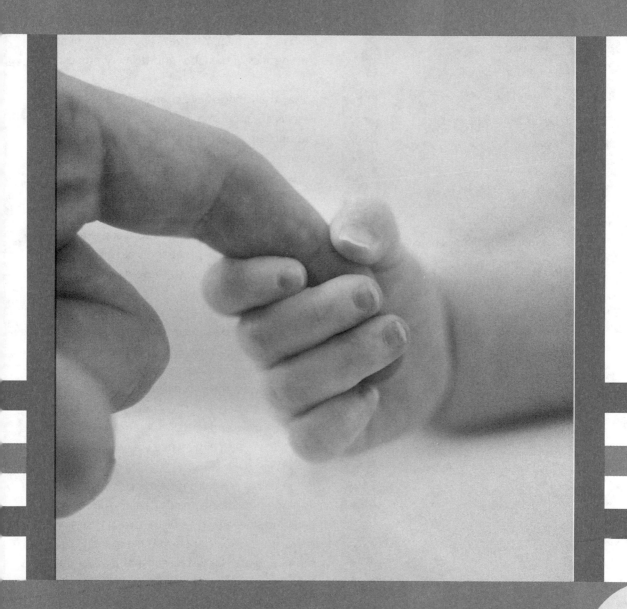

I

Contents

*N*ot too long ago, pregnant women in this country had limited options when it came to how and where they delivered their babies: Just about every woman received care from an obstetrician and gave birth in a hospital, with very little control over the specifics of the labor and delivery process.

To say that things have changed in recent years is an understatement. Soon-to-be mothers are reclaiming control over pregnancy and childbirth and making their own decisions about issues such as prenatal testing, episiotomies, epidurals and anesthesia, and electronic fetal monitoring during labor. You might have strong feelings about some or all of these medical procedures already—or you might prefer to leave these decisions in a doctor's hands.

Whatever your personal philosophy and approach, it is important that you do some research before selecting an obstetric health care provider and a place to deliver your baby. The choices you make will affect your prenatal and maternity care and partially determine what kind of childbirth experience you will have.

If you feel overwhelmed at the prospect of finding an obstetric health care provider and deciding where to give birth, take a deep breath and relax. (If you're the expectant mom, you are going to hear that a lot in the next few months!) The chapters that follow will help you make the decisions at hand. You'll learn about the options (a certified nurse midwife versus an obstetrician, for example, or a hospital versus a home birth) and how to decide which ones are right for you. You'll also find information about newborn testing, how to select a pediatrician, and how to get a birth certificate and a Social Security number for your new addition.

 BABYCENTER RESOURCES

If you're looking for a comprehensive resource on pregnancy and childbirth. BabyCenter.com provides answers to all of your pregnancy and childbirth-related questions, from fetal development to pregnancy dos and don'ts. Just log on to www .babycenter.com/topicsaz to get started. Also, see the book *BabyCenter's Essential Guide to Pregnancy and Birth: Expert Advice and Real-World Wisdom from the Top Pregnancy and Parenting Resource,* by Linda J. Murray, Jim Scott, and Leah Hennen (Rodale Books, 2005).

Be Sure to Check Out Your Health Insurance Coverage

Before you can tackle the important tasks of selecting an obstetrician or midwife and a place to deliver your baby, you'll need to understand the terms of your health insurance coverage so that you can make financially prudent health care decisions. See Chapter 15 for complete details on health insurance coverage during pregnancy, how to enroll your baby in your employer-sponsored group plan, and insurance rights when you lose or quit a job.

 ADDITIONAL RESOURCES

Your state department of health can provide useful information on doctors, midwifes, hospitals, and birth centers. If you want to check the licensing and certification of a physician, midwife, hospital, or birth center, get in touch with your state department of health. You can also find a complete list of state departments of health at the federal Food and Drug Administration (FDA) website at www.fda .gov/oca/sthealth.htm. ■

Chapter I

Selecting a Doctor or Midwife

As soon as you find out you're pregnant, you'll need to decide who's going to provide prenatal care and deliver your baby—that is, who will be your obstetric health care provider. While most women use an obstetrician, there are other options, including midwives. You'll be seeing your obstetric health care provider on a regular basis, especially in the final weeks of pregnancy, and relying on this person's professional guidance at a significant time in your life. This chapter will help you find a physician or midwife whose qualifications you respect and whose approach to pregnancy and childbirth is in line with your own.

Basic Information About Obstetric Health Care Providers

Although the remainder of this chapter discusses each type of obstetric health care provider in detail, this section provides a preview—along with factors to consider when choosing among them.

I just found out that I am pregnant. What are my options when it comes to providers? There are five main types of obstetric health care providers:

- **Obstetricians.** Physicians who have extensive training in pregnancy and childbirth-related issues. Obstetricians are bona fide specialists in the baby-delivering business and are by far the most popular type of provider.

- **Maternal-fetal medicine specialists (or perinatologists).** Obstetricians who have several additional years of specialized training in high-risk pregnancies. Look for a specialist if the expectant mother is in a high-risk category—for example, she is older than 35, delivered a baby prematurely, or has a history of health problems.

- **Family physicians.** Doctors who manage a wide range of basic medical conditions and can provide everything from prenatal care for Mom to pediatric care for baby. You might choose a family physician if you already have a relationship with a doctor whom you know and trust.

- **Certified nurse midwives.** Registered nurses with special training in midwifery (the art of welcoming babies into the world). You might select a certified nurse midwife if you're hoping for a natural delivery, but also want a provider with formal medical training who practices in a hospital setting.

- **Direct entry midwives (or lay midwives).** People who have childbirth experience and perhaps even some formal midwifery education, but who lack a nursing degree or other professional medical qualification. You might choose a direct entry midwife if you want a home delivery.

 FAST FACTS

Curious to know whom other soon-to-be mothers are choosing? According to a report issued by the Centers for Disease Control, in 2002 more than 91% of pregnant mothers in the United States chose physicians to deliver their babies.

Choosing a Physician or Midwife: Key Issues to Consider

- What will your insurance cover?
- In what type of setting would you like to deliver your baby?
- Is the pregnancy high risk?
- What type of prenatal tests do you want?
- What type of delivery do you envision?

What factors should I consider when selecting an obstetric health care provider? Choosing an obstetric health care provider is a personal decision, one based on your values, beliefs, and priorities, as well as your age and health. Here are some factors to consider:

- **What will your health insurance cover?** Your health insurance may only cover in-network providers and hospitals—or make you pay substantially more to go outside the plan's network. Some plans will not cover birth center deliveries, and many plans do not cover home births. See Chapter 15 for details on these and other health insurance issues.

- **Where would you like to deliver your baby?** This is an important question because the provider you choose will determine where you will deliver. Most obstetricians, for example, have privileges at only one or two hospitals. And some midwives handle home births only. So it's best to decide in advance where you would like to deliver and then choose a health care provider accordingly. If you've heard great things about a particular hospital, make sure the doctor you choose has privileges there.

- **Is the pregnancy high risk—for example, are you older than 40 or a diabetic?** If so, your options are likely limited to an obstetrician or maternal-fetal medicine specialist.

- **What types of prenatal tests—such as amniocentesis—do you want?** The more high tech you want the care to be, the more it makes sense for you to choose an obstetrician or maternal-fetal medicine specialist.
- **What type of delivery do you envision?** Your views on issues such as medication and setting will determine the type of obstetrical health care provider that's best for you.

The sections that follow discuss each option in detail and provide you with a list of questions to ask before choosing an obstetric health care provider.

Obstetricians

For most pregnant women in this country, obstetricians are the easy choice. Obstetricians (or OBs) have years of medical school and residency training under their belts, and prenatal and maternity care is their life's work. What's more, OBs are experts at using medical and technological advances to make pregnancy and childbirth safe and relatively pain free. For these reasons, obstetricians deliver the vast majority (about 80%) of babies in the United States.

What are the advantages of using an obstetrician?

There are plenty of reasons why the vast majority of soon-to-be mothers opt for an obstetrician:

What Makes a Pregnancy High Risk?

Periodically in this book, we refer to high-risk and low-risk pregnancies. Some relatively common situations that make a pregnancy high risk include the following:
- a preexisting medical problem, such as heart or kidney disease
- advanced age of the mother
- carrying twins
- a problem that develops during pregnancy, such as pregnancy-induced hypertension, gestational diabetes, a baby in breech position near or on your due date, or placenta previa
- a previous preterm delivery.

Add a Doula to Your Team

A doula is an experienced labor coach who provides continuous emotional and physical support to the mother during and after labor. Although a hospital nurse might come and go, a doula will remain by your side for every single contraction—holding your hand, massaging your back, and doing everything she can to ease your pain and discomfort. A doula can also take some pressure off your partner, who may be unsure of how best to support and care for you while you are in labor.

Several research studies have associated the use of doulas with lower C-section rates, lower rates of forceps and vacuum extraction deliveries, shorter labors, less need for Pitocin or other labor-inducing drugs, and fewer episiotomies. And after labor, women who have used doulas to help out at home are less likely to experience postpartum depression. In addition, they breastfeed for longer periods of time.

Ask your doctor, midwife, or childbirth class teacher if they have suggestions for doulas. Before you choose a doula, be sure to check out her training, experience, fees (at least a few hundred dollars or more depending on where you live), the types of services she provides (before, during, and after birth), and her personal philosophy on issues such as epidurals and medications during labor. Get recommendations and talk with other mothers who have used this doula.

If you want to learn more about doulas, you can find plenty of helpful articles at the Doulas of North America website at www.dona.org.

Look for the "Consumer Information" link. This website also includes a list of certified doulas.

- Obstetricians are physicians with extensive specialized training in prenatal and maternity care.
- Obstetricians are skilled in using medical technology—from prenatal testing for genetic disorders to epidural anesthesia during your labor.
- In most cases, obstetricians will not pressure you to consider natural childbirth.

What are the disadvantages?

Before deciding to use an obstetrician as your health care provider, consider the following issues:

- Some people feel that obstetricians intervene too much in the natural process of childbirth.
- Drug-free childbirth is not a priority. If your goal is to give birth with as little pain relief as possible, an obstetrician might not support or encourage your decision as much as a certified nurse midwife might.
- You may not get personalized attention during pregnancy or labor. Hand-holding and emotional support aren't taught at medical school. Your busy OB might have only a few minutes to spend with you during prenatal visits and may just drop in occasionally during the nonpushing stage of your labor. A certified nurse midwife, on the other hand, would probably provide you with substantial support and nurturing during pregnancy and labor.
- Obstetricians deliver only in hospitals. With very few exceptions, obstetricians do not practice in birth centers. So if

you want an obstetrician to deliver your child, you'll almost certainly have to choose a hospital. Still, all is not lost. Many hospitals now offer services similar to birth centers. You can learn more about hospital deliveries in Chapter 2.

What are the education and training requirements for obstetricians?

To qualify as an obstetrician, a physician must have graduated from medical school and completed at a four-year residency in obstetrics and gynecology.

Is there a difference between an obstetrician and an OB/GYN?

The term "OB/GYN" is an abbreviation for "obstetrician/gynecologist." All obstetricians are actually OB/GYNs because they are trained in both obstetrics (pregnancy and labor issues) as well as gynecology (the care of the female reproductive system) during their residencies.

 TIPS

Not every OB/GYN delivers babies. Because obstetrics and gynecology is a somewhat broad field, some OB/GYNs choose to limit their practices to just a couple of areas. For example, an OB/GYN might decide to concentrate only on gynecology—which means that the doctor who handles an expectant mom's annual Pap smear might refer her to a colleague instead of delivering the baby.

What does it mean for an obstetrician to be licensed?

Each state's department of health licenses the physicians in that state, so the particular requirements vary. Generally speaking, however, a license means that the physician graduated from an accredited medical school and successfully completed the United States Medical Licensing Examinations. You can find out whether an obstetrician has an up-to-date license by contacting your state's medical licensing board. For contact information, log on to the Federation of State Medical Boards website at www.fsmb.org, click on "State Medical Board Info," and then click on "Board Directory."

A license doesn't mean as much as you might think. Although it would be illegal for an obstetrician to practice without a valid license, having a license is no indication that an obstetrician is well-trained in the art of delivering babies. This is because physician licensing is not specialty-specific. In other words, your state government will issue the same license to a surgeon, a pediatrician, and an obstetrician.

Find out whether an obstetrician is board certified on your own. You don't have to wait until your initial consultation to learn whether your obstetrician is board certified. Simply log on to the American Board of Medical Specialties' website at www.abms. org and click on "Who's Certified" in the left-hand navigation bar. You'll be able to learn whether your doctor is board certified with just a couple of clicks of your mouse after you register on the site. For more detailed information on board certification status, you'll have to send a written request plus a small fee to the American Board of Obstetrics and Gynecology. Contact the board directly at 214-871-1619 or log on to the Board's website at www.abog.org to learn more about this service.

What does it mean for an obstetrician to be board certified?

Board certification is a good sign that an obstetrician knows his or her stuff. To achieve this qualification, the American Board of Obstetrics and Gynecology requires an obstetrician to pass both a written and oral examination and keep up with rigorous recertification requirements. An obstetrician can apply for board certification only after he or she has practiced for at least two years after completing a residency.

How can I find a good obstetrician? The first thing to do is to decide what you are looking for. Does it matter whether the obstetrician is a man or a woman? Is it important that the doctor's office be close to your home? (You'll be visiting the office often, especially the last month or so of your pregnancy, when a long drive might not be appealing.) Do you need an obstetrician who can speak your native language? Would you prefer that your obstetrician work in a small, intimate practice, or would you feel more comfortable with a larger, or hospital-based, obstetrics group? Are you looking for an obstetrician who encourages natural childbirth?

With your basic requirements in hand, ask friends, family members, and your family physician for recommendations. If you have a regular gynecologist whom you trust and respect, check to see whether his or her practice includes obstetrics. If not, get a recommendation.

If you still need names, check out the American Board of Medical Specialties' website at www.abms.org to get a list of board-certified obstetricians in your area.

☑ CHECKLIST

Finding and Checking Out a Physician or Midwife

Whether you decide to go with an obstetrician, midwife, or some combination, here's how to find a good one:

❑ Make a clear list of what you want in an obstetric health care provider, including office characteristics, such as size, services, and location; specialties, such as high-risk pregnancies; admitting privileges in a particular hospital; personal characteristics of provider (man or woman, speaks your native language, sensitive to your preferences for labor and delivery); and anything else that's important.

❑ Get recommendations from family, friends, coworkers, and your other doctors and health care providers—or check the list of obstetric health care providers participating in your health insurance plan.

❑ Check out websites (if any) of potential obstetricians or midwives for basic information on the practice and staff training and qualifications.

❑ Call the office if there's no website or if you need additional information on insurance accepted, fees and payment arrangements, hospital affiliation.

❑ Make sure your health insurance covers the specific provider you want to use or the type of provider, such as a midwife.

❑ Schedule an initial appointment with the doctor or midwife and come prepared with a list of questions.

CAUTION

Check with your health insurance company in advance. It may provide you with complete benefits only if you choose an in-network obstetrician. If so, use the plan's list of participating obstetricians as the starting point for your search. See Chapter 15 for more on health insurance.

Will I need a referral from my primary care doctor to see an obstetrician?
Fortunately, most health insurance companies do not require a referral. But to be on the safe side, ask.

I've made an appointment for an initial consultation with an obstetrician I am considering. What questions should I ask?
There are numerous medical books about pregnancy that discuss in depth what questions you should ask prospective obstetricians to ensure you get the type of medical care and delivery that you want—for example, their views on medication during labor, their experience with high-risk pregnancies, and what labor procedures they routinely use, such as fetal monitoring. Because those questions veer so much into the medical realm, this book does not cover them.

On the practical side, ask about:
- What insurance does the obstetrician accept?

- What are the obstetrician's fees and payment arrangements? Most, but not all, obstetricians will bill your insurance company directly.
- At what hospital does the obstetrician deliver? An obstetrician can deliver at hospital(s) only at which he or she has privileges, so when you choose an obstetrician, you are also choosing a hospital. Make sure you are as comfortable with the hospital as you are with the obstetrician (see Chapter 2 for guidance on choosing a hospital).
- What is the obstetrician's educational and residency training background? You might be able to get a copy of the obstetrician's curriculum vitae online at the American Board of Obstetrics and Gynecology's website at www.abog.com. If not, the office staff should be able to fill you in.
- How long has the obstetrician been in practice?
- Is the obstetrician board certified?
- How many other obstetricians are in the practice? It's good to choose an obstetrician with at least one partner, so that there will be someone whom you can contact in the event that your obstetrician is unavailable. Ask someone in the office whether he or she can tell you about the other obstetricians in the group or whether there is an information packet he or she can send you about the practice. After all, there's a good chance that one of your obstetrician's partners will end up delivering your baby.

- What are the obstetrician's office hours? If your work schedule makes daytime doctor's appointments difficult, make sure you'll be able to schedule prenatal visits in the mornings, evenings, or on weekends.

- What happens if the obstetrician is not on call when you go into labor? Not even a solo obstetrician is available around the clock, seven days a week, so find out who else could deliver your baby if your chosen doctor is not on duty. Find out as much as you can about the obstetrician's partners (or colleagues) who could be handling your care when you go into labor. Do these obstetricians take a similar approach to labor and delivery as the obstetrician you are considering? Are these obstetricians just as well trained and experienced? Do these other obstetricians also accept your health insurance? Will you have an opportunity to meet these obstetricians during your prenatal visits?

- What happens if you have a question or concern between visits? Can you page your obstetrician at any time? Will the obstetrician respond to questions via email?

Understanding a Physician's C-Section Rate and Other Statistics

There's not much point to asking for numbers—such as a doctor's C-section rate—if you don't know the national average for comparison. Here are some relevant numbers from a Centers for Disease Control and Prevention report on birth trends (published in 2002) that you might want to have on hand as a point of comparison:

- Electronic fetal monitoring was used in more than 85% of deliveries.
- More than 20% of deliveries were the result of labor induction.
- Nearly 6% of deliveries required forceps or vacuum extraction.
- More than 26% of deliveries were C-sections—the highest rate ever. (The U.S. Department of Health and Human Services (DHHS) has said that the current C-section rate is too high. DHHS has set a target rate of 15% for first-time C-sections by 2010.)

And if you're wondering how many women rely on pain medication during labor, a recent study reported by the *New England Journal of Medicine* found that 60% of all laboring women use epidural anesthesia.

Check first with the office staff.
Don't pester your obstetrician for information that you can learn on your own or by talking to the office staff. Obstetricians are busy people—so you probably won't get your relationship off to a good start if you arrive at the office with a three-page list of questions. Although you'll want to discuss the medical issues with the doctor, bring practical questions first to the staff.

 BABYCENTER RESOURCES

If you'd like a cheat sheet.
BabyCenter.com's "Ob-Gyn or Family Physician Interview Sheet" lists questions to ask when interviewing obstetricians, such as the types of tests the physician routinely performs during pregnancy. This form includes the medical side of the equation that this book does not cover. You can find a copy on the *Parent Savvy* page of Babycenter.com (www .babycenter.com/parentsavvy).

I want to check up on the obstetrician I am considering. Do you have any advice?
Find out if any state's medical board has disciplined the obstetrician. A medical board's disciplinary committee is responsible for reviewing patient complaints against obstetricians and other physicians, and it deals with everything from incompetence and negligence (for example, an obstetrician's failure to perform a C-section when medically necessary) to fraud and substance abuse (such as an obstetrician who delivers babies while under the influence of narcotics).

To find out about disciplinary actions, use the Federation of State Medical Boards' "Doc Info" tool, which provides access to a physician's disciplinary history in all 50 states, as well as disciplinary information from the U.S. Department of Health and Human Services and Drug Enforcement Administration. You can find the tool at www.docinfo.org. You will have to pay $9.95 per search, but you'll have your answer with just a few clicks of your mouse.

Alternatively, you can contact your state's medical board directly. (For state-by-state contact information, go to the Federation of State Medical Boards' website at www .fsmb.org, click on "State Medical Board Info," and then click on "Board Directory.") Bear in mind, however, that your state's medical board may tell you about disciplinary actions taken by your own state's board only—not actions taken in other states.

If you need some more help researching your obstetrician. ChoiceTrust (www.choicetrust .com) and HealthGrades (www .healthgrades.com) are Internet services that rate health care professionals. For less than $10, either company will give you an instant online report telling you: when and where the obstetrician completed medical school and residency training, whether the obstetrician is board certified, and whether there have been any disciplinary actions against the obstetrician.

How can I find out about an obstetrician's medical malpractice history?

Some states have services that provide this information. For example, Maryland's Health Care Alternative Dispute Resolution Office can tell you the number of malpractice suits against a Maryland physician, as well as the outcome of each suit. Contact your state's department of health or medical board to find out whether your state offers such a service.

Preparing a Birth Plan

A birth plan is a document that sets forth your preferences when it comes to important labor and delivery issues, such as having an episiotomy or using pain medication.

Having a birth plan is no guarantee that your labor and delivery will go exactly as you hope. Still, putting your views down in writing will help you to communicate them to your doctor or midwife. You can then discuss what is and isn't possible given your medical needs and the policies of the facility where you plan to give birth. And if you're a first-timer with no set views when it comes to labor and delivery, creating a birth plan can help you to understand your choices and plan ahead.

Although birth plans tend to be individualized documents, you don't have to start with a blank slate. BabyCenter.com's "Create Your Own Birth Plan" tool allows you to put together a birth plan in minutes—covering everything from the type of birth environment you want (the number of people present, videotaping the birth) to your feelings regarding inducing labor. You can find a copy on the *Parent Savvy* page of Babycenter.com (www.babycenter.com/parentsavvy). Another wonderful resource is *Pregnancy Today*'s online birth planner, available for free at www .birthplan.com.

Review your birth plan with your provider, making sure what you are asking for is both safe and practical. For example, your obstetrician might tell you that your hospital requires all laboring mothers to be on IV hydration—so there isn't much point in saying that you don't want IV hydration in your birth plan unless you switch facilities. Revise your birth plan as necessary and give a final copy to your obstetrical health care provider. Tuck a couple of copies into the bag you have packed for the hospital or birth center.

The obstetrician I am considering has been sued for medical malpractice twice. Does this mean I should find another obstetrician? Not necessarily. Obstetricians are among the most frequently sued of all physicians—and the more babies an obstetrician has delivered, the more likely it is that he or she has been sued more than once. Before rejecting an obstetrician solely because of a lawsuit, contact an attorney for help in finding out the basis for the lawsuit and the outcome.

I'm unhappy with the obstetrician I've selected. Can I switch to a different obstetrician midway through my pregnancy? Absolutely. Sometimes, it takes a few prenatal visits to learn that the doctor who initially seemed perfect isn't meeting your needs. Once you've switched, your new obstetrician will obtain a copy of your file from your prior one, so you won't have to repeat tests and procedures.

Maternal-Fetal Medicine Specialists

If you already know that you fall into a high-risk category—perhaps you've got a health condition that makes your pregnancy challenging—the safest course of action is to begin seeing a maternal-fetal medicine specialist from day one. These specialists are also known as perinatologists, and they are obstetricians with advanced training in managing high-risk pregnancies.

CROSS REFERENCE

Read the Obstetricians section, above. Many of the same issues and considerations that arise when choosing an obstetrician apply to maternal-fetal medicine specialists.

What are the education and training requirements for maternal-fetal medicine specialists?
These specialists complete the same training as standard obstetricians and then complete fellowships in maternal-fetal medicine.

Are there board certification standards for maternal-fetal medicine specialists?
Yes. The American Board of Obstetrics and Gynecology awards board certification only to maternal-fetal medicine specialists who do all of the following:

- complete at least three years of training in maternal-fetal medicine following a basic obstetrics and gynecology residency
- pass a written and oral examination in maternal-fetal medicine, and
- maintain certification.

You can learn more about the certification requirements for maternal-fetal medicine specialists at the American Board of Obstetrics and Gynecology's website at www.abog.org.

How can I find a good maternal-fetal medicine specialist?

First, find out whether you really need this kind of specialist by talking to your family physician, gynecologist, or obstetrician. And then ask these same individuals for a referral (indeed, your health insurance may require one).

What questions should I ask before choosing a maternal-fetal medicine specialist?

Find out if the individual you are considering has expertise in the particular area that makes your pregnancy high risk. For example, if you're carrying triplets, ask about the specialist's experience with multiple births.

In addition, ask many of the same questions that you would ask when choosing an obstetrician, but remember that in your case, a doctor's baby smarts and book smarts are infinitely more important than his or her bedside manner.

Also bear in mind that your choices are limited, because there may be only a handful of specialists in your area who handle the type of complications or risks that you are experiencing.

ADDITIONAL RESOURCES

To learn more about maternal-fetal medicine. The Society for Maternal-Fetal Medicine, a non-profit organization dedicated to improving perinatal care, has useful information on its website at www.smfm.org about when and why you might consider choosing a maternal-fetal medicine specialist over a standard obstetrician.

Family Physicians

You might be surprised to learn that family physicians provide prenatal and maternity care. Family physicians practice medicine the old-fashioned way, treating a wide range of basic health conditions and offering preventive care for people of all ages. In some parts of the country, it's standard for women to continue using their usual family physician when they become pregnant. What's particularly nice about using a family physician is that he or she can continue serving as your doctor even after you've delivered. In fact, you could even decide to have your family physician care for your newborn, instead of giving the job to a pediatrician whom you don't know nearly as well. See Chapter 3 for advice on choosing a doctor for your baby.

CROSS REFERENCE

Read Obstetricians, above. Even if you've already decided to have a family physician deliver your baby, some of the information that applies to obstetricians applies to family physicians as well.

What are the education and training requirements for family physicians?
The doctor must have graduated from medical school and completed a three-year residency training program in family medicine.

Can family physicians be board certified?
Yes. To do so, a family physician must successfully complete the American Board of Family Medicine certifying examination (in addition to meeting the requirements listed above). You can learn more about the training and certification requirements for family physicians at the American Board of Family Medicine's website at www.abfp.org.

How can I find a good family physician?
If you don't already have a family physician, or if your physician does not include obstetrics as part of his or her practice, then ask friends and relatives for recommendations. Look for a family physician who has delivered a baby for someone you know. After all, the family physician who does a terrific job managing your Aunt Martha's arthritis might not be particu-larly experienced or qualified when it comes to pregnancy and childbirth.

Also refer to the American Board of Family Medicine's website at www.abfp.org and click on "Directory of Diplomates" in the left-hand navigation bar. There you will find a list of board-certified family physicians in your area.

Once you have a list of prospective family physicians, do two things: First, find out whether the doctor is included within your health insurance network. Second, call the doctor's office to see whether obstetrics is part of the doctor's practice. Although family physicians are qualified to deliver babies, only about 28% of them actually care for women during pregnancy and childbirth.

What questions should I ask before choosing a family physician to manage my pregnancy and delivery?
Ask the same questions you would ask if you were interviewing an obstetrician (see **Obstetricians**, above). In addition, it's especially important to inquire about the doctor's expertise with prenatal care and deliveries. Ask the physician to give you some estimate of the number of deliveries he or she has handled, and find out whether prenatal care and childbirth is a substantial part of his or her practice. Also ask about experience handling pregnancy-related complications. Find out under what circumstances the physician would ask an obstetrician to comanage your case or even take over your care completely. Finally, ask whether the physician would be able to care for your new baby—or whether you should look for a separate pediatrician for your little one.

Certified Nurse Midwives

More and more women these days view labor and delivery as an emotional and meaningful experience, not just as the final hurdle that must be endured to enter the ranks of parenthood. If you have strong feelings about how you want your childbirth to proceed—for example, you want to deliver your child without pain medication or other medical interventions—then a certified nurse midwife may be the right choice for you.

Certified nurse midwives are registered nurses who specialize in pregnancy, labor, and delivery. Although they emphasize natural childbirth, most practice in hospital settings and have the medical training and clinical experience necessary to handle the average delivery. Certified nurse midwives deliver nearly one in ten American babies.

What are the advantages of using a certified nurse midwife?

There are some compelling reasons to consider a certified nurse midwife as your provider:

- If you want a natural delivery, a certified nurse midwife will encourage and support that choice.
- Certified nurse midwives place less emphasis on tests and medical interventions than do physicians. For example, recent statistics show that certified nurse midwives have significantly lower episiotomy and C-section rates than do their physician peers.
- Certified nurse midwives offer personal and highly individualized care. In contrast to a busy obstetrician, who might see you for only a few minutes during each visit, a certified nurse midwife will spend the time necessary to answer your questions and explain the changes pregnancy brings. Typically, a certified nurse midwife will stay by Mom's side during most of labor, instead of popping by every hour or two as an obstetrician might.
- Studies have shown that it's just as safe for a healthy woman with a normal pregnancy to deliver with a certified nurse midwife as an obstetrician.

What are the disadvantages?

Although a growing number of women are turning to certified nurse midwives for pregnancy and childbirth care, there are some reasons why most soon-to-be mothers choose physicians instead:

- Certified nurse midwives do not attend medical school or complete a residency training program.
- A certified nurse midwife must call an obstetrician if complications arise during pregnancy or childbirth. When you have an obstetrician handling your care, on the other hand, that individual can usually do whatever is needed—including an emergency C-section—without assistance.
- Some, but certainly not all, certified nurse midwives might frown on your decision to have pain medication during labor. Even if you have every intention to proceed with a natural childbirth, you may find the pain so unbearable that you need medication to continue.

 TIPS

Find out who is your certified nurse midwife's consulting obstetrician. It's a good idea to talk with this person before your due date in case complications develop during childbirth.

What are the education and training requirements for certified nurse midwives?
Certified nurse midwives must do both of the following:

- Graduate from a nurse-midwifery education program accredited by the American College of Nurse-Midwives Division of Accreditation. Although the precise requirements vary, most programs require students to obtain a bachelor's degree in nursing and a master's degree in midwifery.
- Pass a national certification examination administered by the American College of Nurse Midwives Certification Council (ACC). You can learn more about this certification examination at the ACC's website at www.accmidwife.org.

Are there licensing requirements for certified nurse midwives?
Yes. Every state licenses certified nurse midwives, and most states require that they have a consultation and referral arrangement with a physician who can step in if a pregnancy or delivery becomes complicated. To learn your state's licensing requirements, contact your state's department of health, which can also tell you whether the certified nurse midwife you are considering has a valid license.

Will my health insurance cover a certified nurse midwife?
Probably—most insurance companies do. In fact, 33 states require private insurance companies to cover nurse-midwifery services. And Medicaid covers these services in all states. Check with your insurance company to find out more.

I would like to use a certified nurse midwife, but I'm not sure about natural childbirth. What are my options?
Provided you deliver in a hospital, epidural anesthesia and other pain medication options

will be available to you even if you use a certified nurse midwife. (An anesthesiologist—and not your certified nurse midwife—would administer the epidural.)

TIPS

Talk to your certified nurse midwife about pain medication in advance. Depending on the certified nurse midwife you choose, she may recommend that you select an obstetrician to provide your care instead. At a minimum, you'll want to get a sense of the certified nurse midwife's view on epidurals and other pain management interventions—because you will want someone who will support your choices on this important issue.

My pregnancy is high risk. Can I still choose a certified nurse midwife?
Probably not. Certified nurse midwives do not have the training and expertise necessary to handle pregnancy and childbirth complications. In fact, depending on the nature of your pregnancy, you may even require the services of a maternal-fetal medicine specialist rather than an obstetrician. But if you're intent on having a certified nurse midwife involved in your care, talk to your obstetrician and/or maternal-fetal medicine specialist about the possibility of having a certified nurse midwife comanage your care. In addition, check with your insurance company to see whether it covers this type of an arrangement.

How can I find a good certified nurse midwife?
Try word of mouth. Ask your gynecologist. Check the American College of Nurse-Midwives' (ACNM) online directory by going to www.midwife.org and clicking on the "Find a Midwife" link in the upper navigation bar. The ACNM also has a variety of useful publications available on nurse-midwifery.

Once you've put together a list of certified nurse midwives in your area, contact your health insurance company to see whether your plan covers them.

What questions should I ask when choosing a certified nurse midwife?
Although it is important to have a connection with your certified nurse midwife, don't base your decision solely on the nurse midwife's bedside manner. Ask the same questions you would ask if you were interviewing an obstetrician. In addition, find out:

• Does the certified nurse midwife accept your health insurance?

• Does the certified nurse midwife practice at the place where you would like to deliver?

• How long has the certified nurse midwife been practicing? Look for someone who's been delivering babies for at least two years—and not just practicing obstetrical nursing.

• Is the certified nurse midwife certified by the American College of Nurse-Midwives (ACNM)? Certification indicates that the nurse midwife has received training in providing prenatal and maternity care and has passed a rigorous examination in nurse midwifery. To check whether your nurse midwife is certified, contact the ACNM Certification Council directly at 301-459-1321 or log on to www.accmid-wife.org. There, click on "Verify Certification" and then click on "Purchase Primary Source Verification."

- Does the certified nurse midwife have a consultation and referral arrangement with an obstetrician? Who is it? (You'll want to check this doctor out, too.) Under what circumstances would the midwife call in the obstetrician to comanage or take over your care?
- What happens if complications arise during delivery? Will there be an obstetrician and an anesthesiologist on call? If you'll be delivering at a birth center, find out which hospital you would go to in the event of complications.
- Will the certified nurse midwife help you develop and implement a birth plan? (See "Preparing a Birth Plan," above.)

CROSS REFERENCE

If you want a home birth. See **Direct Entry Midwives**, below, for a list of questions to ask a midwife whom you are considering for a home birth.

BABYCENTER RESOURCES

For a list of certified nurse midwife interview questions. BabyCenter.com has an interview sheet to help you get the information you need to choose the best certified nurse midwife for you. You can find a copy on the *Parent Savvy* page of Babycenter.com (www.babycenter.com/parent savvy).

Direct Entry Midwives

If you want a home delivery, you might decide to use a direct entry midwife (also known as a lay midwife). Unlike certified nurse midwives, direct entry midwives are not registered nurses and have had no nursing training. Their expertise in pregnancy and childbirth comes from apprenticeships, workshops, formal classes, or some combination of these.

What does the law have to say about direct entry midwives?

The legal status of direct entry midwifery varies dramatically from state to state. Twenty-one states issue licenses or otherwise legally regulate direct entry midwives, including California and Florida. Other states, such as Maryland and North Carolina, strictly prohibit the practice of direct entry midwifery. And some states don't take a position, neither issuing licenses nor restricting the practice.

ADDITIONAL RESOURCES

For a state-by-state list of midwifery laws. Citizens for Midwifery is a nonprofit organization that promotes the use of midwives for prenatal and maternity care. You can find a chart summarizing state midwifery laws on the organization's website at www.cfmidwifery.org. This website has a lot of other useful information and resources on midwives.

Are direct entry midwives credentialed?

There are two main types of credentials that a direct entry midwife may have: certified midwife or certified professional midwife.

The American College of Nurse Midwives (ACNM) offers the certified midwife credential to people who graduate from an ACNM-accredited midwifery program and who pass a certification examination.

CAUTION

Don't confuse certified midwives with certified nurse midwives. Certified midwives are not nurses and have had no formal training in nursing. To learn more about the certified midwife credential, log on to www.accmidwife.org.

The North American Registry of Midwives (NARM), an international certification agency for direct entry midwives, offers the certified professional midwife credential to people who meet certain educational and clinical experience standard (including training in either a formal program or through an apprenticeship) and who pass a certification examination. You can learn more about the certified professional midwife credential at NARM's website at www.narm.org.

CAUTION

A credential is no substitute for a license. Even credentialed midwives need licenses to practice in states that require it. And if your state prohibits direct entry midwifery, it is illegal for even a credentialed direct entry midwife to practice there.

How can I find a good direct entry midwife?
If you don't know anyone who can recommend someone, contact the North American Registry of Midwives at 888-842-4784 for a list of certified professional midwives in your area. For information on this organization, see their website www.narm.org. In addition, contact the Midwives Alliance of North America, a professional organization representing midwives in the United States and Canada, via email at membership@ mana.org. The organization will send you a list of member midwives in your state. It cannot, however, verify that people on the list are credentialed, nor can it confirm they have the appropriate education and experience to provide prenatal and maternity care.

What questions should I ask before choosing a direct entry midwife?
Ask the same questions that you would ask when choosing an obstetrician or a certified nurse midwife. In addition, find out the following:

- Is the midwife credentialed? You can contact one of the organizations listed above for this information.
- Does the midwife have any formal training?

- If the midwife attended a formal program, is it accredited by either the American College of Nurse Midwives Division of Accreditation or the Midwifery Education Accreditation Council (MEAC)? The MEAC is a nonprofit organization that the U.S. Department of Education has approved as an accrediting agency. To date, MEAC has accredited only nine midwifery education programs. Find out more at MEAC's website at www.meacschools.org.
- What types of apprenticeships or other hands-on training and experience does the midwife have? This question is particularly important with midwives who have no formal education. Find out how many babies the midwife has delivered entirely on her own.
- Ask for the names and contact information of women whose babies the midwife has recently delivered so you can check out their experiences. In particular, ask for a patient who had complications during her delivery so that you can get a personal account of how the midwife would transfer your care to a physician.

Informed Consent: A Patient's Rights and Responsibilities

A health care provider cannot perform any nonemergency procedure on your body—for example, amniocentesis or induction of labor—without your informed consent. Your health care provider must give you enough information for you to decide whether to undergo the procedure. Although the specifics of informed consent laws vary, all states require your health care provider to explain to you the following:

- the procedure's purpose
- the risks and benefits
- any alternatives and the risks and benefits of those alternatives, and
- the consequences of choosing not to have the procedure.

As a practical matter, your provider may not always give you clear explanations of the procedures he or she recommends. It's your job to make sure you consent to medical procedures only after you gather enough information to make your decision.

So, if you have questions, don't be shy about asking them. You are legally entitled to answers. The law also gives you the right to request and receive a copy of your medical records and to seek a second opinion any time that you are uncertain about your health care provider's recommendations.

Educate yourself about your care and communicate questions and concerns promptly to your health care provider. Being proactive about your prenatal and maternity care will make you feel more comfortable with the care you receive and will ensure that you make educated decisions.

If you want more information about a particular procedure your health care provider has recommended, do a search on WebMD .com. ■

Chapter 2

Deciding Where to Give Birth

No law requires women to give birth in a hospital. In fact, plenty of women have successfully given birth to babies everywhere from taxicabs to cornfields, but here are the three most conventional options:

- **Hospitals.** Where the vast majority of babies in the United States are born. There's more variety to hospitals than you might think: There are community hospitals and teaching hospitals, hospitals with separate birthing facilities, and even hospitals with doulas on staff.

- **Birth centers.** Independent, cozy facilities that emphasize natural birth and respect for the mother's wishes. Birth centers can be a good middle-ground option for women who want the comforts of home but the reassurance of on-site medical equipment and on-call obstetricians.

- **Home.** A safe option for many women. This chapter explains your different choices and how to get the best care no matter where you decide to give birth.

FAST FACTS

Hospital deliveries are still the norm. According to a Centers for Disease Control and Prevention report, in 2002 more than 99% of American babies were born in hospitals. Among the 1% nonhospital births, 65% were at home and 27% were in free-standing birthing centers.

Hospitals

Most pregnant women feel that a hospital is the safest choice, particularly because immediate medical attention is always available if something unexpected happens, such as the need for an emergency C-section. Although all hospitals offer similar levels of basic care for the average delivery, they vary in the amenities they offer, the approach they take to labor and delivery, and the level of newborn care they offer.

What are the advantages of delivering my child in a hospital?

If you're wondering why 99 out of every 100 American babies is born in a hospital setting, here are a few good reasons:

- You'll be cared for by a team of medical professionals. In addition to your own obstetric health care provider, your hospital will have obstetric nurses, anesthesiologists, and pediatricians on hand to care for you and your newborn.
- You'll have immediate access to emergency medical care. If you opt for a birth center delivery or home birth, on the other hand, you'll have to be transferred to a hospital in an emergency.
- You'll have access to an epidural. Unless you're certain that you won't want an epidural no matter how bad the pain becomes, it's good to know that an anesthesiologist can be called in if you need some pain relief.

What are the disadvantages?

Here are a few drawbacks to consider when deciding whether a hospital is the right delivery facility for you:

- You'll have significantly less control. Many hospitals have established policies when it comes to issues such as whether you may eat and drink during labor, the number of friends and family members who may attend your birth, and whether you may videotape your delivery. At a birth center, on the other hand, your personal preferences are more respected. And at home, you have the most control of all.

- You may be subjected to routine medical procedures, such as fetal monitoring and intravenous hydration (IV). If you feel strongly that labor is a natural process that requires as little medical intervention as possible, a hospital may not be the best place for you.
- You may not be able to labor, deliver, and recover in the same room. However, many hospitals now offer the option of birthing suites so that you can get the medical benefits of a hospital delivery while still enjoying some of the comforts of a birth center.
- The hospital's policies may interfere with your plans to bond with and breastfeed your baby. Depending on the hospital you choose, your baby may be whisked away to the nursery for examination and observation shortly after the birth. The hospital staff might also feed your baby formula or sugar water unless you specifically instruct them not to do so.
- A hospital can feel like a sterile and impersonal place to deliver a child. Because childbirth is an intimate and emotional experience, it might feel strange to have your baby in an institutional environment.

How can I find a list of hospitals in my area that offer obstetric care?

A terrific resource is the U.S. News/American Hospital Association National Directory, available online at www.usnews.com/usnews/health/hospitals/hosp_home.htm. The search feature allows you to look for hospitals by state and specialty. What's particularly nice is that you can search specifically for hospitals with neonatal intensive care units and birthing rooms—two key features that expectant parents often look for.

What factors should I consider when choosing a hospital for my delivery?
Below you'll find a list of things to think about before selecting a hospital. You can find the answers to many of these questions on your own, by browsing the hospital's website, or reviewing the hospital's informational brochure.

The Basics

- Is the hospital conveniently located to your home?
- Does the hospital accept your health insurance? How much should you expect to pay if you have a normal vaginal delivery? (Keep in mind that you won't know the exact costs until after you give birth, but it's a good idea to get a rough idea of costs before you give birth.)
- Is the hospital accredited by the Joint Commission on Accreditation of Healthcare Organizations (JCAHO)? Accreditation means that a hospital has met national health and safety standards and passed on-site reviews of its facilities and services. You can find out whether your hospital is accredited at the JCAHO's website at www.jcaho.org. Click on "Quality Check" in the left-hand navigation bar.

Staff and Specialties

- Is there a maternal-fetal medicine specialist on staff? If your labor becomes unusually complicated, your obstetrician may need to call for a specialist's help.
- Is an on-site anesthesiologist available 24 hours a day? If the hospital's anesthesiologist is simply on call—rather than on site—it may take longer for you to receive pain relief. Also find out whether the anesthesiologist specializes in obstetrics.
- Is an obstetrician always on hand? In the event that you need some immediate assistance and your own obstetrician is en route, it's important that the hospital have an obstetrician who can step in.
- Does the hospital have a neonatal intensive care unit (NICU)? Only hospitals with NICUs have the capacity to care for premature infants or babies with significant health complications. Level II NICU's are acceptable, but if you want a hospital with the best possible facilities, look for a Level III NICU, the highest level available. If the hospital you're considering has no NICU, ask what happens when babies require high-level medical attention.
- What is the nurse-to-patient ratio? Unless you have a doula, you'll be relying heavily on your obstetric nurse. The American College of Obstetricians and Gynecologists recommends a one-to-two ratio during early labor and one-to-one ratio during the pushing stage.
- Is the hospital a teaching hospital? Although teaching hospitals tend to offer the most cutting-edge services and

well-qualified staff, some people aren't comfortable with the visits from obstetric residents and medical students.

Hospital Policies, Practices, and Rooms

- What is the hospital's approach to labor and delivery? There are many medical and comfort issues to consider, from whether you will be allowed to move about the hospital during labor to the hospital's policy on using drugs such as Pitocin to speed up labor.
- What is the hospital's C-section rate? (See "Understanding a Physician's C-Section Rate and Other Statistics" in Chapter 1.)
- Will you have the option of laboring, delivering, and recovering in the same room? These rooms are typically called "birthing rooms" or "birthing suites."
- Are private rooms available? Will you have to pay extra for one?
- How many visitors will be allowed during your labor? Will your partner be allowed to stay with you at all times, even if you have a C-section?
- Will the hospital allow you to use a doula (labor coach) or does it have doulas on staff?
- Will the hospital allow you to videotape your delivery? Some hospitals prohibit videotaping for legal reasons.
- Will you be able to share a room with your newborn? This is called "rooming in." This is particularly important if you plan to breastfeed.

- Are there reasonable sleeping arrangements for your partner or other family member to remain with you overnight?

Care After the Birth

- What breastfeeding support does the hospital offer?
- What tests are routinely conducted on newborns? Typical ones include a hearing test and genetic tests. (See Chapter 4 for more about this issue.)
- Does the hospital offer childbirth or newborn care classes?

Once you've identified a hospital as a possibility, take a tour. While there, pay attention to your surroundings and the staff members you meet. Is the hospital clean? Do you feel comfortable inside the facilities? Are staff members pleasant and helpful?

If you have other children, ask if they provide a tour for siblings.

I've found a hospital where I'd like to deliver my baby. What's the next step?
Preregister with the hospital's labor and delivery department by completing a set of forms, which will ask for everything from your address and Social Security number to your health insurance information. You will also have to complete some consent forms. Taking these steps ahead of time will make it easier for you to get settled when you arrive at the hospital to deliver your child.

Finding and Checking Out a Hospital or Birth Center

Whether you decide to go with a hospital or independent birth center, here's how to find a good one:

❑ Make a clear list of what you want and need in a place to deliver your child.

❑ Get recommendations from family, friends, coworkers, and your doctors and health care providers—or check the list of hospitals and birth centers participating in your health insurance plan.

❑ Check out websites (if any) of potential hospitals or birth centers for basic information on the practice and staff training and qualifications.

❑ Call the facility if there's no website or if you need additional information on insurance accepted, fees and payment arrangements, or hospital affiliation.

❑ Make sure your health insurance covers the specific hospital or birth center you want to use, and get complete information on fees and administrative procedures.

❑ Schedule an initial appointment and come prepared with a list of questions.

Birth Centers

If you have visions of delivering your baby naturally in a cozy, home-like environment, a birth center may be a wonderful choice for you. Birth centers emphasize drug- and intervention-free deliveries, and they offer comforts—such as whirlpool baths and massage—to help ease the pain of labor. Moms get to labor, deliver, and recover in the same room.

For many expectant parents, a birth center offers the best of both worlds—an intimate and personal setting that can also handle minor medical situations and transfer you to a hospital immediately for more advanced medical care should the need arise.

 CAUTION

You can't use a birth center if your pregnancy is high risk. Because birth centers aren't equipped to perform C-sections or handle complications during labor, they only accept women whose pregnancies are low risk. This means that if you're carrying twins, for example, or you've previously had a preterm delivery, you won't be able to deliver at a birth center.

What are the advantages of delivering my child in a birth center?

There are many reasons why you might decide to deliver your baby in a birth center rather than a traditional hospital setting:

- You'll have as natural a delivery as possible. A birthing center won't use Pitocin to speed up your contractions, for example, and you won't be tied down to an IV or an electronic fetal monitor during your labor process. Birth centers focus on natural childbirth and won't administer epidural anesthesia under any circumstances.
- You'll enjoy many of the comforts of home during your labor and delivery. In marked contrast to the sterile, institutional nature of many hospitals, quality birth centers often seem like charming country inns—complete with overstuffed chairs, flowering plants, and soothing artwork. Your room might have a rocking chair, a Jacuzzi tub, or even a bed large enough for your partner to lie down beside you as you work through your contractions.
- You'll receive lots of personal attention and care during your labor. In contrast to a hospital, where obstetricians generally just look in on their patients only occasionally until the pushing stage of labor, your birth center's certified nurse midwife will probably remain by your side for your entire labor.
- You'll labor, deliver, and recover in the same room. If you opt for a traditional hospital, you'll probably deliver in one room and then be moved to another room once your baby is born.
- You'll have more control over your labor and delivery. For example, you'll get to decide how many family members and friends you'd like to have present. You'll also get to wear your own clothes, eat and drink normally, and move about during labor.
- You'll be able to stay with your child in the first few hours. In contrast to hospital staff, who often whisk newborns away for testing and observation, birth center professionals allow parents to remain with their babies from the moment they are born. They will examine the baby in your presence and give you the chance to cuddle and bond with your little one in those important few minutes and hours after delivery.
- You'll get plenty of breastfeeding support. Birth center staff will give you the opportunity to breastfeed right away and assist you if you need help.
- You might end up saving some money. If you have to pay some or all of the costs of your delivery out of pocket, you'll be happy to know that it costs about one third less to have your baby at a birth center instead of a hospital.

What are the disadvantages?

Although birth centers can provide wonderful childbirth experiences for many women, there are two important drawbacks to consider:

- You'll have to be transferred to a hospital if complications arise. Indeed, fully 12% of women who begin labor in a birth center are transferred to a hospital midcourse, and the statistics are even higher for first-time births.

- You won't be able to get an epidural even if you find the pain unbearable. Many women plan on delivering without medication, only to be overwhelmed by pain once childbirth starts. Because birth centers do not offer epidurals, you'd have to be transferred to a hospital to get one.

I want to deliver in a birth center. What is the next step?

Call a birth center in your area and talk to one of the staff members about whether you are a good candidate for a nonhospital delivery. The staff member will probably ask you a few basic questions about your health history—such as whether you suffer from high blood pressure or if you've previously delivered by C-section. If there are no obvious high-risk indicators, you'll be able to schedule an initial prenatal visit at the center. One of the center's health professionals will do a comprehensive health assessment, including a complete physical exam and blood testing, to determine whether a birth center delivery would be a safe choice for you.

The center will keep tabs on you as your pregnancy progresses to ensure that you remain a good candidate for a birth center delivery. If things change, the center may refer you to an obstetrician for a hospital-based delivery.

Is there a licensing process for birth centers?

Currently, three quarters of all states license birth centers (Minnesota and Montana are among the states that don't). To find out what your state does—and to check whether the birth center you are considering has an up-to-date license—contact your state's health department.

My state licenses birth centers, but I know these standards are minimal. How do I find out if the center I am considering is top-notch?

Look for accreditation by the Commission for the Accreditation of Birth Centers (CABC). The CABC accredits centers only after a thorough review that includes the facilities, staff, and philosophy. To date, the CABC has accredited only 50 centers. For more information, visit the CABC's website at www.birthcenters.org.

Will my insurance company cover a birth center?

Most major health insurers—such as Aetna/US Healthcare and Blue Cross/Blue Shield—cover birth centers. Contact your insurance company to learn more.

How can I find a birth center in my area?
A good place to start is the National Association of Childbearing Center's online directory at www.birthcenters.org. This organization supports birth centers by developing quality standards, educating the public about birth centers, and advocating on behalf of birth centers with respect to insurance and legal issues. The NACC directory lists birth centers by state and tells you which ones have CABC accreditation. Log on to www.birthcenters.org and click on the link marked "Find A Birth Center."

By looking on the Internet, I've found a birth center that seems like a good fit for me. Now I'd like to interview the director and tour the facility. What basic questions should I ask?
The interview will likely take a while, because there is a lot of information to gather:

- Is the center accredited by the CABC?
- How long has the center been in operation?
- How many deliveries has the center handled?
- How many deliveries take place in an average month?
- What are the center's fees?
- Do the fees include prenatal care, childbirth, and postnatal care?
- Are the following items included in the fees or do you have to pay extra charges for them: childbirth education classes, lodging and food, doula services, lactation consultant services, massage therapy, the consulting obstetrician's fees, and the consulting pediatrician's fees?

- Does the center accept your insurance?
- What fees will you owe if transferred to a hospital?
- Does the center offer childbirth education classes? Other classes?
- Will the center help you apply for a birth certificate and Social Security number for you child?
- What are the staff's qualifications and experience levels? Certified nurse midwives provide the majority of care at birth centers. Some centers also employ obstetricians and pediatricians on a consulting basis. If you can, meet with staff members and make sure you are comfortable with them.
- What types of medical situations can the birth center's professionals handle on their own? Birth centers are usually equipped to take care of the basics, such as repairing a tear, for example. Some birth centers can even handle more complex medical situations, such as resuscitating a newborn.
- Is a consulting obstetrician on call at all times? Find out what will happen in the event of a complication—will the obstetrician actually come to the center or just offer advice over the phone?

What about prenatal care?
As part of your interview, be sure to get details on the kind of prenatal care the birth center offers, including the number and frequency of your prenatal appointments and what types of tests the center can perform. Ask about the circumstances under which you'd switch your care to an obstetrician.

What about the labor and delivery process itself at birthing centers?

Be sure to tour the part of the center where you will labor and deliver and ask detailed questions about the labor and delivery process. Find out:

- Who will be present during labor and delivery? Birth centers pride themselves on offering more support and encouragement during the labor process than hospitals, so you should be able to count on having a certified nurse midwife by your side for much of the process.
- How will the center make you comfortable during labor? Is there a whirlpool for you to relax in? Will massage therapy be available?
- What pain medications will be available? You won't be able to find an official birth center that administers epidurals, but some centers do offer non-narcotic pain medication.
- Will the center do an episiotomy if necessary? As a general rule, birth centers take a no-intervention approach to childbirth—and this usually means no episiotomies.
- How will the center monitor the baby's health during labor and delivery? Hospitals rely on electronic fetal monitors to assess the baby's well-being; birth centers usually use hand-held ultrasound devices.
- Will the center allow you to eat and drink during labor? Will it allow you to move around? Most hospitals have strict limitations on eating and drinking during labor, preferring to hydrate women

through an intravenous line. But most birth centers let women do whatever feels natural when it comes to eating, drinking, and moving.

- Will the center allow as many family members and friends as you wish to be present? If you have another child whom you'd like to include, be sure to ask about this.

I'm concerned that I might need to be transferred to a hospital. What then?

This is another area to cover when visiting a birth center. Find the answers to the following questions:

- Under what circumstances would you be transferred to a hospital?
- Which hospital does the center use? Call your insurance company and make sure the hospital would be covered if you needed to be transferred there.
- Do the center's certified nurse midwives have admitting privileges at that hospital? If not, then the hospital's on-call obstetrician would likely take over your care.
- What are the center's statistics on transfer rates? A center's overall transfer rate should be in the neighborhood of 12%; but the rate for first-time mothers can be substantially higher.

What should I ask about post-delivery at a birth center?

You definitely want to find out what happens after delivery at a birth center, including the answers to the following questions:

- Who will examine your baby? Does the center have a consulting pediatrician?
- What tests does the center perform on newborns? If the center does not conduct a basic hearing test and screening for genetic disorders, will the center make arrangements for you to have these tests performed at your local hospital?
- What happens if you baby needs immediate pediatric attention? Will the center's consulting pediatrician be called in, or will you and your new baby be taken to a hospital?
- What kind of postpartum care will you and your baby receive? How long will you be able to stay at the center? Will your spouse, your other child, or friends or family members be allowed to stay with you?
- What breastfeeding support does the center offer? Does the center have a lactation consultant or experienced nurse on staff to assist you?

Before leaving the center, ask the director for the names of at least three mothers who have used the center's services. To get a sense of what happens when complications arise, ask for the name of one mother who began laboring at the center but ended up being transferred to a hospital.

I like the idea of a birth center delivery, but I want to have access to an epidural in case my labor is very difficult. What are my options?

Epidural anesthesia runs counter to the natural birth philosophy of birth centers, so this will not be an option for you at an official birth center. However, some hospitals are now creating their own centers that offer the best of both worlds—including epidurals. For example, St. John's Hospital in Illinois offers doula services and massage therapy to laboring mothers while at the same time providing top-notch medical care by obstetricians and anesthesiologists.

ADDITIONAL RESOURCES

To learn more about birth center deliveries. You can find information and view videos of birth center deliveries at the National Association of Childbearing Centers' website at www.birth-centers.org.

Home Births

Although the majority of American women deliver their babies in hospitals, most women around the world continue to give birth at home—surrounded by family members and attended to by caring midwives. This section will help you decide whether a home birth is right for you and will give you the information you need to ensure that your home birth is safe for you and your baby.

What are the advantages of giving birth at home?

There are two main reasons why you might want to consider a home birth over other alternatives: You'll have complete control over your labor and delivery, and you'll labor, deliver, and recover in a comfortable and familiar environment.

What are the disadvantages of home birth?

There is a reason most American women choose against delivering at home. The disadvantages are significant:

- Your choices of an obstetric health care provider will be limited. Not many health professionals handle home births. You'll be hard-pressed to find a physician who's willing to deliver your baby at home; the same holds true for certified nurse midwives. Likely, your only choice will be a direct entry midwife. And depending on the state in which you live, direct entry midwifery may be illegal.
- Immediate medical attention will not be available if complications arise. Although most women with low-risk pregnancies have uneventful childbirths, there is always the possibility of a complication that threatens your health or the health of your baby. With a home birth, you'll have to risk the delay of getting to a hospital for care.
- You won't be able to get an epidural—no matter how painful labor gets. Although you may be committed to the idea of natural childbirth, you might change your mind once you experience the intensity of labor contractions (many women do). You'll need to be transferred to a hospital if the pain becomes too intense.

What factors should I consider when deciding whether home birth is for me?

The decision of where to give birth is a personal one. Still, it's important to take practical considerations into account. For example, is your home close to a hospital? Home birth is a reasonably safe choice if you can drive to a good hospital in a few minutes. But if it will take more than 20 minutes to get to a quality medical facility, then reconsider.

In addition, home birth is reasonable only for women with low-risk pregnancies. Consult an obstetrician or certified nurse midwife before you make your final decision.

Find out how much it will cost. Will your health insurance cover it? You may have heard that home births are generally much more economical than hospital births. However, your out-of-pocket costs may be higher with a home birth if your insurance doesn't cover the tab.

Finally, do a little research to make sure you truly understand and are comfortable with what it means to give birth at home. A good starting point is the American College of Nurse-Midwives (ACNM), which has a committee dedicated to home birth. You can contact the ACNM at 240-485-1800 or log on to its website at www.acnm.org.

What questions should I ask when choosing an obstetric health care provider for my home birth?

When you give birth at home, your obstetrical health care provider (usually a direct entry midwife) is the only health professional who will be immediately available to assist you and your newborn baby. Find out the answers to the following questions:

- How many home births has the provider handled? Look for someone who has delivered at least 50 babies in a home environment.
- What complications has the provider handled alone? For example, has the provider ever resuscitated an infant? What medical equipment does the provider use?
- What will happen if your baby or you require immediate medical attention? Find out which hospital and which obstetrician will take over your care—and make sure they are covered by your insurance.
- Under what circumstances would the provider refer you to an obstetrician or certified nurse midwife for a hospital birth?
- What types of preparations will you have to make for your home birth? Will the provider help you to gather the necessary supplies?
- What kind of postbirth support does the provider give? For example, will the provider help with cleanup and laundry after the delivery? Will the provider make postpartum visits?
- Will the provider help you apply for a birth certificate and Social Security number?

In addition, find out who will examine the baby immediately after birth and who will conduct newborn testing. If you're not comfortable with having your obstetric health care provider examine your baby, find a pediatrician who will come to your home. And you may also need to arrange for a hearing test and genetic screening on your own.

Ask for references—including someone who suffered complications during her home birth and had to be transferred to a hospital midcourse.

ADDITIONAL RESOURCES

To learn more about home birth. Two excellent books on the subject are Rahima Baldwin's *Special Delivery: A Guide to Creating the Birth You Want for You and Your Baby* (Celestial Arts) and Diana Korte and Robert M. Scaer's *A Good Birth, A Safe Birth* (Harvard Common Press). Another good resource, if you can find it, is Sheila Kitzinger's out-of-print book, *Homebirth* (Dk Publishing). ■

Chapter 3

Choosing a Pediatrician

Once you've selected an obstetric health care provider and a place to deliver your baby, you'll have at least one more key medical decision to make: Choosing a doctor for your little one. Not only will this person treat your child's medical problems and handle regular checkups and immunizations, he or she will give you advice on parenting issues—such as how best to handle your child's picky eating—that are not strictly medical in nature.

 FAST FACTS

Plenty of doctor visits in your future. On average, new parents visit their baby's doctor 11 times in the first year.

When should I begin looking for a doctor for my baby?
Ideally, you should line up your baby's doctor before you give birth. This is because a doctor will have to examine your baby short-

ly after birth. To allow for time to interview prospective physicians, not to mention the possibility of a premature birth, start looking about three to four months before your baby's due date. Some popular pediatricians limit the number of new babies they accept in their practice each month—another good reason to start your search early.

What are my choices when it comes to doctors who could care for my baby?
Your two main options are a pediatrician or a family physician.
- **Pediatricians.** Physicians specially trained in caring for infants, children, teenagers, and young adults. To become a pediatrician, a physician must complete medical school and a three-year pediatrics residency. Pediatricians are the most popular choice for parents.
- **Family physicians.** Doctors with training in the basic medical problems that affect people of all ages. To become a family physician, a doctor must graduate from medical school and complete a three-year family medicine residency. The great thing about choosing a family physician as your child's doctor is that

every member of your family can be cared for by one doctor whom you all know and trust.

How can I find a good doctor for my baby? As always, the first step is to ask friends and family members for recommendations. In addition, there are a couple of free online referral services that you can use:

- The American Board of Pediatrics (ABP) website has a list of board-certified pediatricians in your area. Log on to www.abp.org and click on the link marked "Locate a Board-Certified Pediatrician."
- The American Board of Family Medicine's website has a list of board-certified family physicians in your area. Log on to www.theabfm.org and click on "Find a Diplomate."

My friends have given me the names of some possible physicians for my child. What is the next step?

Do some research. We've provided three lists of questions for you: One for the office staff, one for the doctor, and one that you can deal with on your own. If you're worried that you'll seem silly visiting a doctor before your baby is even born, don't be. Doctors expect soon-to-be parents to do this.

Questions for the office staff:

- What health insurance does the doctor accept?
- Where did the doctor attend medical school? When did he or she graduate?
- Where and when did the doctor complete residency training?

- Where and when did the doctor obtain a license to practice?
- What are the office hours? Any weekend hours?
- Is the doctor a fellow of the American Academy of Pediatrics? To become a fellow, a pediatrician must be board certified or have some similar qualification (such as certification by the Royal College of Physicians and Surgeons in Canada).
- Who are the other physicians in the group? What are their qualifications? Most physicians these days practice in group settings in which the group members cover for one another. So when you pick a doctor, you are also picking a group.
- Does the office have an advice nurse on call?
- Does the office organize support groups for new parents?

Questions for the doctor:

- Will the doctor examine your newborn in the hospital (or wherever you choose to deliver)? This is a nice service, for it can be comforting to have a familiar person answer your initial questions and respond to your concerns right after you've given birth.
- How does the doctor feel about parenting issues that are important to you? Such issues include breastfeeding, circumcision, immunizations, alternative medicine (such as acupuncture or homeopathy), and attachment parenting (such as cosleeping). Although parent-

ing issues may not seem as important as medical ones right now, they will once your baby arrives. For example, if you don't want to breastfeed your baby, you want a doctor who will support your choice, not make you feel guilty.

- How do you get questions answered between appointments? Can you call or email your doctor with your concerns, or will your doctor ask you to hold any nonemergency questions until your next scheduled appointment? How quickly will your call be returned if your question does not involve an immediate health crisis? (A good turnaround time is 24 to 48 hours for these types of calls.) Does the doctor provide access to a 24-hour advice service?
- Is the doctor—or someone from the group—on call around the clock to offer guidance in the event your child becomes sick or injured after hours? How quickly will your call be returned if you are concerned about an immediate health problem?
- Does the doctor offer same-day appointments to children who are ill?
- If your child requires immediate medical attention, to what hospital will the doctor admit your child?

When you interview the doctor, ask yourself how you feel about the doctor as a person. Did you trust what the doctor had to say? Would you feel comfortable phoning the doctor to ask about nonemergency issues, such as your baby's difficulty weaning to a bottle or your toddler's sleep terrors? Having a good relationship with your child's doctor will go a long way toward keeping your child in good health—and yourself sane.

When you visit the office, see if you are comfortable there. Is it clean and pleasantly decorated, with plenty of toys and books to occupy your baby? Is the atmosphere calm and supportive?

Questions you can answer on your own:

- Is the doctor's office conveniently located to your home, with easy parking?
- Is the doctor board certified? For pediatricians, you can find out through the American Board of Pediatrics by logging onto www.abp.org and clicking on the link marked "Verification of Certification." For family physicians, you can find out through the American Board of Family Medicine by logging onto www.theabfm .org and clicking on "Find a Diplomate."
- Is the doctor in good standing with your state's medical licensing board? To find out, contact your state's medical board. For contact information, look at the Federation of State Medical Boards' website at www.fsmb.org.

If you'd like an interview checklist. BabyCenter.com has an interview sheet that can help you cover all the bases during your pre-birth consultation. You can find a copy on the *Parent Savvy* page of Babycenter.com (www .babycenter.com/parentsavvy).

For some terrific advice on your baby's health. If you're looking for as much parenting guidance as you can get, you might want to add the American Academy of Pediatrics website (www.aap.org) to your favorites folder. The Parent Center section has helpful information on everything from teething to separation anxiety. ■

Chapter 4
Medical Tests for Your Newborn

Shortly after birth, someone will examine your baby to see if he or she is in good health and suffered no trauma during the delivery. Your newborn will receive eye drops (usually erythromycin) to prevent infection and a Vitamin K injection to help his or her blood to clot. Your child will also be given a hearing test and be screened for certain genetic disorders.

The precise newborn testing that your baby will undergo will depend on the state in which you live and the facility where you deliver. No federal law sets a nationwide standard for newborn testing; each state has established its screening requirements—and these requirements vary. For example, if you give birth in Virginia, your newborn will be screened for nine genetic disorders; but if you deliver your baby across the border in West Virginia, your newborn will be tested for only four.

What newborn tests do most states require?
All states currently require testing for phenylketonuria (PKU) and hypothyroidism—two genetic disorders that have a dramatic effect on a baby's brain development if left untreated. Most states also require testing

for galactosemia, a genetic disorder that can cause infant death or mental retardation if left untreated. More than 40 states require testing for sickle cell anemia, and more than 25 states mandate testing for congenital adrenal hyperplasia (CAH) (a deficiency of certain hormones).

In addition, most states require that newborns be screened for hearing loss. Thirty-six states require that newborns be given a hepatitis vaccine before leaving the hospital. And a couple of states mandate HIV testing for babies.

How can I learn what my state requires?
The National Newborn Screening and Genetics Resource Center—an organization dedicated to providing information and education about newborn screening and genetics—provides state-specific newborn screening information at http://genes-r-us.uthscsa.edu/resources/consumer/statemap.htm. There, you can find a link to each state's newborn screening program website.

Your doctor or midwife can tell you what newborn tests are routinely given at the hospital you plan to use.

What tests do health experts recommend?
A panel of experts convened by the U.S. Department of Health and Human Services and the March of Dimes recommends newborns be screened for 30 genetic disorders that can be detected through a simple blood test. These disorders include phenylketonuria (PKU), hypothyroidism, cystic fibrosis, sickle cell anemia, and galactosemia. All of the disorders can be treated using relatively simple interventions, such as changing a baby's diet or feeding more frequently. Early intervention can literally mean the difference between life and death for affected children.

The Centers for Disease Control and Prevention, the March of Dimes, and the American Academy of Pediatrics also recommend that all newborns be tested for early hearing loss before leaving the hospital.

FAST FACTS

Hundreds of babies fall through the cracks. Each year, approximately 1,000 babies born with treatable genetic disorders are not diagnosed early enough to prevent the terrible consequences of these disorders, which range from problems with brain development to death.

ADDITIONAL RESOURCES

To learn more about recommended newborn testing. The March of Dimes, an organization whose mission is to prevent birth defects and infant mortality, provides information about newborn screening on its website at www.marchofdimes.com/pnhec/298_834.asp.

My state falls short of the expert recommendations. What should I do?
Few states mandate the comprehensive newborn screening that health experts recommend. If you would like your baby to be tested for more disorders than your state law currently requires, discuss this with your doctor or midwife. See if you can make arrangements with a laboratory for supplemental newborn screening. The cost is quite low: For example, the Institute of Metabolic Disease at Baylor University (800-4BAYLOR) will test your newborn for 30 genetic disorders for about $25. You can find a list of organizations that offer supplemental newborn screening at the National Newborn Screening and Genetics Resource Center's website at http://genes-r-us.uthscsa.edu/resources/newborn/commercial.htm.

Genetic disorders are quite rare. When deciding whether to pursue supplemental newborn screening, bear in mind that only one in about every 5,600 babies is born with a genetic disorder.

To find out if your state offers an exemption to newborn genetic testing. The National Conference of State Legislatures has a state-by-state summary of opt-out laws on its website at www.ncsl.org/programs/health/screeningprivacy.htm. ■

I do not want my baby tested for genetic disorders. What are my rights?

Although you generally have the freedom to make medical decisions affecting your own body, you don't have the same broad rights when it comes to your baby's health. This means that you can only opt out of mandatory genetic testing for your newborn if your state provides for an exemption. Currently, 23 states offer exemptions to parents with religious objections; two states—Florida and Wyoming—offer exemptions to parents who object on any ground.

Chapter 5
Applying for a Birth Certificate

A birth certificate is a legal document that serves as proof of your baby's name, date of birth, citizenship status, and parentage. You will need a copy of your child's birth certificate when enrolling your child in school, applying for a passport for your child, traveling with your child by plane, and many other important events in your child's life.

How do I apply for a birth certificate for my baby?
You will need to complete a birth registration form and submit it to the department in charge of issuing birth certificates in your state (often called the department of vital statistics). The birth registration form will ask you for your name, the name of your child's other parent, your child's date of birth, and your child's name.

What's in a Name?
In most states, you may give your child any first, middle, and last name you like. Whether you are married or not, you don't have to give your baby the last name of either parent if you don't want to, and the child does not have to have the father's last name to be "legitimate."

If you deliver your baby in a hospital, the hospital staff or a representative of the local health department will provide you with a copy of the birth registration form, ask you to complete it before discharge, and submit it to the appropriate agency. Some states automatically send new parents a copy of the birth certificate; in other states, parents have to make a formal request to the pertinent department and pay a small fee.

If the baby isn't born in a medical facility, the mother and/or the physician or midwife assisting in the delivery must notify health officials of the birth. Contact your state's department of health or bureau of vital statistics for more information.

Having trouble choosing a name for your baby? Check out Baby-Center.com's Baby Name Finder, a tool that lets you search for baby names by country of origin, first letter, number of syllables, and (of course) gender. See the *Parent Savvy* page of Babycenter.com (www.babycenter.com/parent savvy) for details. Once you've come up with your top choices, you can ask your friends and family members for their input by creating your very own baby name poll at BabyCenter.com.

Special legal issues for un-married couples and lesbian and gay couples. For a general overview of legal issues facing unmarried couples having children, including naming the baby, naming the father, adoptions, and inheritance rights of unmarried parents, see *Living Together: A Legal Guide for Unmarried Couples,* by Ralph Warner, Toni Ihara, and Frederick Hertz (Nolo). For legal issues specific to lesbian and gay couples—such has how to complete a birth certificate if you are a lesbian who has given birth to a child conceived by donor insemination or egg donation or if you are a gay man who has used a surrogate—see *A Legal Guide for Lesbian and Gay Couples,* by Hayden Curry, Denis Clifford, and Frederick Hertz (Nolo).

My child's father and I are not married. Are there any special legal rules for us?
Yes—in fact, you've raised an important issue. Here's the problem: When a married couple has a child, the law automatically presumes that the husband is the child's father. There is no such legal presumption when it comes to unmarried couples.

What this means is that your partner will need to sign a voluntary acknowledgment of paternity to be legally recognized as your child's father. If you deliver in a hospital, the staff can provide you with this form. Or you can get a copy from your state's department of vital statistics. Most states will not permit you to list your partner on your child's birth certificate unless he first signs an acknowledgment of paternity.

If your child's father is unwilling to sign an acknowledgment of paternity, you will need to bring legal action to prove that he is the father. If you don't legally establish paternity, you will not be able to compel your child's father to pay child support, and your child will miss out on other valuable benefits, such as dependent health insurance coverage offered through the father's employer. ■

Chapter 6

Obtaining a Social Security Number

A Social Security number is the federal government's way of identifying your child. You will need it to claim child-related tax breaks, to add your new baby to your health insurance plan, to set up a college savings plan or bank account for your little one, or to apply for government benefits for your child.

How do I apply for a Social Security number for my baby?

The easiest way is through the birth registration form, which has a box you can check. You will need to provide both parents' Social Security numbers. Your child's Social Security card should arrive in about six to 12 weeks.

Or you can visit your local Social Security Administration (SSA) office and request a number in person. This process requires you to do three things:

- Complete Form SS-5 (*Application for Social Security Number*) and provide both parents' Social Security numbers on the form. To save time, download and complete Form SS-5 from the SSA website (www.socialsecurity.gov/online/ss-5.pdf) before you go.

- Provide at least two documents proving your baby's age, identity, and citizenship status. One document should ideally be your child's birth certificate. The other document can be your child's hospital birth record or other medical record.

- Provide proof of your own identity. Your driver's license and passport are both acceptable.

Find the SSA office nearest you by logging on to the SSA's Office Locator at www.socialsecurity.gov/locator. If you'd prefer, you can send in a completed Form SS-5 along with your identification documents to your local SSA office by mail. However, you'll have to send originals or certified copies of all identification documents. For this reason, most people apply in person.

Once you've submitted your application, you should receive a Social Security card in about six to 12 weeks. It may take substantially longer to process your application if your child is one year of age or older, because the SSA will contact your state's department of vital statistics to confirm that the birth certificate you have provided is a valid one.

Is Your Baby a U.S. Citizen?

Every baby born in the United States is a citizen, regardless of the parents' status. This means your baby can be a citizen even if you and your spouse are aliens or even illegal immigrants. All that is required is that your baby be born on U.S. soil. (There is one very minor exception to this rule for certain children of diplomatic personnel—but this exception does not apply to the vast majority of people who live in the United States.)

There is no special paperwork to complete to establish your child's citizenship status—your child's birth certificate will serve as proof of your child's citizenship.

The citizenship rules are much more complex for children born outside of the United States to U.S. citizen parents. If you and your child's other parent are both citizens and you are married at the time your child is born, your child will be a citizen provided that either you or your spouse actually lived in the United States at some point before your child was born. Different (and more complicated) qualification requirements apply if you and your child's other parent are not married. To find out whether your foreign-born child meets the standards for citizenship, contact your local U.S. consular office.

If your foreign-born child qualifies for citizenship, you will need to register your child's birth with your local U.S. consular office and obtain a Consular Report of Birth Abroad of a Citizen of the United States of America (also known as an FS-240).

You can find contact information for your local consular office at http://usembassy .state.gov. To learn more about the citizenship rules that apply to children born abroad, log on to http://travel.state.gov/family /family_issues/birth/birth_593.html and http://travel.state.gov/law/info/info_609 .html.

My husband and I are both illegal immigrants, but our child was born in the United States. Can we still obtain a Social Security number for our baby?

Yes. Just follow the instructions above, but leave items 8 and 9 (which request the parents' Social Security numbers) on Form SS-5 blank. ■

2. Mother's Milk
(And Your Right to Supply It)

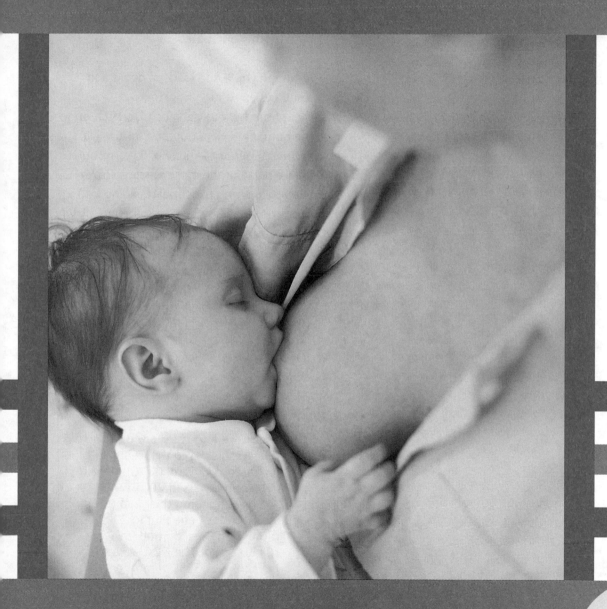

Contents

*I*f you're a mother who plans to breastfeed her baby, you're part of a trend. More and more new moms these days are opting to breastfeed, thanks to a growing recognition of the health benefits of breastfeeding for both mother and baby.

Although you'll find loads of books and resources explaining how to do it—everything from how to get a baby to latch on to the number of days pumped milk will last in the refrigerator—many of these resources ignore some of the more practical issues you'll face trying to fit breastfeeding into a busy, modern lifestyle: Can someone ask you to stop nursing your baby in public because they are uncomfortable? Do you have a right to a private place to pump breast milk after you return to work? The chapters that follow discuss these practical issues and more.

 FAST FACTS

Breastfeeding rates are on the rise. According to the Centers for Disease Control (CDC), only 27% of mothers in 2001 were still breastfeeding their infants at six months of age. But in 2003, more than 36% of mothers were still doing so. The CDC aims to have at least 50% of mothers still breastfeeding their babies at six months of age by the year 2010.

BABYCENTER RESOURCES

Everything you want to know about breastfeeding—and more! BabyCenter.com has tons of useful articles about the value of breast-feeding and how to do it. To find them, go to the *Parent Savvy* page of Babycenter.com (www.babycenter .com/parentsavvy).

 ADDITIONAL RESOURCES

For more answers to your breastfeeding questions. Breast-feeding isn't always as easy or trouble free as new mothers are often led to believe. If you need more advice on how to make breastfeeding work for you, Me-dela—the leading manufacturer of breast pumps—has plenty of information and troubleshooting advice available on its website. There are also weekly online chats with a lactation consultant, and many of the articles are available in six different languages. Just log on to www.medela.com and click on "Breastfeeding Information/ FAQs" or "Online Advice" in the left hand menu bar. ■

Chapter 7

Nursing in Public

If you choose to breastfeed your baby, you may be concerned about your right to nurse in public places, such as shopping malls and restaurants. Fortunately, breastfeeding in public is legal—everywhere. Whether or not people can ask you to stop—and how much you should cover up—are murkier topics, however.

BABYCENTER POLL

Wondering how many other moms breastfeed in public? In a recent BabyCenter.com poll, 60% of the 70,000 respondents said they were comfortable nursing in public places.

Is there any federal law that gives me the right to breastfeed in public?
Sort of. The federal Right to Breastfeed Act, signed into law by President Clinton in 1999, gives you the right to breastfeed anywhere on federal property that you and your child have a right to be—for example, federal courthouses and national parks. It is impor-

tant to understand that this law applies to federal property only. If you're on private property or state property—such as a shopping mall or state courthouse—then the Right to Breastfeed Act does not protect you. You'll have to rely on state law (see below).

> EXAMPLE: *Andrea was touring the National Gallery of Art, a federal government-owned museum, when Andrea's baby began to wail. It was perfectly legal for Andrea to sit down on a bench and breastfeed her little one in the museum, because the museum is federal property.*

Is there any place where it is illegal for me to breastfeed?
No. There is no state that outlaws breastfeeding.

Does that mean that I have the right to breastfeed anywhere I'd like?
Not necessarily. In the states that specifically give mothers the right to nurse in public, you do have the right to breastfeed anywhere—and people cannot ask you to stop.

If your state does not have a law specifically giving you the right to breastfeed in public, then you can still legally do so, but people who control property—such as shop owners and restaurant managers—can ask you to stop. Whether or not their action is legal is an open question.

Refer to the "State Laws on Breastfeeding in Public" chart, below, to find out about the law in your state.

ADDITIONAL RESOURCES

To learn more about state breastfeeding laws. La Leche League, a nonprofit organization dedicated to promoting and supporting breastfeeding, has a comprehensive list of state-by-state breastfeeding laws on its website at www.lalecheleague.org/Law/summary.html.

Does the law require me to cover up when I breastfeed in public?
It depends on where you live. A few states specifically give mothers the right to nurse in public, even if the mother's breast is partially exposed. These states are: Florida, Illinois, Michigan, Minnesota, Montana, Nevada, New York, North Carolina, and Utah. One state, Missouri, provides that mothers may breastfeed in public "with as much discretion as possible." (For tips on nursing discreetly, see below.) If you live in any other state, there's no clear-cut rule that specifies whether you have to cover up when breastfeeding in public.

No matter where you live, the best thing to do is to use your judgment and cover up whenever you feel the situation demands it. Some cities, even some neighborhoods, are more conservative than others; if you want to avoid stares or disputes, adjust your nursing style to fit the place where you happen to be.

Regardless of the law, I'd like to be discreet while nursing in public. Any advice?
La Leche League International says that the easiest way to breastfeed discreetly is by wearing lose fitting clothing that you can lift up or unbutton to give your baby access to your breast without exposing yourself. There are also special nursing blouses that you can sew or buy that have hidden but strategically placed slits or panels. In addition, some women find it helpful to wear their baby in a sling.

ADDITIONAL RESOURCES

To read more tips for discreet nursing. You can read La Leche League's entire article on the subject at www.lalecheleague.org/FAQ/discreet.html.

What should I do if I'm nursing in public and someone asks me to stop?

Tell the person that breastfeeding is legal and normal. Remind the person that by asking you to stop, he or she is asking you to deny your baby food. If your state has a law specifically giving you the right to breastfeed in public, tell the person that it is he or she—and not you—who is violating the law. Do not accept suggestions that you nurse in the restroom—it is unsanitary and unnecessary.

If this doesn't work, see if you can resolve the situation by talking to a manger or shop owner. If not, it may be best to leave the establishment and pursue the matter later, instead of making a scene (and upsetting your baby) right then and there.

What to do next is an open question. You can refuse to patronize the establishment again—and suggest that your friends and family do the same. You can write a letter to the local newspaper describing what happened. You can write to corporate headquarters. It's really up to you—and depends on how much of an advocate you want to be.

A local café recently asked me to stop nursing my baby. I'd like to sue—just to make a point. What are my rights?

A couple of states—namely, Hawaii and Illinois—have laws in place that specifically give women with the right to sue in civil court for these types of violations. In other states, you may have to bring suit under your state's sex discrimination or civil rights law. In any case, you should talk to a lawyer.

For Some, Burgers and Breasts Don't Mix

Even if you live in a state that has a law specifically protecting your right to breastfeed in public, your rights may not always be respected. This is because many people simply don't understand or follow the letter of the law when it comes to breastfeeding in public.

Just take the example of Catherine Geary, a Utah resident who began nursing her baby at her local Burger King. Even though Utah law specifically gives moms the right to nurse in public, a Burger King employee told Catherine that she either had to move to the bathroom or leave the restaurant. Although Catherine didn't make a scene at the time—or sue the restaurant—she told her story to the local press, effectively getting egg all over Burger King's face.

The moral of the story is that changes in the law are not always enough to bring about a change in people's attitudes and beliefs. Until breastfeeding in public gains more widespread acceptance, the rights of breastfeeding mothers to nurse in public will probably continue to be violated from time to time.

State Laws on Breastfeeding in Public

States that give mothers the right to breast-feed anywhere they have a right to be.	Colorado, Delaware, Florida, Illinois, Indiana, Iowa, Louisiana, Maine, Missouri, Nevada, New Jersey, New Mexico, New York, North Carolina, Oklahoma, Oregon, Texas, Utah, Virginia (limited to Virginia state property).
States that give mothers the right to breast-feed anywhere they have a right to be with their child.	California (but the law does not apply to private homes), Georgia, Maryland, Minnesota, Montana, Vermont.
States that make it illegal to interfere with a mother's right to breastfeed her child in public.	Connecticut, Hawaii, Illinois, Louisiana, Maryland, New Hampshire, New Jersey.
States that specifically exempt breastfeeding in public from the obscenity laws.	Alaska, Florida, Illinois, Louisiana, Michigan, Minnesota, Montana, Nevada, New Hampshire, New York, North Carolina, Oklahoma, Rhode Island, South Dakota, Utah, Virginia, Washington, Wisconsin. ■

Chapter 8

Breastfeeding and the Working Mom

Although breastfeeding after you return to work is challenging, it's doable—and with organization and practice, it can even become second nature. Once you figure out the logistics—finding a time and a place to pump, figuring out where to store your milk, figuring out how to clean your breast pump—all that's left to do is the pumping.

What are my rights to express and store my breast milk at my workplace?

Despite the recognized health benefits of breastfeeding for both mother and child, there is no federal law that gives you the right to express milk at work—something that is necessary if you are going to continue breastfeeding after returning to work.

However, a handful of states do require employers to provide nursing mothers with both a reasonable amount of unpaid break time to express milk and a convenient, private place (other than a toilet stall) in which to do it.

A few other states encourage—but do not require—employers to accommodate nursing mothers.

To find out about your state's law on expressing breast milk at work, see the chart, below.

State Laws on Expressing Breast Milk at Work

States that require employers to allow women to use break time to express milk.	California, Connecticut, Hawaii, Illinois, Minnesota, Tennessee
States that require employers to make reasonable efforts to provide a private space, other than a toilet stall, for expressing milk.	California, Connecticut, Illinois, Minnesota, Rhode Island, Tennessee
States that prohibit discrimination against women for expressing milk.	Connecticut, Hawaii
States that simply encourage employers to accommodate nursing mothers.	Georgia, Texas, Washington, Wyoming

I'd like to make arrangements to express milk at work. What should I do?

Here's a step-by-step guide for making arrangements to express milk at work:

- Know your rights (see the "State Laws on Expressing Breast Milk at Work" chart, above). This way, you'll know where you stand if your employer resists.

- Find out how other new mothers have done things. There's no need to reinvent the wheel. If someone else at your company has recently continued breastfeeding after returning to work, find out her strategies for success.

- Figure out where you can pump at work. Do you have a private office where you could express your milk? Or is there a small conference room that is almost always empty?

- Devise a tentative schedule for expressing milk. If you already have a break and lunch schedule, ask yourself whether you could squeeze in a few minutes with your breast pump during this time.

- Decide how you will store and transport your breast milk. Your boss might feel odd about having your breast milk kept right next to his lunch in the office refrigerator—or he might not. Many breast pumps come with insulated bags to store your expressed milk, so this might not be an issue at all. If you suspect you'll face some resistance, however, think about the logistics— such as whether you could bring in a small fridge for your office or store your milk in a special cooler during the day.

- Present a clear plan to your employer as to when and where you plan to pump at work.

 TIPS

Buy the right equipment. If you're serious about expressing milk at work, a hand-powered, single-breast pump just isn't going to do the trick. You'll need an electric two-breast pump (Medela makes some terrific models) to express your milk efficiently at the office. In addition, don't forget to pick up breast pads, containers for storing your milk, and a cooler pack to cart your milk home at the end of the day.

☑ CHECKLIST

Arranging to Pump at Work

If you want to pump at work, you'll have to figure how the logistics. Here's what to do:
- ❑ Know your rights.
- ❑ Find out how other new mothers in your workplace have arranged things.
- ❑ Find a place at work where you can pump.
- ❑ Devise a tentative pumping schedule.
- ❑ Decide how you will store your milk at work (and how you will transport it home).
- ❑ Present a clear plan to your employer.
- ❑ Purchase the right equipment (pump, pads, storage bags or containers, and so on).

My state does not have a law requiring employers to accommodate pumping breast milk at work. I've talked to my boss, and he says he doesn't want me to do it. Is there anything I can say to convince him?

A lot depends on your boss and why he is reluctant. If it's purely a matter of thinking that it isn't feasible, you can start by coming up with a concrete, workable plan for doing it (see above). If he is uncomfortable with breastfeeding in general, talk to him about the benefits for you and your baby—and for the workplace. For example:

- working mothers who continue nursing generally miss less time from work due to baby-related illnesses than nonbreast-feeding mothers
- working mothers who continue nursing tend to have higher morale than non-breastfeeding mothers because of the mother-child bond that breastfeeding promotes, and
- on average, mothers who are able to continue nursing after they return to work take shorter maternity leaves.

 TIPS

Talk to your boss about breast-feeding before you go out on maternity leave. Your boss may be more willing to work with you if he or she feels that accommodating your breastfeeding goals will encourage you to return to work sooner.

My employer says that if I want to pump, I have to do it on my lunch break. Is that legal?

Yes. Even if your state requires accommodations for nursing mothers, expect to spend your lunch hour with your breast pump. It is perfectly legal for your employer to insist that you pump during your regular meal and other break times. For example, if you are already entitled to take a one-hour lunch beak and two 15-minute coffee breaks at your job, your employer does not have to give you additional break time to express your breast milk. Or you could agree to work a little later each day to accommodate breastfeeding.

I work in a large, open room, and there is no private place for me to express milk. Even my supervisor's office has glass walls. What should I do?

Even if your state provides workplace rights for nursing mothers, the law probably won't help you. This is because these laws simply require that your employer make "reason-able efforts" to provide you with a private place to express your milk. Given the nature of your work environment, it may impos-sible for your employer to give you a private place—because there are no private places whatsoever. Your best bet under these circumstances may be to work from home until you are no longer breastfeeding. If this is not a practical option, then you may have to make do with pumping in the ladies' room until you feel your child is ready for infant formula.

My boss refuses to let me express milk at work—even though I live in a state that requires employers to accommodate breast-feeding moms. What should I do?

First, tell your employer that you have a legal right to some accommodations. Second—if that doesn't do the trick—contact your state labor department. It may be that your employer needs a crash course in the law (and some harsh words) from a state labor official to accommodate your request. Or you may have to take more serious action—such as filing a formal complaint against your employer under your state's law.

ADDITIONAL RESOURCES

For more information about breastfeeding at the workplace. La Leche League's website (www .lalecheleague.org) has tons of information on just about every aspect of breastfeeding, including your right to continue breastfeeding after you've returned to work. You might also want to pick up a copy of *Nursing Mother, Working Mother: The Essential Guide for Breastfeeding and Staying Close to Your Baby After You Return to Work*, by Gale Pryor (Harvard Common Press). The book offers practical tips on nursing while working, as well as encouragement to help you stay the course.

BABYCENTER RESOURCES

Read BabyCenter.com's advice for working moms who want to continue breastfeeding. Baby-Center.com has tons of information for moms who are balancing breastfeeding with work. Be sure to read "Breastfeeding and the Working Mom" and "Pumping and the Working Mom." And if you're worried about producing enough milk for your baby while working full time or appearing professional while pumping at the office, you'll find tips and advice from other BabyCenter.com moms in the "Pumping and Expressing" section, which you can find on the *Parent Savvy* page of Babycenter .com (www.babycenter.com/parent savvy). ■

3 · Balancing Work and Family

Contents

*B*abies have a way of rearranging our lives—even our professional ones. The time we spend away from work takes on new importance, and our jobs must now compete with our babies for our attention. Although it can be highly rewarding to have both a job and a family, balancing the two can be quite a challenge. In this part of the book, we provide the information you need to meet this challenge. Sometimes, laws will help, such as the Family and Medical Leave Act. In other cases, you'll have to rely on company policy and the kindness and flexibility of your boss or coworkers to come up with acceptable solutions.

The following chapters cover the full range of work-related issues when you're starting a family—from figuring out your rights to maternity and paternity leave to exploring family-friendly work schedules to deciding whether you can afford to stay at home. This part of the book also covers the important job benefit of health insurance during pregnancy and after your child's birth.

 FAST FACTS

If you are a working parent, you are not alone. According to a recent report from the National Partnership for Women and Families (www .nationalpartnership.org), in 78% of today's families, both parents work for pay. The typical American couple now works close to 90 hours per week, with each partner giving 40 or more hours to the job. ■

Chapter 9

Before Your Baby Arrives

The challenge of balancing work and family starts long before your baby is even born. Pregnant women must cope with significant physical changes that may make it difficult for them to do their jobs; adoptive parents must deal with the requirements and red tape of the adoption process. And everyone must break the news to bosses and coworkers—and face the possibility of negative attitudes.

The good news is that sometimes the law can help—by prohibiting discriminatory treatment, for example. And many bosses and coworkers will be happy for you and will gladly help you in the transition from being a working individual to being a working parent.

BABYCENTER RESOURCES

Check BabyCenter.com for expert advice on working while pregnant. Pregnant moms can find plenty of tips on surviving their pregnancy at work—from how to handle first trimester nausea without seeming unprofessional to how best to break the big news to their boss. To get started, log on to the *Parent Savvy* page of Babycenter.com (www.babycenter.com/parentsavvy).

CROSS REFERENCE

Taking time off from work. No matter what type of parent you are—mother or father, birth or adoptive—you may need to take some time off before your baby arrives. Pregnant moms may need time to attend doctor's appointments or to cope with extreme morning sickness, for example, and expectant fathers may want to attend appointments with the mother or take time off to care for her. Adoptive parents may need time to prepare for the adoption. There are laws that provide for leave in all of these situations. In fact, they are, for the most part, the same laws that provide for maternity and paternity leave. See Chapter 10 for a discussion of all the types of leave that you can take—before and after your baby arrives.

Breaking the News at Work

Sharing the news of a baby on the way with family members and friends is usually a happy occasion, marked with hugs, photos, and perhaps a little bubbly. But announcing a pregnancy or planned adoption to your employer can be a serious (and stressful) business. You might worry that your boss won't be supportive of your new addition, perhaps because you'll soon be taking a few weeks (or months) of leave. Or you may be concerned that your boss will view you differently once he or she learns that you're a soon-to-be parent—and work may no longer be your top priority.

I'm nervous about telling my boss that I am expecting. When do I have to do it? Although you might prefer to wait until the last possible minute, your right to take leave usually hinges on giving your employer sufficient notice. (For example, under the federal Family and Medical Leave Act, you must give at least 30 days' notice.) This is true for expectant fathers, mothers, and adoptive parents. The amount of notice you must give depends on the type of leave you are taking—private leave through your employer, federal leave, or state leave.

Otherwise, you're free to tell your boss the big news anytime you'd like. Many people wait until after the first trimester because of the decreased risk of miscarriage. Others keep the news under wraps even longer—until they've had an amniocentesis and confirmed that the fetus has no genetic abnormalities.

But don't wait too long. Breaking the news sooner rather than later is considerate—and savvy. Good bosses appreciate the advance notice, because it gives everyone time to figure out who will do your work while you are on leave. Also, it's much better that your boss hears the news from you, rather than the office gossip mill.

Many soon-to-be parents find it helpful to time the announcement to coincide with a workplace accomplishment. This sends a message that you are valuable—and that you are worth whatever inconvenience the pregnancy and new baby may cause.

If you are the expectant mother, your changing body may force your hand—either because your burgeoning belly gives you away or because morning sickness, fatigue, or other physical difficulties require you to take time off from work.

BABYCENTER POLL

Curious as to when other soon-to-be parents shared the good news with their bosses? Out of 8,030 responses to a recent BabyCenter .com poll, 35% of parents waited until after the first trimester, 23% broke the news immediately, and 14% let their bellies do the talking for them.

My wife and I are on a waiting list for a domestic adoption. Do I have to tell my boss about the waiting list, or can I wait until we know that we'll be adopting a baby?
It can take literally years to get off of a waiting list and actually adopt a baby, so there's no legal requirement that you tell your boss while you are on the waiting list. If you know that you are getting closer to the top of the list—and therefore closer to getting a baby—you might think about letting your employer know, just as a courtesy. When you get a definite date for your baby's arrival, your right to take leave will hinge on giving your boss adequate notice. See Chapter 10 for more about taking leave and giving notice.

Is there anything I should do before I break the news to my boss that I am expecting a baby?
Whether you are an expectant mother or father, preparation is the key to ensuring a warm workplace reception for your news. Although no law requires this, it's a good idea to learn in advance how much leave you are entitled to and decide how and when you want to take it. (Chapter 10 can help you do this.) If any coworkers have had a baby recently—and if you trust them—find out about their experiences and get their advice. Look at your work schedule and put yourself in your boss's shoes: Are there deadlines that you will be unable to meet? Projects that you won't be able to complete? Seminars, trainings, or company events that you won't be able to attend? You aren't legally required to help your employer with the problems that

will arise—but it's a considerate and smart thing to do. Help your boss; be prepared to suggest ways that your work can be handled while you are on leave.

Dealing With Unfair Treatment

Although many companies have become more family friendly in recent years, some employers still believe that expectant parents won't work as hard or as well as they did before—and they treat these expectant parents accordingly by withholding promotions, handing out less desirable work assignments, failing to include them in meetings and trainings, and so on.

Although some laws protect pregnant women from workplace discrimination, there's no clear law protecting expectant fathers, partners, or soon-to-be adoptive parents—instead, those parents have to rely on company policy and the goodwill of employers and coworkers.

I am pregnant. What laws protect me from discrimination?

The federal Pregnancy Discrimination Act (PDA) prevents employers with 15 or more employees from treating women differently just because they are pregnant. This means employers can't:

• fire a woman because she is pregnant or intends to become pregnant

• demote a woman or compensate her differently because she is pregnant or

intends to become pregnant, or

- refuse to hire a woman because she is pregnant or intends to become pregnant.

The PDA also prohibits employers from treating pregnant women differently in the terms and conditions of employment—that is, pay, benefits, training, harassment, and so on.

Some states also have laws that protect pregnant women from workplace discrimination. These state laws are often broader than the PDA and apply to smaller employers. For example, California law prohibits companies with as few as five employees from discriminating against pregnant women. Contact your state department of labor or fair employment office to find out about the law in your state.

I have received a raise every one of the past five years because I am a very productive salesperson. This year, however, my pregnancy has made me too tired and too nauseous to work as hard as usual. As a result, my sales have dropped, and I didn't get a raise. What are my rights?

The PDA and similar state laws only prohibit employers from making employment decisions because of pregnancy. When there are legitimate reasons for not giving a raise—such as a drop in sales, in your case—then it is perfectly legal. This is true even if a woman is performing poorly at work because of pregnancy-related symptoms. The law does not guarantee special treatment for pregnant employees, only equal treatment.

TIPS

Talk to your supervisor if your performance at work is slipping. Although your supervisor is not legally required to cut you any slack at work during your pregnancy, he or she may be sympathetic if you have an honest conversation about how your pregnancy is affecting your performance.

TIPS

Consider taking time off before your baby arrives. If your pregnancy symptoms make it virtually impossible for you to get your job done, think about taking some leave. You may even qualify for a paid (or partially paid) leave if you are eligible for disability benefits through your employer or your state's disability program. See Chapter 10 to learn more about your leave options.

After I announced my pregnancy, my company filed for bankruptcy and laid me off along with the rest of my department. Is this legal?

Yes. No law protects a pregnant woman from being fired for nonpregnancy related reasons, such as company-wide staff reductions or poor performance.

My boss has been treating me differently ever since I announced my pregnancy. He no longer sends me on business trips to meet with out-of-state clients, and he often excludes me from evening meetings. How can I resolve the situation?

Your boss may think that he is doing you a favor by minimizing travel and late night obligations during your pregnancy. Resolving the situation may be as simple as telling your boss that you are healthy enough to continue your usual job responsibilities.

On the other hand, if your boss is restructuring your job because he doesn't trust a pregnant woman with important work responsibilities, then you have a problem. By demoting you to lower profile work responsibilities solely because you are pregnant, your boss is discriminating against you. If your company is covered by the PDA or a similar state law, then the discrimination is illegal.

Start by talking to your boss and educating him about your abilities and the law. Request he give you back your previous work responsibilities. If he doesn't comply, use your company's complaint procedures or take the issue to your human resources department. If you still can't resolve the problem, then consider filing a formal complaint with a government agency— either your state fair employment office, state department of labor, or the federal Equal Employment Opportunity Commission (EEOC), the federal agency that enforces the PDA.

☑ CHECKLIST

How to Deal With Unfair Treatment at Work

- ☐ Find out whether you're covered by the Pregnancy Discrimination Act or a state law that protects pregnant women from workplace discrimination.
- ☐ Try to resolve any problems with your boss or the company's human resources department.
- ☐ Contact a nonprofit organization such as Equal Rights Advocates or 9to5 for advice.
- ☐ If you can't resolve the problem, file a formal complaint with your state fair employment office, state department of labor, or the federal EEOC.

Can my boss fire me if I file a formal complaint of pregnancy discrimination?

No. It is illegal for your employer to fire you or take any other negative action against you (for example, demote you or give you less desirable work assignments) for asserting your rights under the PDA or a similar state law.

For free advice and information on the rights of pregnant women in the workplace. It's not always easy to tell whether you've been the victim of pregnancy discrimination. And even if you are sure, you may need some help figuring out what to do about it. Two terrific nonprofit organizations that focus on women's rights in the workplace are Equal Rights Advocates (ERA) and 9to5. Both have hotlines where you can get confidential advice and guidance on your situation, and both have informative websites: For ERA, call 800-839-4ERA or refer to www.equalrights.org/personal/faqs.asp. For 9to5, call 800-522-0925 or refer to www.9to5.org.

Another excellent resource is Workplace Fairness, a nonprofit organization that promotes employee-friendly policies and practices. Log onto www.workplacefairness.org for information about your rights in the workplace and things you can do if you feel those rights have been violated.

Thousands of employers violate the PDA each year. In 2004, more than 4,500 women filed charges against their employers with the EEOC for treating them unfairly during their pregnancies. That same year, the EEOC collected more than $11 million in financial penalties for victims of pregnancy-based discrimination.

Working at a Strenuous or Dangerous Job While Pregnant

Some jobs are not suitable for pregnant women—either because they are too physically demanding or because they are hazardous to the fetus's health. This section will help you understand your rights when it comes to handling a strenuous or hazardous job during your pregnancy.

My job involves heavy lifting, which my doctor has prohibited in my second trimester. However, my boss refuses to reassign me to a less strenuous job. What are my rights?
If your company is covered by the federal PDA (see above), then your boss has to reassign you only if he or she has made similar accommodations for other temporarily disabled employees in the past. For example, if one of your coworkers broke his leg and

your boss reassigned him to clerical work while his leg healed, then your boss would have to reassign you to clerical duty for the rest of your pregnancy. But if your boss sent your broken-legged coworker home and docked his pay until he could work again, then your boss has no legal obligation to treat you any better.

Fortunately, some state laws are considerably kinder towards pregnant women. In California, for example, your boss would be legally obligated to reassign you to a less strenuous position for the duration of your pregnancy. Contact your state labor department or state fair employment office to find out what your state law requires.

I work at a chemical plant and I'm concerned about exposure to toxic substances during my pregnancy. What should I do? You are right to be concerned about contact with chemicals at your workplace. Certain substances—such as lead, mercury, and organic solvents—are known reproductive hazards. Exposure to these substances during your pregnancy (or sometimes even before you become pregnant) can lead to miscarriage, preterm delivery, structural birth defects, or abnormal infant or fetal development. Women who work in chemical factories are not the only ones who need to be aware of this potential problem. You could be exposed to risky substances in a variety of workplaces, such as operating rooms and pottery studios.

If you suspect that there are reproductive hazards at your workplace, check with your employer. Health and safety laws require employers to prepare something called a "Materials Safety Data Sheet" (MSDS) if there are hazardous chemicals at the workplace. Ask your employer for a copy and share your company's MSDS with your obstetrician, who may recommend that you change your work responsibilities or find a new job altogether to minimize the risks.

My obstetrician has informed me that it would be reckless to continue working at my current job because of exposure to reproductive hazards. Do I have any rights to a job transfer within the company? Unfortunately, you are not entitled to a job transfer under federal law even if your job exposes you to reproductive hazards during your pregnancy. You may, however, be entitled to a job transfer under your state's laws. In California, for example, employers with five or more employees must accommodate a pregnant woman's request to transfer to a less strenuous or hazardous position. Contact your state labor department or state fair employment office for more information.

To learn more about reproductive hazards at the workplace. If you'd like more information about exposure to toxic substances at work during your pregnancy, check the National Institute for Occupational Safety and Health's website at www.cdc.gov/niosh. Just go to the menu entitled "Workplace Safety and Health Topics" and select "Reproductive Health." You can also learn more about your rights to a safe workplace at the Occupational Safety and Health Administration's website at www.osha.gov.

One of my coworkers is a chain smoker, and the smoke often wafts over to my office cubicle. My obstetrician has cautioned me against exposure to second-hand smoke during my pregnancy. What are my rights?
There are no federal laws that prohibit your coworker from smoking in the workplace. However, many states and cities have laws and ordinances either prohibiting smoking altogether in office buildings or requiring employers to take steps to protect the health of nonsmokers—for example, by limiting smoking to separate lounges. You may be able to use your state's law or city's ordinance to force your coworker to smoke outside. Contact your state labor department for more information.

Looking for a New Job While Pregnant

If you decide to embark on a job search during your pregnancy, you may worry that potential employers will be reluctant to hire you. This section will help you make sense of your legal rights and responsibilities when it comes to the challenging sport of job-hunting while pregnant.

I just began my second trimester, but I don't look pregnant. Must I tell prospective employers that I am expecting?
No. The law does not require you to reveal your pregnancy. And it's illegal for employers covered by the PDA (or similar state law) to ask whether you are pregnant. (See **Dealing With Unfair Treatment**, above, to find out whether an employer is covered by the PDA or similar state law.)

From a practical perspective, however, honesty is the best policy when it comes to looking for a new job during your pregnancy. Although you don't need to send a copy of your ultrasound along with your resume or mention your pregnancy during the initial interview, it's a good idea to tell your employer that you are pregnant once you're offered the job and before you accept it. This sends a message that you are sensitive to your employer's needs. Let's face it: You'll eventually have to come clean, and a new employer may be unpleasantly surprised to learn that you will be taking time off so soon after starting a new job. This could get your relationship off to a rocky start. Besides, if an employer is going to react badly to a pregnancy, it's probably not a very family-friendly place anyway—something that is better to find out sooner rather than later.

I'm interviewing for the job of my dreams, but I'm scared I won't have a shot at getting the offer because of my big belly. Can an employer refuse to hire me because I am pregnant?

If the job is one that you would be perfectly capable of performing while pregnant—a copyediting position, for example—and the company is covered by the federal PDA or a similar state law, then the company cannot reject your application simply because you are pregnant. (See **Dealing With Unfair Treatment**, above, to find out whether the company is covered by the PDA or similar state law.)

But if you are applying for a position that is too strenuous or hazardous for a pregnant woman—a construction job that involves lifting cement blocks, for example, or a power plant job with high risk of radiation exposure—then it would be legal for a company to refuse to hire you on the basis of your pregnancy, even if the company is covered by the PDA or similar state law.

Of course, an employer is always free to reject you in favor of another candidate so long as pregnancy isn't a reason.

Will I still be entitled to take maternity leave if I switch jobs midway through my pregnancy?

Maybe, maybe not. It depends on what kind of leave you want to take and the state that you live in. For example, in order to qualify for leave under the federal Family and Medical Leave Act, you must work for the employer for at least a year. You can learn more about eligibility requirements and various types of leave in Chapter 10

In addition to maternity leave, many new parents use accrued vacation time and sick days to add to their official leave. But if you change jobs, you won't have any. ■

Chapter 10

Taking Leave

Work can enrich our lives, but when it comes to babies, it can really get in the way. This is why taking leave from work during pregnancy and after your child is born is of paramount importance to parents. Unfortunately, arranging a fair and financially practical pregnancy, maternity, paternity, or adoption leave can be difficult. This chapter can help.

Although most people talk about leave as if it is one discrete thing, the leave you will take during pregnancy and after your baby is born is really a bunch of different kinds of leaves put together. The most well-known leave is through the federal Family and Medical Leave Act (FMLA), which guarantees eligible workers 12 weeks of unpaid leave. But depending on who you are and where you live, you can find leave in all kinds of places, not just through the FMLA. The following are potential types of leave for you to take, provided you meet eligibility requirements:

- unpaid FMLA leave for parents before and after birth or adoption (see **FMLA Leave**, below, for more information)
- unpaid state leave for parents before and after birth or adoption (see **State Leave and Benefits**, below, for more information)
- paid or unpaid company leave for parents after birth or adoption (see **Employer Leave, Policies, and Benefits**, below, for more information)
- accrued sick leave for mothers coping with difficult pregnancies or who need to attend doctor appointments (see **Employer Leave, Policies, and Benefits**, below, for more information), and
- accrued vacation time for parents before and after birth or adoption (see **Employer Leave, Policies, and Benefits**, below, for more information).

FAST FACTS

Many countries are more supportive of new parents than ours. More than 160 countries guarantee women the right to paid maternity leave, and 45 countries provide men with the right to paid paternity leave.

FAST FACTS

The FMLA is far from perfect. The law does not cover everyone. In fact, more than 41 million Americans—or 40% of the private sector workforce—do not qualify for FMLA leave. And those employees who are covered face significant financial barriers to taking unpaid time off from work. According to a 2000 study by the U.S. Department of Labor, nearly two out of five workers had to cut their FMLA leaves short for economic reasons.

FMLA Leave

The FMLA guarantees eligible working parents the right to take up to 12 weeks of unpaid leave after the birth, adoption, or foster placement of a child. FMLA also allows soon-to-be parents to take leave for pregnancy-related needs or to prepare for an adoption. Since the law's enactment in 1993, more than 35 million Americans have taken advantage of its provisions to take time off from work to care for their families or deal with health issues.

How can I tell if I am eligible to take FMLA leave?

You probably qualify to take FMLA leave if:

- you work for an employer with at least 50 employees
- you have worked for that employer for at least one year, and
- you have worked at least 1,250 hours— or about 24 hours per week—for that employer in the last year.

We say "probably" because there are a few exceptions to this general rule.

First, you are not guaranteed FMLA leave if you are among the highest-paid 10% of all employees at your company. The reason for this exception is that a company may not be able to continue functioning if one of its top executives took a leave of absence for three months. As a practical matter, however, many companies give their highest-paid employees the same rights to take unpaid FMLA leave as they give to the rest of their workers.

Second, you are not eligible for FMLA leave if you work for a company that has fewer than 50 employees within a 75-mile radius, even if the company is quite large and has tens of thousands of employees nationwide. This rule can be unfair, particularly if you happen to work for a tiny branch office of a multinational corporation. For the purposes of this rule, count all employees on the payroll—including part-time workers and employees on leave—when determining whether there are 50 employees within a 75-mile radius.

TIPS

The FMLA extends well beyond the corporate world. Provided you meet the eligibility requirements, you are entitled to the law's benefits even if you work for a state or local government agency or a nonprofit corporation.

I am eligible to take FMLA leave. Under what circumstances can I take it?

The FMLA allows you to take an unpaid leave from your job for any of the following reasons:

- the birth or adoption of a child
- the placement of a foster child in your home
- a serious health condition that prevents you from performing your job, such as a significant pregnancy-related complication, or
- a serious health condition affecting your child, your spouse, or your parents. (For example, if your wife has been ordered to remain on bed rest, you could take FMLA leave to care for her.)

FAST FACTS

Babies are responsible for more than a quarter of all FMLA leaves. According to a 2000 study by the U.S. Department of Labor, more than 26% of all FMLA leave-takers took time off from work to care for a new child, deal with a pregnancy-related health issue, or prepare for an adoption.

What will happen to my job and benefits while I am away on FMLA leave?

Your employer must hold your job open for you during your time off and keep you at the same seniority level. Your employer must also continue your health insurance coverage on the same terms during your FMLA leave. For example, if your employer currently pays two-thirds of your health insurance premiums, your employer must continue paying two-thirds of your health insurance premiums while you are on leave. (You may need to make arrangements with your employer for you to pay your share of the premiums while you are away, however.)

Your employer does not have to continue contributing to your retirement plan—such as your 401(k)—during your FMLA leave. Your employer can also stop the clock, so to speak, on vacation and sick leave accrual, seniority level advancement, and pension benefit accrual while you are away.

How much unpaid leave can I take under the FMLA and when can I take it?

The FMLA allows you to take a maximum of 12 weeks of unpaid leave in any given 12-month period. This means that if you take FMLA leave for pregnancy complications, you will have to subtract that time from your unpaid leave after your baby arrives. Similarly, if you took some FMLA leave at the beginning of the year to care for your ailing father, you will have to subtract that amount of leave from the total available to you once your baby arrives.

> EXAMPLE: *Gloria had planned on working until the day she delivered. However, her doctor ordered her to remain on bed rest for the final four weeks of her pregnancy. Because Gloria took four weeks of FMLA leave while she was pregnant, she was only entitled to take eight weeks of FMLA leave after her baby was born.*

The same holds true if you take time off from work to deal with preadoption obligations, such as court appearances. Your FMLA leave after your child is placed with you for adoption will be reduced by the amount of time you took off from work prior to the placement.

What should I do if my employer refuses to let me take FMLA leave?

If your employer denies your request for FMLA leave, or otherwise interferes with your FMLA rights, first try to resolve the problem on your own by talking to your employer. Sometimes, employers refuse to provide FMLA leave because of a genuine misunderstanding about the law. Make sure that your employer knows that you want to take unpaid leave pursuant to the FMLA, and give your employer a copy of the U.S. Department of Labor's fact sheet on the FMLA (available online at www.dol.gov/esa /regs/compliance/whd/whdfs28.htm). Other times, the employee is the one who misunderstands. For example, your employer may refuse your FMLA leave request because your employer already offers 16 weeks of paid leave. If this is the case, then your employer's refusal is perfectly legal.

Second, lodge a complaint with your company's human resources department or file a grievance with your union. Your human resources administrator or union representative may be able to work out the situation for you.

If you still meet with no success, consider filing a formal complaint with the U.S. Department of Labor's Wage and Hour Division. Often, a quick call to an employer from a Department of Labor representative is all it takes to solve the problem. To find a division office near you, log on to www.dol.gov.

The only kind of leave I am entitled to is FMLA leave, but I want to take more than 12 weeks off. Is there anything I can do?
If you don't have accrued vacation time—and if you aren't entitled to any state leave—then you're stuck. If you take more than 12 weeks of leave, your employer can let you go and hire a replacement.

Taking FLMA Leave During Pregnancy

My doctor has ordered me on bed rest for the last part of my pregnancy. Can I take FMLA leave for this?
You can take up to 12 weeks if you're suffering from a serious pregnancy-related health condition, such as preterm labor. But remember: Any time you take off during your pregnancy will cut short the amount of FMLA leave you can take after your baby arrives.

CAUTION

You may have to provide proof of your health problem. Don't be surprised if your employer asks you to provide written confirmation of your pregnancy-related health condition before approving your request to take unpaid leave. This is perfectly legal. In fact, your employer can request up to three medical certifications, provided your employer is willing to cover the costs of the second and third medical opinions. (Most employers, however, are satisfied with just one.)

My wife is suffering from severe morning sickness and cannot take care of herself. Can I take time off from work to care for her?
Yes, you can use FMLA leave to care for your wife, but remember: The time you care for her will reduce the FMLA leave you can take after your baby arrives.

CAUTION

Unmarried parents not eligible to take FMLA leave to care for pregnant partners. The FMLA does not entitle you to take time off from work to care for a pregnant woman you are not married to—even if you are the baby's father. However, your state law may help. Contact your state labor department to find out.

Because my pregnancy is high risk, my obstetrician has insisted that I work a reduced schedule. Can I?
Yes, because it is medically necessary. However, any days you take off from work during your pregnancy will count against the FMLA leave you can take after your baby is born. For example, if you take one day off a week for five weeks during your pregnancy, then you will be entitled to only 11 weeks of unpaid leave after your baby arrives.

My obstetrician does not offer weekend or evening appointments, so I often have to leave work during the day to see her. My boss is very unhappy about this. What are my rights?

The FMLA does not entitle you to take time off from work to attend regular doctor's appointments. So unless you're willing to switch to a more flexible obstetrician, your best bet is to use accrued vacation or sick leave to attend your appointments.

I've taken six weeks of FMLA leave to deal with a pregnancy complication that is now resolved. However, my employer is insisting that I remain on leave until my baby is born. Is this legal?

No. If you work for a company with 15 or more employees, the federal Pregnancy Discrimination Act (PDA) prohibits your boss from forcing you to remain on leave until your child is born. If you work for a smaller company, a state law may protect your right to return from pregnancy leave. Contact your state labor department to learn more.

Taking Leave After Your Baby Arrives

Do I have to take my maternity leave immediately after my child arrives?

Although most parents begin their FMLA leaves as soon as their babies are born (or even slightly before), some soon-to-be parents would rather take time off from work a bit later because a spouse will be home with the baby for the first few weeks. Fortunately, the FMLA gives you one full year after your child arrives to take advantage of your 12 weeks of unpaid maternity/paternity leave—so feel free to schedule your leave whenever it makes the most sense for you and your family.

Must I take my leave in one chunk?

Generally, yes, if you are taking the leave to bond with a newborn or newly adopted child. If you would rather stagger your FMLA leave—for example, by working a reduced schedule for half the year instead of taking 12 weeks off in a row, or by taking off one week each month—you can do so only with your employer's prior approval.

My state has a family leave law. Can I take my state leave in addition to my FMLA leave?

In most cases, no. You get to use the law that is most beneficial to you, but you can't use both. For example, if your state provides for 16 weeks of unpaid leave following the birth of a baby, you can take a maximum of 16 weeks of maternity/paternity leave—not 28 weeks (which would be your state family leave plus your FMLA leave).

I have accrued two weeks of paid vacation time. Can I add that to my FMLA leave to get a total of 14 weeks off?

Only if your employer says it's okay. It is legal for an employer to count your vacation time as part of your FMLA leave—and limit your total time off from work to a maximum of 12 weeks.

My husband and I work for the same company. Can we both take FMLA leave after our baby is born?

Yes, but your employer may limit your combined time off to 12 weeks. So if one parent takes ten weeks of leave, for example, the employer is free to limit the other parent to two weeks.

My boss is pressuring me to take a shorter maternity leave than I had planned. He has even promised me a small bonus if I return to work after six weeks. Is this legal?

No. Employers cannot interfere with an employee's plans to take FMLA leave. This means that your boss cannot threaten to fire or demote you for taking time off under the FMLA, nor can your boss offer to pay you more or promote you for cutting short your FMLA leave.

I'm a teacher, and I have taken my 12 weeks of FMLA leave. We are in the middle of a term, and the principal wants me to remain on unpaid leave until next term. Is this legal?

Yes. If you are a teacher or an instructor, your employer can require you to postpone your return to work until the beginning of the next term or semester, to avoid disrupting the class. However, your employer must give you back your same job or an equivalent job when you resume working and must also continue your health insurance coverage on the same terms during the entire time that you are out on leave.

I just returned to work after a 12-week maternity leave, and my job is totally different. What are my rights?

It depends on what is different about your job. The FMLA requires your employer to give you back your old job, or an equivalent job, when you return from leave. An equivalent job means one with the same pay and bonus opportunities, the same seniority level and status, the same work schedule, and at the same job location (or very close to it).

> EXAMPLE: *Before Violet left on maternity leave, she had a high-level position at her advertising company. Violet supervised a staff of ten people and she had a tremendous amount of client contact. When Violet returned from maternity leave, she was given a job paying only 80% of her former salary. Her job responsibilities had also changed. She no longer supervised other employees, and her days were filled with clerical work, not client contact. Violet's new job was not equivalent to her old job under the FMLA, so her employer has violated her rights under the FMLA.*

There are two exceptions to this rule. First, if your employer would have eliminated your job anyway, then you are not entitled to the same or equivalent job when you return from leave.

Second, your employer does not have to give you back your old job or an equivalent job if you are in the highest paid 10% of your company's employees and it would cause your employer substantial economic harm to hold your job open for you during your leave. For example, if you are the company's chief financial officer, your company may not be able to continue functioning unless it hires a replacement for you during your leave. If you fall into this category, your employer must let you know before you take FMLA leave that you may not get your job (or an equivalent job) when you return.

Taking Leave for Adoption Under the FMLA

My partner and I are adopting a child. Can either of us take time off from work under the FMLA?

Yes. Adoptive parents have the same rights as biological parents to FMLA leave.

Do I have to wait until my child's adoption is final before taking FMLA leave?

No. You can take time off under the FMLA as soon as your child is placed with you for adoption.

Can I take FMLA leave to deal with preadoption requirements?

Yes. You can take FMLA leave for meetings and other obligations that are necessary for your adoption to proceed. For example, you can take FMLA leave to travel abroad to interview with a foreign adoption agency or to attend a midday meeting with the lawyer who is handling your adoption. But remember: The time you take arranging for the adoption counts against the FMLA leave you can take after your child is placed with you.

State Leave and Benefits

Most states have their own family and medical leave law. In many states, the law parallels the protections provided by the FMLA. In some states, however, the law provides greater benefits or protections than the federal FMLA. For example, state law may cover smaller employers not covered by the FMLA, or may cover employees who have worked for an employer for less time than the FMLA requires, or may provide greater total job-protected time off than the 12 weeks the FMLA provides.

To find out about the family leave law in your state, refer to the booklet "Expecting Better: A State-By-State Analysis of Parental Leave Programs," published by the National Partnership for Women and Families. You can view (and download) a copy at www.nationalpartnership.org.

In addition, a handful of states provide some form of wage-replacement benefits for which mothers can apply while on an unpaid family or medical leave from work. Five states (California, Hawaii, New Jersey, New York, and Rhode Island) provide temporary disability benefits to women who are unable to work due to pregnancy and childbirth.

California provides an additional six weeks of partial wage benefits during a worker's unpaid time off to bond with a newborn, newly adopted, or new foster child, or to care for an ill parent, child, spouse, or domestic partner. So, for example, a mother and father could obtain these benefits while they are on unpaid family leave to bond with their new child. Or a father could obtain these benefits while on unpaid family leave to care for an ailing pregnant spouse. To learn more about the California law, go to the state's official website at www.edd .ca.gov/fleclaimpfl.htm..

Employer Leave, Policies, and Benefits

Many employers are now choosing to provide family and medical leave benefits above and beyond what state and federal law requires of them. For example, smaller employers that are not covered by state or federal family and medical leave laws may choose to provide unpaid, job-protected leave anyway, or employers who are required to provide only unpaid leave may choose to provide a certain amount of paid leave for their employees.

Many parents want to use accrued vacation and sick leave to pad out the other types of leave that are available to them. Whether this is an option for you is up to your employer. Some employers require parents to use their accrued vacation as part of their federal or state leave. Other employers, allow employees to take both.

Finally, some employers offer temporary disability benefits to women who miss work because of pregnancy and childbirth. Be sure not to miss out on any additional benefits your employer provides. Talk to your benefits administrator for details.

Calculating Your Leave

- ❏ Determine if you are eligible for unpaid leave under the FMLA.
- ❏ Determine if you are eligible for state leave.
- ❏ If you are eligible for both state and federal leave, choose the leave that is most beneficial to you.
- ❏ Determine if you are eligible for company leave. If you are, find out how that fits in with any federal or state leave to which you are entitled.
- ❏ Find out how much accrued vacation and sick leave you have. Find out how that fits in with any federal, state, or company leave to which you are entitled.
- ❏ Find out whether you are eligible for any wage replacement during your leave— for example state temporary disability benefits or your company's own private disability policy. ■

Chapter II

Not Returning to Work

Although you might have every intention of returning to work, you may change your mind once you're holding your newborn in your arms. You may not want to miss a minute of your child's early years. Or you may be overwhelmed by the prospect of juggling a demanding career with a baby.

It's a tough decision, one that involves questions about money (Can I really afford to stop working?) and questions about your sense of self (Who am I if I'm not working?).

 FAST FACTS

More new mothers are choosing to stay at home. More than five million American moms have chosen to put their careers on the back burner to stay home with their children, and 42% of stay-at-home moms have children younger than three.

I don't want to continue working after my baby is born, but finances are a serious concern. How do I know if I can afford to stay home?

Depending on your family's financial circumstances and the lifestyle you'd like to enjoy, quitting your job to raise your child may be a realistic and affordable option for your family. Why? Because when you take into account taxes and work-related expenses, you might be earning far less than you think.

Let's talk about taxes first. Under the federal tax system, your tax rate depends on your income. The more you earn, the higher your tax rate. If you make less than your spouse, your income might be pushing your family into a higher tax bracket, which means that you take home a smaller percentage of every dollar that you earn.

EXAMPLE: *Keith earned $59,400 per year as a pharmaceutical sales representative and his wife, Nancy, earned $35,000 per year as a legal assistant. After the birth of their son, Christopher, Nancy wanted to stay home, and the couple worried about making ends meet. They consulted with a financial planner and were surprised to learn that highest* marginal tax rate for the first $59,400 of their income (Keith's salary) was only 15%, but the tax rate for the remaining $35,000 of their household income (Nancy's salary) was taxed at 25%. In other words, Nancy was giving up 25 cents of every dollar she earned. The financial planner explained that the reason for this was that Nancy's added income moved the couple from the 15% marginal tax bracket to the 25% marginal tax bracket that year.

Your additional income might also be preventing your family from enjoying valuable tax breaks, such as the child tax credit and the dependent exemption. This is because you can only claim these child-related tax benefits if the total of your income plus your spouse's income is within certain dollar limits. Chapters 28 through 33 discuss these tax breaks in detail, but for now consider this quick example:

EXAMPLE: Ellen earned $50,000 as a freelance writer; her husband, Mark, earned $100,000 as an accountant. Because their adjusted gross income exceeded $130,000 in 2005—the year that their daughter, Eliza, was born—they could not claim the child tax credit that year. This meant that they lost $1,000 in tax savings that they would have enjoyed had Ellen not been working.

Taxes are not the only issue to consider when deciding whether your family can make it on just one income. You also have to think about child care bills, commuting costs, paying for business clothes and lunches out, and other work-related expenses.

EXAMPLE: Reed earned $40,000 as an assistant district attorney while his partner, Tara, earned $90,000 through her interior design business. After their twins were born, Reed decided that he would rather stay at home with their two children than spend his days prosecuting white-collar criminals. Tara was nervous at first about whether they could survive on her income alone, but Reed explained that his salary would leave them with almost no extra money each month after they paid child care bills and other work-related expenses. The two decided that making simple changes, such as making do with one car and eating out less often, would enable them to continue enjoying a comfortable lifestyle on Tara's salary alone.

If you're still unsure whether your family can afford to cut back to just one salary. Consider making an appointment with a financial planner who can run the numbers for you. You can find a list of certified financial planners in your neighborhood—as well as valuable advice on choosing a financial planner—at the Certified Financial Planner Board of Standards' website at www.cfp.net. You can also refer to two useful books on downscaling from two incomes to one: *You Can Afford to Stay at Home with Your Kids,* by Malia M. Wyckoff and Mary Snyder (Career Press), and *Miserly Moms: Living On One Income In a Two Income Economy,* by Jonni McCoy (Bethany House).

I've decided not to return to work after my maternity leave. When do I have to tell my employer?

There are no legal rules to worry about, so the answer to your question depends mostly on your situation. It may make sense to postpone telling your employer to keep your options open in case you change your mind. But it is also important to be considerate and give your employer enough time to find and train a replacement for you. You don't want to burn bridges, for you may want to return to work for this employer some-day—or you may want a reference from this employer if you ever decide to work for someone else.

BABYCENTER POLL

Wondering when other parents informed their bosses? According to a recent BabyCenter.com poll, 54% of the 550 responding parents who knew they would not be returning to work after their babies were born waited until the end of their parental leave to let their bosses know of their decision. Why did they wait so long? Sixty-nine percent explained that they waited so that they would remain covered by their company's health insurance plan during their leave.

If I don't return to work, do I have to pay back the wages I received while I was out on leave?

That depends on the nature of the wages you received and your company's policy. If you were paid for accrued vacation time or sick leave, then you don't have to pay them back. The same holds true for private and state disability benefits. However, if your company provided you with paid family leave, your company can ask you to pay back the compensation you received during your leave.

My company paid my health insurance premiums while I was on leave. I've decided not to return to work. Do I have to reimburse my employer?

If your employer asks you to, yes.

I've decided to stay at home with my baby, but I'm worried about my future career options. What can I do to keep from falling behind?

Although it can be challenging to reenter the workforce after spending a few years as a stay-at-home parent, there are things you can do to keep your skills current and grow your resume while you're at home with your child:

- **Stay in touch with your colleagues.** You've probably built up a network of friends and contacts in your field. It's easy to lose touch with these people when you've got a baby underfoot, but making the effort to stay connected is a smart professional (and personal) move. Your colleagues keep you in the loop during your years away and may even help you get your foot back in the door down the line.

- **Read up on your profession.** Instead of unwinding with a good magazine when your baby naps, curl up with a professional journal or newspaper instead.

- **Get involved with professional organizations.** It may seem silly to attend meetings and conferences when you're not practicing your profession. But active membership in a professional organization can be a great way to network and stay current in your field. You may even be able to take on a leadership role of some kind—such as chairing a committee, for example—that could help to fill the gap on your resume.

- **Go back to school.** If you can afford it (and if you can find the time away from your baby), taking classes or seminars in your area of expertise can be a terrific way to stay marketable during your time off.

- **Take on freelance assignments in your field.** You don't have to commit to a full-time job to get interesting and relevant work experience. If you're lucky, you may be able to do occasional short-term projects in your area of expertise.

- **Volunteer your professional skills.** You may be able to use your professional skills while you're at home with your child, even if you don't get paid to do it. For example, if you used to be a marketing executive, you might be able to volunteer your expertise to help publicize the PTA fundraiser. Volunteering can help keep your skills from getting rusty—and you'll make some new friends while you're at it.

If you need some help deciding whether to become a stay-at-home parent. If you are still struggling with choosing between home and work, pick up a copy of *Staying Home: From Full-Time Professional to Full-Time Parent,* by Darcie Sanders and Martha M. Bullen (Spencer & Waters).

BABYCENTER RESOURCES

For advice and support from fellow stay-at-home parents. BabyCenter.com's Stay-At-Home parents message board can connect you to other parents who have taken a break from the working world to raise their children. To find it, log on to the *Parent Savvy* page of Babycenter.com (www .babycenter.com/parentsavvy). You can also check out BabyCenter.com's other message boards by clicking on "bulletin boards" in the "community" menu bar at www .BabyCenter.com.

TIPS

When you're ready to return to the workforce. It's not always easy to reenter the job market after you've taken a few years off to raise your child. But with a little prodding from forward-thinking organizations such as Women for Hire, employers are realizing that former stay-at-home moms can be valuable employees. Membership in Women for Hire—an organization designed to help women find jobs and career satisfaction—is a worthwhile investment when you're ready to start sending out your resume. With a basic membership, you'll get access to career resources and guidance, as well as networking opportunities. Learn more at www.womenforhire.com. ■

Chapter 12

Returning to Work: Creating a Family-Friendly Work Schedule

One of the best strategies for balancing work and family is to adjust your schedule. If you want to stay home with your baby while keeping a foot in your career, perhaps you can work part time or job share until your child starts school. If you are a nursing mother, maybe you can work from home so that you can continue to breastfeed. Or if you want to work but don't want anyone other than a parent to care for your child, perhaps you and your partner can both switch to part-time or flextime schedules so that one of you is always home. This chapter introduces you to family-friendly work arrangements and provides advice on how to convince your employer to approve your plan.

 FAST FACTS

Not enough employers offer flexible work options. According to a recent study by the Families and Work Institute (www.familiesand-work.org), only 43% of employees have access to traditional flextime, and only 47% have access to part-time work arrangements. This is a shame, because nearly a quarter of women working full time and 13% of men working full time would prefer to be able to work part time.

Now that I'm a mom, I'd love to find an alternative to my 40-hour, Monday-through-Friday workweek. What are my options? Your imagination and your employer's flexibility are the only real limits on what you can do, but to get you started, the following are some common arrangements:

- **Telecommuting.** Just a fancy word for working at home. You'll still be considered a full-time employee, and you'll still keep your full salary and benefits. The only difference? You can go to work in your pajamas, while your child watches *Sesame Street* in the next room.

- **Flextime.** A schedule that you mold to your needs, so long as you work the required number of hours. For example, if you normally work from 9 a.m. until 6 p.m., flextime would allow you to begin work at 7 a.m. and leave work at 4 p.m.—leaving you enough time to pick your baby up from day care and get dinner started before the sun sets.

- **Compressed workweek.** A schedule that squeezes five days of work into four (or even fewer) days. For example, suppose you currently work eight hours a day, five days a week. With a compressed workweek, you might work ten hours a day, four days a week—getting a day off each week without taking a pay cut.

- **Job sharing.** Splitting one job between two people. There's no set formula for job-sharing arrangements. In some cases, job-share partners divide the work week, with each person working two and a half days a week. In other cases, job-share partners divide the work that needs to be done, instead of the time that needs to be worked.

- **Part time.** Working fewer hours and receiving less pay than a full-time commitment. For example, you might choose to work three days a week instead of five and receive 60% of your usual salary.

You can learn about the pros and cons of these family-friendly work arrangements, and get some help deciding which arrangement would be right for you, in the pages that follow.

FAST FACTS

A family-friendly work arrangement is also good for your employer. According to recent research from the Families and Work Institute, a nonprofit organization that addresses work-life issues, employees who enjoy family-friendly work arrangements are more engaged in their jobs, more committed to helping their company succeed, more likely to plan on staying with their employer, and more satisfied with their jobs. In fact, 46% of companies that offer flexible work arrangements report a positive return on their investment in these programs. You can learn more at the Families and Work Institute's website at www.whenworkworks.org.

How do I go about asking my employer for a family-friendly work arrangement?
Before you can approach your employer about a family-friendly work arrangement, you'll have to do some research and preparation. Here are the steps to take:

First, see what family-friendly work options your employer already offers. Talk to your coworkers, check with your human resources department, and review your company policy manual.

Second, decide what type of work arrangement you want. Don't expect your employer to come up with a solution for you. Instead, carefully evaluate your own needs and your employer's needs and craft a plan that will work for you both. It may be that your company already offers the work arrangement you have in mind. But you don't have to limit yourself to tried-and-tested arrangements. Many parents have successfully made arrangements that their employers have never attempted before.

Third, put together a detailed proposal for your ideal work arrangement. Unless your employer has a well-established part-time or flextime policy that requires no special approval, you'll need to write a plan that will tell your employer the following:

- the hours and days you plan to work
- the job responsibilities you will be able to handle during this time
- the salary and benefits you are seeking
- how you can be reached if an issue arises during a time when you are not in the office

- if you plan to telecommute, the child care and home office arrangements you have made and the number of days you plan to work from home
- if you are requesting a job-sharing arrangement, the name and qualifications of your proposed job-share partner (include a resume if you can) and the specific details of how you will break up your job responsibilities, and
- why the family-friendly work arrangement you are proposing is in your employer's best interests.

Make sure the plan is businesslike and focuses on your employer's needs, not your own. Experts even recommend keeping words such as "baby" and "home" out of the proposal entirely, so that you make a business case—rather than a personal plea—for the plan's approval.

Finally, set up an appointment with your supervisor to discuss your proposal.

ADDITIONAL RESOURCES

Turn to WorkOptions.com for a customized proposal. If you're worried about drafting a proposal for a family-friendly work arrangement entirely on your own, then log on to WorkOptions.com for a customizable template. Recommended by *Working Mother* and *The Wall Street Journal,* WorkOptions.com is the easiest and most stress-free way to prepare a winning proposal. The site is also crammed with useful tips on coming up with a flexible work plan, getting your boss to approve your plan, and making the arrangement work well for everyone. Another useful resource on the subject is "Workplace Flexibility: A Guide for Employees," a free pamphlet published by the Families and Work Institute. To find it, log on to www.whenworkworks.org and click on "Flex Tips for Employees, Supervisors and Companies" in the left-hand navigation bar.

Requesting a Family-Friendly Schedule

Preparation and planning are the key to winning your employer's approval of a family-friendly schedule. Before making your request, do the following:

❑ Research the family-friendly options that your employer already offers by talking to coworkers, consulting with human resources, and reading your employee handbook.
❑ Decide what type of arrangement would work for both you and your employer.
❑ Draft a detailed proposal describing the arrangement and its value.
❑ Meet with your supervisor to discuss your proposal

If you are worried, you're not alone. According to a 2004 study by Catalyst, a research and advisory organization focusing on women in the workplace, only 15% of surveyed women and 20% of surveyed men reported that they could use a flexible work arrangement without any career consequences.

Do I have a legal right to a flexible work arrangement?
No. If your employer refuses to offer you a more family-friendly schedule, you only have two options: Convince your boss to change his or her mind or find a new job.

I want to switch to a flexible work arrangement, but I'm concerned about the effect it will have on my career. Do I have any legal rights?
Your employer is not legally required to treat employees using flexible work arrangements the same as traditional full-time employees when it comes to career opportunities, such as pay raises and promotions. If you make job changes to improve your family life, you may suffer professionally in some—but certainly not all—work environments.

Temping may be the answer. If you can't find the perfect family-friendly job, then signing up with a temp agency can be a good solution. Temp agencies aren't just for replacement receptionists anymore. These days, employers are turning to temp agencies to fill a wide range of positions—from consultants to lawyers to engineers. Approximately 2.5 million people are employed by temp agencies every day, and 43% of these employees take on temporary work because they need to spend more time with their families. And if you're worried about losing benefits, many temporary staffing companies offer health insurance, paid vacations, and retirement plans. To learn more about temping, log onto www .staffingtoday.net, which is the website for the American Staffing Association, an umbrella organization for the nation's temporary staffing agencies. On this site, you'll get answers to your temping questions.

Telecommuting

What are the advantages of telecommuting? There's more to telecommuting than the ability to pad around in your pajamas in the middle of the workweek. Here are a few reasons why telecommuting is so popular:

- It will allow you to structure your own day. For example, you could do some of your work in the evening—leaving you free to take nursing breaks during the day or take your baby to the park in the afternoons.
- You will avoid the time and stress of commuting.
- You'll work more efficiently: All of those trips to the water cooler and the casual chats with your coworkers can take a big bite out of your working day. Chances are you'll get your work done in less time in the comfort of your own home. In fact, employers regularly report double-digit productivity gains among employees who telecommute.
- You'll get flexibility without a pay cut.

What are the disadvantages of telecommuting?
Before you take the plunge and ask to work from home, there are some drawbacks to consider:

- You'll still have the same amount of work to do. If your workload is the problem, working at home isn't the solution.
- You'll still need full-time child care. It's difficult enough to get the laundry done with a baby underfoot, let alone keep up with the demands of a full-time job.

- Your boss might think you're not working as hard. When you don't put in the same "face time" at the office, it's easy for your boss to think that you're not doing as much work as everyone else.
- You might get passed over for plum assignments or promotions—because out of sight can mean out of mind.
- You might feel lonely. You won't have the pleasant distractions of office chit-chat and coffee breaks with your coworkers.
- You may not get the same sense of satisfaction from clocking in a long day at your home office as you do at your work place.
- You might be distracted. For many people, working at home means fewer distractions—because there are no coworkers to gossip with or meetings to attend. But for a parent with in-home child care, there may be no place more distracting than home. Your child may seek your attention, or you may take frequent breaks to cuddle with, play with, or feed your baby—instead of working straight through the day.
- Work is always there. You won't be leaving work at the office, because your home is your office.

How do I know if telecommuting is the right solution for me?
Not every job can be done from home, but if all you need to do your job is a tele-phone, a computer, and an Internet connec-tion, then telecommuting is a good option.

Of course, the job is not the only issue to consider. You also have to think about you—your work habits, your child care arrange-ments, and your home. Are you a self-starter, or do you work best when your boss is standing in your doorway? Do you prefer to work alone and without interruptions, or do you feel lonely when your favorite coworkers are away on vacation? Do you plan on using in-home child care, or will your child be away at day care center? Is there space in your home for a dedicated home office, or will you have to do your work on your laptop at the kitchen table?

Flextime

What are the advantages of flextime?
Little changes can sometimes make a huge difference. Here are the main advantages of flextime:
- You choose when you work and when you don't. If you want to spend your mornings with your baby, for example, you could begin your day at noon and end at 8 p.m.
- Because you'll be shifting your hours—not cutting them—you won't have to give up even a dime of your salary or benefits.
- Unlike with a telecommuting arrange-ment, people will see you working, which will keep you in the office loop—and make your hard work visible to your boss.

What are the disadvantages of flextime?
Although flextime is popular, it's not the right option for everyone for two main reasons.

First, you won't have more time with your family, just different time. And the more hours you can spend with your family, the less time you'll have to yourself. For example, you may have your afternoons free to take your child to the park, but you'll have to begin your workday at the crack of dawn to earn that privilege.

Second, you might have trouble finding child care to match your schedule. Unless you've got a spouse or partner who can care for your child while you're at work, you may have a tough time finding a nanny willing to begin work at 6:30 a.m. or end her day at 9 p.m. And day care centers may be out of the question.

Does flextime mean that I can choose a different schedule every day?
It depends. For some employers, flextime means that you decide what schedule will work for you and stick to that same schedule every day. Other employers will let you change your schedule every week or even every day, just as long as you work the same number of hours each day and get your work done.

How do I know if flextime is the right solution for me?
First, think about your job responsibilities. Are there certain hours when you really have to be at work, or can you do your work at any time of the day? If you're a stock trader, for example, you have to be at work when the market is in session. But if you're an editor at a publishing house, it may not matter whether you're working at 7 a.m. or 7 p.m. And in some cases it might not matter that you're getting a chunk of work done on weekends, when your partner or spouse is available for child care.

Second, consider your family's needs. Are you looking for just a couple of extra hours in the morning or the evening to be with your child? Or do you want to work fewer hours overall, so that you can have more time for your family (or yourself)? If it's the latter, then part-time work, not flextime, is what you need.

Compressed Workweek

What are my options when it comes to a compressed workweek?
The most popular option is to work four ten-hour days instead of five eight-hour days. But that isn't the only way to go. For example, you could work five nine-hour days one week and four nine-hour days the next—taking one day off every other week. Or you could work three ten-hour days and two five-hour days—taking two afternoons off each week. It all depends on what you can work out with your employer.

Take your day off in the middle of the week. Experts recommend against taking Mondays or Fridays off even though a three-day weekend can be tempting. You'll have a better image with your boss and coworkers—and be more available for meetings and update sessions—if you choose a Tuesday or Wednesday as your day at home.

What are the advantages of a compressed workweek?

You get to spend time with your family while remaining a full-time employee—with full-time benefits and salary. In addition, you might save a little on child care. For example, let's say you work ten hours a day, four days a week. If your spouse watches your child for the extra two hours into the evening that you are working, you only have to pay for child care for 32 hours a week instead of 40.

What are the disadvantages of a compressed workweek?

It may sound ideal in theory, but a compressed workweek has drawbacks just like every other family-friendly work arrangement. The longer days can be grueling. Especially if no one else in your department is working longer hours, it can be tough to stay in the office two extra hours after everyone else has gone home.

Arranging for child care can also be tricky, depending on the hours you are working.

How do I know if a compressed workweek is the right solution for me?

First, think about your job. If your job involves regular client contact, for example, your clients might not get the service they need if you're out of the office one day a week. But if you work independently most of the time, you may be able to tackle your duties in just four days a week.

Second, think about what you and your family need. Do you want the freedom of having one entire weekday to spend with your child—even if that means that you'll see less of your child on the other four days? Or are you looking for a way to reduce the total amount of work on your plate? If it's the latter, you want part-time work, not compressed time.

Job Sharing

What are the advantages of job-sharing?

Job-sharing is still somewhat unusual, but with any luck more new parents will start to embrace this family-friendly work arrangement. You get to keep your job, but cut the amount of work—or the amount of time at work—in half. Job-sharing tends to have less of a negative impact on people's careers and responsibilities. Part-time work sometimes means career stagnation, with no promotions or advancements for some time to come. But if you can set up a really good job-sharing arrangement, you and your partner may be able to climb through the ranks at the same pace that you would have had you continued working full time.

What are the disadvantages of job sharing?

The politics of managing the job-share relationship can be challenging. Your job-share partner will be doing half of your job, so your partner's job performance will affect your own. Unless your job-share partner is as talented and diligent as you are, your combined work product might not be as good as what you could do on your own. And you'll need to communicate perfectly with one another to keep from duplicating work and to make sure everything gets done properly and on time. If you and your partner don't get along well, your work could suffer. And if your job-share partner decides to switch jobs, you'd be in quite a bind.

If you choose to job share, you'll have to absorb a significant cut in pay. And you may even have to forfeit some of your benefits to seal the deal. Of course, you may save money as well. You won't need full-time child care, for example, and you'll save on commuting costs.

How do I go about finding a job-share partner?

The best place to look is within your own company—so you won't be proposing a radical change in your work arrangement and a new hire at the same time. Is there a coworker who has recently had a child and is looking for a more family-friendly work arrangement? Or do you know someone who is struggling with other issues, such as caring for an aging parent or coping with

a health problem? Don't limit your search to candidates at your same seniority level or even in your own department. Instead, focus on finding someone who is well-qualified and can be trained to do your job.

If you can't find a suitable job-share partner within your own company, then ask around at your next professional association meeting. Consider posting an ad in a professional publication, to cast a wider net.

What factors should I consider when choosing a job-share partner?

The person should be qualified to do your job, have work habits that are similar to your own, and have a personality that is compatible with yours. It's also nice if you and your partner have similar professional goals. Pick someone who is flexible and able to cover for you on days when something unexpected comes up—for example, your child has a medical emergency.

How do I know if a job-share arrangement is the right solution for me?

First, consider whether your job is amenable to a job-sharing arrangement. Is your job one that you could easily hand off to another person in the middle of the week? If you're a documentary filmmaker or a stock analyst, for example, it may be hard for someone else to step into your head and pick up where you left off. But if you're an information technology support person, or an administrative assistant, it may be possible for someone else to do your job a couple of days a week.

Next, think about your personality and work style. Do you tend to work well with other people, or do you work best on your own? Are you well-organized and meticulous, or do you tend to work in a state of healthy chaos? To survive a job-share arrangement, you'll need to be organized enough for someone else to step in where you left off.

Finally, evaluate your family's financial needs. Will you be able to survive on just half your income? Will you have access to health insurance through your spouse's plan, if you will no longer be eligible for health insurance coverage with your new arrangement?

 FAST FACTS

Fewer employers are offering job-sharing opportunities. According to the Society for Human Resource Management, an organization representing human resources professionals, the number of employers offering job sharing fell from 26% in 2001 to 17% in 2004.

Working Part Time

What are the advantages of working part time?

Working part time gives you the best of both worlds—a work life and a family life. With a part-time schedule, you'll work just a few days a week—without having to work longer hours to earn your days off as you would with a compressed workweek. And you won't have to deal with the hassles of a job-share arrangement.

What are the disadvantages of working part time?

Financially, the cut in salary can be difficult to absorb. And you may lose your benefits.

Practically, you may end up working more than you are getting paid for. Often, people get part-time pay, but full-time assignments.

And professionally, your career may suffer. Depending on your workplace, it may be more difficult to snag high-profile assignments. Your boss might view you as someone on the mommy (or daddy) track and pass you over for promotions in favor of full-time workers.

Finally, you may have more difficult time arranging child care on a part-time basis (although share care might be a good option under these circumstances, as discussed in Chapter 18).

How do I know if working part time is the right solution for me?

First, ask yourself whether your job is one that could be done on a part-time basis. Some jobs just can't be done in 20 hours a week. Second, take a hard look at your family's finances. Could you afford to live on just a fraction of your regular salary? What would happen if you no longer qualified for health insurance coverage? Would you be able to obtain coverage through your spouse's plan?

Chapter 13
Taking Time Off for Child-Related Issues

After your baby arrives, you may find that you need more time off from work than ever before. When your child is young, you'll need to stay at home on days when your child is sick or your child care falls through. As your child gets older, there will be parent-teacher conferences to attend, school field trips, and doctor's appointments.

In some circumstances, the law will require your employer to give you time off. In others, you'll have to rely on your employer's good will and flexibility.

My six-month-old son has the stomach flu, and I want to take a few days off from work to care for him. What are my legal rights? Three states—California, Minnesota, and Washington—require employers to let workers use sick leave to care for a sick child. If you don't live in one of these states, your only hope is that your employer's own policies allow you to use sick leave or vacation time.

Our toddler was just diagnosed with a treatable form of cancer. Do I have the legal right to take time off from work to care for him? If you and your employer are covered by the federal Family and Medical Leave Act (see Chapter 10 for more about the FMLA), then you are entitled to take up to 12 weeks of unpaid leave per year to care for a child with a serious health condition—and cancer certainly qualifies as serious.

You can take your 12 weeks of leave all at once or stagger your time off over the course of several months. If you'd prefer, you can even work a reduced schedule—say, four days a week rather than five—until you've used up your 60 days of unpaid leave.

Even if you are not covered by the FMLA, you may be entitled to take unpaid leave under your state family leave law. State family leave laws are sometimes more generous than the federal law, and they often cover a wider range of employers. To learn the details of your state's family leave law, check out the booklet "Expecting Better: A State-By-State Analysis of Parental Leave Programs" from the National Partnership for Women and Families. You can find the booklet at www .nationalpartnership.org.

Do I have a legal right to take time off from work to attend my child's doctor's appointments?

Only Massachusetts and Vermont require employers to give workers time off to take their children to see a doctor or a dentist for routine appointments. If you are taking time off because your child is sick, however, you can use sick leave if you live in California, Minnesota, and Washington—or if your employer's own policies allow it.

My child's school holds midday parent-teacher conferences a couple of times a year. Can I take time off from work to attend?

A handful of states give parents the right to miss a certain number of work hours each year because of their children's school activities. These states are: California, the District of Columbia, Illinois, Louisiana, Massachusetts, Minnesota, Nevada, North Carolina, Rhode Island, and Vermont. Otherwise, you'll have to rely on your employer's own policies on this issue. ■

Chapter 14

Dealing With Unfair Treatment Because You're a Parent

Now that you are a parent, you might find your boss, your coworkers, and potential employers treating you unfairly just because you have a child. For example, your supervisor might pass you over for a lucrative promotion, commenting that you wouldn't be able to handle the stress and long hours with a little one at home. Or a potential employer might suddenly become much less enthusiastic about your job application once you mention the existence of your six-month-old twins. If you suspect that your new status as a parent is getting in the way of your current and future job prospects, this section will help you understand your legal rights under both federal and state law.

I applied for a great job as an editor. Unfortunately, I just received a rejection letter. The head of the company said he was concerned that my two children would affect my work performance. Is this legal?

Federal law does not prohibit discrimination against parents. A handful of states do, however. To find out about your state, contact your state fair employment office or labor department.

 TIPS

Federal government employers must treat parents the same as nonparents. Thanks to Executive Order No. 11478, parents are entitled to equal employment opportunities in the federal government.

My wife was recently passed over for a promotion because her boss felt that someone without children could better handle the job's hours and responsibilities. Our state does not prohibit discrimination based on parental or familial statues. Does this mean she has no rights?

No. It just means that she has a much more challenging legal battle on her hands. Because there is no parental antidiscrimination law in place, she may have to file a complaint against her employer for gender discrimination—something that is illegal under federal law and the laws of most states—if she can show that the employer treats men with children better than it treats women with children. Another route is to file a lawsuit against her employer for violating the public policy of the state. This is a complicated issue beyond the scope of the discussion here, but suffice it to say that it's worth talking about with a lawyer.

Where can I find more information about parental status discrimination or find a lawyer who specializes in this area?

If you believe that you have been treated unfairly by an employer simply because you are a parent, a terrific way to learn your rights is to contact American University's Program for WorkLife Law—a research and advocacy organization that aims to eliminate discrimination against parents and caregivers of aging parents. You can find it on the Internet at www.worklifelaw.org. If you have a problem you'd like to discuss, a staff attorney will discuss your situation with you at no cost and will let you know whether you might have a legitimate parental discrimination case on your hands. If need be, the WorkLife lawyer will also give you the name and number of a conveniently located private lawyer with experience in this area. You can reach WorkLife Law by telephone at 202-274-4488 or by email at info@worklifelaw.org. ■

Chapter 15

Health Insurance Issues

When you're having a baby, good health insurance is more important than ever You will need health insurance for everything from prenatal and maternity care for Mom to pediatric visits and immunizations for baby. Health insurance is also a key to your family's financial security. Without it, your family could be bankrupted by medical bills if one of you suffers a serious and unexpected accident or illness. Or you or your child could have to forgo quality health care because of cost concerns.

Although the United States does not provide universal health coverage to its citizens, most employers offer their employees some type of group insurance plan, and that's the focus of this chapter. It explains your rights to health insurance coverage during pregnancy and the ins and outs of enrolling your new baby or adopted child in an employer-sponsored group health plan. This chapter provides useful advice on how to choose the right health insurance plan for your family, and also covers your health insurance rights when you lose or quit a job.

Health Insurance Resources

Throughout this chapter are a number of resources that can give you additional information about health insurance. Here is a summary:

- **State laws that affect your right to health insurance and specific programs.** An excellent place to start is the Georgetown University Health Policy Institute's publication "A Consumer's Guide to Getting and Keeping Health Insurance." There, you can find state-specific health insurance guides. To download the guide for your state, log on to www.healthinsuranceinfo.net. If that doesn't give you what you want, check out the Health Insurance Law and Benefits Tool at Insure.com, a comprehensive online consumer information service, at http://info.insure.com/health/lawtool.cfm. Your state department of insurance might also be a good resource. To find your state's website, check with the National Association of Insurance Commissioners at www.naic.org. Click on the link marked "Insurance Dept. Contacts or "State Insurance Web Sites."

- **Programs for uninsured families.** Check with your state department of health for information on Medicaid and comparable state programs. To find your state health department, go to your state's home page on the Web. You can also find a complete list of state departments of health at the federal Food and Drug Administration (FDA) website at www.fda.gov/oca/sthealth.htm.
- **Public health insurance programs available to children and their families.** See Insure Kids Now!, a division of the U.S. Department of Health and Human Services, www.insurekidsnow.gov.
- **Private health insurance.** Check with your state department of insurance as well as the online consumer information service www.insure.com.
- **Federal laws.** These laws include the Health Insurance Portability and Accountability Act (HIPAA) and the Consolidated Omnibus Budget Reconciliation Act (COBRA). They affect health insurance when you lose a job or reduce your hours. To get started, log on to the website of the U.S. Department of Labor (DOL), and check out the Benefits Advisor tool at www.dol.gov/ebsa/consumer_info_health.html. You'll find other resources in discussions of specific federal laws covered in this chapter such as HIPAA and the Newborns' and Mothers' Health Protection Act.

CROSS REFERENCE

Information about health care tax breaks. Although they aren't terrific, there are a few tax breaks that cover health care expenses. See Chapter 30 for details.

Basic Information About Employer-Sponsored Health Insurance

If your employer offers health insurance benefits, you'll need to know everything from your right (and that of family members) to be covered by the plan to whether you are subject to a preexisting condition exclusion period.

Must employers provide health insurance? No federal law requires employers to provide health coverage, but a few states (for example, Hawaii), counties, and cities do. To learn whether you're covered under a state law of this nature, contact your state's insurance department (see "Health Insurance Resources," above, for contact information).

Fortunately, even when the law does not require employers to provide health insurance, the majority do so—to attract quality employees and to be fair. In fact, three out of every five American workers have employer-subsidized health insurance benefits—although plans vary greatly in terms of policies, premiums, and coverage. (Of course, this statistic does not include people who are not working. Those people are most likely uninsured, unless they are on a spouse's plan.)

ADDITIONAL RESOURCES

Wondering which companies provide the best health benefits? Check out *Fortune* magazine's ranking of companies that offer the most comprehensive employee health insurance coverage. The list is available to subscribers online at www.fortune.com.

My employer offers health insurance benefits to full-time workers only. Is this legal?
Probably. Federal law allows this practice. However, a state or local law might prohibit it. To find out whether such a law applies in your case, contact your state's insurance department.

If my employer offers health insurance benefits, must the benefits cover my spouse and child as well?
No federal law requires plans to cover dependents, but some state laws do. To learn whether your state law does, log onto Insure.com's Health Insurance Law and Benefits Tool at http://info.insure.com/health /lawtool.cfm. Or contact your state's insurance department for more information.

TIPS

Husbands and wives must be treated equally. If your employer has 15 or more employees and offers health benefits that extend to employee spouses, the federal Pregnancy Discrimination Act requires that your employer offer the same level of health insurance coverage to both husbands and wives of employees. The purpose of this rule is to prevent employers from limiting their pregnancy and childbirth-related health care costs by offering more coverage to husbands than to wives. See Chapter 9 for detailed information on the Pregnancy Discrimination Act.

Can my employer deny me health insurance coverage or charge me higher premiums because of a health condition?
No. A federal law called the Health Insurance Portability and Accountability Act (HIPAA) prohibits employers from refusing to provide health insurance benefits or charging higher premiums simply because of a medical condition or health history, such as diabetes.

My employer offers several different health insurance plans. How do I choose one that's best for my family?
If your employer offers more than one type of health insurance plan, count yourself lucky. It's important to make your choice

carefully, after reviewing the coverage and cost differences among the plans. Although you might be tempted to go with the cheapest option, bear in mind that you usually get what you pay for when it comes to health insurance. Less expensive plans generally have more restrictions on the health care providers and hospitals you may choose, and some plans provide no coverage whatsoever for things such as prenatal testing and immunizations—which means your out-of-pocket costs could be quite substantial.

Comparing health plans can be challenging, to say the least. Fortunately, there are some wonderful (and free) resources available to help you with the chore. The Agency for Healthcare Research and Quality, a division of the U.S. Department of Health and Human Services, offers several useful publications explaining how different health plans work, how to check the quality of the health plans you are considering, and how to choose the best plan for your family's needs. Visit the agency's website at www. ahrq.gov and click on "Health Plans" under "Consumers & Patients."

Another good resource is the National Committee for Quality Assurance (NCQA), an independent nonprofit organization dedicated to improving the quality of health care in America. The NCQA offers a health plan report card that lets you compare how different plans rank according to the services they provide (for example, coverage for preventive care measures and the quality of the provider network). To get started, log on to www.ncqu.org and click on "Report Cards" in the right-hand menu bar.

Health Insurance When You Start a New Job

Before starting a new job, be sure to get complete details on health insurance benefits, including your out-of-pocket costs and what family members are covered. Be sure to ask the benefits administrator when health insurance benefits start. This may not be the first day of work, because many employers impose a waiting period before a new employee becomes eligible for health insurance coverage. In addition, if your new employer's plan is a health maintenance organization (HMO), you might have to endure a waiting period imposed by your HMO as well. If there's no general waiting period, there may be a preexisting condition exclusion period before coverage begins for certain conditions (pregnancy is not one of them). See "Understanding the Preexisting Condition Exclusion," below, for details. If you'll face a gap in health insurance coverage, your best bet is to enroll in continuing benefits from your old job so that you and your family can remain covered under your previous employer's group health plan until your new benefits take effect. You can learn more about your rights to continuing benefits in **If You Lose or Quit Your Job,** below.

Coverage During Pregnancy

Now that you or your partner is pregnant, you need high-quality health care more than ever. If you are the mom, you'll need regular prenatal care to ensure that your pregnancy is progressing smoothly. You'll need maternity and postpartum care when the time comes for you to deliver your little one. And you'll need access to specialists in maternal-fetal medicine and neonatology if something goes wrong along the way.

This section will tell you what you need to know about a woman's right to health insurance coverage during her pregnancy. You'll also find a list of questions to ask your health insurance company so that you can plan and pay for your—or your partner's—prenatal and maternity care.

I just learned that I am pregnant. What do I need to find out about my health insurance coverage?

First of all, congratulations! Although your head is probably spinning right now with all of the excitement and anticipation that comes with a pregnancy, you'll need to come back down to earth to select a doctor or midwife and a place to deliver your baby. (You can learn all about your options in the first part of this book.) Before you can tackle those tasks, however, you'll need to understand the terms of your health insurance coverage so that you can make financially prudent health care decisions.

Below you'll find a list of questions to ask early on in your pregnancy. If you've been

with your health plan for some time, you'll probably be able to answer some of these questions yourself. You should be able to get the rest of the information you need from a document called the "summary plan description" (more about that in "Learning About Your Health Insurance Plan," below), through a quick call to your plan's customer service line, or from your benefits administrator.

- **Does the plan cover prenatal and maternity care?** If you work for an employer with 15 or more employees, your plan must cover your pregnancy-related medical bills.

- **Will I need preauthorization for any of my prenatal or maternity care?** Some plans require you to complete and submit a preauthorization (or precertification) form for your medical care to ensure that your bills will be covered. If your plan is one of them, find out what care requires preauthorization, what forms you'll need to complete, and the deadlines for submitting them.

- **Must I contact the health insurance company when I am admitted to the hospital for my labor and delivery?** This question is so important that we wanted to put it near the top of the list. Some health plans will penalize you financially—by reducing the percentage of your medical bills that the plan will cover, for example—if you don't call your health insurance company shortly after your admission.

- **Must I select an in-network obstetrical health care provider?** If your health plan is an HMO, then it may cover you only if you choose an in-network physician. Be sure to ask where you can find a directory of in-network obstetrical health care providers.

- **How much will I owe out of pocket if I choose an in-network health care provider?** For most plans, you'll be on the hook only for copayments (usually $10 or $20 a visit) with an in-network provider.

- **How much will I be reimbursed if I choose an out-of-network physician?** Some plans do offer out-of-network benefits, but you'll probably have to foot a substantially higher percentage of your medical bills if you choose this option.

- **Will I need a referral from my primary care doctor to see an obstetrician?** What if I require the services of a maternal-fetal medicine specialist? Most plans don't require you to get a referral to see an obstetrician, but you might need prior authorization or a referral to see a specialist.

- **Will the plan cover the cost of a certified nurse midwife?** Most plans do cover certified nurse midwives, but you may have to use one who is part of your plan's network.

- **Will the plan cover the cost of a doula?** A doula is a birth assistant whose job is to care for and coach the mother during labor. If you would like to use a doula, don't be surprised if your plan doesn't pay for it (but ask just in case).

- **Does the plan cover the cost of prenatal testing—such as ultrasounds and amniocentesis procedures?** These tests can be pricey, so find out whether you'll be the one covering the cost.

- **Must I select an in-network hospital for my delivery?** If so, can you provide a list of network hospitals in my area? Some plans limit your choice of hospitals to those that are in-network.

- **How much will I have to pay if I choose an in-network hospital for my delivery?** There are different components to a hospital bill, so find out which costs you'll be responsible for.

- **How much will I be reimbursed if I choose an out-of-network hospital?** Bear in mind that hospital bills can be quite steep, especially if you end up delivering by C-section.

- **Will the plan cover the costs of my hospital stay following my delivery?** Under the federal Newborns' and Mothers' Health Protections Act, your health insurance company must cover a minimum postpartum stay for you if it pays for hospital stays following a delivery (read more about this law below).

- **Will the plan cover the costs of an extended hospital stay for me, if medically necessary?** Hopefully your delivery will go smoothly, but if something happens that requires you to stay in the hospital for longer than expected, you'll want to know that your hospital bills will be covered.

- Will the plan cover the costs of a birth center delivery? Some health plans do cover birth centers.
- **Will the plan cover the cost of a home birth?** Most health insurance companies will not cover an obstetrical health care provider's fees for delivering a baby in your home, but they will cover prenatal and postpartum care regardless of where you choose to give birth.
- **Will the plan cover my newborn's nursery charges?** Remember that your newborn's hospital bill will be separate from your own. Typically, a health insurance plan will provide coverage only if you enroll your child for dependent benefits within 30 days of birth.
- **Will the plan cover the costs of a neonatal intensive care unit (NICU) stay for my newborn, if medically necessary?** NICU charges can be high, because newborns with medical problems require sophisticated care.
- **What is the procedure for adding my new baby to my health insurance plan?** It's useful to find out before your child is born whom you'll have to call and what forms you'll need to complete.
- **Does the plan cover well-child care, such as my baby's first set of pediatrician appointments and vaccinations?** Not every health plan covers well-child care (see below for more details).

- **What are the plan's rules with respect to emergency room visits?** Some plans will cover only those visits to an in-network hospital.
- **Will I have to reach a certain deductible amount before the plan's coverage will begin?** Some plans have a deductible amount—usually in the range of $500 to $1,000—that people have to spend before the health insurance company will begin paying bills.
- **Does the plan have any annual reimbursement limit?** Some plans have an annual coverage limit, beyond which they will not pay for any of your health care costs. You probably won't get anywhere near the reimbursement limit for a normal delivery, but you could exceed the limit if you or your baby has an extended hospital stay.

Must my employer-sponsored health plan cover prenatal and maternity care?

If you work for an employer with 15 or more employees, and your employer offers health insurance benefits, the federal Pregnancy Discrimination Act (PDA) requires that your employer-sponsored health plan cover pregnancy and childbirth-related medical bills. Your plan must also reimburse pregnancy-related medical expenses the same way that it reimburses other medical costs.

For more information about the PDA, see Chapter 9.

Must my health insurance plan cover the costs of my postpartum hospital stay?

If your plan covers childbirth-related hospital stays, the federal Newborns' and Mothers' Health Protection Act (Newborns' Act) requires the plan to cover your postpartum hospital stay for at least 48 hours following a vaginal delivery or 96 hours following a C-section.

For the purposes of the Newborns' Act, the clock starts when you actually give birth to your child, not when you are admitted to the hospital for your delivery.

> EXAMPLE: *Violet is admitted to the hospital's maternity ward on Sunday afternoon. After 14 hours of rather miserable labor, Violet finally gives birth to a cherubic baby girl at 4 a.m. on Monday. Under the Newborns' Act, Violet's health insurance plan must cover her hospital stay until at least 4 a.m. on Wednesday—48 hours from the time her daughter was born.*

CAUTION

The Newborns' Act does not apply to all employer-sponsored health plans. If your plan is insured by an insurance company rather than self-insured by the plan itself, then the Newborns' Act does not apply to your coverage. Confused? You can find out your plan's status by checking your summary plan description or calling your benefits administrator. Even if the Newborns' Act doesn't apply to your plan, a similar state law might. Ask your benefits administrator or contact your state's insurance department for details.

ADDITIONAL RESOURCES

For more information about the Newborns' Act. Check out the U.S. Department of Labor's website at www.dol.gov for details on the Newborns' Act. A good place to start your reading is a publication entitled "Questions & Answers: Recent Changes in Health Care Law," available for free at www.dol.gov/ebsa/pdf/hippa.pdf.

I am switching jobs and therefore health insurance plans midway through my pregnancy. Must my new employer cover the costs of my prenatal and maternity care?
It depends. The good news is that your new employer cannot deny coverage for your pregnancy on grounds that it is a preexisting condition. However, your new health insurance benefits may not take effect immediately because of an employer-mandated waiting period and/or an HMO affiliation period.

What this means is that you could be without health insurance coverage for several months, while you are waiting to qualify for health insurance benefits under your new plan. A few weeks without health insurance may not be a major concern if you are in your first trimester. But if you're in your eighth month of pregnancy, you certainly don't want to go without comprehensive health insurance coverage for even a few days.

There are other concerns as well: If your new employer has fewer than 15 employees, its plan might not cover prenatal and maternity care at all. And even if it does, the terms may be different from your present coverage. For example, the new plan may require you to switch to a different obstetrician because your current one is not an in-network provider.

Given these wrinkles, the best thing to do is to find out the details of your new employer's benefits before you start your new job. If you'll have to wait a few months for your new coverage to kick in or if the new coverage differs substantially from your current plan, then consider continuing your current health insurance to bridge the gap. You can learn more about your rights to continue your current health insurance coverage under the federal Consolidated Omnibus Budget Reconciliation Act (COBRA) in **If You Lose or Quit Your Job,** below.

I just lost my job. What are my rights to continued health insurance coverage for the rest of my pregnancy?
It's terrible timing for a job loss, but the good news is that you can continue your current health insurance coverage for up to 18 months provided you pay the premiums. (The same holds true if you are covered through your husband's or partner's employer-sponsored health plan, and your husband or partner loses a job midway through your pregnancy.) To learn more about your rights to continue your health insurance coverage, turn to **If Your Lose or Quit Your Job,** below.

Coverage for Your Newborn

Immediately upon birth, your baby will begin a life that is independent of yours—and this independent life includes independent medical care. Your baby will get his or her very own medical bills, even at only a few days or weeks old. In fact, a medical bill is likely to be the very first piece of mail your baby receives.

For this independent care, your baby will need his or her own coverage. This section will tell you what you need to know about your rights to add your little one to your—or the other parent's—health plan.

I receive health insurance through my employer. Must it also cover my child?
No federal law requires your employer to provide your child with health insurance. However, some states have laws that do. You can find out if your state is one of them by checking Insure.com's Health Insurance Law and Benefits tool at http://info.insure.com/health/lawtool.cfm. You can also contact your state's insurance department

Fortunately, most employers extend health insurance benefits to the children of employees regardless of the law. If you use your employer's plan, you can almost certainly enroll your child in it—although often at an additional cost. Check with your benefits administrator for details.

Must my employer-sponsored health plan cover well-child care, such as immunizations?
Although no federal law requires a plan to cover well-child care, such as your baby's first set of scheduled pediatrician appointments or immunizations, some states have laws that do. To learn whether your state is one of them, check Insure.com's Health Insurance Law and Benefits Tool at http://info.insure.com/health/lawtool.cfm. You can also contact your state's insurance department.

Most insurers recognize the importance of well-child care and cover it regardless of the law. Read your summary plan description or contact your benefits administrator for more information.

Can I add my unborn baby onto my health plan while I am still pregnant?
Although it would be convenient to get this detail out of the way before you've got your hands full with a newborn, you'll have to wait until your baby is actually born to enroll him or her.

Do I have to wait for the enrollment period to add my child to my plan?
No. Your plan must give you a 30-day window after your baby's birth to enroll your baby. Coverage will be retroactive to the date of your baby's birth.

EXAMPLE: *Anthony's son, Nicholas, is born premature. He is in the NICU for his first two weeks of life—leading to a pretty hefty hospital bill. Three weeks after Nicholas's birth, Anthony adds him to his plan. Even though Nicholas was not enrolled for health insurance coverage until he was nearly 20 days old, Nicholas's health insurance plan covers the NICU stay because the coverage is retroactive to Nicholas's birth date.*

Can my plan impose a waiting period on my baby's health insurance benefits?
No. As long as you are covered under your employer-sponsored health plan and the plan offers dependent benefits, your baby is entitled to receive health insurance coverage from the day he or she is born.

Can the plan limit coverage if my baby is born with health problems—such as a genetic disorder?
No. Regardless of the severity of your child's health problems, your employer-sponsored health insurance cannot deny coverage to your child or charge you a higher premium for your child's health coverage.

Be sure to enroll your baby within 30 days of birth. If you miss this cutoff period, the plan may impose a preexisting condition exclusion period with respect to your baby's health problems. This means that your health plan may refuse to cover your baby's health condition for up to 12 months—leaving you to foot the bills.

My spouse and I both work for companies that offer health insurance. Should we enroll our child in both plans?

It sometimes makes sense to enroll your child in more than one health plan, particularly if the cost is minimal. When two health plans offer different types of benefits—for example, one plan offers better well-child care coverage and the other offers better catastrophic health event coverage—then enrolling your child in both plans may result in a higher level of coverage for your child. The drawback is that doing so is complicated thanks to an insurance industry practice known as coordination of benefits.

Coordination of benefits is designed to ensure that you won't get reimbursed twice for the same health care bill. Here's how it works: One of the two health plans will be your child's primary plan. You usually don't get to choose which plan will be the primary plan. Rather, the plan of the parent whose birthday falls earlier in the year will be the primary plan.

Your child's primary plan will cover the costs of your child's health care as if it were your child's only health insurance plan. Then, your child's other plan (the secondary plan) will cover any expenses that were not covered by the primary plan—but only if the expenses are covered benefits under the secondary plan. For example, let's suppose your child's primary plan covers 80% of the cost of immunizations, but your child's secondary plan doesn't cover immunization costs at all. In that case, you'll be responsible for 20% of the cost of every immunization—even though your child has two insurance plans.

Before you enroll your child in more than one health insurance plan, compare the plans and talk to the benefits administrators about coordination of benefits.

Coverage for Your Adopted Child

Some special issues arise when you seek health coverage for an adopted child.

Is my adopted child eligible for health benefits through my employer-sponsored health plan?

Your employer must provide you with the same level of health care benefits, and at the same cost, for your adopted child as it would for a child that was born to you.

Is my child's birth mother eligible for dependent health benefits through my employer-sponsored health plan?

Although soon-to-be adoptive parents sometimes pay the birth mother's medical expenses for prenatal and maternity care, no federal law requires your plan to cover her. And since most plans limit dependent benefits to spouses and children only, birth mothers don't count.

TIPS

Your state may have a special law on insurance for birth mothers. A few states have cutting-edge laws that allow adoptive parents to purchase coverage for the birth mother's prenatal and maternity care through their group health plan. To see if your state is one of them, check with a qualified adoption attorney in your state. If you don't already have a stellar adoption attorney handling your case, a great place to find one is through the American Academy of Adoption Attorneys (AAAA), which is an invitation-only organization whose membership consists exclusively of attorneys who have each handled at least 50 adoption proceedings. You can learn more about the AAAA at www.adoptionattorneys.org

Can I enroll my child before the adoption is finalized?

Yes. Your child becomes eligible for dependent health benefits when placed with you for adoption, which happens when you assume financial responsibility for your child. This means that you can enroll your child in your health plan the moment he or she is born if that is when you will begin covering your child's medical and other expenses.

Do I have to wait for the enrollment period to add my adopted child to my plan?
No. You can enroll your child within 30 days following the adoption or placement of adoption of your child, and the coverage will be retroactive to the date of your baby's adoption or placement for adoption.

Can my employer impose a waiting period on my adopted child's health benefits?
No. Your adopted child is entitled to coverage from the first day that your child is adopted or placed with you for adoption.

My soon-to-be adopted child has several health problems. Can my employer deny or limit coverage?
No. Your employer cannot deny coverage for your adopted child or charge you higher premiums for the same level of coverage just because your child has serious health problems. This is true regardless of the nature of your child's health problems or the costs of treating those problems.

 CAUTION

Don't let more than 30 days pass. Add your child to your plan as soon as your child is placed with your family for adoption, because if you miss the 30-day enrollment period, your plan could impose a preexisting condition exclusion period and refuse to cover your child's medical care for conditions that your child had before the adoption, for up to 12 months.

Special Issues for Unmarried Parents

This section will tell you what you need to know about health coverage when you and your child's other parent are not married.

My partner and I are expecting a child. Can I obtain health coverage for my prenatal and maternity care through my partner's employer-sponsored plan even though we are not married?
There is no federal law that entitles you to coverage under your partner's employer-sponsored health plan. However, if you and your partner have formally registered your domestic partnership, a state or local law may require that your partner's employer-sponsored health plan give you the same health benefits offered to spouses. Contact your state's insurance department to find out.

Even if there is no state or local law to help, all is not lost. More than 8,000 employers now voluntarily offer benefits to domestic partners, so check with your benefits administrator. (About a third of these plans are limited to same-sex partners, however, so you may be out of luck if you and your partner are of opposite sexes.)

My company offers domestic partner benefits. What will we have to do to obtain them?
You and your partner will probably each have to sign an affidavit of domestic partnership. Typically, these forms state that:

- you and your partner have lived together for a certain period of time (usually at least six months)
- you and your partner are responsible for one another's financial welfare
- you and your partner are not currently married to anyone
- you and your partner are registered as domestic partners (if your state or locality offers this option), and
- you and/or your partner will inform the company in the event that your relationship ends.

Your employer might also ask for proof that you and your partner are actually living together and/or are financially dependent on one another. For example, your employer might want to see copies of your joint mortgage or joint checking account statements.

I am not married to my son's father. Is my son nonetheless eligible to be covered under his father's plan?

Yes, but the plan may require the father to sign an acknowledgment of paternity.

CAUTION

You may owe taxes on your partner's benefits. Although spousal benefits are not considered taxable income, an employee may be taxed on the value of employer-sponsored benefits for his or her domestic partner. Check with your human resources department or benefits administrator about this tricky issue.

ADDITIONAL RESOURCES

For more information about domestic partner benefits. The Human Rights Campaign (HRC), an organization dedicated to obtaining equal rights for gay and lesbian individuals in the workplace and beyond, has a comprehensive online database of employers that offer domestic partner benefits. To find it, log on to www.hrc.org, click on the link marked "Work Life," and then click on the link marked "Domestic Partner Benefits." If it turns out that your employer does not offer domestic partner benefits, HRC's website also offers a helpful manual on how to advocate for domestic partner benefits.

TIPS

A child support order can include health coverage. If you have custody of your child and a court is ordering your child's other parent to pay child support to you, ask the court to include a medical support order that requires the other parent to add your child to his or her employer-sponsored health plan until your child is an adult.

If You Lose or Quit Your Job

Life is rarely predictable, particularly when it comes to jobs. You may have lost your job in a company-wide layoff, or you might have quit because the work-life balance was, well, out of balance. Whatever the reason, the end of a job brings with it the end of employer-subsidized health insurance for you and your family. Fortunately, you don't have to become uninsured when you become unemployed. The federal Consolidated Omnibus Budget Reconciliation Act (COBRA) allows you to maintain coverage under your former employer's health insurance plan. You'll learn the basics of your COBRA rights in the questions and answers that follow.

Understanding the Preexisting Condition Exclusion

If you or any of your dependants has an ongoing health condition (such as cancer), you may be worried that you'll lose health insurance coverage for the condition if you lose your job. Fortunately, people who go immediately from one job to another (or who use COBRA benefits when they are between jobs) usually don't have to worry about this issue. This is because insurance companies can only deny coverage for preexisting conditions on people who have a gap in coverage.

If you've had a gap in health insurance coverage, however, you need to understand preexisting conditions and your rights in the face of them. For example, if you leave your job to care for your child and go uninsured for a period of time, you'll have to deal with the preexisting condition exclusion when you return to the workforce. The same holds true if you switch to part-time work and lose your health insurance benefits as a result.

To avoid getting caught off guard with surprise medical bills, know your rights when it comes to preexisting condition exclusion periods before you leave a job, start a new job, or lose your benefits because of a switch to a more family-friendly work schedule. A terrific resource is HIPAA Online, an interactive tool sponsored by the Center for Medicare and Medicaid Services (a division of the U.S. Department of Health and Human Services). To find it, log on to http://cms.hhs.gov/hipaa/online/default.asp. Another useful resource is the U.S. Department of Labor's publication entitled "Questions & Answers: Recent Changes in Health Care Law," available free at www.dol.gov/ebsa/pdf/hippa.pdf.

Losing health insurance because of a part-time schedule. You don't have to quit your job or get fired in order to become eligible for continued group health insurance coverage under COBRA. If you lose your health insurance coverage when you cut back to a part-time work schedule, you are also entitled to the COBRA health benefits described in this section.

State law may provide you with additional rights to COBRA benefits. For example, some states require even small employers (those with fewer than 20 employees) to allow former employees to continue health insurance coverage. Also, some state laws provide a longer period of coverage. Contact your state insurance department to learn more.

I just lost my job. How do I know if I am eligible to continue my health insurance benefits under COBRA?
You (and your dependents) qualify to keep health insurance coverage under COBRA if you worked for an employer with 20 or more employees and you lost your coverage under one of the following circumstances:

• You were laid off.
• You were fired for ordinary reasons, such as poor performance or low productivity or an inability to fit in.
• You quit your job.

If you have a domestic partner who has received benefits under your employer's plan, COBRA does not require your employer to extend those benefits. Many employers will do so anyway. Check with your company's human resources department.

I'm eligible for COBRA. For how long can I keep my health insurance benefits?
Generally, you and your dependents can continue coverage for up to 18 months. And if you become disabled during that period, you and your family members can keep your health benefits for up to 29 months (although you may have to pay an additional premium charge for the last 11 months.)

How much will I have to pay to continue my benefits through COBRA?

Unfortunately, COBRA health benefits come at a price: Your employer can charge you as much as 102% of the premiums.

> EXAMPLE: *Morton was the head chef at a prominent steakhouse. The steakhouse's group health insurance plan charged $500 in monthly premiums to cover the cost of health insurance benefits for Morton, his wife, and their two children. Because the steakhouse subsidized Morton's health benefits, Morton only paid $200 per month for his family's health insurance coverage. Recently, the steakhouse fired Morton for chronic tardiness. Morton signed the family up for COBRA benefits, fully expecting to pay only $200 or so for the monthly premiums. But his first bill was for $510, which is 102% of the premium.*

My COBRA premiums are so high. Is it really worth it for me to pay for continued health insurance coverage?

Yes. Here's why:

- What if you or a family member suffers an accident or illness while you are uninsured? Many a family has been financially devastated by medical bills. Don't let this happen to yours.
- Continuous insurance coverage ensures that you won't have to worry about satisfying a preexisting condition exclusion period for your next job. If you have a break in health care coverage of 63 days or more, your next employer's group health plan can deny coverage for your preexisting health conditions for up to 12 months.
- Even if you're switching jobs, it might take a few months for your health insurance coverage to kick in—and you don't want to be left uninsured during that time.
- As expensive as they are, COBRA benefits are much cheaper than buying an individual insurance policy.

How do I sign up for COBRA benefits?

You'll have to submit a COBRA election notice to your employer within 60 days from the date you lose your health insurance coverage or the date you receive a COBRA election form from your employer, whichever is later. Check with your benefits administrator for details.

I'm pregnant and on COBRA benefits. If my baby is born while I am still on COBRA, will he or she be eligible for health benefits under my former employer's health plan?

Yes, provided that the plan offers coverage for the children of current employees. You'll have to pay additional premiums for your new baby's coverage, of course. And your baby's health benefits will only last as long as your own COBRA coverage.

If you adopt a child. COBRA treats adopted children the same as biological children.

Watch out for the preexisting condition exclusion. If you have a gap in coverage because you've run out of COBRA benefits before finding a new job, you'll likely be subject to the preexisting condition exclusion. See "Understanding the Preexisting Condition Exclusion," above, for more information.

I've exhausted my COBRA benefits but still haven't found a new job. Do I have any legal rights when applying for individual health coverage?

Yes. Federal law requires insurance companies to grant your health insurance application provided that:

- you've elected and used all of your available COBRA coverage
- you've had at least 18 months of continuous health insurance coverage under a group health plan with no break in coverage of 63 days or more, and
- your group health insurance coverage was not terminated because of fraud or nonpayment of premiums.

The law does not limit the amount that an insurer can charge you for this coverage, however, which can be quite expensive, particularly if you're used to group health plan premiums.

To learn more about COBRA coverage. A good starting point for more information about COBRA is the U.S. Department of Labor's online publication entitled "Frequently Asked Questions about COBRA Continuation Coverage." To find it, just log on to www.dol.gov/ebsa/faqs/faq_consumer_cobra.html. ■

4 · Who's Minding the Baby? Choosing and Managing Child Care

Contents

*F*or most working parents, child care is a major concern. There are at least seven major types of care for you to choose from—from nannies to day care centers—and within each of those are several variations. Advice from friends and family can only provide so much guidance, for selecting the right child care arrangement is necessarily a personal decision. Different families have different needs and priorities, so the solution that works wonderfully for your neighbor might not work well for you. And picking a type of care is only the beginning: You must still find potential care givers or centers, investigate your options, make a choice, and then manage the relationship.

The chapters that follow help with all of these issues. Chapter 16 provides some general information about your child care options and helps you choose the type that is best for your family. Chapters 17 through 22 provide in-depth material on the advantages and disadvantages of each particular child care option, guidance on how to interview child care providers and check references, advice on the legal rules that apply in each situation, and tools for managing your relationship with the provider you chose.

Chapter 16

Deciding What Type of Child Care to Use

The initial question of what type of child care to choose can be overwhelming. There are so many choices and considerations that it may be difficult to figure out what is best for your family. A nanny gives great individual attention, but can you afford one? A day care center means lots of playmates, but will your child get lost in the group? Rest assured that every parent struggles with choosing a type of child care, but every parent also finds a workable solution. This chapter will help you make the choice that is right for you and your child.

BABYCENTER POLL

Feeling guilty about leaving your baby with someone else? You might feel better knowing that plenty of other parents are making the same choice. In a recent BabyCenter.com poll, 72% of 7,700 parents responding said they will use some form of child care during their child's first year of life.

When should I start thinking about finding child care—and how long will it take?

If you are still pregnant or gave birth just days ago, you've got plenty of other things on your mind—and worrying about child care should not necessarily be one of them.

That being said, the more time you can give yourself, the better. Researching, interviewing, and signing on the dotted line with a child care provider takes time and energy—and luck and perseverance—so start the process two to three months before you need the care. You may have to put your child on a waiting list, or you may interview scores of nannies without finding the right one, so giving yourself a nice time cushion is important (after all, you don't want to have to pick a caregiver who is less than ideal just because you're due at work the next day).

If you have a child with special needs—or if you have unusual schedule requirements—you might need even more time.

What are my choices when it comes to child care?

New parents have more child care options than ever. Here is a quick overview of the pros and cons of each type. You can find more detailed information in the chapters that follow.

Day care centers provide a structured environment with teachers, some of whom are trained in early childhood education. Although centers don't give children the same one-on-one attention as do nannies, children get the chance to socialize with other children throughout the day. You might sleep better, too, knowing that day care centers are licensed and inspected by your state government. (See Chapter 20 for more about day care centers.)

Although **preschools** are similar to day care centers, they focus on your child's academic, social, and physical development.

Preschool will become an option once your child nears age three. (See Chapter 21 for more about preschools.)

In **home-based day care (or family care) centers,** one or more people care for children in a home. Some parents feel that home-based day care combines the advantages of both nanny care and day care centers: Your child will have the opportunity to play with other children throughout the day, but will still enjoy the comforts of a home-like environment. (See Chapter 22 for more about family care.)

A **nanny** is, quite simply, the closest substitute to a stay-at-home parent, giving your child consistent, one-on-one care in your own home. There are advantages for parents as well: No need to worry about set drop-off and pick-up times or scrambling for backup care when your child is ill, for example. The comfort and convenience of a nanny comes with a hefty price tag—nannies are generally the most expensive child care option around. (See Chapter 17 for more about nannies.)

If you like the idea of a nanny but can't quite foot the bill on your own, **share care** might be the best option for you. With share care, one nanny cares for children from two (or more) families at the same time. You won't have quite the same convenience and flexibility that you would with a nanny devoted to your child only. Still, the cost savings and built-in playmates that come with share care make it quite appealing to many families. (See Chapter 18 for more about share care.)

For parents in search of affordable one-on-one care for their children, the **au pair** program can be like a dream come true. An au pair is someone from another country who lives with your family and cares for your child for one or two years as part of a cultural exchange. You'll pay an au pair substantially less than what you would pay a nanny, but there are some limitations: An au pair can work only 45 hours per week and must return to her home country within two years of her start date. In addition, you don't get the chance to meet the au pair before she shows up to work. (See Chapter 19 for more about au pairs.)

Nana as Nanny

Some parents are lucky enough to have a relative who's willing to step in and help out with child care, often at little or no cost. When you sign up a relative as your nanny, there will be no need for background checks or nanny cams—your child is with someone you love and trust. But relative care is not without its pitfalls: You'll have to navigate the challenging and sometimes awkward relationship issues that are part and parcel of employing a relative. Although this book does not provide details on relative care, you'll find the discussion of **Getting Your Nanny Started** in Chapter 17 helpful.

For an overview of the pros and cons of relative care and how to make the relationship work, see the articles on relative care on the *Parent Savvy* page of Babycenter .com (www.babycenter.com/parentsavvy).

There are so many child care options! How do I choose the one that is right for me? All parents want the best child care possible for their child. Choosing child care is a very personal decision, one that depends on your own family's particular needs and priorities.

Here are some key factors to consider:

- the age and number of your children
- any special needs your children have
- your work schedule (hours, days, flexibility)
- your budget
- the location and size of your home
- availability of backup child care (another parent, friend, or relative, for example), and
- your personal preferences (one-on-one attention in your home versus socialization opportunities in a day care center, for example).

One couple might hire a nanny to avoid the struggle of getting the child dressed and out the door before the morning commute; another couple might choose a day care center because they want a structured environment and curriculum. You may know you want someone in your house, or maybe you're just not sure. Depending on factors such as the age of your child and your work situation, you may even put together a combination of care—a day care center three days a week and Grandma two days, for example.

TIPS

Child care needs will change. The type of care you choose for your six-month-old baby will likely be different from what you would choose for that same child two or three years later. Nannies may come and go. A day care center may switch directors, spurring you to move on. You may cut back on your work hours and need another type of care. So child care is a topic that you may revisit many times before your child starts school.

I have a child with special needs. What do I need to know?
Finding good care for a child with a disability or other special need is challenging at best. How it affects the type of care you choose depends on your child's particular issue. No matter what, however, you must be frank with potential caregivers about your child, and you must address your child's special needs when questioning caregivers. For example, find out if the caregiver has experience with these issues. What are the caregiver's attitudes toward people with disabilities in general and your child's disability in particular? If therapists or other professionals will be working with your child, will the caregiver take advice and instructions from these people?

The law provides you with some protection in this area. The federal Americans with Disabilities Act makes it illegal for child care centers and home-based day care centers to discriminate against children with disabilities. Among other things, this means that it is illegal for them to charge you more because of your child's special needs.

The ADA does not apply to nannies and other individual caregivers, however, so you may find yourself rejected by nannies after you explain your child's needs—or charged more money.

ADDITIONAL RESOURCES

For detailed advice on finding care for children with special needs. Bananas Inc. is a child care referral service in Northern California that has a number of wonderful materials on its site for choosing and managing child care. Download "Choosing Child Care For A Child With Special Needs" for free from www.bananasinc.org.

I've heard all kinds of figures for child care costs. How much can I expect to pay?

Child care costs can range from a few hundred dollars a week to thousands of dollars a month, depending on the type and amount of care (live in or live out, day care center or nanny) and the qualifications of the child care provider. Where you live is also a key factor.

Here are some ranges for monthly costs of full-time child care:

Nanny:	$1,600 to $2,600
Share Care:	$1,300 to $1,600
Au Pair:	$1,160 plus room and board
Home-Based Care:	$700 to $1,000
Day Care Center:	$500 to $1,250

Ways to Lower Your Child Care Costs

- Take advantage of the child care credit and dependent care accounts.
- Consider less expensive variations (share care instead of a nanny, for example, or family day care instead of a center).
- Shift your work schedule to lower the number of hours your child is in nonparental care.
- Start a babysitting co-op.

How can I minimize child care costs?

Child care can really break the bank—and it can be frustrating to feel like you are signing over your weekly paycheck to your nanny. Child care is often the single largest expense for working parents—topping even the mortgage or rent in some cities. Fortunately, there are ways to cut costs.

If you qualify, take advantage of child care tax credit and dependent care accounts. They can lower your out-of-pocket expenses and help offset the cost of child care. (See Chapter 29 for more information on these child care tax breaks and how to claim them.)

If your first choice is too expensive, consider a less expensive variation. For example, share care gets you most of the advantages of a nanny for half the cost.

Think about shifting your work schedule. For example, you might be able to work four ten-hour days instead of five eight-hour days to save on one day's worth of child care bills. Or you may want to talk to your partner about coordinating your schedules so that one of you can care for your child while the other is at work.

If you work part time, connect with other parents. Although we don't cover them in this book, babysitting co-ops, in which parents watch each other's kids, can be an inexpensive, or even free, way to go. For general information on babysitting co-ops, go to the *Parent Savvy* page of Babycenter .com (www.babycenter.com/parent savvy). Also, Bananas Inc. sells a guide titled "Parent-Created Child Care—Exchanges and Babysitting Co-ops." Order it through the organization's website at www .bananasinc.org.

Backup Child Care Plans

Regardless of which child care option you choose, you won't always have care when you need it. There will be days when your child is ill or when your nanny calls in sick. Unless you have a plan for backup child care, you're going to have to call in sick yourself or use vacation time to stay home with your child.

The best backup plan is a flexible job and an understanding boss—but few people have that, so here are some options for the rest of us:

- **See whether your company offers emergency backup day care.** Some family-friendly companies have backup care for when an employee's child care plans fall through.
- **Contact a nanny or babysitting agency.** Some agencies will send over a caregiver with just a couple of hours' notice—but expect to pay a premium.
- **See if a friend's nanny can pinch-sit.** Your friend may be willing to let you drop off your child at her house when your nanny calls in sick, if you promise to do the same when her nanny is away.
- **Ask grandma to be on call.** You may be able to enlist your relatives (or even your close friends) as backup troops, but be careful not to abuse this privilege.
- **Telecommute.** Now that we're in the digital age, working from home is considered perfectly respectable—so you might be able to stay home with your child without wasting a vacation day. If you plan to use this as your backup child care plan, talk to your boss in advance to see whether it is okay. And don't plan on getting as much done as you would at the office, because you'll have to care for your child in addition to doing work. But you may get away with taking only a few hours of vacation time, instead of a full day.

If the numbers still don't add up. Believe it or not, it might actually be more cost-effective to stay at home than to work outside the home and pay for child care. Chapter 11 can help you decide whether staying home makes financial sense for you.

Babysitter Basics

This book does not cover child care that is irregular or after work hours, such as a teenager who babysits your child on a Saturday night. BabyCenter.com has several articles on finding and using babysitters, plus a useful checklist for medical and emergency contact information. You can find these resources on the *Parent Savvy* page of Babycenter.com (www.babycenter.com/parentsavvy).

If this book doesn't answer all of your questions. BabyCenter.com is packed with invaluable child care guidance—covering everything from how to ensure that your child care arrangement runs smoothly to planning for backup child care. Just go to the *Parent Savvy* page of BabyCenter.com (www.babycenter.com/parentsavvy).

Child Care Options at a Glance

	DAY CARE CENTER	PRESCHOOL	HOME-BASED DAY CARE
Does my child have to be a certain age?	It depends on the day care center. For example, many centers do not accept infants.	Yes. Preschools generally require that your child be at least two and a half or older.	It depends on the center you choose. Some providers do not accept infants.
Is there any state licensing procedure?	Yes.	Yes.	Yes. However, the licensing standards for home-based day care centers are less rigorous than those for regular day care centers.
Will my child care provider be professionally trained in early childhood education?	Yes.	Yes.	Probably not, but it depends on whom you hire.
Will I be able to choose my own child care hours?	No.	No.	Perhaps. Some home-based day care providers are less rigid than others when it comes to drop-off and pick-up times.
Will my child be cared for in my own home?	No.	No.	No.
Will my child enjoy one-on-one attention all day long?	No.	No.	No.
Will my child benefit from a formal curriculum of activities?	Yes. However, some day care centers have more of a set curriculum than others.	Yes.	Maybe—it depends on the center.
Will I be able to choose how my child spends her day?	No.	No.	No.
Is my child likely to catch minor illnesses from exposure to other children?	Yes.	Yes.	Yes.
Will I have to find backup care when my child is ill?	Yes.	Yes.	Yes.

Child Care Options at a Glance

	NANNY	SHARE CARE	AU PAIR
Does my child have to be a certain age?	No.	No.	Yes. Au pairs cannot care for infants younger than three months without supervision.
Is there any state licensing procedure?	No.	No.	No. However, there are some qualifying requirements for au pair candidates (such as English fluency).
Will my child care provider be professionally trained in early childhood education?	Probably not, but it depends on whom you hire.	Probably not, but it depends on whom you hire.	Yes. All au pairs must have a minimum amount of training (24 hours) in early childhood education.
Will I be able to choose my own child care hours?	Yes.	Yes, but you'll have to accommodate the scheduling needs of the other family as well.	Yes, but you cannot ask your au pair to work more than 45 hours in a week or ten hours in a day.
Will my child be cared for in my own home?	Yes.	It will depend on your arrangement with your nanny and the other family.	Yes.
Will my child enjoy one-on-one attention all day long?	Yes.	Yes, to an extent. It depends on how many other children your nanny is caring for at the same time.	Yes.
Will my child benefit from a formal curriculum of activities?	No.	No.	No.
Will I be able to choose how my child spends her day?	Yes.	Yes. However, you'll have to accommodate the needs of the other child(ren) in the share.	Yes.
Is my child likely to catch minor illnesses from exposure to other children?	No.	Yes. However, there will be fewer illnesses than at a day care center or preschool.	No.
Will I have to find backup care when my child is ill?	No.	It depends on the sick child policy you've agreed to with the other family.	No.

Chapter 17

Nannies

If you want individual care for your child in your home, and are willing to pay for it, a nanny may be your best option, particularly if your child is very young and both parents work.

This chapter will take you step by step through the process of finding, screening, and hiring an excellent nanny, whether on your own or with an outside agency. It provides advice on paying your nanny, preparing a child care employment agreement, and getting your nanny relationship off to a good start and keeping it that way.

Pros and Cons of Nannies

Nannies can be a godsend to working parents—providing convenience and flexibility to the parents and highly personalized care to the child. But they have their drawbacks as well, not the least of which is their high price tag. Find out more in this section.

What are the advantages of hiring a nanny? For some families, a nanny is the only child care option—and for good reason. Here are some of the many benefits of having a quality nanny:

- Your child will receive one-on-one nurturing all day long in your own home—an environment that you control and that contains familiar toys, books, and other comforts.
- Your child will build a close relationship with another caring adult who can become part of your extended family during your child's important early years.
- You'll have all the scheduling flexibility you need. Unless you hire a nanny with significant personal commitments (such as a child of her own), you'll generally get to choose the hours that your nanny works. Depending on your arrangement, your nanny can stay in the evenings and tuck your little one into bed when you're working late.
- A nanny is convenient. You won't have to get your child fed, dressed, and out the door before you leave for work, because your child care provider will come to your home.
- Your nanny might take care of some basic household chores, such as your child's laundry. Although most nannies don't mop floors or prepare dinner for the whole family, many handle light

housekeeping in addition to child care duties.

- A nanny can enrich your child's life through outings—for example, to the park, to story time at the library, to music class.
- With a nanny, your child won't be exposed to other children on a regular basis—which means your child will endure fewer colds and illnesses than children in group care settings.
- If your child does become ill, your nanny can still provide care. In a group care setting, you'd have to keep your child at home.

What are the disadvantages of hiring a nanny?

If you have visions of Mary Poppins arriving at your doorstep each morning to care for your child, keep in mind these drawbacks:

- You'll be dependent on one person for child care. There will invariably be days when your nanny comes down with the flu or needs to take time off for personal reasons—days when you'll be stuck without child care. Life can also be turned upside down if your nanny quits—especially if your child has grown attached to her.
- The government doesn't license nannies, so it will be entirely up to you to make sure that the nanny you hire is competent and skilled at child care.
- Unless you work at home, there won't be anyone watching your nanny. In a group care situation, other caregivers—and the center's director—provide supervision.

- You (or your nanny) will have to schedule play dates or enroll your child in classes if you want your child to spend time with other children during the day.
- The relationship between you and your nanny can be challenging. Because she will care for your child and spend her workday in your home, your nanny will become more like a family member than an employee. It's tougher than you might imagine to ask a nanny to love your child as her own, but to still respect you as her boss.
- It can be a headache to hire and pay your nanny legally. If you do it by the book, you'll have to deal with paperwork and maybe even use a payroll service.
- Last, but not least, a nanny is the most expensive child care option around—unless you have a live-in nanny or more than one child.

Deciding What You Want in a Nanny

Every family needs a nanny who is loving, trustworthy, patient, and armed with plenty of childrearing smarts. Beyond these obvious qualities, however, there is no simple formula for the perfect nanny. Different families need different types of nannies depending on the age and number of their children and the parents' work schedules.

Before you start looking for a nanny, think carefully about what you want in terms of schedule, responsibilities, pay, and other important issues. For example, some families want a nanny who is fluent in English, while other families might actually prefer someone who speaks a different language. Suburban families might need a nanny with a valid driver's license, while urban parents might just need someone with enough common sense to navigate the public transportation system. You might prefer an older woman with lots of experience from raising her own children or someone younger with plenty of energy for your active toddler.

Before you begin your nanny search in earnest, devise your own wish list, using the "Nanny Priorities" checklist, below, as a guideline of important issues (all of which are discussed in this section). Otherwise, you'll end up spinning your wheels by interviewing nannies who just don't fit the bill.

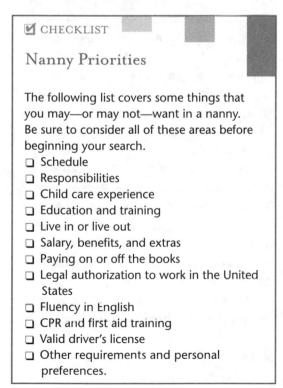

CHECKLIST

Nanny Priorities

The following list covers some things that you may—or may not—want in a nanny. Be sure to consider all of these areas before beginning your search.

- ❏ Schedule
- ❏ Responsibilities
- ❏ Child care experience
- ❏ Education and training
- ❏ Live in or live out
- ❏ Salary, benefits, and extras
- ❏ Paying on or off the books
- ❏ Legal authorization to work in the United States
- ❏ Fluency in English
- ❏ CPR and first aid training
- ❏ Valid driver's license
- ❏ Other requirements and personal preferences.

TIPS

Know your priorities. Finding the right nanny is often a matter of give and take, so decide now which features are nonnegotiable and which are not. For example, you might ideally want a nanny who's willing to do all of your family's laundry while your child naps—but you might end up settling on a nanny who doesn't mind doing your child's laundry but draws the line at hand washing your underwear.

Schedule and Flexibility

What hours and days do you want the nanny to work? Five days a week from 8:30 a.m. to 5:30 p.m.? Two days a week from 10 a.m. to 3 p.m.? Four full days plus a regular weekend night? Depending on your schedule, you may need a live-in nanny if you want exceptionally long or unusual hours. If you need a lot of flexibility because you work different hours on different days, you might have to pay a premium.

When thinking about schedule, make sure you build in time to talk to the nanny before and after work—you'll want to give her information about your child before the day begins (what time your child woke up, for example, or whether you suspect your child is coming down with a cold), and you'll want your nanny to tell you how the day went.

Do you want a nanny who is available nights and weekends for babysitting? Some nannies appreciate the opportunity to earn a little extra income, while others prize their personal time.

Child Care Responsibilities

It goes without saying that you want a nanny who takes excellent care of your child. But what does this mean? Parents often disagree about important issues, such as what activities are appropriate for the child and how the child should be disciplined. Do you want a nanny who will comfort your child to sleep, or do you want someone who will sleep train your child by putting your child on a schedule? Do you want a nanny who plans the day down to the last minute, or one who will let your child choose activities as the day unfolds? Nannies have to make decisions in the moment—without a parent there to tell them what to do. So you should pick a nanny who has the same child care philosophy that you have—or at least has one that is close.

Household Responsibilities

Do you want your nanny to do housework in addition to caring for your child? It is perfectly reasonable to expect your nanny to do your child's laundry, make meals and snacks, clean up after your child (and herself), and keep your home neat and tidy. But heavy housework—such as polishing the floors and scrubbing the tub—and cooking dinner for the family every night are probably too much to ask. You don't want your

nanny spending too much time cleaning and not enough time loving and nurturing your child.

Child Care Experience

It's best to find a nanny with experience caring for children the same age as yours. If you have twins, look for a nanny who has cared for twins in the past—or at least two children very close in age. If you have a child with special needs or health problems, try to find a nanny who has experience with similar issues.

Unfortunately, the ideal nanny may simply not be available at the time you're looking or may want more pay than you can afford or a schedule that you can't accommodate. Think carefully about how much experience you need. A first-time nanny might be willing to work with you on issues such as salary and schedule, but be sure you're comfortable with the idea of leaving your child with someone who has never formally worked as a nanny. Also, keep in mind that someone who's worked several years as a teacher or camp counselor might be fine.

And don't forget the hands-on experience offered by a nanny who's raised her own children. There is a flip side, however: If your nanny has a young child, you may run into more scheduling difficulties and require more backup child care. This is because your nanny will have to prioritize the needs of her own child—for example, staying home when her child is ill—rather than taking care of yours.

Education and Formal Training

Do you have specific educational requirements for your nanny? Although a bachelor's degree in early childhood education is an unreasonable requirement (unless you're offering a very comfortable salary), it's certainly fair to expect that your nanny have first aid and CPR training. You might even want to insist that the nanny have a high school diploma.

Live In or Live Out

Depending on your schedule and family needs, you may want your nanny to live in your house. Hiring a live-in nanny is a big step—one that can have quite an impact on your personal and family life—so be sure that a live-in nanny is the right choice for you before taking the plunge.

What does it mean to have a live-in nanny?
As the name suggests, a live-in nanny is someone who will live in your home and care for your child. Usually, she'll need her own room (and ideally her own bathroom). If you have visions of being served hand and foot by your live-in nanny—enjoying breakfast in bed on

Saturdays and complimentary babysitter coverage on Friday nights—think again. A live-in nanny will expect a schedule of the hours and days she will work (and be paid). Although a live-in nanny may always be just a few steps away, don't expect to call on her at all hours of the day and night (unless you are willing to pay for this privilege). You also can't expect a live-in nanny to also serve as your full-time housekeeper just because she happens to live in your home. Basically, a live-in nanny is the same as any other nanny—except that you'll provide her with room and board in addition to a cash salary.

What are the advantages of hiring a live-in nanny?
There are a number of benefits to having a nanny who lives in your home:

- You won't have to pay as much out of pocket. Because room and board are part of the nanny's compensation package, a live-in nanny will accept a lower salary than a live-out nanny. So if you're house rich and cash poor, a live-in nanny may be a good way to go, especially if you have more than one child.
- Your nanny will become like a true member of your family. There's no ice breaker like padding around in your pajamas with someone. Your child may develop a closer bond with a live-in nanny as well, because he or she will have more opportunities to spend time with the nanny.
- You'll have lots of scheduling flexibility. Because there's no commute to worry about, a live-in nanny will generally be able to begin work early or stay late if

need be. If you and your partner both work long and stressful hours, you might have no choice but to hire a live-in nanny to get the kind of child care coverage you need.

- You won't have to worry about a nanny arriving late because she missed the bus or got stuck in traffic. This may sound insignificant, but rushing out to work in the morning when you have a child is challenging enough. When a nanny arrives even a few minutes late, your entire day can get off to a terrible start.

- You'll have someone to help with middle-of-the night feedings and diaper changes. Particularly if you've been blessed with twins, it can be tough to handle the night shift on your own. A live-in nanny can be a godsend for this purpose (but remember that you cannot ask your nanny to be on call 24 hours a day without paying her for those hours).

What are the disadvantages of hiring a live-in nanny?

No child care option is perfect. Here are a few of the biggest drawbacks to hiring a live-in nanny:

- You'll have to give up your privacy. Unless you live in a sprawling mansion, a live-in nanny will know about every argument you have with your spouse, every time you lose your temper with your child, and other personal ups and downs. Even simple things such as enjoying breakfast with your partner and child can be different when a nanny is popping into the kitchen to grab a cup of coffee and some toast. Here's a good way to gauge your ability to deal with this lack of privacy: If you don't handle houseguests well, you probably can't handle a live-in nanny.

- You'll know much more about your nanny than you otherwise would. You might hear the door shut when your nanny returns from a late night out, for example, or have to comfort her at the kitchen table after a bad breakup. This intimacy can strain and complicate your relationship with your nanny.

- You'll have to give up some space. Depending on the size and layout of your house, you may have to forego an important room—such as a study or guest room—to accommodate the nanny.

Salary

How much do you want to pay your nanny? To come up with a reasonable figure, find out what other parents in your area are paying their nannies. Consider using a salary range rather than a fixed figure. For example, you might be willing to pay a premium rate of $14 per hour for a top-notch nanny but only $11 per hour for someone with minimal nanny experience. Or you might pay a flat fee of $1,500 per month for a live-in nanny who has room and board and other benefits. Also, be prepared to pay more for part-time help or a more flexible schedule. See **Paying Your Nanny**, below, for more on setting a nanny's pay.

Benefits and Extras

Will you be offering any perks in addition to salary? You might be able to attract the best candidates even with an average salary if you're willing to provide other benefits, such as health insurance or a gym membership. Think creatively here—for example, you might be able to offer a live-in nanny her own phone line or a computer for minimal out-of-pocket cost.

Paying On or Off the Books

If you would like to pay your nanny legally—that is, making deductions for Social Security and taxes—you may have a more difficult time, because many otherwise well-qualified nanny candidates don't want to pay taxes on their income. Moreover, your nanny might even ask for a higher salary if she's on the books, to make up for the tax bite. For more about this issue, see the discussion on income and payroll taxes in **Paying Your Nanny**, below.

Legal Authorization to Work in the United States

Even though some of the best nannies are not "legal"—that is, they are not authorized to work in the United States—there are several downsides to hiring an illegal immigrant as your nanny:

- You cannot pay an illegal immigrant nanny on the books or comply with other legal requirements, because she is not legally authorized to work in the United States. (For more on this, see **Legal Requirements for Employing a Nanny**, below.)

- It's more difficult to conduct a background check on someone who is not officially part of the system—so you might be taking more chances when you hire an illegal immigrant as your child's nanny. (See **Arranging a Nanny Background Check**, below, for details.)

- An illegal immigrant may not be able to get a valid driver's license in your state, an important issue if you want a nanny to drive your children to the park, play dates, and the like.

- A nanny who is not legal will not be able to travel with your family by plane or train.

Having said that, many families do build very successful relationships with nannies who are not legally authorized to work in the United States. You might find that these nannies command lower salaries and are more willing to do housekeeping chores in addition to child care duties. If you decide to hire an illegal immigrant to care for your child, be especially careful to check her references before she begins working for you.

Fluency in English

You may be willing to hire someone who doesn't speak English very well. That's your call. But keep in mind that communicating may be very difficult, especially if you have a newborn and want to know all the details of the baby's day. You'll want to make sure that the nanny understands all your instructions and preferences and, most importantly, knows how to deal with an emergency. Keep in mind that speaking English may not be enough—you may want your nanny to read and write in English. Although a nanny's education level may not be important to you, a nanny who cannot read English might not be able to read signs, warning labels, or other important day-to-day documents. This may affect your child's health and safety—for example, if your child is allergic to eggs, your nanny should be able to read the ingredients on cookie boxes and other food items.

CPR and First Aid Training

All nannies should know CPR and have basic first aid skills. These courses are short and relatively inexpensive, so don't make this a sticking point if you meet a candidate whom you otherwise adore. Consider paying for the training yourself—to ensure that the nanny completes it soon after she begins working for you.

Valid Driver's License

If your nanny will be driving your child around, she'll need a valid driver's license. Be sure to check that your nanny has a safe driving record before she takes your child out or uses your car. (See **Arranging a Nanny Background Check,** below, for more about checking driving records.) Also consider test driving your potential nanny—by asking her to take you on a long ride—to see if you feel comfortable with her road skills before you hire her.

Do you want your nanny to have her own car or will you allow her to use yours when caring for your child? In either case, make sure there is appropriate insurance coverage in place. If your nanny will be driving your car, you'll have to add your nanny to your auto insurance policy. (She's probably not automatically covered since she's not a family member.) If the nanny will be driving her own car, her own policy may not cover accidents that happen while she is driving your child (because some policies do not provide coverage for business use of an automobile). Ask the nanny to check the terms of her policy and—if needed—to expand her coverage to include business use. (You might have to offer to pay any difference in premiums.)

No Problem With Parents Working at Home

If you will be in the home when your nanny is there, quiz your candidates about their feelings on this issue. Some nannies prefer not to have the child's parents home during the day because it distracts the child and makes it more difficult for the nanny to do her job. Other nannies are perfectly comfortable working in this type of situation.

Other Requirements and Personal Preferences

There are a host of other issues that may be important to you and may spell disaster in an otherwise great nanny. For example, do you want a nanny who shares your same religion or politics (or at least is not the complete opposite)? If you're a complete neat freak, does your nanny need to be also? Do you want a nanny willing to keep a Kosher home? If you don't smoke, do you want a nonsmoking nanny? If you have a pool, you'll want a nanny with adequate swimming skills.

☑ CHECKLIST

Finding a Nanny on Your Own

If you don't hire an agency to find a nanny for you, the process can seem overwhelming. It doesn't have to be. Just follow these steps:

❑ Write up a brief description of what you are looking for in a nanny—in terms of schedule, responsibilities, live in or out, experience, salary, legal status, fluency in English, valid driver's license, and other requirements.

❑ Ask friends, family, and coworkers for recommendations on prospective nannies.

❑ Look at nanny-recommended ads in newspapers and online resources.

❑ Place nanny-wanted ads in community papers and on Internet bulletin boards.

❑ Prescreen prospective candidates over the telephone to see if they meet your needs.

❑ Call each qualified candidate's references to verify nanny information and ask about the nanny's strengths and weaknesses.

❑ Arrange in-person interviews with nannies who pass your prescreen.

❑ For good candidates, call references again with follow-up questions.

❑ Schedule a second meeting with the two or three best candidates.

❑ Consider ordering a background check on the nanny candidate you like the most.

❑ Make an offer to your first choice.

❑ Spend a few days with the nanny before making a firm commitment.

❑ Create an employment agreement covering all the details of the job.

❑ Prepare nanny training materials such as an emergency contact sheet.

❑ Establish a system for communicating regularly with your nanny.

Searching for a Nanny

This section provides an overview of a typical nanny search and gives you the information you need to find the best nanny for your family.

How long will it take me to find a nanny?
Finding a quality nanny is no quick task. To avoid feeling compelled to hire the first reasonable candidate you meet, give yourself at least eight weeks if you are conducting a nanny search on your own. (You can get away with less lead time—about four weeks—if you are using an outside agency. See **Working With a Nanny Placement Agency**, below.) Be sure to build in enough time to stay at home and train the nanny before you go back to work.

CAUTION

If you find a nanny too quickly. You may be lucky enough to meet your dream nanny in the first week or two of your search. But if you've given yourself a full eight weeks for your search, your nanny might be unwilling to wait until your desired start date to begin work. You'll then have to choose between paying a nanny for several weeks when her help is not needed or—if that's not financially practical—passing on a nanny you like very much.

Where do I begin my search for a nanny?
The parent grapevine is the best place to start. Canvas friends, neighbors, work colleagues, and even your pediatrician's office for leads. Ask about nonprofit organizations in your area that help parents to find quality in-home child care. Other parents' nannies may know of candidates.

Many parents swear by the list of nanny-recommended ads in newspapers and local parenting websites. Sometimes, a family must let a beloved nanny go because the family is moving out of town, the children are starting school, or one parent has decided to stay at home. These families often go out of their way to ensure that their former nannies find a good home.

What about advertising? I don't want to have to screen dozens of applicants.
If you exhaust the word of mouth technique and you have no luck with the nanny-recommended ads, post your own nanny-wanted ad in your local newspaper or on a community message board. You'll get a lot of ideas by looking at other nanny-wanted ads. To avoid being bombarded by applicants who don't meet your needs, provide job details in your ad—for example:

Family looking for live-in nanny for our three-month old twins. Salary, room, board, and benefits. English speaking, nonsmoker. Must have valid California driver's license. Experience with infants and references required. 415-555-5678.

Another good option is to aim your ad at families who are looking for new homes for their nannies, rather than targeting potential nanny candidates themselves. For example, your ad might read as follows:

Dear Fellow Parent: Are you letting your beloved live-in nanny go for reasons not related to her performance? We may be able to provide a good position for her. Please contact 555-222-2222 to learn more.

Although it might be the nanny—and not the mom herself—who is scouring the ads, phrasing the ad this way will ensure that you receive responses only from candidates with experience.

Prescreening Nannies Over the Phone

Hopefully word-of-mouth and ads will generate good candidates for your nanny job. Rather than invite every prospective candidate over to your home, prescreen each potential nanny over the phone. This will help make sure that a nanny meets your basic requirements before you take up your time (and hers) with an in-person interview.

What's the best way to screen nannies over the phone?
Describe your child, the basic details of the job (schedule and responsibilities), and requirements. (See the "Nanny Priorities" checklist, above, for a list of issues for you to consider deciding about requirements.) Then ask questions about the nanny's experience, qualifications, and interest in the job.

You'll want enough information to see if the candidate has potential and is worth interviewing in person.

TIPS

Postpone salary discussions if you can. Unless the salary you are offering is particularly generous, you might accidentally weed out the best candidates if you discuss pay issues over the phone. If pressed, say that the salary is negotiable, based on the nanny's qualifications and experience. This will ensure that you keep your options open, at least until you've had the chance to meet the most promising candidates. Who knows? You might be willing to sweeten the deal—by offering a slightly higher salary or adding a few perks—for the right nanny. Many parents start their search with one salary in mind but end up increasing their budget when they meet someone they love.

If a nanny meets your job requirements, jot down the nanny's full name, address, and contact information. Also ask for the names and numbers of at least two references—ideally former employers. You'll want to talk to the nanny's references before scheduling an in-person interview to avoid wasting time with nannies whose previous employers have less than glowing things to say about them.

Trust your instincts. Don't schedule an interview with anyone you don't feel comfortable with on the phone. And if someone rubs you the wrong way—by being rude or abrasive on the phone—it definitely doesn't make sense to go forward. If your nanny is reluctant to give her current or former employer as a reference, ask why. If her answers aren't satisfactory, don't bother arranging an interview—especially if this nanny has a history of short-term positions.

Checking Nanny References

Checking references is one of the most important steps in any nanny search. No matter how great a nanny sounds on the phone, it's essential to contact at least two or three former employers. Do this before you meet the nanny in person.

Checking a Prospective Nanny's References

Be sure to ask the following questions when you call the reference of a prospective nanny:

- ❑ How long did the nanny work with you?
- ❑ Why did the nanny leave your family?
- ❑ How old were your children when the nanny cared for them?
- ❑ What hours and days did the nanny work for you?
- ❑ Did the nanny live in your home?
- ❑ What were the nanny's responsibilities?
- ❑ Did the nanny arrange play dates for your child?
- ❑ How did your child like the nanny?
- ❑ Did you find it easy to work with the nanny?
- ❑ How well did the nanny communicate?
- ❑ Was the nanny reliable?
- ❑ Did you like the nanny as a person?
- ❑ What did you like most about the nanny? Least?
- ❑ Describe any emergencies that arose and how the nanny handled them.

What should I ask when I call my prospective nanny's references?

Although it may feel awkward to call a stranger and ask for the sometimes personal details of a nanny relationship, reference checking is a standard part of the process, so the parent and the nanny will be expecting you to call.

Start by calling the most recent references and those for whom the nanny worked the longest and where the job was the most similar (age of children, hours, live in or out). You basically want to confirm that what the nanny told you (in terms of previous jobs) was true and that she is a good candidate for the nanny position and worth an interview.

 TIPS

Careful reference checks take time—and good notes. Set aside at least 20 minutes for every reference check. If you catch the parent at a bad time—when he or she is rushing out the door, for example—ask if you can reschedule the call. Also, be sure to keep good notes. You may think you'll remember every detail of the conversation, but if you'll be talking to a couple of references for several nanny candidates, your memory can get muddled fast. Especially if you'll be discussing the references with your spouse or partner, you'll want to keep a good record of what people say.

Here are the basic questions to ask each reference:

- How long did the nanny work with you? It is, of course, much more helpful to speak with someone who worked with a nanny for three years rather than just three months.

- Why is the nanny no longer employed by your family? You can breathe a sigh of relief if the reference tells you that the family had to let their beloved nanny go because the family moved out of state or because the child started preschool. But if you get a vague answer, be concerned: The family may have asked the nanny to leave because things weren't working out.

- How many children do you have? How old were they when the nanny cared for them? If you're looking for a nanny to care for your one-month-old baby, it's important to find someone with experience caring for infants. If you have two preschoolers, you'll want someone with experience caring for one than one active child.

- What hours and days did the nanny work for you? There are many reasons why you might want to know this. For example, if the nanny only worked for the employer two afternoons a week, the reference might not be able to tell you what it would be like to have this person work full time.

- Did the nanny live in your home? If you are hiring a live-in nanny, it's ideal to find parents who have lived with the nanny before and can answer questions about this.
- What were the nanny's responsibilities? This will give you an idea of the scope of the nanny's former job—and whether she can take on similar responsibilities with you. You might also get ideas for ways that the nanny can help you. Did the nanny prepare meals for and bathe the child? Did the nanny take the child on outings—to the park or the zoo, for example?
- Did the nanny arrange play dates for your child? Particularly if you're concerned that your child may be lonely at home with your nanny, it's good to know whether the nanny will take the initiative to set up play dates with neighborhood children.
- How did your child like the nanny? If a parent tells you that her child absolutely adored the nanny and still occasionally calls the nanny just to say hello, you should put the potential nanny at the top of your list. Children know when someone cares for them, and a nanny with a big heart and genuine fondness for children is a gem.
- Did you find it easy to work with the nanny? Managing a nanny can be challenging enough—so you don't want the added burden of a difficult personality. You'll want to know whether the nanny followed the parent's directions (at least most of the time) and how well the

nanny handled criticism. In addition, ask whether it was easy to deal with issues such as pay and holidays. You might want to steer clear of a nanny who pestered her employer for pay increases every couple of months.
- How well did the nanny communicate? Did you feel fully informed about your child's day and any issues that arose? This is especially important if the nanny speaks limited English or seems very shy.
- Was the nanny reliable? For example, did she arrive to work on time (on most days)? How often did the nanny call in sick? Did the nanny frequently request personal days in addition to scheduled vacations?
- Did you like the nanny as a person? Especially if you or your child's other parent will be working from home, you'll want a nanny who's personable and pleasant to be around.
- What did you like most about the nanny? What did you like the least? No nanny is perfect, so ask the parent to share her criticisms of the nanny. Try to elicit an honest assessment of the nanny's strengths and weaknesses, not just a rosy picture of the nanny's best features.
- Did any medical emergencies ever arise while your child was in the nanny's care? If the nanny successfully handled a choking episode, or rushed the child off to the emergency room when the child had a bad playground fall, that's a good sign. But be wary of a nanny who has handled too many emergencies, as this

may indicate inadequate supervision.

- Did you ever check up on your nanny or ask someone else to do so? Nannies sometimes behave differently when they are alone with a child, so it helps to know that the parent regularly made unannounced lunchtime visits or asked a neighbor to keep an eye on the nanny at the park.

- Did you trust the nanny's judgment? It's hard to leave behind precise instructions on every aspect of your child's care. Often, your nanny will have to make many basic child care decisions, so you want a nanny whose judgment you trust.
- How much did you pay the nanny? It helps to know a nanny's prior salary so that you have a sense of the nanny's salary requirements. You might also want to find out whether the family paid the nanny on the books.

During your conversation, pay careful attention to the parent's tone of voice and any awkward silences. A parent who sounds hesitant or gives short answers might be trying to keep from saying something negative and interfering with the nanny's future job prospects. Also, don't be too scripted: Some of the most useful tidbits of information will come in the form of anecdotes rather than from direct answers to your questions.

Interviewing Nannies in Person

After you've screened a nanny on the phone and checked references, you're now to ready to meet good candidates in person.

What are some general tips on interviewing nannies?

Nanny interviews are different from other job interviews, because the nanny-employer relationship is personal. In essence, you're trying to find a new addition to your family—so don't make the interview too formal or businesslike.

The best place to meet prospective nannies is in your own home. Set aside at least an hour for each interview and avoid scheduling more than two interviews in any given day. Offer the candidate a cup of tea or glass of water when she arrives, and show some interest in the nanny as a person (and not just as a prospective employee). The nanny will be interviewing you as well, so be as warm and courteous as you can.

Have notes from your telephone screening and from your reference check handy, in case you want to follow up on anything. Take detailed notes during the interview; you'd be surprised how difficult it is to keep track of who said what when you're talking and meeting with several prospective nannies.

Should my child sit in on the interview?
Your child should be present for at least some of the time so that you'll get a chance to see how the nanny interacts with your child. But don't expect miracles: A child who cries around strangers isn't going to take an instant liking to even the best nanny. Still, if the nanny handles the crying well and doesn't get flustered, then that's a good sign. Look for a nanny who pays attention to your child and who attempts to hold or play with your child. Ask yourself whether the nanny seems intuitively caring and nurturing and whether you could see yourself leaving your child in this person's care.

What questions should I ask?
Here are some specific questions you can ask. You can tailor these to your particular situation. Just make sure that you cover all points that are really important to you. A nanny interview is likely to be more of a conversation than a traditional job interview, so don't worry about asking these questions in a particular way or order.

☑ CHECKLIST

Nanny Interview Topics

When interviewing a prospective nanny, be sure to cover the following topics:
- ❏ Interest in the job
- ❏ Educational background
- ❏ Nanny's family (number of children)
- ❏ Previous positions
- ❏ Other child care experience
- ❏ Typical day
- ❏ Feeding and meals
- ❏ Naps
- ❏ Discipline
- ❏ Playtime
- ❏ Comforting
- ❏ CPR/first aid training
- ❏ Medical emergencies
- ❏ Smoking
- ❏ Driving record
- ❏ Health problems
- ❏ Personal interests
- ❏ Availability after hours
- ❏ Ideal position
- ❏ Legal authorization to work in the United States
- ❏ Pay on or under the table.

- **Interest in the job.** Find out why this person has chosen to be a nanny—and what she likes most and least about the job. These are nice icebreaker questions that give the nanny a chance to explain who she is and why she'd like to care for your child. Look for someone who actually wants to be a nanny and enjoys working with children—not someone who fell into the job because other careers didn't work out.

- **Educational background.** Has the nanny completed high school? College? Does she have any formal training in early childhood education? Although it's fine to ask these questions, keep in mind that there probably aren't going to be many nannies with extensive education and training.

- **Nanny's family.** Ask about the nanny's current living situation and whether she has children of her own. If so, find out her parenting philosophy. If the nanny's children are adults, what are they doing now? If they are still young, who cares for them while the nanny is working? Will there be any logistical challenges (for example,

if your nanny must return home by a certain time each evening to relieve her child's caregiver)? Does the nanny have other family responsibilities, such as caring for an elderly parent, that may affect her schedule?

- **Previous positions.** Find out the details of the nanny's current and previous child care positions, including the names and ages of the children the nanny has cared for, the number of years the nanny worked at each job, why the nanny left, what the nanny's job responsibilities were at each position, and what the nanny liked most and least about each job. Take your time and get as many details as possible.

- **Other child care experience.** If you're interviewing someone with only a year or two of nanny experience, find out whether she has any other child care experience—for example, as a babysitter or camp counselor—that might make her a more attractive candidate.

- **Typical day.** Ask the nanny to describe how she'd spend a typical day with a child the age of yours. This is a good way to start learning about the nanny's childrearing philosophies.

- **Feeding and meals.** Would the nanny feed your baby on demand or according to a schedule you set? Would the nanny prepare meals for your child? How does your nanny feel about snacks in between meals? Would the nanny insist that your child sit in a high chair or would she feed your child wherever is most comfortable? Would the nanny let your child watch television or play with toys during mealtimes?

- **Naps.** Does the nanny believe in nap schedules, or would she put your child down for a nap whenever your child seemed sleepy? Would the nanny be comfortable letting your child cry to sleep, or would she instead rock or sing your child to sleep? Does the nanny feel it's best for a child to nap in the crib, or would the nanny let your child sleep wherever is most comfortable for your child (such as the stroller, perhaps)?

- **Discipline.** How would the nanny set limits for your child? How would the nanny handle toddler temper tantrums? Would the nanny use time outs? Has the nanny ever shouted at or spanked any of the children she has cared for in the past?

- **Playtime.** How would the nanny entertain your child? Does the nanny believe it is important for children to get fresh air each day? If your child is still a baby, would the nanny include a mix of activities—such as tummy time and reading board books? For an active toddler, how would the nanny keep your child occupied on rainy or snowy days?

- **Comforting.** How does the nanny calm an upset child? How does the nanny deal with separation anxiety?

- **CPR/first aid training.** Has this nanny had this type of training? If so, how long ago? If not, would she agree to take a class if you paid for it?

- **Medical emergencies.** Has the nanny had to take a child to the hospital or called poison control? Why? Has she had to deal with any accidents or illnesses?

- **Smoking.** Many parents won't hire a nanny who smokes. If you hire a nanny who smokes, find out how much and if she smokes on the job. If she does, she will expose your child to secondhand smoke.

- **Driving record.** If the nanny will be driving your child, ask about her driving record.

- **Health problems.** Find out if the nanny has any health issues that would affect her ability to care for your child. If she has a bad back, for example, this could become a problem as your child gets older—and heavier. If you have pets, ask about allergies. Some parents even pay for a basic physical examination and tuberculosis test (because of the contagious nature of the infection) before hiring a nanny.

- **Personal interests.** Ask the nanny what she likes to do in her spare time. Particularly if you are looking for a live-in nanny, you'll want to get a sense of the nanny's lifestyle—especially when it comes to things such as drinking and staying out late. A young nanny who hits the party scene every Thursday night, for example, might not be fresh and alert enough to care for your child on Fridays.

- **Availability after hours.** If you want a nanny who's willing to babysit on weekend nights or travel occasionally, be sure to bring this up.

- **Ideal position.** Before giving details of the position you are offering, find out what type of job the nanny would like—so that you can present your position in the best light possible. Ask about the nanny's preferred working hours, job responsibilities, and salary range. If light housework is part of the job you are offering, ask whether the nanny has any objection to simple chores. If yours is a live-in position, ask the nanny what type of live-in arrangement would best suit her needs. For example, would she mind sharing a bathroom? Does she prefer to eat meals with the family?

Some parents use hypothetical situations to get a sense of the nanny's child care instincts. For example, you might want to ask what the nanny would do if your child woke up a few minutes into a nap hysterically screaming. (An experienced nanny might tell you that she would first comfort the child as best she could and then examine the child to see whether something external—such as a soiled diaper—was the cause of the problem.)

If you haven't done so already, describe the position in more detail, including job responsibilities, salary and benefits, live-in logistics (for example, will the live-in nanny have her own room and private bathroom?), work schedule, start date, and any special requirements, such as a valid driver's license and a clean driving record.

Finally, ask the nanny whether she has any questions for you. Thank her for her time and let her know when you will be contacting her to inform her of your decision.

 CAUTION

Don't drag your heels when you meet the right person. The best nannies are very much in demand—no matter where you live—so don't wait to make an offer if you meet someone you really like with great references. Otherwise, your dream nanny could get quickly snapped up by another family before you've had a chance to hire her.

Following Up on Your Nanny Interview

Unless you've met your ideal nanny, it's a good idea to do more checking before hiring someone—for example, you might want to talk with her references again.

Is just one meeting enough, or should I schedule a second interview before making an offer?

It's best to interview potential nannies at least twice before extending an offer. A second meeting will give you the chance to confirm your original good feelings about the nanny and to make sure that the nanny is a good fit with your family.

Instead of another short interview, you might want to consider asking the nanny to come spend the day with you. (You'll have to pay the nanny for her time if you decide to do this.) You'll see how the nanny interacts with your child at different times of the day (when your child is sleepy, for example, or hungry). You'll also get the chance to chat more with the nanny if you spend a whole day together.

TIPS

Many parents do a trial week instead. Although you are legally entitled to let your nanny go at any time, it's good to feel comfortable with a potential nanny before extending a formal offer of employment. For this reason, you might want to have the nanny work with you for a few days or even a week before you offer her the job. Be sure to be at home as much as possible during the trial period, so that you can see the nanny in action.

I've met so many wonderful nannies! How do I choose among them?

If you're lucky enough to have several great candidates, all with glowing references and several years of experience, any one of them would probably make a fine nanny for your child. So choose the nanny you like the best. For example, whose personality is the best fit with yours and your child's? Whose child care philosophy do you respect the most? What do your instincts tell you? If you still can't decide, then ask a friend or relative to meet the candidates and help you make your choice. It can be helpful to get someone else's perspective, particularly because a friend or relative might see qualities (or drawbacks) that you didn't notice in a nanny.

Maybe no nanny will do. If you've interviewed several nannies with excellent references, but still haven't found one you want to hire, it may be that a nanny simply isn't the right child care choice for you. Perhaps you have unvoiced concerns about how well a nanny would care for your child when you are not around, or you might be worried that your child would be bored or lonely in a nanny's care. Whatever the reason, it's probably time to begin exploring other child care options—such as neighboring day care centers. If you still can't find a good match after expanding your child care search, then the real problem may be that you want to stay home with your child instead of returning to work. Look at Chapter 11 for advice on how to decide whether staying home is financially practical for your family.

Arranging a Nanny Background Check

Although some might think it's a bit paranoid to do a thorough background check on a potential nanny—particularly if she has excellent references and years of experience—the reality is that the nanny will be spending many unsupervised hours with your child. As a parent, you owe it to your child to rigor-ously screen prospective nannies to ensure you don't accidentally hire someone with falsified credentials or a criminal record. According to the International Nanny Association, approximately 5% of nanny applicants have a criminal conviction on their records.

I've found a wonderful nanny, but I want to conduct a more thorough background check before she begins working for me. How do I do this?

A thorough nanny background check has several important components:

- verification of identity and Social Security number
- verification of educational and employment history
- a criminal records search, including a search of sex offender registries, and
- a driving records search.

This seems really complicated and time-consuming. Are there outside agencies that do background checks on nannies?

For a few hundred dollars, you can hire an experienced screening agency to do the heavy lifting for you—for example, searching the records of your local criminal courthouse or verifying the nanny's Social Security number. One company to consider is ChoiceTrust (www.choicetrust.com), which will provide you with a reasonably comprehensive background check for about $100. You can also order nanny background checks at www.nannynetwork.com and www.nannybackgrounds.com.

Do I need the nanny's permission to do a background check?

If you hire a service to do a background check, the federal Fair Credit Reporting Act (FCRA) requires that you inform the nanny and obtain her consent in advance. (This means that you can't do a secret background check on your nanny.) The service you hire should provide you with all of the necessary documents for complying with the FCRA. If it doesn't, then find another service.

What can I reasonably expect a nanny background check to involve?

Different screening agencies offer slightly different services, so it's a good idea to ask about the scope of the check before signing a contract. Some important questions to ask are:

What's included in the criminal records check?

Screening agencies generally cannot provide you with information relating to an individual's federal criminal record because the FBI does not make that information public. If the agency claims it will do a national criminal record search, the agency will probably turn to a criminal record database that currently contains data from 37 states. This database does not contain data from California, Delaware, Hawaii, Louisiana, Massachusetts, Maryland, New Hampshire, New Mexico, Pennsylvania, South Dakota, Vermont, West Virginia, or Wyoming. Moreover, the database is generally limited to records for felony convictions that resulted in state prison sentences. Information about misdemeanor convictions—for example,

convictions for petty thefts—is not included in the database for most states. The better practice is for your screening agency to conduct a state- and county-specific search of felony and misdemeanor records. No agency will search the records of every single state and county (unless you're willing to fork over a small fortune) because this would entail checking the files of more than 3,300 courthouses. However, your agency should check the state and county criminal records for each state and county in which your nanny has lived.

Is there an extra fee to conduct a sexual offender check? If there is, it may not make sense to pay it. Many states maintain sexual offender registries that you can search on your own, either on the Web or by calling a hotline number. To find out how to access your state's sex offender registry, contact the Parents for Megan's Law (PFML) hotline at 888-ASK-PFML. Or you can go to www.pfml.org and click on "Megan's Law nationwide and registry links" in the left-hand menu bar.

What's included in the driving records check?

Your background check might only include a driving record for the state in which your potential nanny currently resides. But to be on the safe side, it should include each state in which your nanny has ever lived. A useful driving record resource is www.drivingrecord.org, which currently charges $29.95 per driving record. Notably, not all states will provide you with a copy of your potential nanny's driving record even if you go through a screening agency. If you live in Alaska, the District of Columbia, New

Hampshire, Oregon, or Pennsylvania, you're going to have to ask your nanny to provide you with a copy of her motor vehicles record. (She can order one from her local department of motor vehicles.)

I've found a great nanny with terrific references, but I'm having trouble getting additional background information because she's an illegal immigrant. What should I do?
If you're thinking about hiring an illegal immigrant as your nanny, you may not be able to use a standard background check service. This is because these services generally use a nanny's Social Security number (something most illegal immigrants do not have) and available public records (which may not include any information about your nanny) to research the nanny's background. In this case, you'll want to check as many personal references as possible.

I don't want to spend the money on an outside agency. Besides checking references, what kind of background check can I do myself?
There are several things you can do yourself. If the nanny will be driving, ask her for a copy of her driving record. You can check your state's sexual offender registry yourself, following the advice on the previous page. You can also ask the nanny to provide proof of any particular training or school records.

Working With a Nanny Placement Agency

If you're like many new parents, you may be too tired, too busy, or simply too nervous to find a nanny on your own. Or maybe you've exhausted all your leads, and advertising just hasn't worked. In these cases, you may want to hire a nanny placement agency to do some or most of the work for you. An agency will sift through its roster of prescreened nannies and introduce you to candidates who are likely to be a good match.

How do nanny placement agencies work?
It would be wonderful if you could simply call a nanny placement agency on Friday and then have your ideal nanny arrive on Monday—but even the best nanny placement agency can't work miracles. A placement agency's real value is in taking much of the work out of the nanny search process. You won't have to advertise for nanny candidates and prescreen them on your own. Instead, a nanny placement agency will send over qualified applicants who meet all—or at least most—of your requirements. You'll still have to interview nannies and choose a nanny for your child, but hiring a quality placement agency will take much of the stress out of the process. A placement agency can also be a good solution if you're short on time, because it will generally take fewer weeks to hire a nanny through an agency than to find one on your own.

How much will it cost me to use an agency? Using a nanny agency comes with a price—and a hefty one at that. Expect to pay at least $2,000—if not more—in placement fees. Some agencies charge a flat fee, while others set their fees as a percentage of the nanny's first year's salary.

Will I find better qualified or trained nannies through an agency?
That's a tough question. Many parents find extraordinary nannies without ever using an agency. At the same time, however, the better placement agencies have stringent criteria for the types of nanny candidates they will represent. Placement agencies generally require that candidates have good references, previous child care experience, and legal authorization to work in the United States. As a result, you'll probably see higher caliber applicants.

 CAUTION

Quality comes at a price. The better nannies command higher salaries—so you might have to pay more to a nanny who comes through a placement agency. For an accurate sense of how much you'll have to pay an agency-referred nanny, ask the placement agency with which you plan to work.

How do I find a good nanny placement agency?
Look for an agency that belongs to the Alliance of Professional Nanny Agencies (APNA)—a nonprofit organization dedicated to promoting professionalism in the nanny placement industry. Although the APNA does not have a formal agency accreditation process, it screens agencies to ensure they comply with its standards. You can find a state-by-state listing of APNA member agencies at www.theapna.org.

Another way to search for a placement agency is by using the International Nanny Association's member directory (available on the Internet at www.nanny.org). The International Nanny Association (INA) is a nonprofit organization that educates nannies and nanny placement agencies. Although the INA does not review or accredit placement agencies, INA member agencies have pledged to adhere to INA standards.

What should I ask before signing on with an agency?
Not all nanny placement agencies are the same, so before you hire an agency, find out what you'll be getting for your money. Here are some questions to ask:
- **How long has the agency been in business?** Make sure the agency didn't open its doors just yesterday.
- **Is the agency a member of the APNA or the INA?** Membership in these organizations is an indication that the agency takes its professional standards seriously.

- **How many nannies has the agency successfully placed?** The more, the better. If an agency is unwilling to share even a ballpark figure with you, keep looking.
- **What are the agency's fees and refund policies?** Some agencies will charge you a nonrefundable application fee (usually a few hundred dollars). In addition, you'll normally have to pay a substantial placement fee of a couple of thousand dollars or more if you find a nanny through the agency.
- **Will I have to sign a contract in order to retain the agency's services?** Reputable agencies will require you to sign a formal agreement before they will begin working with you. The contract will cover important issues such as the agency's fee structure, refund policy, and satisfaction guarantee.
- **What is the selection process for nanny candidates?** Find out whether the agency has any specific criteria—such as fluency in English—for the nannies it represents. Look for an agency that interviews all applicants in person and checks references. Find out whether the agency conducts drug and health checks (such as tuberculosis testing).
- **Does the agency conduct background checks and, if so, at what stage in the process?** Ideally, you'll want an agency that does a comprehensive background check on its candidates as part of its selection process—before you even meet the nannies.
- **Does the agency charge any fees to the nannies it represents?** If so, find out exactly how the fee is calculated. Charging nanny applicants a fee makes for a poor incentive structure, because an agency might be eager to find a home for even a mediocre nanny in order to collect its placement fee from the nanny.
- **What is the average salary paid to nannies placed by the agency?** Unless the salary you plan to offer is within this range, it makes little sense to use the agency because a nanny referred by the agency is unlikely to accept your offer. Also ask whether there is a minimum salary you must be willing to pay.
- **How are potential nanny candidates matched with families?** You'll want an agency that spends time assessing your family's needs—so that the candidates the agency sends your way will meet your criteria. If possible, look for an agency that will speak with you in person—rather than just over the phone—before introducing you to applicants.
- **How many candidates can I expect to meet through the agency?** Although you want an agency to present you with many good choices, you also don't want to be bombarded with candidates. Somewhere in the neighborhood of five to ten nannies is generally a good number.
- **On average, how long does it take for families you represent to find their nannies?** The answer should be a month or so.

- **What if I can't find a candidate I like through the agency?** Ask the agency how often a family simply can't find the right nanny. (If the agency tells you that it's never happened before, be skeptical.) You'll want to know exactly what fees you'll owe even if the agency can't find you a good match.
- **What if I end up finding a nanny on my own?** Though it may not be likely, it's certainly possible that the perfect nanny could fall into your lap without the agency's help. A good friend might decide to stay at home, for example, and suggest that you take her trusted nanny. You'll want to know whether you'll owe the agency any placement fees in that event.
- **Will the agency assist me with extending an offer to the nanny and preparing a nanny employment agreement?** Look for an agency that's going to deal with most of the hassles that are involved in hiring a nanny. If the agency won't help you prepare an employment agreement, keep looking.
- **Will the agency help me comply with the tax and immigration requirements for hiring a nanny legally?** At a minimum, the agency should be able to answer your questions about the legal requirements for hiring and paying a nanny.
- **What happens if I am unhappy with the nanny?** You'll want an agency that will help you locate a new nanny at no additional charge and will refund at least part of its placement fee if you are not satisfied. Don't just take the agency at its word on these important issues; look for language in your contract on how the agency deals with unhappy customers.
- **What happens if the nanny leaves within just a few months?** A good placement agency will help you find a new nanny at no additional cost if the nanny leaves within one year of her start date (assuming you were not to blame).
- **What types of continued support does the nanny agency offer?** Some nanny agencies offer additional services—such as backup child care.

Keep good notes. Ask the agency for at least three parent references. Call each of the agency's parent references and ask how the agency handled the search process, whether the family still has the nanny placed by the agency, and how the agency resolved any problems along the way.

Screening Nanny Agencies

When choosing a nanny agency, be sure to ask the following questions:

- ❑ How long has the agency been in business?
- ❑ Is the agency a member of the APNA or the INA?
- ❑ How many nannies has the agency successfully placed?
- ❑ What are the agency's fees and refund policies?
- ❑ Will I have to sign a contract?
- ❑ What is the selection process for nanny candidates?
- ❑ Does the agency conduct background checks? What do they cover?
- ❑ Does the agency charge any fees to the nannies it represents?
- ❑ What is the average salary paid to nannies placed by the agency?
- ❑ How are nanny candidates matched with families?
- ❑ How many candidates can I expect to meet through the agency?
- ❑ On average, how long does it take for families to find a nanny through the agency?
- ❑ What if I can't find a nanny?
- ❑ What if I end up finding a nanny on my own?
- ❑ Will the agency help me extend an offer to a nanny and draft a nanny employment agreement?
- ❑ Will the agency help me comply with tax and immigration requirements?
- ❑ What happens if I am unhappy with my nanny?
- ❑ What happens if the nanny leaves shortly after starting work?
- ❑ Does the agency offer any support after placing a nanny?

What will the agency process be like? After you've checked references from families who have used the agency, and you're satisfied with the answers to your questions, you're ready to sign up. The first step will be to retain the agency's services, usually by signing a contract and paying a registration fee. The next step will be to give the agency a job description and let the agency know what you are looking for in a nanny. See **Deciding What You Want in a Nanny,** above, for advice on setting your nanny priorities. Some agencies will ask you to come in for a face-to-face discussion of your needs; others will send you a lengthy questionnaire to complete. The agency will then review your dream nanny profile and begin scheduling interviews. You'll then interview nanny candidates much as you would if you were searching for a nanny on your own. Once you find a nanny you like, the agency should be able to help you with the process of extending an offer to your nanny and—if the offer is accepted—creating a nanny employment agreement.

Be thorough when you interview an agency nanny. You might be tempted to cut a few corners when interviewing a nanny sent to you by a placement agency. But the most an agency can do is match you with candidates who seem like they might be a good fit. Only you can decide whether a candidate is the right choice for your family.

Legal Requirements for Employing a Nanny

When you hire a nanny, you become your nanny's employer and are subject to several federal and state employment laws. In this section, you'll learn about your legal obligations to verify your nanny's immigration status, report your new hire to your state government, and purchase workers' compensation insurance for your nanny.

CROSS REFERENCE

This section doesn't cover taxes and the like. You can find out about your legal obligations with respect to your nanny's pay, benefits, and work schedule—such as your duty to pay Social Security and Medicare taxes on your nanny's salary—in "Paying Your Nanny", below.

I've met a wonderful nanny through my agency. Should I still check the nanny's references, even though the agency already did so?

Absolutely. Although you shouldn't have to worry about falsified credentials with an agency-referred nanny, you'll still want to talk to the nanny's previous employers to get a good sense of what it's like to work with the nanny. It might turn out that a nanny with glowing references is not the right one for you—for example, because the nanny's approach to child care is too different from your own.

Immigration and Other Laws That Cover New Employees

Do I have any obligation to make sure that my nanny is legally authorized to work in the United States?

When you hire someone, even someone who was born and raised in the city where you live, you must review documents such as a passport or naturalization certificate, that proves the nanny's identity and employment eligibility. Within three days of your nanny's first day of work, you must confirm that she is legally authorized to work in the United States by completing USCIS Form I-9 (*Employment Eligibility Verification*). You can download a copy of Form I-9 from the U.S. Citizenship and Immigration Services website at www.uscis.gov. You do not need to submit a completed Form I-9 to the government; just keep a signed copy for your records for three years after the date of hire or for one year after employment is terminated or whichever is later.

Do I have to let the government know when I hire my nanny?

Yes. You'll have to file a new hire form with your state labor department. The information on the form becomes part of the National Directory of New Hires, used primarily to locate parents so that child support orders can be enforced. Government agencies also use the data to prevent improper payment of workers' compensation and unemployment benefits or public assistance benefits. Contact your state department of labor for a copy of the form and instructions for filing it.

Workers' Compensation Insurance

Do I have to purchase workers' compensation insurance for my nanny?

It depends on the state in which you live. The following states require parents to purchase workers' compensation insurance for both full- and part-time nannies: Alaska, California, Connecticut, Delaware, District of Columbia, Hawaii, Iowa, Kansas, Maryland, Massachusetts, Minnesota, New Hampshire, Ohio, Oklahoma, and South Dakota. The following states require workers' compensation insurance for full-time nannies only: Colorado, Illinois, Kentucky, Michigan, New Jersey, New York, and Utah. (Check with your state's insurance department to learn what "part time" means.) See The Insurance Information Institute website at www.iii.org for a list of state insurance departments. You do not have to purchase workers' compensation insurance if you live in any other state.

What does workers' compensation insurance cover?

Workers' compensation will cover your nanny's medical expenses and lost wages if she is injured on the job. Workers' compensation protects you from liability for any work-related injuries suffered by your nanny.

Isn't my homeowner's insurance policy enough to cover my nanny if she is injured on the job?

No. First of all, if your state's law requires you to purchase workers' compensation insurance for your nanny and you fail to do so, your homeowner's insurance policy will not provide you with coverage for your nanny's on-the-job injuries. However, your policy may cover you if your state does not require you to purchase worker's compensation—but check with your insurance company to learn the precise terms of your coverage.

Second, it's possible that your nanny could get injured while she is caring for your child away from your home—for example, while playing in the park or driving your child to school. In no event will your homeowner's policy provide coverage for accidents that do not take place in your home.

My state requires me to purchase worker's compensation insurance for my nanny. How do I go about doing this?

This depends on where you live. In some states, you must purchase workers' compensation insurance through your state's insurance fund. In other states, you can simply add a workers' compensation rider to your existing homeowner's insurance policy. The best thing to do is to contact an insurance agent in your state who handles workers' compensation policies.

ADDITIONAL RESOURCES

Learn more about your state's rules and how to go about purchasing workers' compensation insurance. For complimentary guidance on your state's requirements and how you can purchase workers' compensation insurance, contact Breedlove & Associates— a payroll and tax service for household employees—at 888-BREEDLOVE (or on the Internet at www.breedlove-online.com). If you'd prefer to deal directly with your state's insurance department, you can find links to insurance departments at the Insurance Information Institute's website at www.iii.org.

Paying Your Nanny

Once you find a nanny, the next task is negotiating a salary and—if you plan to pay your nanny on the books—complying with the many requirements for paying your nanny legally. This section will give you the scoop on both the legal rules and the real-life concerns involved in nanny compensation.

☑ CHECKLIST

Paying Your Nanny Legally

Complying with the law when it comes to paying your nanny is not as hard as it might seem. Just follow these steps:

❑ Figure out your nanny's schedule. Will she be working more than 40 hours in a week or eight hours in a day?

❑ Learn your state's overtime rules. Will you have to pay overtime if your nanny works more than eight hours in any given day? If so, at what rate?

❑ Set an hourly rate and an overtime rate. Overtime is usually set at one and a half times your nanny's hourly rate.

❑ Decide how often you will pay your nanny. Weekly paychecks are the norm.

❑ Ask your nanny whether or not she would like you to withhold taxes from her paycheck. If so, you'll need to have your nanny complete a W-4 form, which you can obtain from the IRS website at www .irs.gov or from your payroll service.

❑ Pick an accountant or payroll service to deal with your tax obligations and generate paychecks and tax documents. Once you do this, all you'll have to worry about is writing a check to your nanny each week.

Setting Nanny's Pay

How much should I pay my nanny? Nanny compensation can be a delicate subject. You should pay your nanny fairly—commensurate with the going rate in your area and your nanny's experience level and responsibilities. Be sure to leave yourself room to handle the annual pay increases and holiday bonuses that most nannies expect.

To come up with a reasonable rate, ask what other parents in your neighborhood are paying. If everyone else is paying $12 per hour, for example, you'll be hard-pressed to find a good nanny who'll accept $10 per hour—unless there is a good reason for the pay difference (for example, the more expensive nanny can drive, but yours can't). Also ask the nanny's previous employers how much they paid her—to ensure that your offer isn't rejected based on salary alone. If you're using a nanny placement agency, ask the agency for guidance on how much to offer.

At the end of the day, you and your nanny can reach almost any agreement on compensation that makes sense for each of you. All the law requires (in cases where you are paying your nanny on the books) is that you comply with federal and state minimum wage and overtime laws—both of which are discussed below.

Money isn't everything. If you can't afford to pay your nanny top rate, think of other benefits you can offer such as a flexible schedule, use of your car, a cell phone, or benefits such as health insurance or membership in your health club.

Do I have to worry about the minimum wage?

Realistically speaking, no. Just about any reasonably qualified nanny—including a live-in nanny—will demand a much higher rate than the minimum wage.

How do the overtime laws work?

If your nanny works more than 40 hours per week, and if she doesn't live with you, federal law requires that you pay your nanny overtime for every hour that she works over 40. Overtime pay is set at one and a half times your nanny's usual hourly rate.

Live-in nannies are not entitled to overtime pay under the federal rules. This means that you can pay your live-in nanny the same standard hourly rate even if she works 60 or 70 hours each week—unless a state daily overtime law applies (discussed, below).

EXAMPLE: *Kim pays her nanny, Natasha, $10 per hour to care for her child. Natasha usually works 40 hours a week. This week, however, Natasha works five extra hours on a Saturday so that Kim can attend a wedding. Kim pays Natasha $10 per hour for the first 40 hours she works and $15 per hour (one and one half times Natasha's usual hourly rate of $10) for the five additional hours.*

What if my nanny works more than eight hours in a day?

Some states require employers to pay daily overtime in addition to the weekly overtime established under the federal law. These daily overtime rules generally apply if you have your nanny work more than eight hours in any given day. In California, for example, you must pay your nanny one and a half times her usual hourly rate for every hour after the first eight that she works in a day.

EXAMPLE: *Bruce and Maggie live in California and hire their nanny, Greta, to work ten hours a day (from 8 a.m. until 6 p.m.), four days a week. Because Greta never works more than 40 hours a week, she is not entitled to overtime under federal law. However, she is entitled to daily overtime under California law. Bruce and Maggie pay Greta $10 per hour for the first eight hours she works each day, and $15 per hour (one and a half times Greta's usual hourly rate of $10) for the next two hours that she works.*

The following states have a daily overtime standard. The number in parentheses shows the number of hours in a day someone can work before getting overtime:

- Alaska (8)
- California (8)
- Colorado (12), and
- Nevada (8).

 TIPS

Spell out your rate structure. Make sure that your nanny understands the standard hourly rate and the overtime rate you will be paying her. Your written agreement with your nanny—see **Preparing a Nanny Employment Agreement**, below—should specify these rates.

Do I have to pay my nanny overtime if she works on weekends or holidays?

The law does not require you to pay your nanny more than her usual hourly rate just because you ask her to work on a Saturday or a holiday. (If your nanny has already worked more than 40 hours that week, however, you will have to pay your nanny overtime on those days.) As a practical matter, however, some nannies do expect to be paid extra for working on weekends or holidays.

I plan to pay my nanny a fixed weekly salary, rather than paying her by the hour. Do I still have to worry about overtime pay?

Yes—but that doesn't mean you have to change the fixed salary you plan to offer. All you need to do is break your salary down into a standard hourly rate and an overtime rate.

> EXAMPLE: *Gordon wants to pay his new nanny, Deirdre, a weekly salary of $550 per week. Deirdre's work hours will be 7:30 a.m. until 5:30 p.m. five days a week—for a total of 50 hours per week. Although this amounts to an average hourly rate of $11 per hour, Gordon knows that he has to figure out a standard hourly rate as well as an overtime rate—rather than just an average hourly rate. Because Gordon lives in a state with no daily overtime rules, all he needs to worry about are the federal overtime laws. With a little help from his calculator, Gordon determines that Deirdre's standard hourly rate is $10 per hour. This rate will apply for the first 40 hours worked each week—amounting to $400. Deirdre's overtime rate will therefore be $15 per hour (one and a half times her usual hourly rate of $10 per hour) for the additional ten hours—or $150. With these rates, Deirdre's weekly salary will still be $550 per week ($400 of standard time plus $150 in overtime pay)—just as Gordon had intended.*

Agreeing to only a fixed weekly salary without breaking the salary down into a standard hourly rate and an overtime rate can lead to problems, because your nanny may later claim that the agreed-upon salary was based only on a 40-hour workweek.

EXAMPLE: *Madeleine agreed to pay her nanny, Vanessa, a weekly salary of $400 per week. The two also agreed that Vanessa would work 45 hours each week, from 10 a.m. until 7 p.m. five days a week. Soon after she began working, Vanessa claimed that she should be paid $445 each week— rather than $400 as Madeleine had agreed. Vanessa argued that the $400 weekly salary was based on a 40-hour workweek, which meant that her standard hourly rate was $10 per hour. Vanessa demanded that she should therefore be paid an overtime rate of $15 per hour for the extra five hours she worked each week.*

 CAUTION

The minimum wage and overtime laws are nonnegotiable. Even if your nanny agrees to be paid less than the minimum wage or is willing to work overtime hours for her usual hourly rate, you are still required by law to pay her the minimum wage and overtime.

Income and Payroll Taxes: Paying Your Nanny on the Books

I want to pay my nanny on the books. What do I have to do?

To pay a nanny legally, you'll need to obtain federal and state employer identification numbers; pay Social Security, Medicare, and federal unemployment taxes on your nanny's salary; and comply with federal reporting requirements by filing a W-2 for your nanny at the end of the year. You'll also have to follow state reporting and tax requirements and—if you and your nanny agree—withhold federal and state income taxes from your nanny's salary.

And doing all of this is even more complicated than it sounds. Many a parent has started out trying to handle payroll taxes on his or her own only to give up in despair. The best thing to do is to hire a payroll service instead. For about $20 per month (or more, depending on the service you choose), a payroll service will calculate your nanny's tax withholdings for you, generate your nanny's paycheck for each pay period, tell you when to file various tax reporting forms, and generate your nanny's tax forms at the end of the year. Take our word for it: Payroll services are well worth the money. If you're not sure whom to call, two services to consider are PayCycle (www.paycycle.com) and Nanny Tax, Inc. (www.nannytax.com).

My nanny is an illegal immigrant. Can I pay her on the books?

No, you can't pay an illegal immigrant on the books.

If you still want to do it your-self. You can find step-by-step instructions for paying a nanny legally in IRS Publication 926, *Household Employer's Tax Guide,* available at www.irs.gov. You'll also need to check with your state department of labor (the appendix includes a list of agen-cies) for state rules that apply.

TIPS

Hang on to important nanny-re-lated documents. Keep the fol-lowing records on file for at least four years: Your state and federal employer identification numbers; the nanny's name, address, and Social Security number; the nanny's dates of employment; the nanny's pay schedule, wages, and taxes paid; copies of all necessary forms, such as the I-9, the W-2, payroll tax returns, payment coupons (for making quarterly payments), and the W-4, if used; and dates and amounts of tax deposits (quarterly payments). It's also a good idea to include interview notes, reference information, and your employment agreement in the nanny's file—all updated as necessary (for example, if you give your nanny a raise or change her hours).

I'm not sure I want to go through all the trouble and expense of paying my nanny legally. Is there any real advantage to paying a nanny on the books?
The benefit to you of paying a nanny on the books is the ability to take advantage of the child care tax breaks (as explained in Chapter 29). These breaks offset the tax burden that comes with paying a nanny legally. When tax advantages are taken into account, it typically costs less than 5% more in out-of-pocket expenses to pay a nanny above the table.

The benefit to your nanny—who, ideally, will love your child and become a trusted member of your family—is that she will be eligible for Medicare, Social Security, and unemployment benefits. Depending on your nanny's financial situation, she might even be able to take advantage of the earned income tax credit—which would allow her to pay almost nothing in federal income taxes for the year.

Paying Your Nanny Off the Books

Many people I know pay their nannies under the table. What exactly does that mean?
If you decide to pay your nanny off the books, you won't need to pay a service to calculate federal and state payroll taxes, nor will you have to purchase workers' compen-sation insurance. All you'll have to do is pay your nanny a nice tidy cash sum every week.

Parents like the off-the-books method for its convenience, and nannies like the ar-rangement because they don't have to pay even a dime of their hard-earned money to Uncle Sam. Many nannies will even charge parents lower rates for off-the-books arrangements because of the tax savings involved. In addition, some nannies have to be paid off the books because they are not legally authorized to work in the United States.

Can I get into any real legal trouble for paying my nanny under the table?

Although it's unlikely that you'll be hauled off to jail for paying your nanny under the table, you can get into some trouble. The IRS will hold you liable for back taxes and penalties if it finds out. You are most likely to get caught if your nanny files a claim for unemployment benefits, workers' compensation benefits, or Social Security benefits—none of which she would be entitled to if she worked off the books. You could also be caught during an IRS audit—particularly if the IRS notices that you are a two-income family with children yet you claim no child care tax breaks.

Giving Your Nanny Time Off

You have no legal obligation to give your nanny paid—or even unpaid—time off for holidays and getaways, but it's the right thing to do, and any experienced, qualified nanny will expect at least a few paid holidays and vacation days as part of her compensation package. You might have difficulty attracting the right kind of nanny if you don't offer any paid time off at all. On the flip side, a generous amount of time off can compensate for a not-so-generous salary in your quest for a wonderful nanny.

Regardless of how much time off you want to offer, decide the following in advance and spell these out in your employment agreement with your nanny:

- **The number of paid vacation days your nanny will receive each year.** Many parents offer two weeks of paid vacation each year. At a minimum, consider giving your nanny at least one paid week off annually—to give her a break from the demands of taking care of your child.

- **Whether your nanny may choose her own vacation days or whether her vacation must coordinate with your vacation schedule.** You might want to agree that one of your nanny's weeks off must coincide with one week when your family is on vacation, but allow her to choose when to take the other week.

- **Whether your nanny will be paid when you are on vacation or out of town.** Many nannies expect to be paid during this time, even if their vacation days have already been used up, so make it very clear if that's not what you plan to do.

- **Whether your nanny will be paid on holidays, such as Christmas.** It's customary to give your nanny major holidays with pay. But be sure to specify what days count as "major" in your book. If you won't be giving your nanny the day off on Columbus Day, for example, let her know that when you hire her.

- **Whether you will pay your nanny on days when she is sick or otherwise requires a personal day.** You might want to offer your nanny two or three paid sick days so that she won't drag herself into work when she's ill (and pass her cold or flu on to your child). You could also do what many companies do these days: Give your nanny a fixed number of personal days that she can use for vacation time, sick leave, or anything she'd like.

No matter what you decide on the issues above, some states require you to give your nanny paid time off for voting or jury duty. Check with your state's department of labor issues for more details on your state's rules.

Offering Health Insurance

In addition to paying your nanny's weekly wages, you might decide to offer health insurance. As with other issues of pay and benefits, be sure to spell out the details of health insurance in your employment agreement.

Does the law require that I provide health insurance for my nanny?
No—it's entirely up to you. Because health insurance coverage can be very expensive, most families don't provide this benefit.

I would like to provide health insurance for my nanny anyway. What are my options?
Unfortunately, you cannot simply add your nanny on to your family's existing health care plan because she does not count as a family member. Rather, you will have to pur-chase a separate insurance policy for your nanny—a benefit that can cost anywhere from $75 per month for a temporary insurance policy to more than $300 per month for a standard policy.

Most families who provide health insurance coverage for their nannies do so through temporary health insurance policies—which you can purchase for $75 to $100 per month. A temporary policy would insure your nanny for a specific period of time (one year, for example), and would cover all health care costs during that time period. But if your nanny developed a health condition during that time—cancer, for example—the policy would cover it only during the original period. If you renewed the policy for an additional term, the policy would not cover the costs of treating your nanny's cancer because the cancer would be a preexisting condition. This strict limitation on coverage explains why temporary policies cost so much less than standard ones.

CAUTION

Not every state offers temporary health insurance. Depending on the state in which you live, you may not be able to purchase a temporary health insurance policy for your nanny. Ask your insurance agent for advice on the subject.

Another option is to purchase catastrophic health insurance, which will cover your nanny's medical expenses in the event of a serious crisis—such as an automobile accident or an illness that requires a stay in the intensive care unit. Catastrophic health insurance typically comes with a very high deductible, which means that the first several thousand dollars of your nanny's medical expenses would not be covered. Moreover, this type of insurance does not cover routine medical care—such as an annual physical examination or a trip to the emergency room for a minor cut. But these policies are affordable: approximately $200 per month.

Finally, you could just purchase a standard health insurance policy for your nanny. These policies generally cost $300 per month or more, depending on your nanny's age and health condition. To get a quick estimate of how much a standard policy will cost, check www.insure.com. You might also want to check www.ehealthinsurance.com, which offers more affordable (but also more restricted) health insurance coverage.

Are there any tax benefits to providing health insurance for my nanny?
Not really. Still, you won't have to pay any taxes on the health insurance premiums you pay on your nanny's behalf, and neither will your nanny. For example, suppose you pay $100 per month towards your nanny's health insurance. You will not have to pay Social Security, Medicare, or federal unemployment taxes on that sum, nor will your nanny owe income taxes on that amount.

How do I go about purchasing health insurance for my nanny?
The first step is to talk to your nanny. She may prefer a higher salary to health insurance coverage. If she does want coverage, the second step is to contact an insurance broker. If you're a savvy Internet user, you can do almost everything online at www.insure.com. Or contact Eisenberg Associates at www.eisenbergassociates.com—a firm that specializes in nanny health insurance.

Are there options other than purchasing a health insurance policy for my nanny?
If you'd like to contribute towards your nanny's health insurance expenses but you cannot foot the entire bill yourself, you have a few other options:

- offer her a fixed sum—say $100 per month—to help lower her out-of-pocket health care costs
- provide your nanny with a health care discount plan—such as Care Entree (www.nannyinsurance.com) or the Pro-Care Benefit Card (www.procarecard.com). For a small monthly fee (about $20), these plans offer substantial discounts on medical expenses.
- pay for your nanny's doctor appointments, such as an annual physical exam.

Preparing a Nanny Employment Agreement

Once you find a nanny, it's a good idea to create an employment agreement to ensure that you and your nanny are on the same page when it comes to hours, pay, benefits, responsibilities, and other aspects of your relationship. No law requires you to have an agreement, but seasoned parents find that it heads off potential problems.

CAUTION

!f your nanny is an illegal immigrant or is paid off the books, be careful about putting the details of your arrangement with your nanny in writing. If you do not follow the laws when hiring and paying your nanny, you could get into trouble if you have a written agreement and it gets into the wrong hands—for example, if your nanny becomes angry with you for letting her go and alerts the IRS.

Your agreement with your nanny doesn't have to be long or complicated. At the end of this chapter, you can find a "Child Care Employment Agreement" form that you can use. Here are the instructions for completing the form:

Clause 1: Parent(s). Write your name and, if you have one, your partner's name here. Include your address and contact information. For share care arrangements, write down the names and contact information for both families.

Clause 2: Child care provider. Write your nanny's full name and contact information here. Be sure to include her Social Security number.

Clause 3: Children. Write down your child's name—or your children's names—here.

Clause 4: Location and schedule of care. Write down your home address, or—if there's somewhere else your nanny will be caring for your child—that address. Also write down the days and hours you expect your nanny to work (for example, Monday through Friday, 8 a.m. to 6 p.m.). For share care arrangements, specify if you expect your nanny to alternate homes every other day or week.

Clause 5: Beginning date. Write down the date your nanny will begin working for you.

Clause 6: Pay. Write down the amount that you will be paying your nanny either on a weekly basis or an hourly basis. Even if you will be paying your nanny a weekly salary, write down your nanny's base hourly rate and overtime rate. Write down whether these numbers are before taxes or after taxes. For share care arrangements, specify the amount that each family will pay.

Clause 7: Taxes. Write down whether you will be responsible for withholding federal and state income taxes from your nanny's salary. For share care arrangements, specify whether each family will withhold taxes.

Clause 8: Pay schedule. Write down how often you will be paying your nanny (for example, every Friday or every other Friday).

Clause 9: Health insurance. Write down whether you will be providing health insurance to your nanny.

Clause 10: Room and board. Write down whether you will be covering your nanny's lodging and meal expenses in addition to her salary. If you'll be providing room and board, write down the details of your arrangement. For example, write down whether your nanny will have her own room, a private bathroom, and/or a dedicated phone line.

Clause 11: Extras. Here, indicate whether you will be providing any fringe benefits—for example, a gym membership or the use of a cell phone.

Clause 12: Paid vacation. Indicate the number of days (or weeks) of paid vacation your nanny will receive each year. Also write down whether there are any restrictions on when your nanny may take this vacation. For example, if your nanny must coordinate her two weeks of vacation with your family's scheduled vacations, you should say so here.

Clause 13: Unneeded time. Write down whether you will pay your nanny when you are out of town or otherwise do not need her. If you plan to count these days as your nanny's paid vacation days, say so here.

Clause 14: Paid holidays. State whether you will pay your nanny on major holidays, such as New Year's Day. Be sure to list the holidays that count as paid time off.

Clause 15: Paid sick leave. Write down the number of paid sick days (if any) your nanny will receive each year. If you plan to count sick days against your nanny's paid vacation time, say so here.

Clause 16: Responsibilities. Summarize your nanny's duties here. Be specific. For example, you might want to say that your nanny must prepare your child's meals and clean up after your child during the day.

Clause 17: House rules. Note any special rules such as no smoking, no overnight guests, and the like.

Clause 18: At-will employment. This clause means that either you or your nanny can end your working relationship at any time and for just about any reason.

Signatures: Ask your nanny to sign and date the agreement. You and your partner (if you have one) should do the same. Give one copy to your nanny and keep a copy for yourself. For share care arrangements, at least one parent from each family—as well as the nanny—should sign and date the agreement.

If you want a form. BabyCenter .com's "Child Care Planner" form is a handy way to keep all your instructions and expectations in one place. You can add to your planner as needed—and update it as your child grows and his or her needs and schedule change. BabyCenter.com also has a useful "Childcare Provider Daily Diary" that your nanny can use every day to record your child's meals, naps, activities, behavior, and any problems or concerns. You can find both of these resources on the *Parent Savvy* page of Baby-center.com (www.babycenter .com/parentsavvy).

Revise your employment agree-ment every time there's an important change. Your arrange-ment with your nanny will evolve. For example, you might hire a nanny expecting her to work from 9 a.m. until 5 p.m., but you might end up needing her to stay until 7 p.m. each evening if you get a new job with longer hours. Each time you alter your nanny's pay or work schedule, revise your agree-ment accordingly. Otherwise, you'll end up with an employment agreement that doesn't accurately reflect your arrangement.

Getting Your Nanny Started

Spend several days with your new nanny and make sure she understands all the details of the job and your expectations for how she will take care of your child. To make sure everything's clear, you should provide written details on your preferences on important issues such as feeding, naps, safety, discipline, television, and diapering or potty training. It's also a good idea to have the nanny provide a daily written log in on your child's day and routine.

Preparing for Emergencies

It's difficult to think about the possibility of something bad happening while you are away from your child, but it's worse not to have a plan in place for what your nanny should do in the event of an emergency. Here's how to get started on emergency planning with your nanny.

What's the first thing I should do?
Put together a list of important phone numbers for your nanny, including:

- work and cell phone numbers for yourself and your spouse or partner
- name and number for your child's pediatrician, and
- names and phone numbers of at least two friends or relatives whom the nanny can contact if she can't reach you with an important question or in the case of an emergency.

Make several copies of this important list of emergency contacts: Give one copy to your nanny, tuck one into the diaper bag, and post one on your refrigerator or near the telephone.

ADDITIONAL RESOURCES

If you want a form. Use Baby-Center.com's "Emergency Names and Numbers Worksheet," available on the *Parent Savvy* page of BabyCenter.com (www.babycenter.com/parentsavvy) as a way to keep track of all this important information.

It's also a good idea to put together important information about your house (like what you would give to a house sitter), such as where to find first aid supplies or a fire extinguisher, how to deal with the alarm, or where to find the water shut-off valve.

How can I ensure that my nanny is prepared for a medical emergency?
There are several steps you can take:

- make sure that your nanny has had some basic first aid training, including CPR
- talk to your nanny about when it is appropriate to seek medical attention
- tell your nanny how to get to the nearest hospital
- give your nanny a medical information sheet for your child that includes the name of your child's pediatrician, your child's medical history (for example, allergies or prescription medications taken), and your child's health insurance information)

- provide your nanny with a copy of your child's health insurance card, and
- arm your nanny with a medical authorization form.

Use the "Authorization for Child's Medical Treatment" form shown at the end of this chapter as a model for preparing your own form. Simply fill in your child's name and date of birth; name, address, and phone number of your pediatrician, dentist, and other medical care provider; health insurance information; your child's allergies (if any); your contact information and that of a close friend or relative. Date and sign the authorization form and give the original to your nanny to use should she need to arrange emergency medical or dental care for your child.

CAUTION

Some hospitals prefer their own form. Check with the hospital that your nanny is likely to use in the event of an emergency to see if it prefers its own form. If it does, use that form, not the one included here.

How to Deal With Problems With Your Nanny

Even if you find the perfect nanny, you may have to let her go some day. For example, you might decide to become a full-time stay-at-home parent. Or you might find that the nanny who initially seemed so wonderful isn't the right fit. This section tells you what you need to know about letting your nanny go.

My nanny is too unreliable, regularly calling in sick or arriving late to work. Can I fire her?

Absolutely. You can let your nanny go at any time and for any reason—provided that you don't have a written agreement in place limiting your right to terminate your working relationship. The same holds true in reverse: Your nanny is free to quit for any reason.

Do I have to give my nanny any notice before I let her go?

You're not legally required to give your nanny even a day's notice if you decide to let her go. Out of fairness, however, consider giving your nanny some notice to enable her to find a new job.

Do I have to give my nanny any severance pay?

No.

Send a poorly performing nanny home immediately. Once you've told your nanny that you will no longer need her services because of a performance-related reason, do not leave your child in her care.

Is my nanny entitled to unemployment benefits?

If you paid your nanny on the books, she should be eligible to receive unemployment benefits until she finds another job. Advise your nanny to get in touch with your state's labor department.

 ADDITIONAL RESOURCES

Learn more about the process of finding and hiring a nanny. You can find information on everything from taxes to taking your nanny with you on vacation at the International Nanny Association's website at www.nanny.org and at www.nannynetwork.com. Another good resource is *The Nanny Book: The Smart Parent's Guide to Hiring, Firing and Every Sticky Situation in Between,* by Susan Carlton and Coco Meyers (St. Martin's Press 1999).

☑ CHECKLIST

Materials to Give Your New Nanny

Before your nanny starts work, be sure to give her the following materials:

- ❑ USCIS Form I-9 (*Employment Eligibility Verification*) (if nanny is paid on the books)
- ❑ New Hire Form (if nanny is paid on the books)
- ❑ W-2 (if nanny is paid on the books)
- ❑ Child care planner and daily log forms
- ❑ Emergency contacts
- ❑ Employment agreement
- ❑ Medical authorization form

FORM: Child Care Employment Agreement

1. Parent(s).

Name(s): _____

Address: _____

Home phone number: _____

Cell phone number: _____

Work phone number(s): _____

Email address(es): _____

Name(s): _____

Address: _____

Home phone number: _____

Cell phone number: _____

Work phone number(s): _____

Email address(es): _____

Name(s): _____

Address: _____

Home phone number: _____

Cell phone number: _____

Work phone number(s): _____

Email address(es): _____

2. Child care provider.

Name: _____

Address: _____

Social Security number: _____

Home phone number: _____

Cell phone number: _____

Email address: _____

3. Children.

Parent(s) contract(s) with Child Care Provider to care for:

_____

_____

4. Location and schedule of care.

Child Care Provider will take care of the children at _____.

Days and hours of child care will be as follows: _____.

5. Beginning date.

Employment will begin on _____.

6. Pay.

_____ shall pay Child Care Provider $____ per ❑ hour ❑ week. The base hourly rate shall be $_____ and the overtime rate shall be $_____. These rates are ❑ before taxes ❑ after taxes.

[For share care] _____shall pay Child Care Provider $____ per ❑ hour ❑ week. The base hourly rate shall be $_____ and the overtime rate shall be $_____. These rates are ❑ before taxes ❑ after taxes.

7. Taxes.

_____ ❑ will ❑ will not withhold federal income taxes from Child Care Provider's salary.

[For share care] _____ ❑ will ❑ will not withhold state income taxes from Child Care Provider's salary.

8. Pay schedule.

Parent(s) will pay Child Care Provider on the following schedule:_____.

9. Health insurance.

Parent(s) ❑ will ❑ will not provide Child Care Provider with health insurance as a benefit of employment. The details of the health insurance will be described in a separate document.

10. Room and board.

Parent(s) ❑ will ❑ will not provide Child Care Provider with room and board as part of this arrangement. Room and board includes the following:

_____

_____.

11. Extras.

Parent(s) will also provide Child Care Provider with the following as part of this arrangement:

_____

_____.

12. Paid vacation.

Child Care Provider will receive __ ❑ weeks ❑ days of paid vacation each year. Child Care Provider shall arrange to take this vacation according to the following:

_____

_____.

13. Unneeded time.

If Parent(s) choose not to use Child Care Provider during time that Child Care Provider has committed to Parents—for example, because of a family vacation—Parent(s) ❑ will ❑ will not pay Child Care Provider for that time.

14. Paid holidays.

Child Care Provider will receive the following holidays off with pay:

_____

_____.

15. Paid sick leave.

Child Care Provider will receive _____ paid sick days per year. Child Care Provider must give Parent(s) as much advance notice as practically possible.

16. Responsibilities.

Child Care Provider will have the following responsibilities under this agreement:

_____

_____.

17. House rules.

Child Care Provider will comply with the following house rules:

_____

_____.

18. At-will employment.

Either Parent(s) or Child Care Provider can terminate this agreement at any time and for any reason that isn't illegal.

Signatures:

_____   _____

Parent   Date

_____   _____

Parent   Date

_____   _____

Child Care Provider   Date

FORM: Authorization for Child's Medical Treatment

Child(ren)'s names and birth dates: _____

_____

Pediatrician's name, address, and phone number: _____

_____

Health insurance: _____

Dentist's name, address, and phone number: _____

_____

Other medical provider's name, address, and phone number: _____

_____

Child's allergies: _____

Parent's contact information: _____

Names and phone numbers of other adults in case parents can't be reached:

_____

Authorization and Consent of Parent(s)

We give our authorization and consent for [name of nanny] to authorize necessary medical or dental care for our children [name(s) of children] _____

Such medical treatment shall be provided upon the advice of and supervision by any physician, surgeon, dentist, or other medical practitioner licensed to practice in the United States.

Signatures:

_____   _____

Parent   Date

_____   _____

Parent   Date

Chapter 18

Share Care

If you love the idea of a nanny but can't handle the expense, consider sharing child care with another family. In a share care arrangement, a nanny cares for children from two different families at the same time, either in one household or two (alternating between homes). The families share the nanny bill, just as they share the nanny.

This chapter will help you decide whether a share care is right for you and how to structure a good arrangement with another family.

CROSS REFERENCE

Read Chapter 17, *Nannies.* With a share care situation, you'll have to deal with many of the same issues that you would if you were hiring a nanny entirely on your own, including deciding what you want (in terms of nanny schedule, responsibilities, salary), interviewing and screening nannies, checking references, complying with legal requirements, and preparing an employment agreement. This chapter covers issues specific to share care.

Pros and Cons of Share Care

A good share care arrangement can be a wonderful—and practical—child care alternative, but there are drawbacks as well. This section looks at the pluses and minuses of sharing child care.

What are the advantages of share care? Here are some of the main reasons you might want to consider share care instead of hiring your own nanny:

- **You'll get many of the benefits of having your own nanny—but at a significant discount.** Although share care is unlikely to cut your nanny bills in half, your child care costs will be dramatically lower with a share care arrangement. What's more, you'll still enjoy the personalized care for your child that comes with hiring a nanny (especially important for infants and young children). Share care often offers the convenience and flexibility of a full-time nanny.

- **Your child will spend the day in a home environment.** Share care takes place in either your home or the other family's. Depending on your arrangement, you may prefer all or most care in the other family's home—for example, if your home is too small or because you work from home.

- **Your child will have company all day long.** One of the nicest things about share care is the sibling-like camaraderie that comes with having your child spend the day with someone else's child. It's a happy medium between a day care center (where there can sometimes be too many other children around) and a standard nanny arrangement (which can get lonely for a child who craves company).

- **You'll be in it together.** Sometimes, dealing on your own with a nanny can be trying, and parents often tire of handling all of the aspects of the nanny arrangement by themselves. With share care, you have a built-in partner to share everything from managing the nanny to providing backup care. The other family can become part of your extended family, especially nice if your own siblings and parents live far away.

What are the disadvantages of share care? Although share care can be great, there are a number of disadvantages to consider.

- **You'll have to work cooperatively with another family.** You'll have to agree on everything from the nanny's salary

to where the nanny works each day to when the nanny may take vacation. If you and the other family have different needs or different child care philosophies, things can get tricky. To avoid problems, try to work out the details before the care begins, following our advice in **Finding a Family to Share With**, below.

- **Changes in the other family's life will cause changes in your own.** If the other family decides to move out of town or put their child in a day care center, for example, you'll be in a pickle until you can find a new share family.

- **You won't usually have the same level of scheduling flexibility as with your own nanny.** It won't always be easy to make last-minute arrangements for the nanny to arrive very early one morning or stay late one evening because you'll have another family's needs to consider as well.

- **Your nanny probably won't have the time to help you out around the house with basic chores—such as doing your child's laundry.** When your nanny is also caring for someone else's child, it's unrealistic to expect her to have time to tackle anything else.

Finding a Family to Share With

The success of your share care arrangement will depend in large part on the other family—how well you work with them and like them, and how well your child gets along with their child. This section provides you with the information you need to find a good share family.

CROSS REFERENCE

Hammer out the details first. As with hiring a nanny on your own, you'll first need to clearly decide what you want in terms of schedule, responsibilities, pay, and other issues discussed in Chapter 17. If you don't do this first, you'll simply be wasting your time talking with potential families and nannies.

What should I do first—find a nanny or find a share family?

It depends on your personal preferences and situation. If you find the nanny first, then you have a lot more control over setting up the details of the share. But if you want help in finding the nanny—and are willing to cooperate with the other family on the details—then finding the other family first is a good idea. And if you want to combine the nanny search and share family search into one step, then look for a family that already has a nanny.

How do I go about actually finding a share care arrangement?

As with looking for a nanny, ask friends and neighbors. Look at ads in your local newspaper or on community bulletin boards. Sometimes, a family who already has a nanny will advertise a share arrangement—so keep an eye out for those types of postings as well.

You can also post an ad yourself—for example:

> *Westwood family seeking nearby family to find and share a full-time nanny. We need flexible hours for our four-month-old baby, three days a week. We're looking for a like-minded family with a child less than a year old. Please call 555-5689 for more details.*

What should I look for when choosing a family with whom to share a nanny?

Make sure that the other family is a good fit with yours. Prescreen the other parents over the phone first. If you have a good phone conversation, then arrange to meet in person in one family's home. If this initial meeting goes well, arrange a second meeting in the other family's home. Take the time to get to know each other. Have your children spend time together, particularly if they are older, to see how they get along.

Here are some crucial areas of compatibility to consider when choosing a family with whom to share your nanny:

- **Childrearing philosophy.** You'll want to find a family with similar views on things such as discipline, naps, food, and television watching, so that your nanny can take a consistent approach with both children. If you're very careful about feeding your child a healthy diet, for example, you'll want to steer clear of a family who's content to feed their child chicken nuggets and fries for lunch.

- **Location of care.** Where does the other family live? Even if you meet the perfect family, a share care arrangement is not going to be practical if the family lives an hour away. Unless the care will take place in your home, you'll want a family that lives in your neighborhood (or very close to it).

TIPS

Check out the other family's home. If the care will take place at the other family's house, be sure to visit. Is the home clean and spacious? Has the family been careful to childproof—putting safety gates on the stairs and covers on the outlets, for example? Is there a backyard or nearby park where your child can play outdoors? Is the neighborhood a place where you would feel comfortable leaving your child?

- **Age of children.** You may want to share with a child close in age to your own so that the children will be good playmates. But if your children are still babies, you might have a tough time finding a nanny who's willing to care for two infants at once—although in some cases, this will be easier if the babies both take naps. Also, some parents like for the children to be different ages—so that the share feels more like a sibling relationship.

- **Nanny requirements.** What are you each looking for in a nanny? The more you agree on what you want in a nanny, the easier it will be to find a nanny who makes everyone happy.

TIPS

Make sure that the other family has realistic requirements. If the other family wants a nanny with a Ph.D. in early childhood education, for example, your nanny search will probably go on for years.

- **Schedule.** Ask what hours the other family needs a nanny to work. You don't need to have the exact same days and hours as the other family for a share care arrangement to work, but it's best to have similar needs for coverage. If you need a nanny five days a week but the other family needs a nanny only three days a week, for example, it may be harder to work out the details of a share arrangement. On the other hand, if you both work part-time flexible hours, a share care can be ideal because you can arrange for each of your children to have a lot of time on their own with the nanny. Whatever you decide, try (for the nanny's sake) to keep a regular schedule.

- **Budget.** How much are you both willing to pay a nanny? A family with too low of a budget might limit your nanny choices.

- **Benefits.** When two families are involved, paying for things such as health insurance becomes more affordable. These types of benefits can help you to attract a truly top-notch nanny, particularly because some of the better nannies try to avoid share care arrangements altogether.

- **Personal preferences and style.** Finally, don't forget the more subjective issues that can make a break a relationship. If you're very religious or political and the other family isn't this may be a problem.

You'll want to be clear on all of these issues before you interview prospective nannies and then spell out everything in a family share care agreement after you hire a nanny.

Putting the Arrangement Together

Once you find a family with whom to share, you must find a nanny and work out the details of the arrangement.

I've found a wonderful family with whom to share. Now do you have any advice on finding a nanny?

Finding, screening, and hiring a nanny for a share care arrangement involves the same steps as any other nanny search (as explained in Chapter 17). The only difference is that you'll have to find a nanny that both you and the other family like and trust and who meets your requirements—which can be difficult. Someone from both families should be present during every nanny interview, so that both families feel equally involved in the process.

In terms of what to look for in a nanny, it would be ideal if you could find a nanny who has experience with share care so that she knows what to expect and how to juggle the needs of two families at once. At a minimum, however, you should look for someone who has previously cared for two children of the same age as yours at the same time—because this can be much more demanding and draining than caring for just one child.

My state requires workers' compensation for full-time nannies. Do both families have to purchase this insurance, or is it okay if just one of us does?

This is a tricky question, so check with your state's labor department. From a practical perspective, however, it is probably wise for each family to purchase a workers' compensation insurance policy. This way, you won't have to worry about covering your nanny's medical bills or lost wages if your nanny gets injured in your home or while caring for your child. See Chapter 17 for more about nannies and workers' compensation insurance.

Are there any other legal requirements for share care that I should know about?

Some states require that nannies in share care arrangements be licensed. To learn your state's rules on this issue, check the National Resource Center for Health and Safety in Child Care's website at http://nrc.uchsc.edu. You can also call 800-598-KIDS to get the contact information for the agency that regulates child care providers in your state.

We want to pay our share care nanny on the books, but the other family does not want to do so. Is this possible?

Yes. You can pay taxes on your share of the nanny's salary. See Chapter 17 for more information about paying a nanny.

We are both paying the nanny on the books. Does that mean we are both eligible for child care tax breaks?

Yes. For more about these tax breaks, see Chapter 29.

Now that I've gone to all the trouble of setting up a share care arrangement, I want to make sure things run smoothly. Do you have any advice for making share care work?

When two families share a nanny, little problems will inevitably arise from time to time. The best way to ensure that these problems don't get in the way of your relationship is good communication. Decide in advance how you will communicate requests or scheduling changes to your nanny. Otherwise, a nanny can feel caught in the middle when one parent says one thing and the other parent says another.

Treat your nanny and the other family respectfully. Bear in mind that a nanny in a share care arrangement has much more to deal with than a nanny who has to answer to just one family, so don't put more pressure on her than necessary. And be careful not to overstep your boundaries with your share care family—for example, don't assume that it's okay for your child to stay at the other family's home for an extra hour or two after the nanny has left for the day. A little courtesy will go a long way in making the relationship work well long-term. ■

Chapter 19

Au Pairs

If you're open to the idea of a live-in nanny, consider hiring an au pair instead. The au pair program is a cultural exchange that allows young women from foreign countries to spend a year or two with a host family in the United States. For dramatically less than you would pay a nanny, an au pair will live in your home and care for your child for up to 45 hours each week.

 CAUTION

This chapter discusses au pair agencies regulated by the U.S. State Department only. There are many other agencies that offer low-cost foreign nannies. Make sure you work with an agency that is legally authorized to place au pairs with American families. Also, the information in this chapter does not apply to nannies on tourist or student visas who are working illegally in the United States.

What are the advantages of hiring an au pair? The au pair program is a very attractive child care option for a number of reasons:

- You'll get the one-on-one attention for your child that comes with hiring a nanny—but without the steep price. Even when all program fees are taken into account, you'll end up paying your au pair about $6 per hour (in addition to room and board) for a full work week. It would be virtually impossible to find a quality nanny willing to work for those rates.

- You won't have to bother with a payroll service. Because au pairs are nonresident aliens, you don't have to pay Medicare, Social Security, or unemployment taxes on your au pair's salary.

- You pay the same amount no matter how many children you have. With a nanny, on the other hand, you would almost certainly have to pay a higher rate if you have more than one child.

- You don't have to worry too much about screening and background checks. Thanks to the U.S. State Department's au pair regulations, authorized au pair agencies must personally interview each candidate; check each candidate's school, employment, and personal references; and conduct a criminal background check before sending the au pair your way.

- You'll have a young, well-educated caregiver for your child. Au pairs must be between the ages of 18 and 26, have a high school diploma, and be proficient in English. Moreover, if you have a child younger than two, the au pair agency must send you someone with at least 200 hours of infant care experience.

- Your au pair will have received formal training in child development and child safety. Au pairs must receive at least eight hours of child safety instruction and at least 24 hours of child development instruction. You would be hard pressed to find a nanny with that kind of formal training.

- Your child will have the opportunity to soak up some culture. It can be a rewarding experience for your child to have a caregiver who hails from another country and speaks another language.

- You'll have scheduling flexibility. Although you cannot ask your au pair to work more than 45 hours a week or more than ten hours a day, you have the freedom to choose the hours that work best for you, including weekends (with the exception that you must give your au pair one full weekend off a month).

What are the disadvantages of au pairs?

An au pair is not for everyone. The following are some drawbacks to the arrangement:

- Your au pair can stay only for a maximum of two years. What's more, many au pairs leave at the end of one year—so you'll be stuck looking for new child care just as your child is developing a close bond with your au pair. Of course, if you plan to send your child to preschool starting at the age of two, this won't be an issue for you.

- It may take many weeks (even months) to get an au pair after you apply.

- You won't be able to interview your au pair in person. Unless you're willing to travel to your au pair's home country (and few families are), you'll have to rely on just a few telephone interviews, email, and the agency's information about the candidate when hiring your au pair. Ask the au pair and her references the same questions you would ask when hiring a nanny, as explained in Chapter 17.

- You cannot ask your au pair to work more than 45 hours per week, or more than ten hours per day, even if you're willing to pay her more money.

- You cannot ask your au pair to do household chores (except for those relating to your child).

- You may not leave your au pair alone with a child younger than three months.

- Your au pair cannot care for your child overnight.

- You will have to pay hefty agency placement and program fees (usually several thousand dollars) before the au pair arrives in the United States. These fees cover the au pair's screening, training, transportation, and other administrative costs.
- If your au pair has never lived away from home, she may be unhappy and depressed to be so far from family and friends.

How much does an au pair typically cost?

An average au pair will cost you about $14,000 for the year—which works out to about $270 per week. This amount includes your au pair's weekly stipend of $139.05, your au pair's annual $500 education allowance (toward of the cost of at least six hours of academic coursework at an accredited educational institution), and the agency's program and placement fees. In addition, you'll have to provide your au pair with room, board, and the opportunity to become like an extended member of your family. Many agencies offer you the option of hiring an au pair with special qualifications—such as a college degree in early childhood education—for an extra fee. Expect to pay around $340 per week if this is the type of au pair you are seeking.

Who qualifies to hire an au pair?

You can only participate in the au pair program if you meet all of the following requirements:
- you can provide the au pair with a private bedroom
- you live within an hour's driving distance of an au pair program coordinator (you'll have to ask the agency you're using if you are within its coverage area)
- you and your partner (if you have one) are United States citizens or legal permanent residents, and
- you and your partner (if you have one) are fluent in English.

How do I go about hiring an au pair?

You'll have to work with an au pair agency—such as Au Pair in America (www.aupairinamerica.com) or InterExchange (www.interexchange.org). You can find a list of authorized au pair agencies at the U.S. Department of State's website at www.exchanges.state.gov/education/jexchanges/about/catalog/aupair.pdf.

The agency will match your family with prescreened au pair candidates who fit your needs, based on a lengthy application form you complete. Next, you interview the candidates you like the best (via telephone) and extend an offer of employment to one of them.

Check Out Au Pair Agencies

Before you select an au pair agency, understand the agency's fee structure (including nonrefundable application fees) and au pair selection process. Agency websites will provide a lot of this information. Ask many of the same questions you would ask when selecting a nanny placement agency (discussed in Chapter 17)—for example, how long the agency has been in business, the number of au pairs it has placed, and how long the process will take. Here are a few other questions to ask:

- What countries do most of the agency's au pairs come from? If you're set on a French or Thai au pair, for example, make sure the agency places au pairs from these countries.
- Does the au pair agency provide any benefits—such as health insurance coverage—to the au pairs it represents?
- What kind of local support does the agency provide to au pairs in your area?
- What happens if you're unhappy with the au pair: Will the agency try to resolve the problem or find you a new au pair?

ADDITIONAL RESOURCES

Learn more about the au pair program. The U.S. State Department website has comprehensive information about the au pair program. To find the au pair section, log on to www.exchanges.state. gov and scroll down until you see the "Au Pair Program" link on the left-hand navigation bar. ∎

Chapter 20

Day Care Centers

For parents in search of reliable and affordable child care, day care centers can provide the ideal solution. A day care center will never arrive late, call in sick, or expect a holiday bonus as a nanny might. What's more, you'll enjoy the benefits of a structured, school-like environment for your child. The information in this chapter will help you decide whether a day care center is right for your family, and it will guide you through the process of finding an excellent home away from home for your child.

What are the advantages of using a day care center?
There are many reasons why you might want to opt for a day care center:
- the state licenses and inspects them
- the teachers who will care for your child have formal training in early childhood education
- your child's caregiver will be supervised most or all of the time
- your child will enjoy the company of other children all day long
- day care provides a rich and stimulating environment

- day care centers cost substantially less than hiring a nanny, and
- you won't have to depend on just one person for child care, so that if your child's usual caregiver is sick or on vacation, another one of the center's caregivers will fill in.

What are the disadvantages?
Although day care centers work well for many families, there are a number of reasons why a day care center might not be ideal for yours:
- many day care centers do not accept infants
- your child won't get one-on-one attention all day long
- there's very little scheduling flexibility
- your child is likely to get sick often, and
- you'll have to call in the backup troops—or stay home yourself—whenever your child is ill.

How much does a typical day care center cost?
Expect to pay between $500 and $1,250 per child per month, depending on the age of your child, the hours you wish to send

your child to day care, where you live, and the particular day care center you choose. Day care centers generally charge more to care for babies and young toddlers than for preschoolers. Moreover, you will pay higher than average rates if you live in a big city, such as New York or San Francisco. For example, it could cost you more than $1,500 per month to send your child to day care at certain top centers in Manhattan.

If you or your spouse is lucky enough to work for a company or organization with on-site day care, chances are good that the center's fees will be lower than market rates.

 FAST FACTS

Day care can be more expensive than college. If you live in a big city, you'll spend more to send your child to day care than to a public college. According to a December 2000 report by the Children's Defense Fund, in some cities, such as Boston, it costs twice as much to send a four-year-old to day care as it does to send an 18-year-old to a public college. To learn more, check out the entire article at www.childrensdefense .org/earlychildhood/childcare/ highcost.pdf.

What does it mean for a day care center to be licensed by the state?

Each state has established basic health, safety, and teacher training standards that day care centers must meet to become licensed, and states enforce these standards through regular inspections. You can learn your state's rules by checking the National Resource Center for Health and Safety in Child Care's website at www.nrc.uchsc. edu. You can also call 800-598-KIDS to get the contact information for the agency that regulates day care centers in your state. That agency can tell you whether the center you are considering has a valid, up-to-date license.

Although you should steer clear of any day care center that does not have a current license, you shouldn't automatically trust a center that does. This is because the state licensing requirements are the minimum standards that a center must meet before your state government will allow it to operate.

A cut above the rest. If you're in the market for a truly amazing day care center, look for one that is accredited by the National Association for the Education of Young Children (NAEYC). The NAEYC is a nonprofit organization committed to improving the quality of educational programs for young children through its accreditation and professional development programs. The NAEYC holds day care centers to stringent standards on caregiver-to-child ratios, caregiver qualifications, and the center's physical environment, among other criteria. Obtaining NAEYC accreditation involves a lengthy review process that can take many months. To date, the NAEYC has accredited only a small fraction (about 10,000) of the more than 100,000 licensed day care centers in the country. This doesn't mean that the other 90,000-odd day care centers are terrible places to send your child. It simply means that if a center is NAEYC-accredited, you can rest assured that is meets some very high standards. You can learn more about the NAEYC's accreditation standards and locate an accredited day care center near you by logging on to the NAEYC's website at www.naeyc.org.

☑ CHECKLIST

Finding a Day Care Center

Finding a great day care center for your child doesn't have to be a complicated and confusing process. Just follow these simple steps:

- Decide what you need in terms of hours, schedule, and budget.
- Put together a list of day care centers in your area.
- Phone each center and collect some basic information, including fees and the availability of a space of your child. Make sure each of the centers you're considering has a valid license.
- Meet with the director of each center that looks promising and tour the facility.
- Check the center's parent references.
- Schedule a second visit with the centers you like the most.
- Review the contract and complete all necessary paperwork.

Where do I begin my search for a day care center?

Word of mouth is the best place to start. Talk to as many other parents as possible—including family members, friends, neighbors, and even your pediatrician—to get a picture of the day care situation in your area. You'll quickly learn which centers are top-notch, which ones aren't so wonderful, and which centers are best for different types of children. If you or your partner is lucky enough to work for a company with on-site day care, be sure to ask coworkers who use the center what they do and do not like about it.

If you still need recommendations, check with a local child care referral agency. These agencies are nonprofit organizations that gather information about local day care centers and help to match parents to the center that best meets their needs. To find the name and number of a child care referral agency in your area, contact the Child Care Resource and Referral Agency (CCRA)—a national organization whose goal is to help parents obtain the best information about quality child care in their area. You can call the CCRA's telephone hotline at 800-424-2246 or log on to the CCRA's website at www.childcareaware.org. That website is also chock full of helpful (and free) publications and useful articles on a wide range of child care topics, so it's worth checking out even if you don't need help finding a day care center.

☑ CHECKLIST

Day Care Center Topics

When touring a prospective day care center, be sure to cover the following topics:
- ❑ Name, address, and phone number of the center
- ❑ Name of center director
- ❑ Name of person giving center tour
- ❑ Basic information (how long in business, up-to-date license, accreditation)
- ❑ Hours and days of operation, including holiday schedule
- ❑ Number and age of children
- ❑ Caregiver-to-child ratio
- ❑ Fees (amount, date due, additional charges)
- ❑ Space available or waiting list
- ❑ Director's qualifications and experience level
- ❑ Staff qualifications and experience level
- ❑ Typical day (activities, meals, naps, diaper changing, potty training, comforting, discipline)
- ❑ Facilities (cleanliness, organization, safety)
- ❑ Sick child policy
- ❑ Drop-in policy
- ❑ Communication between teachers and parents
- ❑ Communication among parents
- ❑ Parent participation
- ❑ How parent concerns are addressed
- ❑ How the center handles medical emergencies
- ❑ Disaster preparedness plans
- ❑ How the center handles children with special needs
- ❑ How center helps children cope with separation and adjustment
- ❑ Center security
- ❑ Names and phone numbers of parent references.

I've made an appointment to talk to the director of a day care center that a friend recommended. What should I ask while I'm there?

It's wonderful that you've made an appointment to talk with the center's director, because parents should not choose a center without first visiting and talking to the people in charge. Make sure your visit includes a tour, because some of the most important information will come from your own observations.

Here are some factors to pay attention to—and to ask the center's director about—during your visit. Especially if you're visiting several day care centers, keep notes on important information. Also, ask for a copy of the center's policies and programs.

The basics. Find out how long the center has been open (the longer, the better) and whether it has a valid, up-to-date license. Ask about special accreditations—such as one from the NAEYC. Ask about the number and age of children who attend the center.

Hours and days of operation. Ask about drop-off and pick-up times, as well as the holiday schedule and periods during the year when the center is closed. If the center's hours don't mesh well with your work schedule, you'll need to find another center—or another type of child care.

Fees. What is the cost? Ask about the payment structure—for example, do you have to pay for the first three months up front or can you pay your child care bills biweekly? Also ask about hidden costs—such as late pickup fees and other additions to your bill (for example, in California, many centers have earthquake kit fees)—as well as the

center's refund policy. Ask for a copy of the center's written agreement (described below) which should provide detailed information on fees.

Whether there's space for your child. Find out if you'll be able to enroll your child immediately. If the center puts your child on a waiting list, find out how long you should realistically expect to wait for space to open up.

The director's qualifications. The director runs the show, so make sure you are comfortable with his or her credentials, experience level, philosophy, and style. At an absolute minimum, the director should have a degree in early childhood education as well as two years of experience in the child care field. Good directors tend to have advanced degrees in early childhood education and extensive experience. Find out how long the director has been with the center you are considering. Continuity leads to stability—so you might want to think twice before enrolling your child in a day care center with a new director. Finally, trust your intuition. If you don't get a good feeling from talking to the director, the center might not be right for you.

The staff. The center's staff members will be the ones directly caring for your child, so find out how the center selects and screens its staff members. Of course, when it comes to caregivers, credentials aren't everything. Ask to meet the staff members and—if possible—observe them in action. Even if the caregivers have outstanding resumes, the center might not be right for you if the caregivers aren't as nurturing, stimulating, or loving as you would like. Be sure to ask about the following:

- **Qualifications and experience.** Although a degree in early childhood education is certainly not a prerequisite for being a good caregiver, there is no question that better day care centers have better educated staff members. Experience is also important.
- **Turnover.** A happy, stable staff is a good sign that the day care center is a pleasant and productive environment.
- **Screening process.** Background checks can be a good safeguard against hiring caregivers with a criminal record or a history of child abuse. Find out whether the center has any formal screening process for caregivers.
- **First aid training.** Ask whether the staff is trained in basic first aid techniques, such as CPR and the Heimlich maneuver.
- **Professional development.** Ask whether the staff members receive training in child care and early childhood education throughout the year.

The caregiver-child ratio: Look for a center where children are clustered together in small groups with enough caregivers to meet the children's needs. The state licensing standards specify limits on caregiver-to-child ratios—for example, New York requires at least one caregiver for every four babies and at least one caregiver for every seven three-year-olds—but smaller is always better when it comes to child care. (After all, could you imagine juggling four crawling eight-month-olds at once?) The more caregivers

there are, the more one-on-one attention your child will receive. The National Resource Center for Health and Safety in Child Care recommends a maximum ratio of 1:3 for babies and 1:5 for children between the ages of 13 and 30 months.

How your child will spend the day. Learn as much as possible about how your child will be cared for and what your child will be doing during a typical day. It is important that the center's approach to child care is a good match with your own. Be sure to ask about:

- **Meals and snacks.** If your child is a baby, find out whether your child will be fed on demand or on a schedule. For toddlers and older children, ask whether the center will provide meals and snacks. If your child has any food allergies or dietary restrictions, ask what steps the center will take to prevent exposure to problem foods.
- **Napping.** Find out the center's napping policies. Is there a nap schedule or will your child be put down for a nap whenever he or she appears sleepy? Are babies left to cry themselves to sleep or will staff members soothe your baby? Are children supervised while they are sleeping? Look at where your child will be sleeping: Is it comfortable and clean?
- **Comforting.** Ask how caregivers handle crying spells and separation anxiety. It's best to pick a center whose comforting philosophy is in line with your own, so that your child enjoys consistent treatment at home and at day care.
- **Discipline.** If your child is still a baby, discipline is not yet an issue. But for

toddlers who are just beginning to test limits, discipline is important. Ask what happens if a child misbehaves and find out whether caregivers ever shout at the children for any reason.

- **Activities**. Is there a formal schedule of activities—such as singing and reading—or are the children left to play freely for most of the day? Do the children go outside or spend their day indoors? Does the center permit children to watch television?

The facilities. Make sure that you are comfortable with the center's facilities. Do you notice any obvious hazards? Is there enough play space and outdoor space for the children to run around? Is the indoor play area filled with stimulating toys? Is the facility clean, especially the bathrooms, food preparation area, and diaper-changing area? Is the facility warm and inviting? Has the staff personalized the area with the children's photographs and art?

The children. Look at the children while you are visiting. Do they seem clean, comfortable, and cared for? Are they happily engaged in activities? Are any of the children watching television? Remember—your baby may be one of those children some day, so you should feel good about what you see.

The sick child policy. Find out when the center requires you to keep your child at home. At some centers, your child will have to stay home every time she comes down with the sniffles. Other centers will turn your child away only if he or she has more serious symptoms—such as fever or

vomiting. Although a strict sick-child policy means you'll have to rely on backup care more often, it also means that your child is likely to stay healthier.

The drop-in policy. In some states—such as California—day care centers are required by law to permit parents to drop in at any time. If you don't happen to live in one of these states, check to make sure that you can swing by the center on your lunch hour or whenever you have a rare afternoon off from work.

Communication. How does the center communicate with parents? Some centers leave notices in mail cubbies and have a notebook that parents can write in; others have more formal systems, such as email updates and monthly meetings. There's no right system; just make sure that you are comfortable with the one that the center uses.

Parent involvement. Find out whether parent participation is required or expected. For example, are parents asked to help out with fundraising and field trips? Are there parent education meetings? Is there a PTA? Although some parents relish the opportunity to become more involved, others dread the pressure to participate in bake sales and field trips. Be sure that the center's expectations (or requirements) match your interest level and ability to be involved.

How parent concerns are addressed. Even if you enroll your child in the best day care center around, chances are that you'll still have concerns or issues you'd like to raise from time to time. Find out who handles parent concerns and how.

Medical emergencies. What will happen if your child ever needs immediate medical attention? Where will your child be taken? How and when will you be contacted? Ask for examples of how the center has handled medical emergencies in the past.

Disaster preparedness. Does the center have a plan in place for disasters such as fires, earthquakes, storms, and blizzards? Does the center conduct regular fire drills?

Children with special needs. If your child has any medical conditions, allergies, or other noteworthy issues, explain your child's needs and find out whether the center is equipped to care for your child. If your child is on prescription medication, ask where the medicine will be stored and how the center will ensure that your child takes the medicine properly each day.

Separation and adjustment. Ask how the center will help your child become comfortable in this new environment. Will the center allow you and your child to visit and spend a few hours there before the first day?

Security. How does the center prevent strangers from entering the facility? Are the doors locked at all times? Is there a security camera or other system for screening visitors before they enter? If your child will ever leave the center's premises—to go play at a nearby park, for example—are additional staff members assigned to keep track of the children? What other precautions are taken to ensure your child's security off-site?

Policy manual. Many day care centers have a manual specifying policies on all aspects of child care. If the center has such a manual, ask if you can review it.

When the day care center may dismiss your child. Just as you are free to withdraw your child from day care at any time, a day care center generally has the right to stop providing care for your child if the fit isn't right for any reason. It's quite rare for a day care center to dismiss a child, but it does happen—usually because of a child's severe behavioral issues. Ask the director whether the center has ever stopped providing care for a child and for what reasons.

References. Ask the director for the names and telephone numbers of at least two or three families who are currently using the center. Call these families and find out the ages of their children, how long they've been using the center, and what they like and don't like about it.

Your instincts. Even if all of the answers to your questions are acceptable and the references are perfect, you may still have a bad feeling about the center. If so, don't ignore your gut. All children are different, and a center that is terrific for one child may not be right for another.

See whether you can visit more than once. First impressions are usually—but not always—right on the money. To get a good feel for a day care center, however, it's helpful to visit at least twice and at different times of the day. This way you will see the children doing different things and will meet all of the staff (some of whom may only work in the mornings or in the afternoons).

BABYCENTER RESOURCES

If you'd like to bring something with you. Some of the information in our discussion comes from BabyCenter.com's "Day Care Center Director/Caregiver Interview Sheet." You can find a copy on the *Parent Savvy* page of BabyCenter .com (www.babycenter.com/par-entsavvy). Another resource is "A Parent's Guide to Choosing Safe and Healthy Child Care," which is a four-page checklist available free at the National Resource Center for Health and Safety in Child Care's website at http://nrc.uchsc.edu.

How can I find out if other parents have lodged any complaints against the day care center I'm considering?

Ask your state's day care center licensing organization. You can find out the name and telephone number of your state's organization by logging on to www.nrc.uchsc.edu or calling 800-426-2246. You might also want to call your local Better Business Bureau (you can find a list at www.bbb.org) and ask if it has received complaints.

I have decided against immunizing my child. Does this mean that I cannot enroll my child in day care?

Not necessarily. Depending on the state in which you live and the reasons for your decision not to immunize your child, you may be eligible for an exemption to the immunization requirements. To learn your state's immunization requirements, log on to the American Academy of Pediatrics website at www.cispimmunize.org and click on "State Immunization Requirements for School Entry." You can also check with your state's department of health for the most recent regulations and for information about exemptions.

My child has special health needs. Will I still be able to enroll her in day care?

It depends on the nature of your child's health needs and the day care center's ability to accommodate them. Under the federal Americans with Disabilities Act (ADA), a day care center cannot refuse to enroll your child simply because of a mental or physical disability. Rather, the center must determine whether it can accommodate your child's needs without incurring tremendous expense or fundamentally changing the nature of its program.

TIPS

You don't need to be disabled to have a "disability" under the ADA. People often think that the ADA only applies to individuals in wheelchairs or with obvious physical limitations, but the ADA is actually much broader. The ADA defines the term "disability" to include a wide range of common health conditions, including diabetes, AIDS, and attention deficit disorder (ADD).

In most cases, a center will have to make reasonable modifications to its program and provide any communication aids and services necessary to enable a child with special health needs to attend. The center cannot charge parents extra fees for making these adjustments.

EXAMPLE: *Linda's son, Alex, is diabetic and needs regular glucose testing and occasional insulin injections during the day. Linda applied to enroll Alex in Sunshine Kids, a neighborhood day care facility. Under the ADA, Sunshine Kids cannot reject Alex just because he suffers from diabetes. Sunshine Kids can easily accommodate Alex's special health*

needs at almost no cost by having one or two caregivers attend short training sessions on administering glucose tests and insulin injections. Because these tests and injections take just a few minutes, Sunshine Kids will not have to make any major changes to its program in order to accommodate Alex's health needs.

A center can exclude a child who would threaten the health or safety of other children. This narrow exception to the ADA applies only in extreme cases—for example, to a child with a highly transferable disease such as tuberculosis. Notably, the exception does not apply to children who have AIDS or HIV.

ADDITIONAL RESOURCES

If you'd like to bring something with you. The Child Care Law Center, a California-based non-profit organization, offers plenty of information on how the ADA applies to child care centers. You can order helpful publications from the organization's website at www .childcarelaw.org.

The day care center I've selected has asked me to sign a written contract in order to enroll my child. Is this typical? And what should I look for before signing the contract?

It is standard practice for centers to ask parents to sign a written agreement. This ensures that there is no confusion about important issues such as the center's fees and hours of operation.

In reviewing the agreement, pay careful attention to:

- **The basic cost of child care.** How much will the center be charging? Are the costs subject to change—for example, does the center increase its fees each year? Will you still owe the basic fees on days when your child does not attend day care—for example, because your family is away on vacation?

- **Additional fees.** Day care centers sometimes charge extra fees above and beyond the basic cost of child care. For example, you may owe a materials fee to pay for art supplies.

- **Penalties.** To encourage parents to follow the rules, day care centers generally charge financial penalties for doing things such as picking your child up late from day care or forgetting to send enough diapers to last the week.

- **The payment schedule.** You may be asked to pay your child care costs weekly, biweekly, or monthly. Pay close attention to the provisions regarding what will happen if you fall behind on your payments for any reason. For example, will the center refuse to accept your child if you are two weeks late on your payments?

- **The deposit amount.** Just as you pay a deposit when you sign a lease, you'll be expected to pay a deposit in order to enroll your child in day care. How much is the deposit? Must the deposit be paid in one lump sum?

- **The cancellation and refund policy.** Even if you find the perfect day care center, you may decide to withdraw your child from day care for any number of reasons. How much notice must you give the center to cancel your child care contract? Will you receive a refund of all or part of your deposit?

Once you've signed the agreement, be sure to keep it in a safe place—along with a copy of the day care center's policy manual and any documentation you provide to the day care center (see below)—so that you'll have the agreement handy if any issues ever arise.

Will I have to provide any other documents to the day care center?

Yes—there's usually a small mountain of paperwork to complete and submit in order to enroll your child in day care, including:

- A **registration form,** which usually asks for your name and address, emergency contact information, and the name and phone number of your child's pediatrician.

- A **medical history,** including past or current medical issues, allergies, and any other special health needs.

- An **immunization record.**

- An **emergency medical authorization form.**

- A **medication permission** sheet (if your child is on medication) that contains written consent to administer medication to your child. The center may also ask for written instructions from your pediatrician as to the dosage amount and medication schedule.
- A **list of individuals** who may pick up your child.
- The **details of any custody or visitation agreement** in place, if you and your child's other parent are separated or divorced. The center will want to know who has primary physical custody of your child; who is authorized to make major medical, educational, and other decisions on behalf of your child; and the visitation schedule. This will ensure that the day care center will release your child to the appropriate parent each day and that the right parent is contacted when important decisions or authorizations are needed.

 TIPS

Keep your information up to date. If you change jobs or cell phone numbers, give the center your new information. Otherwise, it will have trouble reaching you if something important comes up.

Now that I've found a wonderful day care center for my child, what should I do to ensure the arrangement works well for everyone?

Begin by providing the center with all relevant information on your child (physical, mental, developmental, social, and the like). This will probably be part of the enrollment papers, but make sure the center has all the information it needs on your child.

Perhaps the most important thing to do is engage yourself in your child's care. At least once a week, spend a few minutes talking with your child's caregiver. Tell the caregiver about important developments in your child's life—for example, if you've managed to wean your child from the bottle or if your child has been having trouble sleeping because of night terrors. If you can, use your lunch break to drop in sometimes. Attend parent conferences and take advantage of opportunities to be more involved—such as chaperoning a field trip.

Follow the center's rules. Don't regularly arrive late to pick up your child, for example, or send your child to day care if he or she shows signs of the stomach flu. Pay your bill on time and send required supplies—such as diapers and formula—so that the center can properly care for your child.

Finally, treat your child's caregivers with the respect and kindness: They spend hours each day feeding, comforting, playing with, and nurturing your child.

How can I be sure that the center is taking good care of my child?

It's natural to be concerned, particularly because you cannot spend the whole day peering through the window to make sure your child is all right. Still, there are ways to find out whether your day care center is taking good care of your child.

Ask yourself is whether your child seems happy and well. For example, is your child glad to see caregivers in the morning? Is your child clean, well fed, and in good spirits at the end of the day? If your child is old enough to speak, does he or she talk to you with enthusiasm about day care?

See for yourself how things are going as often as you can. Drop in at lunchtime or playtime, to give your child a hug and to see what your child is doing. Is your child busily engaged in play or enjoying a cuddle from one of the caregivers when you arrive? Or is your child crying in the corner, without anyone paying attention?

Finally, pay attention to how your child's caregivers treat you and your child. Do they seem genuinely interested in your child—telling you excitedly about your child's accomplishments during the day and praising good behavior? Do they let you know when your child is having trouble in a particular area—for example, if your child cannot fall asleep at nap time or is having problems getting along with other children?

I'm concerned that my child's caregiver isn't reading to my child enough during the day. What should I do?

You'll invariably have differences of opinion with respect to the way your day care center provides care. The best thing you can do is address these issues explicitly with the caregiver. For example, you might explain that you'd like your child to be read to more often during the day. If you don't get a positive response, then call the center's director. A good director will promptly intervene (assuming you're not asking for something ridiculous—such as insisting that the caregiver carry your six-month-old baby in a sling all day long). But if the director isn't helpful, then you may want to rethink what you are asking for. If you still think you are being reasonable, then reconsider whether this particular center is the right choice for your family. After all, this is probably not going to be the only problem you'll have as time goes on—and you need a center that will work with you to address your concerns as they arise.

I've decided to withdraw my child from day care. What do I need to know?

You're free to withdraw your child at any time and for any reason. All you need to keep in mind are the center's cancellation and refund policies, both of which should be clearly spelled out in your contract. Most centers require that you provide a minimum amount of notice—often two weeks' or a month—before withdrawing your child. Although you will not have to send your child to day care during the notice period, you will have to pay fees for that time. If you paid a deposit or any advance fees to the day care center, your contract will also govern whether you get a refund. ■

Chapter 21

Preschools

Once your child has left babyhood behind (at age three or so), you might consider a preschool. Keep in mind that the primary purpose of a preschool is to encourage your child's development and lay the foundation for your child's education—not to provide substitute care for your child while you are at work. A preschool can nonetheless be a wonderful and stimulating child care option for working parents, particularly because many preschools now offer extended day programs that combine the best features of preschools and day care centers.

CROSS REFERENCE

Read Chapter 20, *Day Care Centers.* Although preschools differ from day care centers in some ways, many of the issues that apply to day care centers—such as state licensing and accreditation by the National Association for the Education of Young Children—also apply to preschools.

What are the advantages of enrolling my child in preschool?

Although preschools offer many of the same advantages as day care centers, they have two additional attributes that you should consider:

- Preschools provide age-appropriate learning opportunities. Although your child is too young for Shakespeare and algebra, all children no matter what age have tremendous capacities to learn. A good preschool will facilitate your child's development in all areas—through activities such as singing, cooking, and reading.
- Preschool teachers are often better qualified than day care center caregivers. Because preschool teachers are educators—rather than just caregivers—you'll find that preschool teachers generally have more training in early childhood education than day care center staff members.

What are the disadvantages of preschools?

There are a number of drawbacks to relying on a preschool as your primary form of child care:

- **Preschools can be significantly more expensive than day care centers.**

Depending on where you live and the preschool you choose, you might find that preschool costs are closer to private school tuition than to day care center fees.

- **The hours are often much shorter than those of a day care center.** Preschools view themselves as educational programs rather than child care services, so the hours tend to be very limited. For example, your toddler might be able to attend preschool for only a few mornings each week—which means that you'll need some other type of child care in place if you work full time. If you've got your heart set on preschool but need full-time child care coverage, don't give up: Some preschools offer an extended day child care component—for an additional fee—so that your child can remain at preschool all day long. Or you could combine a preschool with a part-time nanny.

- **You may be asked to donate to the school.** If you're already a bit shell-shocked by the high cost of preschool, you're in for quite a surprise: Most preschools actively solicit (and expect) parent donations to help round out their budgets.

 TIPS

Cooperative preschools cost less. By definition, cooperative preschools engage the services of parents to do much of the work of running the school. This generally means lower preschool tuition bills. So if you've got more time on your hands than money, then a cooperative preschool might be a good choice for you.

What factors should I consider when choosing a preschool?

Pay attention to the same types of factors you would consider when choosing a day care center—such as the caregiver's qualifications, the adult-to-child ratio, and how your child will spend the day. In addition, make sure you thoroughly understand the school's educational philosophy.

If you're not a teacher yourself, you might be surprised to learn that different preschools have very different views on how young children learn best. For example, the Montessori method emphasizes individualized, real-world activities; the Waldorf philosophy engages children in group activities in a home-like environment. Some preschools combine elements of more than one educational approach. And even though two preschools may claim to follow the same educational philosophy, their programs may be very, very different. So don't just rely on a preschool's label if you want to learn how the school is run.

Here are some other factors to think about:

- How much of the day is spent in free play—where your child can choose whether she wants to play with blocks or puzzles, for example?

- How much of the day is spent on organized group activities—such as baking or story time?

- How much does the school emphasize traditional academics—such as learning the alphabet or basic counting?

- Are academics taught through traditional classroom teaching or through play activities?

- Does the school emphasize children's social, emotional, and physical development just as much as their academic development?

- Are the children in mixed age groups?

- How much parent involvement is permitted or expected?

There are no "right" answers to these questions; you just need to make sure that the answers fit your and your child's style.

BABYCENTER RESOURCES

If you want to learn more about preschool. ParentCenter has plenty of helpful articles on how to choose a good preschool for your child. To find the preschool section, log on to http://parentcenter.babycenter.com/preschooler/ppreschool/index. ∎

Chapter 22

Family Day Care

A less expensive, more flexible alternative to a formal day care center is family or home-based day care. Run out of a caregiver's home, a home-based day care center can be a good choice for families looking for a cozy environment and personalized attention on a tight budget.

 CROSS REFERENCE

Read Chapter 20, *Day Care Centers.* Although home-based day care might seem very different than a day care center, choosing a quality home-based program involves many of the same steps as finding a good day care center.

What are the advantages of using home-based day care?

Many parents feel that home-based day care combines the best features of day care centers and nannies. Here are some of the key benefits:

- Your child will spend the day in a homey environment.
- Your child's caregiver will almost certainly be a parent herself.
- Your child will be part of a small, mixed-age group of children.
- Your child will have plenty of playmates.
- You might have more scheduling flexibility than with a day care center.
- Home-based day care is an inexpensive child care option.

What are the disadvantages?

Although home-based day care offers plenty of built-in advantages, the list of disadvantages is just as long. Here are some reasons why you might decide against a home-based program:

- The state licensing process is much more lax for home-based day care. Very few states conduct formal inspections of home based day care centers, and in some states, all one has to do to get a license is to mail in a form and pay a small fee.
- Most home-based day care providers have no formal training in early childhood education.

- Your child will not get as much one-on-one attention in a home-based center as in a nanny or share care situation.
- Because of exposure to other children, your child will catch a fair share of colds, flu bugs, and other infections.
- You'll be dependent on a single child care provider. Most home-based day care programs are primarily run by just one person—usually a mom herself. When the caregiver is ill or out of town, you'll have to come up with backup child care plans.
- There probably won't be any supervision for your child's caregiver. Unlike day care centers, where there's a good number of staff members around at all times, a home-based day care provider may very well be the only staff member on hand.

What factors should I consider when choosing a home-based day care?

Pay attention to the same types of factors you would consider when choosing a day care center—such as the caregiver's qualifications and how your child will spend the day. Because the quality and style of home-based day care programs vary dramatically, research the center before enrolling your child. Some additional factors to consider are:

- **Licensing.** Some home-based day care providers do not obtain a license before opening their doors for business, so it is essential to know whether the center you are considering has a valid, up-to-date license. (For more about licensing, see Chapter 20.)

- **Accreditation.** Look for a home-based day care center that is accredited by the National Association of Family Child Care (NAFCC), which is a nonprofit organization that supports and represents home-based day care centers. The NAFCC's accreditation process is quite rigorous and can take up to three years. To learn more about the accreditation process and to find an accredited home-based center in your area, log on to the NAFCC's website at www.nafcc.org.

- **The caregiver's qualifications and style.** In a home-based program, there is often only one caregiver—making it doubly important that you be comfortable with the caregiver's background, experience, and child-rearing approach. Has the caregiver had any formal training in early childhood education? Is the caregiver trained in CPR and other emergency medical procedures? Does the caregiver have any children of her own? Are you comfortable with the caregiver's parenting style?

- **The home environment.** Your child will be spending the day in the caregiver's own home, so it's critical that you feel comfortable with it. Is there enough space for your child to play and explore? Is the home clean and organized? Does the home seem safe—for example, are there outlet covers and stair guards in place?

- **The other children and families.** Ask about the other children and their families. How old are the other children? How many other children are cared for at the same home? The National Resource Center for Health and Safety in Child Care and state law both call for lower caregiver-to-child ratios in home-based centers than in day care centers. A solo home-based day care provider should not care for more than two children younger than two years of age. Ask for contact information for the parents so that you can talk to them about their experiences with the provider. Find out whether you and the other parents agree on important issues, such as television watching, for example, so that you know how much stock to put in their assessment of the child care.

- **Vacation/sick time.** What happens when your child's caregiver is ill or is away on vacation? This isn't an issue at a day care center, where there are plenty of other staff members to fill in for your child's caregiver. But with a home-based day care program, your child's caregiver is often the only caregiver. Be sure to ask whether you will have to pay for days when the caregiver is out of town or sick. Also ask whether the caregiver has any backup child care arrangements in place, so that you won't be left in the lurch whenever your child's caregiver has the flu or is otherwise unavailable to care for your child.

- **The caregiver's business practices.** Does the program have a professional feel to it? For example, is there a formal policy manual and child care contract? Though a child care program's business practices may not seem all that

relevant, a program that takes a professional approach to its business is likely to take a professional approach to caring for your child.

BABYCENTER RESOURCES

BabyCenter.com has useful information on choosing a home-based day care center, including an interview sheet. You can find a copy on the *Parent Savvy* page of Babycenter.com (www.babycenter.com/parentsavvy).

I'm paying my home-based day care provider "off the books." Are there any risks to this arrangement?

Unlike a nanny, a home-based provider is not your employee, so you have no tax-related responsibilities: You don't have to report your payments to the federal government, and you are not responsible for payroll taxes. If your provider chooses to take money off the books, it's the provider's worry, not yours.

CAUTION

No child care tax breaks for off-the-books arrangements. Although an off-the-books provider might offer you discounted rates, you won't be able to claim the child care tax credit or take advantage of a dependent care spending account. This is because the IRS will require the home-based day care provider's Social Security number (or tax identification number) for these tax breaks—something your provider will be loath to give you for fear of alerting the IRS to the fact that she isn't reporting her income. See Chapter 29 for information about child care tax breaks. ■

5 · Saving for the High Cost of Learning

Contents

*A*ll parents want their children to achieve their fullest potential—and most agree that education is the key. Indeed, in our culture there are few things more highly valued than a good education. Not only is it considered the path to economic independence and even wealth, many believe that a good education makes a good person.

All of this, of course, comes with a price—and a hefty one at that. From preschool through graduate school, education bills will be among your heaviest financial burdens as a parent. Fortunately, there are a number of strategies that you can use to maximize the savings you sock away for your child's education. This part of the book explains the ins and outs of those strategies, and it guides you through the process of choosing and implementing the savings plan that is right for your family. And if you're not sure whether you should begin putting money into your child's education fund just yet, don't fret: Chapter 23 gives you some practical advice on how to prioritize your family's many different financial planning goals, such as buying a house, saving for retirement, and—of course—building up an education savings plan for your new addition.

Resources for More Information

Chances are, this part of the book will provide all of the education savings information you need for now. But if you're still hungry for more, here are a few outstanding additional resources:

- www.savingforcollege.com, a leading website on Section 529 college savings plans and other ways to save and pay for college
- www.finaid.org, a comprehensive website covering everything from the federal financial aid methodology to smart strategies for saving for college to grants, scholarships, and military aid.
- www.collegeboard.com, sponsored by the folks responsible for the SAT, this website has lots of useful information on application requirements, choosing a college, and paying for college.
- *The Standard & Poor's Guide to Saving and Investing for College,* by David J. Braverman (McGraw-Hill 2003), a book that will help you save for college in a strategic fashion, by maximizing your child's financial aid potential and saving as much in the way of taxes as possible. ■

Chapter 23

Deciding Whether and When to Start Saving

If you're like many new parents, you find it a challenge just to pay for your baby's current needs, much less worry about saving for college and other educational expenses. Fortunately, there is no rule that everyone has to begin a college savings fund as soon as a child is born; it all depends on the particular situation. Depending on your circumstances, it might make sense to start immediately, or it might be smarter to put off education savings in favor of other needs, such as buying a home. This section will help you decide whether and when your family should begin saving for your child's education.

My child hasn't even started walking yet; isn't a bit early to start thinking about saving for my child's education?

No. You should start thinking about saving for your child's education as early as possible, even before your child starts kindergarten.

Why Start Saving Early?

Here are four good reasons, which are explained more fully in the main discussion:

- It's the only way to keep up with spiraling tuition costs.
- You'll have to save much less in the long run, because your investment earnings will compound the power of your money.
- You won't have to worry about the ups and downs of the economy because a long investment horizon will help you weather the bad times.
- It's easier on the family budget, because starting early means you can set aside a little each month, rather than face a big bill down the line.

Why should I start saving early?

A lot of reasons. First, because college tuition costs generally grow at about double the rate of inflation, if not more. The only way to keep up with these spiraling costs is to save early and to save often.

Second, you'll have to save much less in the long run because your investment earnings will compound the value of your money. In other words, your money will work harder for you with every passing year because you will earn money not only on your original investment but also on that investment's appreciation. Thanks to the compounding power of money and the tax breaks built into some of the education savings plans discussed in the following chapters, even a little bit of money saved each month can take a big bite out of your child's future education bills.

EXAMPLE 1: *You start saving just $50 each month on the day your child is born, using a tax-advantageous Coverdell education savings account. By the time your child is ready to go to college, you will have saved nearly $20,000 (assuming an average investment return of 6%). What's more, you won't owe even a dime in capital gains taxes on the earnings so long as you use them to pay for your child's college tuition.*

EXAMPLE 2: *The year his child was born, Alvin invested $10,000 in a bond fund that grew by 5% each subsequent year. Alvin did not add any more money to the account in the years that followed. In the first year, Alvin earned $500 on his investment. In the second year, Alvin earned $525 on his investment even though the fund's growth rate did not change. Alvin's profits increased because he earned a 5% rate of return on his original $10,000 investment, as well as on the $500 of profits from the year before ($10,500 x 5% = $525).*

Third, you won't have to worry about the ups and downs of the economy. Having a long investment horizon will allow you to benefit from good economies and survive the financial storms of bad economies without stress or worry.

Finally, setting aside a small sum of money for your child's education on a regular basis is infinitely easier on the family budget than facing a giant bill down the road.

BABYCENTER POLL

Most parents start sooner rather than later. According to a recent BabyCenter.com poll, 73% of 400 new parents responding had already begun college savings accounts for their children.

Now that we have a new baby, money is extremely tight. Do we really need to begin saving for our child's education right now? Not necessarily. Although saving early is a good idea (see above), it isn't the best idea for all families. In fact, financial experts say that you shouldn't even think about saving for your child's education until your family is in good financial health overall. Priorities that are more important than education savings include:

- **Paying off high interest debt.** Nothing can get in the way of your family's financial future like credit card and other high interest debt. Before creating an education savings account for your new baby, pay off all debt with an interest rate of 10% or higher.

- **Building an emergency fund.** Every family needs a small stash of cash to cover unexpected expenses. Having a financial safety net in place will ensure that your family can comfortably weather life's ups and downs.

- **Making sure that you are fully insured.** Part and parcel of getting your financial house in order is purchasing adequate life, health, and disability insurance coverage to ensure that your family will be provided for regardless of what lies ahead. (You can learn more about health insurance in Chapter 15 and life insurance in Chapter 37.)

- **Saving for retirement.** You might be surprised to learn that experts recommend that you fully fund all available pretax retirement accounts—such as a 401(k) or IRA—before putting away a single dollar for your child's education. Why? Although it may not be ideal for your child to rely on financial aid or scholarships to foot college tuition bills, it would be far worse for your child to be burdened with the obligation to support you throughout your retirement—or, worse yet, for you to be stuck in dire financial straits in the event your child doesn't have the resources to help you. After all, your child can take out loans to help pay for education; you cannot do the same to help pay for retirement.

- **Time with your family.** If saving for your child's education means you have

to work extra-long hours, forgo family vacations, or otherwise sacrifice the quality of life with your family, don't do it—or at least, do it to a lesser degree.

ADDITIONAL RESOURCES

Resources that can help you get your family's finances in shape. Bookstores have shelves and shelves full of personal finance bestsellers, but you can get most of the information you need for free on the Internet. Two terrific websites to check out are those sponsored by the personal finance publisher Kiplinger at www .kiplinger.com and *MSN Money* at www.moneycentral.msn.com.

TIPS

Collect free cash for college along the way. You can still begin making a dent in your child's future college bills even if you don't have a dime to spare for your child's education fund. With education rewards programs such as UPromise, you can earn cash-back rewards on purchases in the form of contributions to your child's college savings account. See Chapter 27 for more about these types of programs.

We are saving for a down payment on our first home. Is it okay to postpone saving for our child's education?

Absolutely. Thanks to the mortgage interest deduction and the investment potential of real estate, buying a home is one of the best financial moves your family can make. Some experts even recommend that you buy a home and pay down your mortgage before you begin contributing to an education savings plan for your child. This is because you can always take out a home equity loan down the line—and deduct the interest on that loan for tax purposes—if you decide to use the money you've invested in your home to pay for your child's education expenses.

TIPS

If you sell your home. There is another tax advantage to saving for your child's education through investing in your own home: If your home goes up in value and you sell it, you won't have to pay taxes on the first $250,000 of profit you make. The deal is even better for married couples, who can keep up to $500,000 in profits tax free. For more information, check out IRS Publication 523, *Selling Your Home,* available at www.irs.gov.

ADDITIONAL RESOURCES

If you want to know more. You can learn more about the tax benefits available to homeowners in IRS Publication 936, *Home Mortgage Interest Deduction,* available at www.irs.gov. For a general overview of tax deductions of home ownership and general articles on buying, owning a home, and selling a home, see the Real Estate section at www.nolo.com (click the "Property and Money" tab at the top of the home page).

We are so cash strapped that it feels like we don't have enough money to save for both retirement and our child's education. Do you have any advice for saving for both at the same time?

A Roth IRA is one of the best ways to save for retirement while keeping open the option of paying for your child's college education. A Roth IRA is a savings account that allows your retirement investments to grow entirely tax free. What's terrific about a Roth IRA is that you can withdraw the funds in your Roth IRA to pay for your child's higher education expenses without paying any penalties. You will, however, owe capital gains taxes on the earnings unless you happen to be 59½ or older by the time your child is ready for school. To learn more about Roth IRAs, check out the discussion in Chapter 26.

A Short-Term Mortgage Can Help Pay for College

If you qualify, can swing the extra payments each month, and plan to own your home for a long time, consider getting a 15-year mortgage rather than a longer term loan. You'll pay less interest and build equity faster, so that your home will be paid off by the time your child goes to college. Take, for example, a $300,000 fixed-rate loan at 6%. Here's how much your monthly and total payments would be for a 15-year and 30-year mortgage:

Term of Mortgage	Monthly Payment	Total Paid
30 years	$ 600	$ 215, 838
15 years	$ 844	$ 151,894

In this case, you'd pay $244 per month more with a 15-year mortgage, but nearly $64,000 less in interest than a 30-year term. If you bought your house when your child was a baby, you would be through with house payments by the time college rolled around! While this example is admittedly simplistic, it highlights the savings available in short-term mortgages. To run the numbers yourself, check an online mortgage calculator, such as the one found in the Real Estate section of "Property and Money" at www.nolo.com, or talk to your banker.

If you don't want to commit to high monthly payments, you can achieve similar savings by voluntarily paying more principal each month on a longer term loan. This gives you more flexibility—you don't legally obligate yourself to the higher payment each month, so you can change your mind and pay less if need be.

There's no way I will be able to save enough to pay for my child's college education in full. Can't I just rely on financial aid or scholarships to cover my child's future education costs? Unfortunately, no. The main sources of financial aid and scholarships are the federal government and the schools themselves—and both take the position that parents have the primary responsibility for paying for their children's education. If your child does manage to qualify for some form of financial aid, chances are that it will be in the form of loans, not grants or scholarships. This means that the less you can contribute to your child's education bills, the more your child will owe in student loan bills after graduation.

Moreover, most financial aid and scholarship programs don't cover all of the expenses associated with higher education. For example, the average federal Pell Grant covers only 23% of the costs of attending a four-year state college. Unless you have savings that you can tap into, you and your family may have a very difficult time making up the shortfall in college expenses.

Won't I hurt my child's chances of qualifying for financial aid by setting up an education savings fund?

Parents often worry that a dollar saved in a child's education fund will be a dollar lost in future financial aid. Fortunately, it usually doesn't work that way. Unless you invest your money in a 529 prepaid college tuition plan or a custodial account for your child (more on both of these in Chapter 26), the financial aid impact of a college savings fund will be minimal for most families.

If you'd like to learn more about financial aid formulas and eligibility. Financial aid—and how one becomes eligible for it—is a complicated topic that is beyond the scope of this book. For this discussion, you'll just have to trust us when we tell you about the affect of a particular type of savings plan on financial aid eligibility. If you want more information about this topic, you can find out everything you need to know and then some at www.finaid.org. Another useful resource is www.studentaid.ed.gov, the website of the U.S. Department of Education's Federal Student Aid (FSA) program.

College Tax Breaks

The federal government offers a number of education-related tax breaks:

- **The college tuition deduction.** Allows parents to deduct up to $4,000 in tuition costs from their taxable income. This $4,000 cap is a maximum per tax return, not per child.

- **Hope tax credit.** Provides parents with a tax credit of up to $1,500 per child for tuition expenses paid during the first two years that the child is enrolled in college.

- **Lifetime learning tax credit.** Provides parents with a credit of up to $2,000 per tax return (not per child) for every year of college or graduate school.

- **Student loan interest deduction.** Allows parents to deduct up to $2,500 for interest paid on a student loan. The catch is that parents can only deduct interest payments if they are actually liable on the loan. If your child receives a federal student loan, for example, your child, and not you (the parents), gets the deduction.

- **Scholarship tax exemption.** Makes scholarship funds tax free provided the funds are used to pay tuition and course-related expenses. Scholarship funds used to pay room and board are not tax exempt.

All of these tax breaks (with the exception of the scholarship tax exemption) phase out for higher income earners.

You can claim the tuition deduction, the Hope credit, or the lifetime learning credit even if you use borrowed funds to pay your child's tuition costs. But if you qualify, you can only claim one of these tax breaks in any given year.

For more information on education-related tax breaks. Check out IRS Publication 970, *Tax Benefits for Education.* ■

Chapter 24

Figuring Out How Much to Save

When it comes to saving for your child's education, you may feel as though you can't possibly save enough. And no wonder. *Smart Money's* college savings worksheet (available in the Personal Finance section of www.smartmoney.com under "College Planning") will tell you that you'll need to invest more than $900 per month for the next 18 years to send your three-month-old to Harvard one day. Few families can afford to do that.

Fortunately (at least in terms of your finances), not all kids go to Harvard. Indeed, only a small percentage of students (less than 10%) attend the really expensive colleges. And nearly three-quarters of students in four-year colleges pay less than $8,000 per year in tuition.

So don't be discouraged if a college savings calculator spits out a number that is larger than your take-home pay. Save what you can, because every little bit helps.

To figure out how much you can save, take a careful look at your income and your expenses and see how much you have left over each month. If you don't have a good sense of your monthly expenses, track your expenses for a couple of months using a

personal finance program such as *Quicken* software. You'll probably be surprised at how much you are spending—and where. For example, you might not realize that you're spending nearly $30 a week picking up coffee and a muffin on your way to work. It's that sort of discretionary expense that can be turned into education savings with a simple adjustment—eating breakfast at home rather than out.

 BABYCENTER RESOURCES

Need a few creative ideas finding spare change for your child's education savings fund? BabyCenter .com's Family Finances section will show you how to save money on everything from your grocery bills to your child's birthday parties. You'll be surprised at just how quickly the pennies will turn into dollars in your child's savings fund. To find the section, log on to the *Parent Savvy* page of BabyCenter. com (www.babycenter.com/ parent savvy). ■

Chapter 25

Choosing an Education Savings Plan

When it comes to saving for your child's education, there is no one-size-fits-all solution. Different savings plans have different advantages and disadvantages, and the plan that works best for your family might not work well for the family down the street. Fortunately, you don't have to be an accountant or a seasoned investor to sort through your options. This chapter will take you step by step through the process, first introducing you to the various plans and then helping you to make your choice. In Chapter 26, you can find a more in-depth discussion of each type of plan.

Education savings accounts come with restrictions and paperwork that I don't want to deal with. What's the matter with using regular savings account or investment account?

The restrictions and paperwork that you are referring to are in place because education savings accounts have significant tax advantages—and it is just these tax advantages that make them better than just socking away money in a regular savings or investment account. Education savings plans allow your investments to grow completely tax free—which means that you will not owe a penny of capital gains taxes when it comes time to pay for your child's educational expenses. Thus, these plans stretch the value of your dollars by allowing you to keep more of what you earn.

> **EXAMPLE:** *Peter purchased $10,000 worth of the Bigwig Company stock when his son Tommy was just three weeks old. Peter kept the stock in a brokerage account in his own name. By the time Tommy was ready to go to college, Peter's Bigwig Company stock had appreciated handsomely to $100,000. When Peter sold the stock, however, he owed 15% in federal capital gains taxes on the $90,000 worth of appreciation—or $13,500. If Peter had invested that same $10,000 in a tax advantageous education savings plan, such as a 529 college savings plan, he would not have owed any federal capital gains taxes whatsoever on the $90,000 worth of appreciation.*

Okay, I'm convinced. What are my options?

Tax-advantageous education savings plans come in many different flavors, and there really is something for everyone. Chapter 26 provides details on all the options. For now, here's a general overview of your choices:

- **Coverdell education savings accounts.** By far the most flexible education savings plan, a Coverdell education savings account (or Coverdell ESA) provides tax-free treatment for your investment earnings. Although this type of account comes with a cap on the amount you can save ($2,000 per year), you can use the money for a broad array of educational expenses—such as private school tuition and academic tutoring—in addition to college and graduate school tuition.

- **529 college savings plans.** These plans allow you save as much as a quarter of a million dollars for your child's higher education expenses every year—and you won't owe any capital gains taxes on the appreciation. The major drawback to this type of plan is that it covers only college and graduate school expenses—so private high school, for example, doesn't count.

- **529 prepaid college tuition plans.** As the name suggests, these plans allow you to pay for tomorrow's college tuition expenses at today's prices. Although they can be quite a bargain, the plans limit your child's college choice to the schools participating in the program. And there's no guarantee the plans will be around forever—as of this writing, one prepaid tuition plan has shut down completely and several others are no longer accepting new enrollments.

- **Education savings bonds.** If you're more concerned about losing your money in an economic downturn than profiting from a bull market, then U.S. savings bonds offer a guaranteed (but small) return on your original investment. You will not owe any taxes on the interest you accrue on a Series EE or Series I savings bond provided you use the money to pay for your child's college or graduate school bills.

Two other options for saving for your child's education are custodial accounts and Roth IRAs. Although neither allows your investments to grow tax free, they do have their advantages:

- **Custodial accounts.** These allow you to give money directly to your child without the expense and administrative hassle of setting up a conventional trust. You don't have to spend the money in your child's custodial account on your child's educational expenses, but can instead spend the money for your child as you see fit. Although there is no tax exemption for custodial accounts, the earnings in the account get taxed at your child's lower rate rather than your tax rate.

- **Roth IRAs.** Although a Roth IRA is technically a retirement plan, a nifty exception allows you to withdraw money from your Roth IRA—without paying a penalty—to cover your child's higher education expenses. The Roth IRA is an excellent choice for slightly older parents, because you won't owe any taxes on the earnings if you withdraw money from the account after you reach age 59½.

There are so many plans to choose from! How do I decide which plan is right for my family?

Selecting the right savings plan isn't nearly as complicated as it seems. Just decide which features matter most to you and choose accordingly. Below, we've matched up some of the most common goals parents have with the savings plans that best meet those goals. This list will help you find the best plan for your family. Chapter 26 discusses each plan in more detail.

Can I contribute to more than one savings plan?

Absolutely. In fact, depending on your circumstances, it's wise to do so, because different plans have different features. For example, many families couple a Coverdell ESA with a 529 college savings plan. That way, they can save for private school tuition (or other elementary and secondary school expenses) as well as for college. Another common combination is for families to invest in a Coverdell ESA along with a Roth IRA, because they can use the money in the Roth IRA to pay for retirement expenses in addition to higher education expenses.

Do I need to worry about estate and gift taxes when contributing to any of these plans?

Yes. For virtually all of the plans discussed in this chapter, you have to worry about gift taxes if you give more than $11,000 per year to your child. The only times you don't

have to worry are when you contribute to an account in your own name or when you buy U.S. savings bonds in your own name.

The $11,000 ceiling applies per parent and per child, so, for example, if you are married and you have two children, you could contribute a whopping $44,000 to your children's education savings plans each year ($11,000 from each parent to each child) without concerning yourself with the gift tax.

If you want to give more than $11,000 per parent per child per year, then talk to an accountant or estate planning expert to understand the tax impact of your gift. You can also read IRS Publication 950, *Introduction to Estate and Gift Taxes*, available free at www.irs.gov.

 TIPS

Use a 529 plan for large one-time gifts. You can contribute up to $55,000 to your child's 529 college savings plan or 529 college tuition plan in any given year without incurring gift tax consequences by electing to treat the gift as having been made over a five-year period. To take advantage of this exception, you cannot make any further contributions to your child's 529 plan (or make any other gifts to your child) for the year in which you make the contribution or the next four years thereafter.

Choosing an Education Savings Plan

IF YOU GOAL IS:	GOOD OPTIONS FOR YOU ARE:
I want to save for private school tuition as well as college.	• Coverdell ESA • Custodial account
I want to be able to use my savings to pay for preschool.	• Saving for your child's education in your own name • Custodial account Note: The IRS considers preschool to be a child care expense rather than an education expense, so examine whether you're eligible for any child care tax breaks. You can find out more in Chapter 29.
I want my savings to grow without being burdened by taxes.	• Coverdell ESA • 529 college savings plan • 529 prepaid tuition plan • Education savings bonds
I want to know that college is paid for. I don't want to have to worry about the stock market or rising tuition costs.	• 529 prepaid tuition plan
I want to be able to access my savings in case of a family emergency or other financial crisis.	• Saving for your child's education in your own name
I don't want to hurt my child's chances of qualifying for financial aid.	• 529 college savings plan • Coverdell education savings account • Education savings bonds • Roth IRA • Saving for your child's education in your own name Note: If financial aid eligibility is a major concern, then steer clear of 529 prepaid college tuition plans and custodial accounts.
I would like to have the option of using my savings for retirement.	• Roth IRA • Saving for your child's education in your own name
I'm very risk averse. I want to know that my investments won't lose value in an economic downturn.	• Education savings bonds • 529 prepaid tuition plan
I want to have complete control over my investment choices.	• Coverdell education savings account • Saving for your child's education in your own name • A Roth IRA
I would like to contribute a large sum of money to my child's savings account each year, so I need a plan with generous contribution limits.	• 529 college savings plans • 529 prepaid college tuition plan • Education savings bonds • Custodial account

Chapter 26

Types of Education Savings Plans

This chapter looks at each of your savings options in depth. It explains each of the options, how they work, their advantages and disadvantages, how to establish them, and restrictions they place on how you can spend the money.

Accounts in Your Own Name

Though the various education savings plans have their benefits, you may be more comfortable with saving for your child's education in your own name. In this scenario, you might put the money in an ordinary savings account or a mutual fund that you have complete access to and control of.

What are the advantages of saving for my child's education in my own name?
There are two significant advantages to saving for your child's education this way:

- **You can spend the money however you wish.** You won't have to worry about whether your education savings plan allows you to use the money for private school tuition or academic tutoring. What's more, you'll be able to access your savings if you ever need the money for some other purpose—such as the down payment for a new house. This flexibility can be particularly important for families with limited savings who are more likely to have to dip into a child's education fund when money is tight.

- **You control investment decisions.** Instead of choosing from someone else's investment portfolios, you'll be the one in charge of how and when your money will be invested.

What are the disadvantages?
Although it's certainly easy to save for your child's education in your own name, there are a couple of important reasons why most parents choose a formal education savings plan:

- **You'll owe capital gains taxes on earnings.** In contrast, education savings plans, such as Coverdell ESAs, protect your savings from these taxes, meaning there will be more money in the account at the end of each year. (But there is a way to minimize the taxes you'll owe. See below.)

- **You may squander the money on other things.** In this case, one of the advantages that we listed above is also one of the disadvantages: It may be hard to resist the temptation to use this money whenever things get tight. But if you save the money in an education savings plan, you won't be able to. The financial penalties and administrative hassles involved in withdrawing the money for noneducation purposes will encourage you to leave the money alone.
- **There's no guarantee you'll save enough for college.** With a 529 prepaid college tuition plan, however, you can buy blocks of tomorrow's tuition at today's prices (see below).

If I choose to save money for college in my own account, are there any ways to avoid high capital gains taxes?

Yes. Even though you won't get the tax protection of a formal education savings account, there are a number of ways to protect the money from a high tax burden. Here are a few ideas:

- **Buy municipal bonds instead of stocks.** Although the average investment returns on bonds aren't as high as on stocks, municipal bonds do offer one big advantage: You won't pay federal, state, or local taxes on the interest you earn. To learn more about tax-free bonds, log on to www.fmsbonds.com, a website devoted exclusively to individual municipal bond buyers. Another useful resource on bonds and other securities is www.bondsonline.com.

- **Purchase index funds or, better yet, fill your portfolio with "spiders."** With a standard mutual fund, you'll end up owing a little bit in taxes each year largely because of interest and capital gains distributions. You can minimize those taxes by purchasing an indexed mutual fund, one that is designed to mirror an index such as the S&P 500. Your tax bill will be even lower if you invest in an exchange traded fund, such as a SPDR (commonly pronounced "spider"). To learn more about investing in stock funds, check out the "Stocks" section of www.smartmoney.com.

How will my savings affect my child's ability to qualify for financial aid?

Not very much. This is because financial aid formulas weigh a parent's assets far less heavily than a child's assets when determining eligibility for financial aid.

Coverdell Education Savings Accounts

When it comes to education savings plans, the Coverdell education savings account—or Coverdell ESA—is almost flawless. First, there are the tax benefits: Even if your investments double or triple in value, you won't owe a red cent in capital gains taxes provided that you use the money for your child's educational expenses. Second, you don't have to wait until your child is ready for college to tap into your savings. You can withdraw money from your child's Coverdell ESA to pay for a wide range of other educational costs as well—such as after-school tutoring for your second grader or Internet access for your fifth grader.

What is a Coverdell ESA and how does it work?

A Coverdell ESA is a savings account that you manage on behalf of your child, who is the account's legal owner. Although you don't technically own the funds in your child's Coverdell ESA, you have complete control over the account until your child reaches age 30. This means that you will be the one making investment and spending decisions with respect to the money, so no need to worry about the possibility of your teenage child wasting the money on a new motorcycle.

You can open a Coverdell ESA at most banks or brokerage houses. Once you deposit money, you can invest it in any stock, bond, mutual fund, or other investment (except for life insurance) offered by the financial institution you choose. You can also change your investment strategy as you see fit, investing in stocks one year and bonds the next. Each year, your financial institution will send both you and the IRS a Form 5498-ESA, reporting the contributions made to your child's Coverdell ESA and the account's current balance. However, you won't owe any taxes on the earnings in the account.

When your child starts first grade, you can begin making withdrawals from the account to pay for qualifying educational expenses (see below). Every time you withdraw money from your child's Coverdell ESA, the financial institution holding the account will send you a Form 1099-Q reporting your withdrawal to the IRS. You won't owe any taxes on your withdrawals if you use the money to pay for qualifying educational expenses for your child. If, however, you use the money for something else, your child will then owe taxes and a 10% penalty on the earnings on the account.

To get a better sense of how a Coverdell ESA works, let's consider a quick example:

> **EXAMPLE:** *Felicity and her husband, Paolo, open a Coverdell ESA for their four-month-old daughter, Patricia. They name Paolo as the account manager. The couple makes an initial deposit of $2,000 into the account, and Paolo invests the money in an index fund. Over the next six years, the couple contributes $2,000 each year. By the end of that period, the couple has invested $14,000 into Patricia's Coverdell ESA. Thanks to a bull market, the account's value is $25,000.*

> *Now Patricia is six years old and ready to start first grade at a private Catholic school. Tuition at the school is $5,000 per year. To pay for tuition, Paolo withdraws $5,000 from the account and writes a check to the school. At tax time, the brokerage house sends the couple a copy of Form 1099-Q, which reports the $5,000 withdrawal from Patricia's account to the IRS. Because Paolo spent the money on a qualifying educational expense, six-year-old Patricia does not owe any taxes on the withdrawal.*

What are the advantages of using a Coverdell ESA to save for my child's education?
The Coverdell ESA has a few features that truly make it a cut above the other education savings plans:

- **No federal taxes.** You'll pay no federal capital gains taxes on the earnings if you use the money for a qualifying educational expense. Depending on your state's laws, the earnings may also be exempt from state taxes. This can amount to considerable tax savings if the market soars after you've made your initial investment.

- **A broad definition of "educational expenses."** For example, you can use the money to pay for elementary and secondary school as well as college and graduate school. If you expect to send your child to private school, then a Coverdell ESA is something you should seriously consider.

- **You control the investments.** Unlike the case with a 529 college savings plan (see below), you call the shots when it comes to investment decisions. If you choose your investments wisely, you'll keep management and administrative fees to a minimum.

What are the disadvantages?
A Coverdell ESA is almost, but not quite, perfect. Here are the drawbacks:

- **Low contribution limit.** The maximum amount you or anyone else can contribute to the account is $2,000 per year. Other plans have much higher contribution limits. If you're trying to save up for four years' worth of Ivy League tuition, consider one of those plans instead of—or in addition to—the Coverdell ESA.

- **You cannot get the money back.** No matter how much you need it, you won't be able to touch the money in the account. This is because the funds in the account legally belong to your child, not to you.

- **You must spend the money by the time your child reaches 30.** Otherwise, the money in the account will be distributed to your child within a month of his or her 30th birthday. Your child will then owe ordinary income taxes on the earnings and will have to pay a penalty of 10% of the earnings to the federal government (ouch!).

- **There's no guarantee you'll save enough for college.** With a 529 prepaid college tuition plan, however, you can buy blocks of tomorrow's tuition at today's prices.

Who qualifies to invest in a Coverdell ESA?
You can open a Coverdell ESA for your child if he or she is younger than 18 and your income is within certain limits. For 2004, the contribution limits were reduced for joint filers earning more than $190,000 and single filers earning more than $95,000. Joint filers earning $220,000 or more and single filers earning $110,000 or more were barred completely from opening this type of account.

How much can I contribute to my child's Coverdell ESA?

You can contribute only $2,000 to your child's Coverdell ESA each year. What's particularly restrictive about the contribution limits is that they apply per child, not per contributor. In other words, if grandma contributes $1,000 to the account, then you can contribute only $1,000 more to the account that same year.

TIPS

> **Set up a separate Coverdell ESA for each of your children.** If you have more than one child, you can contribute $2,000 to each child's Coverdell ESA per year. For example, a couple with three children could contribute up to $6,000 to their children's Coverdell ESA accounts each year.

Can I ever obtain a refund of my investment?

No. Once you deposit money into a Coverdell ESA, the money legally belongs to your child. This means that you cannot withdraw the money even if your family runs into a financial crisis.

Can anyone else contribute to my child's Coverdell ESA?

Absolutely. If friends or family want to contribute, they simply write a check to the financial institution holding your child's Coverdell ESA, making sure to note your child's account number on the check. Just remember that the total contribution to your child's Coverdell ESA cannot exceed $2,000 in any given year, so it might be wise to coordinate contributions.

What happens if we exceed the contribution limits?

Your child will owe a hefty 6% tax on the excess contribution.

What types of education expenses can I use the money for?

Your can use the money to pay for virtually all of your child's college and graduate school expenses—for example, tuition, fees, books, supplies, and even room and board for students who are enrolled at least half time.

Some foreign schools, trade schools, and technical schools qualify as well. If your child decides to attend Oxford or the French Culinary Institute, for example, you will be able to use the account money to cover the bills. The only requirement is that the school your child selects qualifies to disburse federal financial aid. To find a list of eligible schools, check out the U.S. Department of Education website at www.fafsa.ed.gov. (The "fafsa" stands for Free Application for Student Aid.)

You can also use the funds to pay for your child's elementary and secondary school expenses, including private school tuition, after-school tutoring, school uniforms, and a computer.

If your child has special educational needs—because of a disability or developmental delay, for example—you can use the funds for those needs as well, such as hiring an occupational or physical therapist.

What happens if I spend the money on something that isn't allowed by the plan? Your child will then have to pay ordinary income taxes on the earnings portion of the withdrawal, as well as a 10% penalty on the earnings. What's tricky about the way this rule works is that the IRS won't let you withdraw your original contributions first. Instead, every withdrawal from your child's Coverdell ESA will include a proportionate share of the account's earnings. (We won't bore you with the math here, but you can find an example of how this rule works in IRS Publication 970, *Tax Benefits for Education*, available free at www.irs.gov).

Will the money in a Coverdell ESA affect my child's ability to qualify for financial aid? Yes, but no more so than any asset in your name (such as your retirement savings account or your home). This is because the federal financial aid formula views a Coverdell ESA as your asset, not your child's.

What if my child doesn't need the money in the Coverdell ESA for educational expenses? If your child does not need the money—maybe your son decided to join the Peace Corps rather than attend college—you'll be able to change the beneficiary to another member of the family, such as one of your other children or a niece or nephew, without paying a penalty or suffering adverse income tax consequences. The only requirement is that the new beneficiary be younger than 30.

If you don't want to change the beneficiary, you can close the account and give the money to your child. The only problem with this option is that your child will then owe a penalty of 10% of the earnings, as well as ordinary income taxes on the earnings. Your child will not, however, owe any taxes or penalties on the original contributions.

What if I grow unhappy with my child's Coverdell ESA and want to switch plans? Not to worry: You can transfer the funds in your child's Coverdell ESA to a new Coverdell ESA at a different financial institution, a 529 college savings plan, or a 529 prepaid college tuition plan without paying any penalties or taxes. Simply withdraw the money from your child's Coverdell ESA and redeposit the funds into a new account within 60 days of the original withdrawal.

CAUTION

Look before you leap. You can only roll over Coverdell assets once in a 12-month period, so make sure you've found a good home for your child's funds before closing your child's original Coverdell account.

Where can I learn more about Coverdell ESAs?
Check out IRS Publication 970, *Tax Benefits for Education*, available for free at www.irs.gov.

How do I enroll in a Coverdell ESA?
You can enroll in a Coverdell ESA at most banks and brokerage houses by completing a simple form. Name your child as the beneficiary and yourself (or your child's other parent) as the account manager. You will also have to name the person supplying the funds for the account (look for box marked "initial depositor" or some equivalent on the form). If you are near the income limits, name your child—rather than yourself—as the one contributing the funds for the account.

529 College Savings Plans

One of the smartest ways to save for your child's college education is to use a state-sponsored 529 college savings plan. The plan is free of the restrictive contribution limits that apply to Coverdell ESAs, but you'll still enjoy similar tax benefits: You won't pay a dime in capital gains taxes on your investment earnings so long as you use the money for your child's college or graduate school expenses. What makes 529 college savings plans even more attractive are the state tax benefits: Depending on where you live, you may be able to take a state tax deduction or state tax credit for the contributions you make to the plan.

What is a 529 college savings plan and how does it work?
A 529 college savings plan is a state-operated education savings plan. Unlike a Coverdell ESA, a 529 college savings plan legally belongs to you—the parent—and not to your child. All states except for Kentucky and Washington now offer their own 529 college savings plans. Although most states allow you to invest in their plans even if you are not a resident, there are often state tax benefits that come with investing in your own state's plan. (Check "State Tax Breaks for 529 Plan Contributions" at the end of this chapter.)

Even though 529 college savings plans are sponsored by individual states, there is no requirement that your child attend a state school. You can use the money at virtually any college or university in the country—and even some foreign schools, technical schools, and trade schools.

You can open a 529 college savings plan through the state agency whose plan you have selected. Once you deposit money into the plan, you won't be free to choose your own investments. Rather, you'll have your choice of investing the money in one of several stock and/or bond portfolios—graded according to your tolerance for investment risk. The state's 529 plan manager (usually a well-known company such as The Vanguard Group or TIAA-CREF) will manage your investments for you.

When your child begins college or graduate school, you can withdraw money from the plan to pay for qualifying educational expenses—and you won't have to pay taxes on the money. Your state's 529 plan manager will send a Form 1099-Q reporting each withdrawal to the IRS. If you use the money for something other than a qualifying educational expense, you'll owe ordinary income taxes and a 10% penalty on the earnings.

To see how a 529 college savings plan works, let's consider a quick example:

> **EXAMPLE:** *Amelie and her husband, Frederick, live in Manhattan and decide to open a 529 college savings plan for their six-month-old son, Luke. After doing a bit of research, they decide it's best to invest in New York's 529 plan because they get a state tax deduction on their contributions. They look at the plan's various investment choices and opt for the Aggressive Growth Portfolio, which consists of all stocks and no bonds, because they have a high tolerance for risk.*

> *The couple invest $5,000 per year for the next 18 years. The Vanguard Group manages the plan, so Amelie and her husband don't have to make any investment choices. By the time Luke is ready to begin his first year at Columbia University, his plan is worth $200,000. To pay Luke's first semester's tuition bill, Amelie and Frederick complete a withdrawal form authorizing the plan administrator to pay the money directly to Columbia University. Their plan administrator reports the withdrawal to the IRS, using Form 1099-Q. Because Amelie and Frederick used the money for a qualifying educational expense, they do not owe taxes on the withdrawal.*

What are the advantages of a 529 college savings plan?

There are many reasons why you might choose a 529 college savings plan. Here are just a few:

- **School choice.** You can use the money at just about any college or graduate school in the country. If you want to preserve your child's right to choose an educational institution, then a 529 college savings plan is a great way to go.
- **The contribution limits are high.** Unless you're a Rockefeller looking to invest a million or two, you'll have plenty of room to maneuver within the $200,000-plus investment limits of most 529 college savings plans.
- **No federal taxes.** You won't owe any federal capital gains taxes on the earnings if you use the money to pay for

college or graduate school expenses. Chances are that you probably won't owe state taxes on the earnings either, which means that you'll get to keep every dollar you earn.

- **You can get the money back if necessary.** Because the money in a 529 college savings plan legally belongs to you—and not to your child—you can get your money back provided you're willing to pay a 10% earnings penalty and ordinary income taxes on the earnings.

- **Expert management.** If you'd prefer to let someone else pick your investments and balance your portfolio, then a 529 college savings plan is a good choice for you.

What are the disadvantages?

Although a 529 college savings plan is a wonderful way to begin saving for your child's education, there are a few drawbacks that you should know about:

- **The tax-free treatment is slated to end in 2010.** Although financial experts predict that Congress will extend the 529 plan tax breaks, you'll end up owing capital gains taxes on the earnings if it doesn't.

- **A narrow interpretation of educational expenses.** Unlike with a Coverdell ESA, you won't be able to use the money to pay for elementary or secondary school expenses.

- **Fees.** You'll have to pay management fees on your account—which can eat into your earnings.

- **There's no guarantee you'll save enough.** With a 529 prepaid college tuition plan, however, you can buy blocks of tomorrow's tuition at today's prices (see below).

Who qualifies to invest in a 529 college savings plan?

Anybody can open a 529 savings plan—including people without children. You can even open up a 529 college savings plan for your own education.

How much can I contribute to a 529 college savings plan?

The contribution limits for 529 college savings plans are enormous: Many state plans allow you to invest more than $200,000 per child—enough to pay for four years at even the most elite universities at today's rates. Of course, you can also invest a lot less. Most states allow you to open a 529 savings plan with as little as $25.

Can anyone else contribute to my child's 529 college savings plan?

Yes. All friends and family need is the 529 plan account number and the name and address of the institution that holds the plan. They can then write checks directly to your child's 529 college savings plan account. Because the contribution limits are so high, you don't need to worry about coordinating contributions, as you would with a Coverdell ESA.

What types of educational expenses can I pay for using a 529 college savings plan?
You can use the plan money to pay for your child's tuition, room and board, books, supplies and equipment, and fees at virtually any college or graduate school in the country.

If your child decides to attend college abroad—or opt for an alternative educational path, such as a technical school or trade school—then you can use the plan money only if the school is authorized to disburse federal financial aid. You can find a list of eligible institutions at the U.S. Department of Education's federal student aid website at www.fafsa.ed.gov.

You can also use the plan money to pay for special education services for your child, if necessary. Check with a tax professional for more information.

What happens if I spend the money on something that isn't a qualified educational expense?
Every time you withdraw money, the plan administrator will send a Form 1099-Q to the IRS reporting the withdrawal. If you decide to use the money for a nonqualifying expense, you will owe a 10% penalty and ordinary income taxes on the earnings portion of your withdrawal. The IRS considers every withdrawal from a 529 plan to include a proportionate share of the account's earnings. For more information, talk to a tax professional.

Will the plan money affect my child's ability to qualify for financial aid?
Yes, but no more so than any asset in your name (such as your retirement savings account or your home). This is because the federal financial aid formula views the plan as your asset, not your child's.

What if my child doesn't need the plan money for educational expenses?
If your child doesn't need the plan money, you will have a couple of options:

- **Change the beneficiary.** You can change the plan beneficiary to another family member or yourself without any financial penalties or tax consequences.
- **Withdraw the money.** If you choose this option, you'll pay a 10% penalty and ordinary income taxes on the earnings. You won't, however, owe any penalties or taxes on your original contributions.

 TIPS

No penalties for scholarships. If your child doesn't need the money because of a scholarship, you won't owe a 10% penalty on the earnings. You'll still owe taxes on the earnings, however.

There are so many 529 college savings plans. How do I know which one to choose? First, find out whether your state offers a state tax deduction or tax credit for contributions to your state's own 529 college savings plan. (See "State Tax Breaks for 529 Plan Contributions" at the end of this chapter.) If the tax break is significant enough, then it doesn't make sense to invest anywhere but your home state plan. Next, check out details on the plans at www. savingforcollege.com. Click on "College Savings 201" in the left-hand menu bar. Then click on "5-Cap Ratings" in the left-hand column. The 5-Cap Ratings reflect savingforcollege.com's opinion of the overall usefulness of a state's 529 plan based on factors such as flexibility, liquidity and availability, ownership rights, fees, and investment approach and safety.

What if I grow unhappy with my 529 college savings plan and want to switch plans? Fortunately, you're not committed to your original choice of 529 plans. You can roll over your original investment to a different 529 college savings plan or 529 prepaid tuition plan without paying penalties or taxes, provided you do so within 60 days of withdrawing the money from your original 529 plan. You can make only one switch per 12-month period.

 CAUTION

Your state may ask for its tax break back. If you enjoyed a state tax deduction or tax credit for your original 529 plan contributions, you may have to pay back that benefit in the form of a higher tax bill when you roll over your 529 savings to another state's plan. Be sure to talk to your accountant if this situation might apply to you.

Where can I get more information about 529 college savings plans?
An excellent place to start is www.savingforcollege.com. There, you can find summaries of each of the different 529 college savings plans available and lots of useful articles and advice on these plans. If you would like more information about the tax consequences of a 529 college savings plan, consult IRS Publication 970, *Tax Benefits for Education*, available free at www.irs.gov.

How do I enroll in a 529 college savings plan?
Once you've settled on a particular state's 529 college savings plan, log onto the plan's website to begin the enrollment process.

529 Prepaid College Tuition Plans

If you find the rising costs of college tuition and the uncertainty of the stock market terrifying, consider a 529 prepaid college tuition plan. These plans allow you to pay part or all of your child's college tuition in advance, but at today's rates. When you prepay for college tuition in this way, you won't have to worry about whether you'll save enough or whether the stock market will plummet before your child is ready to start school. It will be taken care of.

If prepaid college tuition plans sound too good to be true, there is a catch: Your child's college choices will be quite limited if you want to reap the full benefits of the plan.

What is a 529 prepaid college tuition plan and how does it work?

A 529 prepaid college tuition plan is a state or private plan that allows you to prepay for your child's future college tuition by purchasing individual credit blocks or by paying for a semester, year, or even all four years of college in advance. The prices and other details vary depending on the particular plan you choose. For example, in 2004 the Florida prepaid college tuition plan allowed you to purchase four years of college for your newborn for the lump-sum price of $10,330 and change. With the Pennsylvania prepaid college tuition plan, that same amount will buy less than two semesters worth of tuition at Pennsylvania State University. Despite their individual differences, the cornerstone of all 529 prepaid college tuition plans is that you can purchase tomorrow's college education at today's prices.

FAST FACTS

Not too many prepaid options.
As of this writing, only 14 states offered new parents the option to enroll in prepaid tuition plans: Alabama, Florida, Illinois, Maryland, Massachusetts, Michigan, Mississippi, Nevada, New Mexico, Pennsylvania, South Carolina, Tennessee, Virginia, and Wisconsin.

If you don't have the money to buy four years' worth of college tuition immediately, don't worry; many plans offer installment payment options so that you can pay off your tuition purchase much in the same way you would pay off a car loan. Once you've paid for your purchase, you can then sit back and relax until your child is ready to begin applying to colleges.

When high school rolls around, your child can apply to the schools covered by your prepaid plan. If your child has her heart set on a nonplan school, however, you'll almost certainly be able to use the money in your 529 prepaid college tuition plan to cover tuition at the nonplan school. The only problem is that you'll then be responsible to make up the difference in tuition costs.

Prepaid tuition is no guarantee of admission. Your child will still have to get admitted to a plan school on his or her own merits. So it's possible that you will pay for tuition at a school that rejects your child's application.

If your child decides to enroll in a plan school—and is admitted—then simply contact your plan administrator, who will handle things from there, arranging to pay tuition and other covered expenses directly to the school of your child's choice.

Let's consider a quick example to get a closer look at how a 529 prepaid college tuition plan works:

EXAMPLE: *Charlie and his wife, Monica, both attended the University of Michigan and decided to raise their family in the state. When their daughter, Paige, is born, the couple agree to invest in Michigan's prepaid college tuition plan. They know she might not choose to attend their alma mater, but they feel that their obligation to educate her will be satisfied if they go the prepaid route. If she wants to attend another school, she can apply the money in the plan to the school of her choice.*

Charlie and Monica enroll in a ten-year monthly payment plan to pay for eight full semesters of college. Although the total price is higher than if they had paid in one lump sum, the payment plan is more affordable. The couple pays $344 to the Michigan Education Trust each month. Charlie and Monica know that their prepaid tuition plan will cover only tuition and mandatory fees, so they set aside an additional $100 per month in a 529 savings plan to cover other expenses. By the time Paige is ten years old, college is paid for.

What are the advantages of investing in a 529 prepaid college tuition plan?

In a crowded field of education savings options, 529 prepaid college tuition plans stand out because of one unique advantage: You will know in advance exactly how much college tuition you are buying for your child.

Another key benefit is that many states offer valuable tax breaks for contributions you make to a 529 prepaid college tuition plan. Check "State Tax Breaks for 529 Plan Contributions" at the end of this chapter to see if your state is one of them.

What are the disadvantages?

As exciting as 529 prepaid college tuition plans seem, you should know that these plans have a number of disadvantages:

- **Limited college choices.** The prepaid plans generally require that your child attend a state university. Your child may not be interested in that choice. And if you're set on a prepaid plan but hoping your child will be admitted to Princeton or Stanford, then your best bet is the Independent 529 Plan, described below.

- **The financial aid consequences are significant.** If you want your child to qualify for financial aid, steer clear of a prepaid plan. This is because every dollar's worth of tuition covered by your investment in the plan will mean one less dollar in financial aid for your child.

- **Many plans let you save for tuition only.** This means that you'll still need a second savings plan for the other costs of college—such as room and board—that can add up to nearly half of the total expense of sending your child to school.

- **The plan terms may change.** Because college tuition expenses are growing faster than the investment returns of many prepaid plans, the plans are in precarious financial shape. This has forced some plans to make drastic changes in the way they operate. In 2003, for example, the Colorado plan offered parents two choices: cash out of the plan or remain in the plan under much less favorable terms.

Who qualifies to invest in a 529 prepaid college tuition plan?

Most plans require you to be a state resident in order to participate. In addition, some plans will allow you to enroll only if your child is younger than a certain age. For example, the Maryland Prepaid College Trust is open to Maryland and Washington, DC, residents only, and the beneficiary must be in the ninth grade or younger.

> ### Independent 529 Plans
> The Independent 529 Plan is a prepaid plan that allows you to purchase tuition certificates good at more than 200 private colleges and universities in the country. This flexibility comes at a price, because the independent rates are much higher to reflect sky-high private college tuition costs. This type of plan is beyond the scope of this book. Check www.independent529 plan.org if you want to learn more about this type of plan.

How much can I contribute to a 529 prepaid college tuition plan?

This varies by plan. Most will allow you to prepay for four years worth of tuition and fees only. Other plans will permit you to prepay for room, board, and supplies as well.

Can I ever obtain a refund of my investment?

Most, but not all, plans will give you a refund if you change your mind or need the money for any reason. The refund policies vary by plan, and you may owe a significant cancellation fee.

Can anyone else contribute to my child's 529 prepaid college tuition plan?

Yes. Ask your plan administrator about the best way for friends and family to make contributions

You may owe taxes and penalties on the interest you've earned. If you cancel your prepaid college tuition plan and spend the money on anything other than your child's undergraduate or graduate education, you will owe a 10% penalty and ordinary income taxes on the earnings. Because most prepaid tuition plans limit your investment earnings to a very small percentage, however, the tax impact should be minimal.

Will the money in a 529 college savings plan affect my child's ability to qualify for financial aid?

Absolutely. Unlike most of the other education savings plans discussed in this chapter, prepaid plans have a dramatic effect on financial aid eligibility. The federal financial aid formula treats 529 prepaid college tuition plans like scholarships, which means that the money you invest in the plan will result in a dollar-for-dollar reduction of your child's federal financial aid eligibility. If you prepay four years worth of college tuition, your child will almost certainly not receive any federal financial aid for college tuition expenses.

What if my child wants to go to a nonplan school—or no school at all?

In either case, most plans will refund you the average cost of in-state public college tuition at the time your child is ready to attend school—an amount that will likely be significantly more than your original investment.

Depending on your situation, a better alternative may be to switch beneficiaries. For example, if your daughter doesn't want to give up her dreams of attending Yale while your son wants nothing more than to attend your state university, then make your son the new beneficiary of the plan. Most plans allow you to change the beneficiary without paying penalties or taxes.

What if my child receives a scholarship to college?

In that case, you should be able to obtain a refund of your original investment (and earned interest on that investment). Another option would be to change the beneficiary to someone else in your family.

What questions should I ask before enrolling in a prepaid college tuition plan?

Prepaid plans come packed with plenty of terms and conditions, so be sure to read the fine print before enrolling. Here are some questions to ask:

- Does my state offer any state tax deduction for investing in its 529 prepaid college tuition plan? (Check "State Tax Breaks for 529 Plan Contributions" at the end of this chapter.)
- What schools does the prepaid college tuition plan cover?

- What is the refund policy if I change my mind for any reason?
- What happens if my child goes to a nonplan school?
- What happens if my child decides not to go to school at all?
- What happens if my child receives a scholarship?
- What happens if my child moves out of state? (Some prepaid college tuition plans will ask you to pay the difference between in-state tuition rates—covered under the plan—and out-of-state tuition rates.)
- Can I change the beneficiary of the plan at any time?

CAUTION

Beware of disappearing plans. The rising costs of tuition have forced some states, such as Texas and Colorado, to close enrollment in their prepaid college tuition plans. This kind of closure means that parents who paid for one year while the plan was open must now pay for the remaining three years of tuition at tomorrow's prices. So be sure to log on to www.savingforcollege.com to do a little research on the plan's financial health before making your investment.

What if I grow unhappy with my prepaid college tuition plan and want to switch plans?
The answer depends on your plan's refund policy. Provided that your plan offers you the option of canceling your contract, you can roll the money in your prepaid college tuition plan into a 529 college savings plan (or a different prepaid tuition plan, if you qualify) without suffering adverse federal tax consequences.

Where can I get more information about 529 prepaid college tuition plans?
Because the details of the plans vary quite a bit, the only way to learn more about any given prepaid tuition plan is to carefully review the plan materials. You can find downloadable brochures and other helpful information at the plans' websites. (To find your plan's Web address, check www.savingforcollege.com.)

How do I enroll in a 529 prepaid college tuition plan?
You should be able to find everything you need to begin the enrollment process at the plan's website.

CAUTION

You may have to pay back your state tax breaks. If you received a state tax deduction or tax credit for your prepaid tuition plan contribution, you may owe your state back taxes when you transfer your money out of the plan. Talk to an accountant in your state if you find yourself in this situation.

Education Savings Bonds

If you are looking for a risk-free, tax-advantageous savings option for your child's college education, consider the U.S. education savings bond program. Although the interest rates are modest, you won't pay any federal taxes on your bond interest earnings provided you use the money to pay for your child's higher education expenses. What's more, you won't pay state or local taxes either, and the federal government guarantees that your investment won't lose value.

What are U.S. savings bonds?

When you purchase a savings bond, you lend the federal government money. In return, the government promises to pay you back with interest when you cash in the bond. Because the federal government backs the bonds, there's no risk.

Once you purchase a U.S. savings bond, it begins to earn interest at a modest rate. The interest is compounded, which means that you earn interest on your interest. What's particularly nice about investing in savings bonds is that your interest earnings are always exempt from state and local taxes.

How does the education savings bond program work?

Savings bonds have become a much more attractive investment option for new parents thanks to the education savings bond program. Under this program, you don't pay federal, state, or local taxes on your savings bond interest earnings provided you use the money to pay for your child's college or graduate school expenses.

Only two types of savings bonds—Series EE savings bonds and Series I savings bonds—qualify for the program. The main difference between the two types of bonds is the way the interest is calculated: Series I bonds have a built-in inflation adjustment. Series EE bonds usually earn a lower interest rate, but are guaranteed to double in value within 20 years.

When you purchase bonds, you don't have to tell the federal government that you plan to use the bonds to pay for your child's education down the road. All you have to do is title the bonds in your own name (not your child's name), and hang on to the bonds until you are ready to redeem the bonds to pay for your child's educational expenses.

Once your child is about to start college or graduate school, you can cash in your bonds at just about any bank. You can then use the proceeds to pay for tuition and other expenses. If you use all of the money to pay for your child's education, then all of the interest you earned will be tax free. However, if you spend less than the total principal and interest of the bonds on education bills that year, then you will have to pay taxes on some of your interest earnings.

You will have to keep careful records of how you spend the proceeds. When the time comes to file your tax return for the year, you'll have to report your interest earnings on your "Interest and Ordinary Dividends" schedule. To enjoy the tax exemption, you will also have to complete Form 8815—which is a worksheet of how you spent your interest earnings—and attach it to your tax return.

Let's consider a quick example of the education savings bond program in action:

> **EXAMPLE:** *Juanita and her husband, Mick, purchase $5,000 worth of Series I savings bonds for their son, Aidan, each year, beginning on Aidan's first birthday. By the time Aidan is 18 years old, the principal and interest on the bonds had grown to more than $120,000, which is more than enough to pay for four years of tuition at Aidan's first-choice school.*
>
> *When Aidan's first semester's tuition bill of $20,000 comes due, Juanita and Mick cash in just enough bonds to pay for that semester's bill. They hang on to the bill and their receipt until tax time. Their accountant files the necessary paperwork, including Form 8815. Because the couple only cashed in the bonds they needed to pay their son's educational expenses for the year, they do not owe taxes on the nearly $7,000 of interest they earned on those bonds.*

What are the advantages of saving for my child's education using United States savings bonds?

There are three significant advantages to the education savings bonds program:

- **Your investment cannot lose value.** No downturn in the economy can stand in the way of your child's college dreams if you put your money in savings bonds, because bonds are federal government-guaranteed.

- **Interest earnings are exempt from federal, state, and local taxes.** The tax savings definitely help to make up for the low investment returns of United States savings bonds.

- **You can cash in the bonds at almost any time and for any reason.** You might sleep easier knowing that you can redeem your savings bond in a pinch, if you ever need the money for anything other than your child's education. Of course, you'll have to pay federal taxes on the earnings.

What are the disadvantages?

There are a couple of important reasons why the education savings bond program isn't for everyone:

- **The investment returns are tiny.** You'll almost certainly earn more in the stock market, particularly if you've got a long investment horizon.

- **If you earn a lot, you lose the tax break.** The interest you earned on the bonds will only be tax free if your income is below certain limits when your child is ready for college. Unless you're very confident that your income will be within these limits many years from now, it may not make sense to invest in education savings bonds.

What are the income limits for getting the tax advantages?

Although anyone can purchase a U.S. savings bond, you will only be able to enjoy the tax advantages (called the "education tax exemption") if your income is within certain limits at the time that you redeem the bonds. For the 2004 tax year, the interest exemption began to phase out for married couples with a modified adjusted gross income of more than $89,750 and for single individuals with a modified adjusted gross income of more than $59,850. The exemption phased out completely for married couples at $119,750 or for single individuals at $74,850.

Unless you have a crystal ball, you probably have no idea what you will be earning at the time your child is ready for college. Your income could very well exceed the applicable limits by then—so you might not qualify for the tax exemption on the interest you earn on savings bonds after all. Be sure to keep this possibility in mind when deciding whether savings bonds are the right investment option for your family.

CAUTION

You cannot claim the exemption if your filing status is "married filing separately." Married couples must file their taxes jointly—and be within the relevant income limits—to qualify for the tax advantages.

CAUTION

If you are a very young parent. You must be 24 years of age or older at the time that you purchase the savings bond to qualify for the interest exemption. If you're younger than 24 but your spouse is older, then put the savings bonds in your spouse's name to ensure that you'll be able to claim the exemption when the time comes.

How much can I invest in education savings bonds?

You can purchase $30,000 worth of Series EE savings bonds and $30,000 worth of Series I savings bonds each year. Your spouse can do the same, because the purchase limit is per person, not per household.

If you're not awash in that kind of dough, not to worry: You can purchase savings bonds in denominations as small as $25.

Can I obtain a refund of my investment?

Yes. In fact, one of the best features of U.S. savings bonds is that you can redeem the bonds at any time after 12 months of your original purchase for any reason. You will owe a very small penalty (three months' worth of interest earnings) if you redeem your bonds within five years of your purchase. If you hold on to your bonds for five years or more before cashing them in, however, you will not pay a penalty.

The rub is in the taxes. Unless you use your bond proceeds to pay for qualifying education expenses, you will have to pay federal taxes on your interest earnings. You won't owe any state or local tax on your interest earnings, however, and you won't have to pay any tax on your principal.

Can anyone else purchase savings bonds for my child's education?
Not if they want to benefit from the education savings bond program. This is because you only get a federal tax break on savings bond interest earnings if you spend the proceeds on educational expenses for yourself, your spouse, or someone whom you can claim as your dependent for tax purposes.

What types of education expenses can I pay for using education savings bonds?
You can spend your bond proceeds only on tuition and mandatory fees for a degree-granting program at a college, graduate school, or other educational institution eligible to disburse federal financial aid. (To find a list of schools that qualify, log on to the U.S. Department of Education's federal financial aid website at www.fafsa.ed.gov.) You cannot spend the money on other higher education costs, such as room and board and supplies, if you want to claim the education savings bond tax exemption.

 TIPS

Use a loophole to get more flexibility. One way around this limit is to reinvest your bond proceeds in a Coverdell ESA, 529 college savings plan, or 529 prepaid tuition plan and then claim the tax exemption. For example, if you want to use your education savings bonds to pay for private school tuition, contribute the money to a Coverdell ESA and then write a check to your child's private school. Check with your accountant for more details on how to take advantage of this loophole.

 TIPS

Savings bonds make wonderful baby gifts. Even though they won't benefit, friends and family members who purchase savings bonds for your child will give you and your child the benefits of owning United States savings bonds—for example, compounding interest on earnings and an exemption from state and local taxes. All your child will owe is federal income taxes on the earnings, which won't amount to much if your child redeems the bonds before he or she has begun earning a real salary.

Moreover, you can use the money only to pay for your own educational expenses, your spouse's educational expenses, or the educational expenses of someone whom you can claim as a dependent on your tax return.

Finally, you must spend your bond proceeds on qualifying educational expenses within the same tax year that you cash your bonds. If you cash in your bonds this year and pay for your child's college tuition next year, you will have to pay federal taxes on your interest earnings—so plan carefully before you redeem your bonds.

What happens if I spend the money on something that isn't allowed by the program?

Spending the money on something else is not a big problem. Although you will have to pay federal income taxes on the earnings, there are no penalties, your interest earnings will remain exempt from state and local taxes, and you will not owe any taxes or penalties on your principal.

Will the education savings bonds affect my child's ability to qualify for financial aid?

Yes, but no more so than any other asset you own (such as a retirement plan or a house). Because education savings bonds must be held in your name (not your child's name), the bonds are considered your assets for federal financial aid purposes.

What if my child doesn't need the bonds for educational expenses?

If your child wins a scholarship or decides not to attend college or graduate school, you can still qualify for the federal tax exemption on bond interest earnings provided that you spend the money on qualifying educational expenses for yourself, your spouse, or one of your other children.

> **EXAMPLE:** *Arthur and his wife, Melinda, purchased $25,000 worth of Series I savings bonds when their daughter, Ella, was five years old. Now Ella is ready to attend college. She receives a full scholarship to Wellesley and doesn't need the money. Ella is an only child, so Melinda uses the money to pursue a longstanding dream of obtaining her master's degree.*

Alternatively, you can redeem your bonds for any other reason—but keep in mind that you will then owe federal taxes on the earnings.

What if I grow unhappy with the education savings bond program and want to switch plans?

You can simply cash in your bonds and redeposit the money in a Coverdell ESA, 529 college savings plan, or 529 prepaid tuition plan for yourself, your spouse, or one of your children. You won't owe any taxes on your earnings if you take this route. However, you will owe a penalty of three months' worth of interest earnings if you switch plans within five years of purchasing your bonds.

Where can I get more information about the education savings bond program?

You can learn more about the education savings bond program online at www.savingsbonds.gov. (This is the U.S. Department of the Treasury's financial services website that lets you buy and redeem securities direct.) To find out more about the tax rules, consult IRS Publication 970, *Tax Benefits for Education,* available free at www.irs.gov.

How can I purchase education savings bonds?

You can buy education savings bonds at www.savingsbond.gov, at any bank or brokerage company, or through your employer if your employer participates in the U.S. Treasury Department's payroll savings plan.

Custodial Accounts

Depending on your financial circumstances, you might want to save for your child's education using a savings or brokerage account in your child's own name. You might be surprised to learn, however, that most states do not allow children to own bank or brokerage accounts by themselves. (This is probably why you don't see many toddlers carrying around their own checkbooks and ATM cards.) To give money or property to your child, you must either use a trust—which can be complicated and expensive—or a custodial account.

For most families, a custodial account is not the right choice for an education savings plan. The tax advantages are minimal if your child is younger than 14, the financial

aid impact is enormous, and you can never obtain a refund of your investment. Still, there are some families for whom a custodial account makes sense for tax and estate planning reasons—particularly because they can use the money to pay for everything from swimming lessons to summer camp. Also, this is one of the few options for very high income families.

CAUTION

Naming yourself as custodian has estate tax consequences. Although the estate planning issues of custodial accounts are beyond the scope of this book, you should know that if you name yourself as the custodian, the money will be part of your estate when you die. So be sure to name someone else—a trusted relative, perhaps—to manage the account if you're opening a custodial account for estate planning reasons. Talk to an attorney if you have more questions about this issue.

What is a custodial account and how does it work?

A custodial account is a simplified trust that allows parents to give assets to their children without the expense and administrative hassle of setting up a conventional trust. Different states use different versions of either the Uniform Gifts to Minors Act (UGMA) or the

Uniform Transfers to Minors Act (UTMA) to set the terms governing custodial accounts. When you set up a custodial account, you are arranging for someone else to supervise assets on behalf of your child, who is the account's legal owner. You can open a custodial account at any bank or brokerage house, just the same way you would open an account for yourself. However, you must choose an account manager—or "custodian"—to manage the account. Many parents name themselves, or another family member, as the account's custodian.

The custodian is in charge of the account and is responsible for investing and spending the money on behalf of your child, until your child reaches an age set by your state. (This age is 21 in most states but some states set it as young as 18—see "The Uniform Transfers to Minors Act: When Will Your Child Gain Control of the Assets in a Custodial Account?" in the appendix, to learn your state's rule.)

Once your child reaches the magic age, your child will gain control over the account. There are no rules on how your child can invest or spend the money at that point. This means, for example, that your 22-year-old child would be free to squander the money on anything from a beachfront condominium in Hawaii to a Harley-Davidson, and there is nothing (except begging) that you could do about it.

TIPS

If you want more control. A custodial account is not a good option if you worry that your child might one day waste your hard-earned savings. If you nonetheless want to put money in your child's name, consider establishing a formal trust, one with stricter limits on when and how your child can access the money.

To get a better sense of how a custodial account really works, let's take a look at a quick example:

EXAMPLE: *At the age of 71, Eleanor decides that it's time to do some estate planning. She takes advantage of the annual gift tax exemption to give away $11,000 per year to her only granddaughter, Penelope. Instead of bothering with a formal trust, she establishes a custodial account for Penelope at her local bank. Eleanor names her daughter, Vera, as the account's custodian. She asks Vera to use the money to pay for private school tuition and ballet classes for Penelope.*

Over the next ten years, Vera invests the money in a conservative mix of stocks and bonds. She withdraws money to pay for Penelope's private school tuition and ballet classes, just as her mother requested. Vera also uses the money to pay for part of Penelope's college tuition expenses. Every year, Vera works with her accountant to make sure that the account's taxes are properly paid.

When Penelope turns 21—the age of custodial account termination in her state—there is only $3,000 left in the account. Vera no longer has any say over how Penelope invests or spends the money. As it turns out, Vera set an excellent example for young Penelope, who invests half of the money in tax-free municipal bonds and uses half to fund a spur-of-the-moment trip to Italy.

What are the advantages of saving for my child's education using a custodial account? Although we've already given you a preview of the disadvantages of custodial accounts, there are some notable benefits to saving for your child's education this way:

- **You can give as much money as you please.** There are no pesky contribution limits to worry about as there are with some of the other plans discussed in this chapter.
- **No income limits.** If you earn a lot of money, you might not be able to take advantage of some of the other college savings options discussed in this chapter. Not so with custodial accounts.
- **Investment control.** Unlike 529 college savings plans, for example, you won't be at the mercy of someone else's investment choices.
- **Spending choices.** The custodian can spend the money on just about anything for your child. There are virtually no limits on how the money in a custo-

dial account can be used, provided the money is spent to benefit your child.
- **Modest tax savings.** The first $800 worth of earnings will be tax free, and the next $800 worth of earnings is taxed at your child's low rate.
- **Significant tax savings once your child is 14.** At that point, all of the account's earnings will be taxed at your child's low rate rather than at your tax rate.

What are the disadvantages?
Before you get too excited about the possibility of investing your money in a custodial account, consider the numerous disadvantages:

- **The earnings are not tax free.** With other savings plans—such as a Coverdell ESA, for example—your child will not owe taxes on the earnings provided the money pays for qualifying education expenses.
- **You can't get a refund.** Once you transfer money to your child's custodial account, the money belongs to your child. You can't take the money back no matter how badly you need it.
- **You can't use the money for other children.** If your child decides not to attend college, for example, you can't simply spend the money on tuition bills for another one of your children, as you would be able to do with some of the other plans discussed in this chapter.
- **Your child will have unrestricted access to the money by age 21 (in most states).** Unless you're confident that you'll spend most of the money in the

account by that time, you should ask yourself whether you are comfortable with the idea of your 20-something child having that much financial freedom.

- **Financial aid impact.** Because your child is the legal owner of the assets in a custodial account, the money will weigh heavily on financial aid calculations.

How are the investment earnings of a custodial account taxed?

Because a custodial account legally belongs to your child, your child (and not you) will owe taxes on any investment earnings. The investment earnings will be taxed at your child's normal rate if your child is 14 or older—which can result in impressive tax savings for your family.

> **EXAMPLE:** *Michael purchases $1,000 worth of the Bumblebee Company's stock in 2000, and the stock appreciates to a staggering $11,000 by 2004. Because Michael's income is high, he will have to pay 15% of his earnings in taxes if he sells the stock himself. To save some money, Michael gives the Bumblebee Company's stock to his 15-year-old son, Jonas, who qualifies for the 5% capital gains tax rate because he is in high school and has very little income or other investment earnings. When Jonas sells the Bumblebee stock, he pays only $500 in taxes ($10,000 in capital gains x 5% tax rate). If Michael had sold the stock himself instead of giving it to his son, Michael would have paid $1,500 in taxes ($10,000 in capital gains x 15% tax rate).*

If your child is younger than 14, however, the account's earnings will be taxed according to a set of rules commonly known as the "kiddie tax." The purpose of the kiddie tax is to prevent parents from transferring income-generating assets to their young children to lower their own tax bills. In 2004, for example, the first $800 in investment earnings was completely tax free. The next $800 of investment earnings was taxed at the child's rate—which is almost certainly much lower than the parents' tax rate. Any earnings over $1,600 were taxed at the parents' tax rate. (The IRS adjusts these numbers each year for inflation.)

Because the kiddie tax rules are quite complicated, consult a tax professional for assistance if your child's investment earnings exceed $800. You should also consult a tax professional if your child is blind, as different kiddie tax rules apply to children who cannot see.

ADDITIONAL RESOURCES

To learn more about the kiddie tax. If you'd like more information about how the kiddie tax works and instructions for completing the necessary tax documentation, take a look at IRS Publication 929, *Tax Rules for Children and Dependents,* available at www.irs.gov.

Who qualifies to open a custodial account?
Anybody can open a custodial account for a child. There are no income limitations and no age restrictions. You can even open up a custodial account for someone else's child—for example, you might choose to open a custodial account for your niece or nephew.

How much can I contribute to my child's custodial account?
The beauty of a custodial account is that there is no limit to how much you can contribute. You can open a custodial account with as little as a dollar or as much as a million dollars—it's completely up to you. Don't forget, however, that the gift tax rules will apply.

Can I ever obtain a refund of my investment?
No. Once you put money into a custodial account, you cannot take it back under any circumstances—even a family financial emergency. The money belongs to your child.

Can anyone else contribute to my child's custodial account?
Yes. Friends and family members can send a check—with the account number—to the financial institution.

What types of expenses can be paid for using the money in my child's custodial account?
There are two main rules when it comes to how the custodian can spend the money in your child's account:

- The custodian cannot use the funds to pay for basic living expenses, such as housing and food. As your child's parent, you have a legal obligation to provide for your child's basic needs. The custodian therefore cannot use the money in your child's account to pay for your family's grocery bill or cover the cost of a new addition to your family's home.

- The custodian must spend the money in a prudent fashion. For example, the custodian cannot use the funds to install an Olympic-sized swimming pool in the basement of your home (unless the child is training for the U.S. Olympic swim team).

Other than these rules, the custodian may generally spend the money on almost anything that would benefit your child. For example, the custodian may use the funds in your child's custodial account to cover private school tuition, figure skating lessons, or summer camp in Europe.

Will the money in my child's custodial account affect my child's ability to qualify for financial aid?
Yes. The money legally belongs to your child (rather than to you). For this reason, custodial account funds will have a serious impact on your child's financial aid eligibility.

If you are worried about financial aid impact, spend the money before your child is ready for college. If Grandma opens up a custodial account for your child, then your best bet is to use the money for other expenses—such as tutoring or tennis lessons. This way, the money won't stand in the way of a good financial aid package at college time.

What if my child doesn't need the money in the account for educational expenses?
One of the great advantages of a custodial account is that the money does not have to be spent on educational expenses for your child. So if your child attends public high school and wins a basketball scholarship to the University of North Carolina, the custodian can spend the money on other things—such as travel and hobbies—for your child's benefit.

What if I grow unhappy with my child's custodial account and want to switch plans?
Your best option is to transfer the funds to a 529 college savings plan, most of which now accept cash rollovers from custodial accounts. If you switch the money to a 529 college savings plan, your child will enjoy tax-free earnings and more favorable financial aid

treatment of the funds in the account in exchange for much stricter limitations on how and when the money may be used.

Some of the original restrictions of a custodial account will still apply. Even if you transfer the assets in your child's custodial account to a 529 college savings plan, you cannot obtain a refund of your original investment or use the money for the benefit of another one of your children.

Where can I get more information about custodial accounts?
You'll find detailed information at www .fairmark.com, the website of Fairmark Press, publisher of books on taxes and investing.

How do I set up a custodial account for my child?
Although you can establish a custodial account at any bank or brokerage house, you must do more than simply title the account in your child's name. Rather, you must use special wording, such as "Samantha Miller as Custodian for Michelle Miller Under the Connecticut Uniform Transfers to Minors Act." Be sure to ask the bank or brokerage company about the correct wording to use in your state when you open the account.

Roth IRAs

Although a Roth IRA is a retirement vehicle—not an education savings plan—it is worth consideration because the Roth IRA offers you the option of using your retirement savings to cover your child's higher education expenses. This makes Roth IRAs a particularly good choice for families that don't have enough money to fully fund both a retirement savings account and an education savings account—but that want to have the freedom to contribute to their child's higher education expenses down the line if possible.

What is a Roth IRA and how does it work? A Roth IRA is a retirement savings account that you fund with after-tax dollars. Although you get no immediate tax deduction for your Roth IRA contribution (as you would with a traditional IRA), you will not pay taxes on earnings if you withdraw the money after you've reached age 59½ and if you've had the money invested in the Roth IRA for at least five years. If you withdraw the money before then, however, you will owe ordinary income taxes and 10% penalty on your earnings, unless one of a number of different exceptions applies.

One of these exceptions allows you to withdraw the money in your Roth IRA at any time to pay for qualifying higher education expenses for yourself, your spouse, or your child. Although you will still owe ordinary income taxes on your investment earnings, you won't have to pay the 10% penalty.

TIPS

No penalty for first time home-owners, either. Roth IRAs also allow you to withdraw $10,000 without penalty to pay for a first home purchase ($20,000 if both spouses are buying a home for the first time).

TIPS

Roth IRAs work wonders for older parents. If you are in your early 40s by the time your child arrives, a Roth IRA is a terrific choice because you will be 59½ when your child is ready for college. This means that you'll be able to use the money in your account to pay for your child's college tuition bills without paying any taxes on your investment earnings.

You might still be wondering why we are even mentioning Roth IRAs in a chapter on education savings plans. Let's consider an example to see why a Roth IRA might be the right choice for some families:

EXAMPLE: *Richard and his wife, Genevieve, have about $8,000 available to save each year. They have a son, Emmanuel. A financial planner advises them to invest for their retirement before saving for Emmanuel's education.*

Both Richard and Genevieve hope to be able to contribute to Emmanuel's college tuition bills down the line, but they also want to ensure that they won't be financially dependent on Emmanuel (or penniless) when they are old and gray. They decide to invest their money in Roth IRAs.

By choosing Roth IRAs, Richard and Genevieve know that their investment earnings will be tax free if they withdraw the money after age 59-1/2. They also know that they will be able to use the money to pay for Emmanuel's education without suffering any financial penalties if they are in a position to do so when the time comes.

What are the advantages of using a Roth IRA to save for my child's education?

Even though Congress did not design Roth IRAs to serve as education savings plans, there are a couple of benefits to saving for your child's education this way:

- **Two birds with one stone.** You can save for retirement and your child's education at the same time. When you're struggling with the day-to-day costs of raising a family, you might not have enough money to invest in both a retirement plan and an education savings plan. A Roth IRA is a two-in-one savings vehicle, allowing you to use the money for either retirement or your child's education—depending on your priorities at the time.
- **Tax free earnings.** Your investment earnings will be tax free if you withdraw the money after you've hit age 59-1/2.
- **Access to the money.** Although you might have to deal with taxes on your earnings and a modest penalty, you can use the money in your Roth IRA for just about any reason. This means that you can tap into your Roth IRA if money ever becomes tight.
- **Investment control.** You're in the driver's seat when it comes to investment decisions. If you're a hands-on investor, then you'll like the complete control that comes with a Roth IRA.

What are the disadvantages?

As with other education savings options, a Roth IRA is certainly not the best choice for every family. Consider these disadvantages:

- **Potential tax liability.** Your investment earnings won't be tax free if you withdraw the money before you turn 59-1/2. With other education savings plans, however, the investment earnings will always be tax free provided you use the money to pay for your child's educational expenses.
- **Penalties for private school.** You can only use the Roth IRA money for higher education expenses. If you want to use the money in your Roth IRA to pay for private elementary and secondary school tuition bills, then you'll have to

fork over a 10% penalty on your earnings—in addition to ordinary taxes on the earnings.

- **Contribution limits.** Each parent can contribute only $4,000 per year. The Roth IRA contribution limits are per parent, not per child. Families with more than one child might need to set up another education savings plan in addition to their Roth IRAs to ensure that they can save enough for their children's educations.

Who qualifies to invest in a Roth IRA? You can contribute to a Roth IRA provided your modified adjusted gross income is within certain limits. For the 2005 tax year, these limits were: $110,000 for single individuals, $160,000 for married couples filing jointly, and $10,000 for married individuals filing separately.

How much can I contribute to my Roth IRA? The maximum you can contribute each year is the lesser of your earned income for the year or $4,000 for the 2005 tax year. The maximum contribution changes slightly from year to year. Moreover, the contribution limits are a little higher ($4,500 in 2005) if you are older than 50.

CAUTION

Lower contribution limits apply to higher income earners. The maximum contribution gets smaller if you are within the ballpark of the Roth IRA income limits. In 2004, for example, the maximum contribution was lowered for married couples filing jointly with an adjusted gross income of between $150,000 and $160,000. To see how the reduction works, check IRS Publication 590, *Individual Retirement Arrangements,* available free at www.irs.gov.

TIPS

If you are a stay-at-home parent. You'll be pleased to know that your spouse can contribute to a spousal Roth IRA on your behalf even if you have no earned income. The only requirement is that your spouse meets the eligibility qualifications for a Roth IRA.

What types of education expenses can I use my Roth IRA for?

You can use the money in your Roth IRA to pay for virtually all college and graduate school expenses—including tuition, room and board, and books—for yourself, your spouse, your child, your grandchild, or your spouse's child or grandchild. The only real requirement is that the school your child selects be authorized to disburse financial aid (check the U.S. Department of Education's federal financial aid website www.fafsa.ed.gov for a list of eligible schools).

What happens if I withdraw the money for some other purpose?

You can withdraw money from your Roth IRA at any time and for any reason. However, you will owe ordinary taxes—rather than the lower capital gains taxes—on your earnings if you have not yet reached age 59½. You will also owe a 10% penalty on your earnings unless one of the various exceptions to the penalty applies. You will not, however, owe any taxes or penalties on your original contributions. To learn the details of the early withdrawal rules governing Roth IRAs, check IRS Publication 590, *Individual Retirement Arrangements*, available free at www.irs.gov.

Will the money in a Roth IRA affect my child's ability to qualify for financial aid?

Because a Roth IRA belongs to you—and not to your child—the money will have a minimal impact on your child's financial aid eligibility.

How do I set up a Roth IRA?

You can set up a Roth IRA at just about any bank, brokerage firm, or mutual fund company. Once you've opened and funded your account, you will be able to invest the money in your Roth IRA however you'd like—but you will be limited to the choices offered by your financial institution. For this reason, make sure that you're happy with the investment options provided by the financial institution you select. Check the fees—such as annual maintenance or account management fees—before setting up your account.

State Tax Breaks for 529 Plan Contributions

STATE	Tax deduction or tax credit?
Alabama	No.
Alaska	N/A (Alaska has no personal income tax.)
Arizona	No.
Arkansas	Yes. Check http://thegiftplan.uii.upromise.com for more details.
California	No.
Colorado	Yes. Contributions (except rollover contributions) are fully deductible for Colorado income tax purposes. Check www.collegeinvest.org for more details.
Connecticut	No.
Delaware	No.
District of Columbia	Yes. Check www.dccollegesavings.com for more details.
Florida	Not applicable. (Florida has no personal income tax.)
Georgia	Yes. Check www.gacollegesavings.com for more details.
Hawaii	No.
Idaho	Yes. Check www.idsaves.org for more details.
Illinois	Yes. Check www.brightstartsavings.com for more details.
Indiana	No.
Iowa	Yes. Check www.collegesavingsiowa.com for more details.
Kansas	Yes. Check www.learningquest.com for more details.
Kentucky	No.
Louisiana	Yes. Check www.startsaving.la.gov for more details.
Maine	No.
Maryland	Yes. Check www.collegesavingsmd.org for more details.
Mass.	No.
Michigan	Yes. Check www.misaves.com for more details.
Minnesota	No.
Mississippi	Yes. Check www.collegesavingsms.com for more details.

State Tax Breaks for 529 Plan Contributions

STATE	Tax deduction or tax credit?
Missouri	Yes. Check www.missourimost.org for more details.
Montana	Yes. Check www.montana.collegesavings.com for more details.
Nebraska	Yes. Check www.planforcollegenow.com for more details.
Nevada	N/A (Nevada has no personal income tax.)
New Hampshire	No.
New Jersey	No.
New Mexico	Yes. Check www.tepnm.com for more details.
New York	Yes. Check www.nysaves.org for more details.
North Carolina	No.
North Dakota	No.
Ohio	Yes. Check www.collegeadvantage.com for more details.
Oklahoma	Yes. Check www.okforsaving.org for more details.
Oregon	Yes. Check www.oregoncollegesavings.com for more details.
Pennsylvania	No.
Rhode Island	Yes. Check www.collegeboundfund.com for more details.
South Carolina	Yes. Check www.scgrad.org for more details.
South Dakota	N/A (South Dakota has no personal income tax.)
Tennessee	Yes. Check www.tnbest.com for more details.
Texas	N/A (Texas has no personal income tax.)
Utah	Yes. Check www.uesp.org for more details.
Vermont	Yes. Check www.vsac.org for more details.
Virginia	Yes. Check www.virginia529.com for more details.
Washington	N/A (Washington has no personal income tax.)
West Virginia	Yes. Check www.smart529.com for more details.
Wisconsin	Yes. Check www.edvest.com for more details.
Wyoming	N/A (Wyoming has no personal income tax.) ∎

Chapter 27
Education Rewards Programs

Believe it or not, education rewards programs allow you to earn free—or almost free—money for your child's education savings plan through your everyday purchases. These programs work much like airline frequent flyer accounts: The more you spend on affiliated products or credit cards, the more money you earn for your child's education. Many of the best education rewards programs have no annual fee, so there's simply no excuse not to enroll.

Although each program has its own rules, the basic structure is the same for them all: You receive small cash-back awards on your everyday food, clothing, travel, and other purchases. Some education rewards programs require you to use a special credit card in order to earn rewards; others, such as BabyMint (www.babymint.com) and the BabyCenter Savings Program (www.babycentersavings.com), offer you your choice of using a special credit card or shopping online at a variety of merchants by first clicking through their website. Although the reward for each individual purchase is usually quite small, the savings can add up over time and put quite a dent in your child's college savings account.

Of the various education rewards programs, UPromise at www.upromise.com is the easiest. All you have to do is register all of your various credit cards, debit cards, grocery cards, and drugstore cards with UPromise, which will take care of tracking your purchases and crediting your UPromise account with cash-back rewards when you buy eligible products or shop at eligible merchants. You can even opt to have your cash back-rewards deposited directly into your child's 529 college savings plan.

 TIPS

Grandma and Grandpa can sign up as well. What's particularly terrific about UPromise—as well as some other education rewards programs—is that friends and family members can also join. This means that every time Grandma makes a trip to the drugstore, a little more money will go into your child's education savings account.

Beware of racking up credit card debt. Even if you sign up for a no-fee credit card that offers very generous credit card rewards, it's never smart to charge more than you can pay off in full each month. Be sure to check the interest rates on your credit cards and pay attention to the due dates for your monthly payments. Otherwise, you'll pay more in credit card interest than you'll earn in rewards—hardly a smart investment.

If you want more options. You can find a much longer list of education rewards programs as well as a description of how each program works at www.finaid.org (search for "credit card rebate and loyalty programs"). ■

6. The Dependent Exemption, Child Care Tax Breaks, and Other Baby Gifts From the IRS

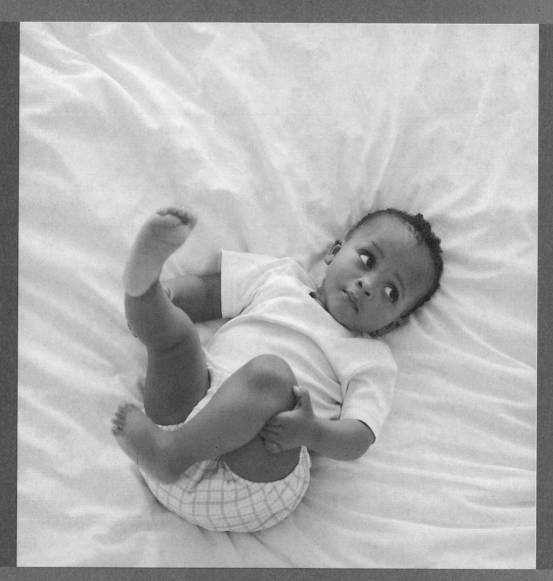

Contents

*N*ew parents often find themselves overwhelmed by the expenses that come with a baby: From nursery furnishings to Onesies to diapers, your little bundle of joy is going to cost you, well, a bundle. Fortunately, the federal government offers a number of tax breaks to offset the cost of raising a child. Although these tax rules can be confusing, it's definitely worth the effort to understand them, because every dollar you don't have to pay to the Internal Revenue Service is a dollar you can spend on your child.

The chapters that follow explain the federal tax breaks available to parents, including information on how the particular tax break could affect your bottom line, how to determine whether you qualify for the tax break, and how to claim it on your tax return.

Finding Your Adjusted Gross Income

As you read through the chapters in this part of the book, you'll see that many tax breaks either phase out or become inapplicable once your income hits a certain number—usually your adjusted gross income (AGI). Your AGI consists of your total annual income minus certain deductions, such as deductible IRA contributions and the tuition and fees deduction. On Form 1040 (if you itemize your deductions), your AGI appears on line 36. On Form 1040A (if you don't itemize deductions), your AGI appears on line 21.

Each tax break described in the chapters that follow has a set of requirements that you must meet to benefit from it—for example, your income must be below a certain amount or your child must live with you for a certain number of months in the year. Look carefully at the eligibility requirements before taking a tax break discussed in this book.

If you and your child's other parent are divorced or separated, only one of you can claim the dependent exemption and most of other child-related tax breaks discussed in this part of the book. Normally, the parent with whom the child resides for more than half the year claims these tax breaks. But it sometimes makes more financial sense for the noncustodial parent to claim these tax breaks instead. Many divorced parents also alternate the tax breaks, with each parent claiming the tax breaks every other year. See a tax professional for more help on this issue.

ADDITIONAL RESOURCES

The IRS website is a great resource. As you read through the chapters that follow, you'll notice references to specific IRS forms, such as the 1040 tax return form, and publications, such as IRS Publication 503, *Child and Dependent Care Expenses.* You can download these for free from www.irs.gov. In addition, you can find a wealth of helpful and (relatively) easy-to-understand tax information on the IRS website. If you still have questions, you can speak to an IRS representative (at no charge) at 800-829-1040. You can also stop by your local IRS office to have your questions answered in person. To find the IRS office nearest you, go to www.irs.gov and click on the link entitled "Individuals" and then click on the link marked "Contact My Local Office."

CAUTION

Don't forget about state tax breaks. The chapters that follow focus on federal tax rules, but you may also be eligible for state tax breaks. Check with either a tax professional or your state's department of taxation for more information. To find your state tax agency, see Yahoo's Finance Tax Center at http://taxes.yahoo.com/stateforms.html.

CAUTION

Stay on top of the ever-changing tax code. Because the tax laws often change from year to year, we strongly recommend that you check with a tax professional or log on to the IRS website for up-to-the-minute tax information before claiming any of the tax breaks discussed in this book. ■

Chapter 28

Tax Breaks for (Almost) All Parents

Although you can't write off the cost of diapers or infant formula on your income tax return, the federal government does offer two money-saving tax breaks to ease the financial burden of caring for your child: the dependent exemption and the child tax credit. The dependent exemption allows qualified parents to deduct a set amount of taxable income for each child ($3,200 per child in 2005). Even better is the child tax credit, which allows qualified parents to subtract a set amount from their total tax bill for each child ($1,000 per child in 2005). To find out whether you qualify for these tax breaks, read the sections below. Both of these tax breaks are available regardless of whether you itemize your tax deductions.

What's the Difference Between Deductions and Credits? A Whole Lot

It's important to understand the difference between tax deductions and tax credits when trying to make sense out of the tax breaks available to parents.

A tax deduction is a dollar-for-dollar reduction of your taxable income. For example, if you are entitled to a $2,000 tax deduction and you have a gross income of $42,000, you would only have to pay income taxes on the first $40,000 of your income (assuming no other deductions apply). In essence, a tax deduction entitles you to pay for something with before-tax dollars, rather than after-tax dollars.

As useful as tax deductions are, tax credits are even better, because they represent a dollar-for-dollar reduction of your overall tax bill. For example, if you are entitled to a tax credit of $1,000, you can subtract $1,000 from the taxes you owe for the year. To put it simply, every dollar in the form of a tax credit means a full dollar in your pocket.

Best of all is a refundable tax credit. If you have overpaid your taxes, you can add the amount of your refundable tax credit to your refund amount. You can even get a refund if you owed no taxes for the year.

The Dependent Exemption

The IRS does not tax every single dollar of your income. Instead, it gives you a very modest tax exemption ($3,200 per person in 2005) to cover your basic living expenses. You can take one exemption for yourself, your spouse, and each of your children. A family of four, for example, could qualify for more than $12,000 in tax exemptions under this rule.

When you add a new child to your family, you can add one more exemption. This means that you get an additional tax deduction of more than $3,000—a nice baby gift from Uncle Sam!

 FAST FACTS

The exemption amount goes up each year. Because the dependent exemption is pegged to the inflation index, the exact amount of the deduction increases slightly from year to year. In 2004, for example, the dependent exemption was $3,100; in 2005, the exemption increased to $3,200.

How will the dependent exemption affect my bottom line?

In terms of actual tax savings, the amount you'll save with the dependent exemption depends on your tax bracket. The higher your tax bracket, the more savings you get—unless your income is so high that you cannot claim the exemption at all (see below for more about how your income affects your ability to claim the dependent exemption). For example, if you are in the 10% tax bracket, you would save about $320 per child with the dependent exemption in 2005. But if you are in the 25% tax bracket, the dependent exemption would save you $800 per child.

☑ CHECKLIST

Are You Eligible for the Dependent Exemption?

Here are the requirements you—and your child—must meet for you to claim the dependent exemption:

❑ your child must be your biological, step, adopted, or foster child (if the child is not, but you support the child nonetheless, additional requirements apply—see below)

❑ your child must live with you for more than half the year (unless an exception applies)

❑ your child must be younger than 19 (unless an exception applies)

❑ your child must be a United States citizen or a resident of the United States, Canada, or Mexico, and

❑ your income must be within the limits set by the tax code.

How young must my child be for me to claim a dependent exemption?

Generally speaking, your child must be younger than 19. There are some exceptions to this rule, however. You can still claim the dependent exemption for an older child if your child is a full-time student younger than 24 or your child is permanently and totally disabled. But if your child marries and files a joint return with his or her spouse, you will generally no longer be able to claim an exemption for your older child.

CAUTION

If your parents can claim the exemption for you. Your parents may still be supporting you, even though you're now a parent yourself. If your parents claim you as a dependent on their tax return, you cannot claim the dependent exemption for your child.

My child has been placed with me for adoption, but the adoption is not yet final. Can I still claim the dependent exemption?

Yes—placement is sufficient, as long as you meet all of the other requirements, such as your child lives with you for more than half the year (see "Are You Eligible for the Dependent Exemption?" above).

I live with my girlfriend, who has a seven-year-old daughter. Can I claim the dependent exemption?

Yes, but different rules apply because your girlfriend's daughter is not legally your child. To claim the dependent exemption, you must meet the following additional requirements:

- the child must live with you for the entire year

- you must provide more than half of the total support for the child for the year, and

- no one else (for example, the child's mother or father) claims the child as a dependent for the tax year.

My daughter is away at boarding school nine months out of the year. Can I still claim the exemption?

Yes. If your child spends time away from home to attend school or travel on vacation, that time will be considered time living at home because you are still supporting your child.

My child was born in October. Can I still claim the exemption for her for this year?

Yes. The birth of a child late in the year is an exception to the rule that the child live with you for more than half the year.

My mother left an enormous trust fund for my child, and that is the money we use to pay most of her expenses. Can we still claim the exemption?

Probably not. If a child can provide more than half of his or her own support through, say, a trust fund or modeling jobs, the parents don't get the benefit of the exemption.

Together, my spouse and I earn more than $225,000 per year. Can we still claim the dependent exemption?

You can probably claim some, but not all, of it. Here's why. As is the case with many of the best tax breaks available, the dependent exemption is phased out for higher earning families. When your adjusted gross income exceeds certain specified limits, the amount of the dependent exemption is reduced proportionately to your income. For the 2004 tax year, for example, married couples filing jointly began losing a portion of their dependent exemption when their adjusted gross income exceeded $214,050, and they lost it completely when their adjusted gross income exceeded $336,550.

How do I claim the dependent exemption?
If you qualify for the exemption, you do not have to file any additional tax forms to claim it. Simply complete line 6c of Form 1040 or Form 1040A, making sure to provide a Social Security number in column 2. (You'll need to provide an Adoption Taxpayer Identification Number if your child's adoption is pending, as explained in Chapter 32.) Also be certain to complete line 41 of Form 1040 or line 26 of Form 1040A. (These lines total up your exemptions.)

FAST FACTS

Changes on the way for high income families. If you do not qualify for the dependent exemption because of your income, you'll be happy to know that the IRS is phasing out the phase-out (how's that for a tongue twister?) beginning in the year 2006. By 2010, all parents will be able to claim the dependent exemption regardless of their income levels (unless the rules change again between now and then, of course).

ADDITIONAL RESOURCES

To learn more about the dependent exemption. IRS Publication 501, *Exemptions, Standard Deduction, and Filing Information,* provides detailed information on the qualification requirements for the dependent exemption—including the income limits and phase-out rules. Another useful resource is IRS Publication 553, *Highlights of the 2004 Tax Changes Revised,* which, despite its title, outlines the 2005 changes to the dependent exemption rules. Download both for free at www.irs.gov.

Although many people think that the best tax breaks are reserved for the wealthy, the earned income credit is a very valuable tax break that only low-income families can use.

If you qualify, you'll get a tax credit of approximately $2,600 to $4,300, depending on the number of children in your family and your filing status. In the 2004 tax year, a family with two children could have saved more than $4,000 with this credit.

Here are two threshold requirements for the credit:

- you must have a low income (for the 2004 tax year, the adjusted gross income of married couples with one child who filed their tax returns jointly could not exceed $31,338; the adjusted gross income of a single parent with only one child could not exceed $30,338), and
- some of your income must be wages from a job (for example, if all of your income comes from investments and you don't work, you don't qualify for this credit).

If you meet these threshold criteria, check IRS Publication 596, *Earned Income Credit,* for details on the other eligibility requirements, information on how to complete the earned income credit worksheet, and help on claiming the earned income credit on your tax return.

The Child Tax Credit

The child tax credit shaves $1,000 per child off your tax bill. Because it is a credit, and not a deduction, that is $1,000 back in your pocket—so it is a very important tax break.

Can I take both the child tax credit and the dependent exemption?

Yes. If you are eligible for both, then you can take both.

How do I know if I am eligible for the child tax credit?

The eligibility requirements are essentially the same as those for the dependent exemption, with two notable exceptions: Your child must be younger than the age for the dependent exemption (17 rather than 19), and your income must be lower than for the dependent exemption (see below for information about how your earnings affect your ability to take the child tax credit). All of the other rules—for example, that your child live with you for more than half the year—are the same.

What are the income limits for the child tax credit?

The child tax credit has much lower income limits than the dependent exemption. For the 2004 tax year, for example, married couples filing jointly began to lose the child tax credit once their adjusted gross income exceeded $110,000, and they could not claim any part of the child tax credit once their adjusted gross income exceeded $130,000.

How do I claim the child tax credit?

Determine the amount of the child tax credit you can claim by completing the child tax credit worksheet contained in IRS Publication 972, *Child Tax Credit*. (You can find this worksheet in the instructions for completing Form 1040 or Form 1040A.) Then enter this number on line 51 of Form 1040 or line 33 of Form 1040A. Complete line 6c of Form 1040 or Form 1040A and provide a Social Security number for each child. (You'll need to provide an Adoption Taxpayer Identification Number if your child's adoption is pending, as explained in Chapter 32.) Be certain to check the box in column 4 of line 6c for each child for whom you are claiming the child tax credit.

If you are owed a tax refund, you may be able to add on a portion of your child tax credit to your refund check—this is known as the additional child tax credit. To claim the additional child tax credit, complete Form 8812, *Additional Child Tax Credit,* and attach it to Form 1040 or Form 1040A. Also complete line 67 of Form 1040 or line 42 of Form 1040A.

ADDITIONAL
RESOURCES

To learn more about the child tax credit. IRS Publication 972, *Child Tax Credit,* provides detailed instructions and examples. Another useful resource is IRS Publication 553, *Highlights of 2004 Tax Changes Revised,* which outlines the 2005 changes to the child tax credit eligibility rules. ■

Chapter 29

Child Care Tax Breaks

Given the price of good child care these days, you'll be relieved to learn that the federal government offers two tax breaks to help offset the cost: the child care credit and dependent care accounts.

General Information About Child Care Tax Breaks

This section provides some basic information common to both the child care credit and dependent care accounts. Subsequent sections provide more specific information about each type of tax break.

How do I know if I am eligible for the child care tax breaks?

You and your child must meet the following requirements for you to be eligible for the child care credit or dependent care accounts:

* your child must be your biological, adopted, step, or foster child (if your child has been placed with your for adoption, he or she still qualifies, even though the adoption is not yet final)

☑ CHECKLIST

Are You Eligible for Child Care Tax Breaks?

In order to claim either one of the child care tax breaks, you, your child, and your child care provider must meet the following requirements:

❑ your child must be your biological, adopted, step, or foster child
❑ your child must live with you for more than half the year
❑ your child must be younger than 13 or permanently and totally disabled
❑ you must pay more than half the cost of keeping up a home in which you and your child live during the year
❑ you (and your spouse, if you are married) must work outside the home (full or part time) or be a full-time student
❑ your child care provider must be a licensed day care provider, preschool, or on-the-books nanny
❑ you must have used the child care to enable you to work, look for work, or attend school full time, and
❑ the payments must have been for child care only, not other household services.

- your child must live with you for more than half the year (time away from home at school or traveling counts)
- your child must be younger than 13 or permanently and totally disabled
- you must pay more than half the cost of keeping up a home in which you and your child live during the year (if your child has a trust fund or other income, he or she cannot provide more than half the support), and
- you (and your spouse, if you are married) must work outside the home or be a full-time student.

If you're not sure whether you pay more than half the cost of keeping up your home, check IRS Publication 503, *Child and Dependent Care Expenses.*

What types of child care expenses qualify for the child care tax breaks?

To qualify, child care expenses must meet all of the following criteria:

- your child care provider must be a licensed day care provider, preschool, or on-the-books nanny
- you must have used the child care to enable you to work, look for work, or attend school full time (for example, you cannot claim a credit for the costs of your Saturday night babysitter), and
- the payments must have been for child care only, not other household services (such as housekeeping).

 CAUTION

No credit after preschool. Educational expenses from the first grade onward—such as private school tuition—are not eligible for the child care tax breaks.

 TIPS

If you are a single parent. Single parents qualify for these tax breaks as long as they are working outside the home or are in school full time even if the child's other parent is not.

I'm a stay-at-home mom, but I still use a babysitter several times a week so that I can run errands. Do either of the child care tax breaks cover this type of arrangement?

No. There are no child care tax breaks available to stay-at-home parents who rely on a nanny or babysitter to help ease their loads. Only working parents or full-time students can claim these breaks.

I pay my nanny under the table. Am I eligible for either of the child care tax breaks?

No. In fact, if you pay your nanny under the table but nonetheless claim these tax breaks, you will wave a red flag at the IRS—and risk being penalized for your arrangement.

My child's home-based day care program is not licensed, and I know that my child's caregiver does not report her income for tax purposes. Can I claim either of the child care tax breaks?

Probably not. Although you aren't doing anything illegal by using the center, your caregiver is. You can only claim the child care tax breaks if you provide the IRS with the caregiver's Social Security number—something your caregiver will not wish to give you if she doesn't pay income taxes on her profits.

My child's family day care center is licensed. What information do I need to claim either of the child care tax breaks?

Ask for a completed Form W-10, *Dependent Care Provider's Identification and Certification.* This form lists the caregiver's Social Security number or the program's tax identification number, which you will need come tax time.

I'm eligible for both the child care credit and a dependent care account. Can I use both?

Yes. However, the money you contribute to your dependent care account will be subtracted from the maximum amount of child care expenses you can claim under the child care credit.

> **EXAMPLE:** *Josh and his wife, Rebecca, have one child, and together they earned more than $100,000 in 2004. The couple contributed $2,000 to Rebecca's dependent care account for that year. If Josh and Rebecca hadn't made any contributions to a dependent care account, they could have claimed a child care credit of 20% of the first $3,000 they spent on child care expenses that year (or $600). But because they contributed $2,000 to their dependent care account, they could only claim a child care credit based on $1,000 of expenses ($3,000 maximum expenses eligible for child care credit minus the $2,000 contribution to the dependent care account)—amounting to a child care credit of only $200.*

Which one should I choose—the child care credit or a dependent care account?

The answer depends on your tax bracket. A good rule of thumb is to opt for an employer-sponsored dependent care account if you are in the 28% bracket or higher. If you're still not sure, you might want to ask a tax professional to run the numbers for you and tell you which is best.

The Child Care Credit

If you qualify, the child care credit could trim more than $1,000 from your federal income tax bill for the child care costs you incur during the year. What's especially nice about the child care credit is that you won't have to do a thing until tax time except hang on to your child care receipts. When you file your tax return, simply tell the federal government how much you paid in child care bills and to whom—and your tax bill will be discounted appropriately.

How will the child care credit affect my bottom line?

The child care credit provides a tax credit of 20% to 35% of the first $3,000 in child care costs you incur per child per year. Your income level determines what percentage of child care costs you can claim as a tax credit. In the 2004 tax year, for example, you could have claimed a tax credit of 30% of the first $3,000 in child care expenses you incurred (or $900) if your adjusted gross income was $24,000 and you had only one child. If your adjusted gross income exceeded $43,000, however, then you could have

claimed a credit of only 20% of the first $3,000 in child care expenses you incurred (or $600).

Notably, the total amount of your child care credit cannot exceed your earned income for the year or your spouse's earned income for the year. (This requirement may be waived if you or your spouse suffers from severe physical or mental limitations that interfere with the ability to work or study.)

EXAMPLE: *Quinn and his wife, Amelia, hired Margaret to take care of their two children on a part-time basis. In total, Margaret earned $10,000 in 2004. Quinn worked as an advertising executive and earned $80,000 that year. Amelia spent most of the year working on her novel and ended up earning only $900 in the entire year. Quinn and Amelia calculated their child care credit as follows: Because Margaret took care of two children, Quinn and Amelia could claim a child care credit based on their first $6,000 of child care expenses. The couple could write off a maximum of 20% of that amount because of their income level. This amounted to $1,200 ($6,000 x 20%). However, because Amelia earned only $900 in the year, the couple could claim only a $900 child care credit on $10,000 worth of out-of-pocket child care expenses.*

How do I claim the child care credit?
Complete Parts I and II of IRS Form 2441, *Child and Dependent Care Expenses,* (if you are using IRS Form 1040) or Parts I and II of Schedule 2 of IRS Form 1040A.) Include the amount from line 11 of IRS Form 2441 on line 47 of IRS Form 1040, or the amount from line 11 of Schedule 2 of IRS Form 1040A on line 29 of IRS Form 1040A.

You will need to provide the IRS with the name, address, and Social Security number or employer identification number of your child care provider, as well as the exact amount paid to your child care provider, in item 1 of either IRS Form 2441 or Schedule 2 of IRS Form 1040A. You do not have to provide an employer identification number if your child care provider is a tax-exempt organization, such as a church or school. In that case, simply write in the words "tax exempt" under column (c) of item 1.

Dependent Care Accounts

A dependent care account is like the 401(k) plan of the child care world: Through your employer (and only through your employer—you can't set one up on your own), you set aside pretax dollars that you can access to pay your nanny, day care, or preschool bills during the year. Setting up a dependent care account does involve some advance planning and administrative hassles during the year. But the trouble is worth your while because a dependent care account can mean sizable tax savings if you're in one of the top tax brackets.

Not all employers offer dependent care accounts. If you work for a small employer, or you are self-employed, you probably do not have the option of contributing to a dependent care account. In that case, you should make sure to claim the child care tax credit if you qualify.

EXAMPLE: *Ellen contributed $5,000 to her dependent care account to cover child care expenses for her son, Duncan. Ellen and her husband, Jim, spent $8,000 on after-school day care for Duncan. Ellen's husband, Jim, was laid off in the beginning of the year. He earned only $3,000 in total for the year. Even though the couple incurred $8,000 worth of child care expenses and contributed $5,000 to Ellen's dependent care account, Ellen could only claim a dependent care account tax deduction of $3,000, the amount that Jim earned.*

How will a dependent care account affect my bottom line?

All of the money you contribute to your dependent care account will be exempt from federal taxes. Your savings will depend on your tax bracket and the amount your employer lets you contribute to your dependent care account. For example, if you are in the 25% tax bracket and you contribute $4,000 to your dependent care account, you will save $1,000 in federal income taxes. You'll also save on other federal taxes, such as Medicare and Social Security. And you may even save on state and local income taxes, depending on your state's rules.

You'll only be able to fully benefit from a dependent care account if both you and your spouse work outside the home. This is because the amount of your dependent care tax deduction will be limited to your earned income or your spouse's earned income for the year, whichever is lower.

If either you or your spouse is a full-time student, you can still pay for up to $250 of your child care expenses ($500 if you have more than one child) using pretax dollars through a dependent care account.

How much can I contribute to a dependent care account?

Regardless of the number of children they have, married people filing jointly can contribute a maximum of $5,000 to a dependent care account, and single people or married people filing separately can contribute a maximum of $2,500.

Not all employers allow you to contribute the maximum amount. Your employer might set a lower maximum (say $2,000). This is legal, and it is binding on you.

How do I enroll in a dependent care account?

If your employer sponsors a dependent care account, you'll have the opportunity to enroll during your general benefits enrollment period.

TIPS

Keep on top of enrollment deadlines. Depending on your company's policies, you may need to re-enroll in a dependent care account every year. Make sure to get your forms in on time to benefit from the program.

How do I access the money in my dependent care account to pay for my child care expenses?

After you spend money on child care, you complete a form and present a receipt to your benefits administrator, who will reimburse you. Consult your employee benefits manual or check with your human resources administrator for more information on your company's reimbursement policy.

What happens if I don't spend all of the money in my dependent care account by the end of the year?

If you don't spend all the money in your account by the end of the year, you'll forfeit it to your employer.

How do I claim the dependent care tax deduction?

Complete Parts I and III of IRS Form 2441 (if you are using IRS Form 1040 to file your annual tax return) or Parts I and III of Schedule 2 of IRS Form 1040A. Include the amount from line 23 of Form 2441 on line 47 of Form 1040, or the amount from line 20 on Schedule 2 of Form 1040A on line 29 of Form 1040A.

CAUTION

Look before you leap. Because you'll forfeit the money if you don't use it, make sure that your child care qualifies before putting the money in the dependent care account.

TIPS

Learn more about dependent care accounts. The best source of information on your employer-provided dependent care account is your employee benefit manual or other publication provided by your human resources department. To learn more about how to claim the dependent care account tax deduction, consult the instructions to IRS Form 2441 (*Child and Dependent Care Expenses*) or Schedule 2 of IRS Form 1040A. ■

Chapter 30

Health Care Tax Breaks

With the cost of health care skyrocketing, even parents with comprehensive health insurance coverage often spend a fair amount out of pocket on health care expenses, such as copayments, deductibles, and prescription drugs. Unfortunately, there aren't too many tax breaks available to trim these bills. The main option for most families is to use a flexible health spending account, which allows you to pay for health care expenses using pretax dollars. If you are self-employed or you work for a small company that offers minimal health insurance benefits, you may be eligible for a tax-advantageous health savings account. Finally, if your family's health care bills are truly enormous, then you may be among the relatively few parents who stand to benefit from the medical/dental expense deduction.

TIPS

Keep health care costs in check. Beyond the tax breaks in this chapter, you can do other things to save on your health care costs. For example, you can use in-network health care providers and ask for generic substitutes for brand-name prescription drugs whenever possible.

Flexible Health Spending Accounts

This type of account allows you to set aside pretax dollars from your paycheck to cover your family's health care costs.

How will a flexible health spending account affect my bottom line?

The savings you'll enjoy with a flexible spending account depends on your tax bracket and the amount you contribute to the account. Let's suppose you contribute $1,000 to your flexible health spending account, and you are in the 15% tax bracket. You'll save $150 in federal income taxes. You'll also save Social Security taxes, Medicare withholdings, and possibly even state income taxes on your contribution. In essence, using a flexible health spending account gives you a discount on all of your out-of-pocket health care bills.

How can I tell if I am eligible to contribute to a flexible health spending account?

If your employer offers this benefit, you are eligible to contribute.

How much can I contribute to a flexible health spending account?

The answer to this question depends on your employer's rules. Some employers limit contributions to a certain percentage of your income. Other employers have a dollar limit on contributions—for example, no more than $2,000 per year.

 TIPS

Some employers will supplement your contributions. If you're lucky, your employer might contribute money to your flexible health spending account—over and above your paycheck deductions.

What types of expenses are covered?

You can pay for just about all of your, your spouse's, and your child's medical and dental expenses using the money in your flexible health spending account. For example, you can use your contributions to cover your obstetrician's fees, the cost of your hospital delivery, and the copayment for your baby's first visit to the pediatrician. You can also pay for a wide variety of drugstore purchases, such as diaper ointment, pregnancy tests, infant pain reliever, and a cold-mist humidifier for your baby's nursery.

For a complete list of qualifying expenses, check your employee benefits manual or consult with your human resources department.

Health insurance premiums are not covered. You won't be able to use the money to pay for your health insurance premiums—even if the premiums are your largest out-of-pocket health care expense.

Don't wait until the end of the year to apply for reimbursement. You can be reimbursed for the full amount you plan to contribute to your health care spending account before you've completed your contribution. For example, suppose you spend $5,000 on fertility treatment in March and April, but you've only contributed $2,000 to your flexible health spending account by that time. As long as you're scheduled to contribute $5,000 to your flexible health spending account by the end of the year, you can be reimbursed in May for the $5,000 you spent on fertility treatment.

How do I enroll in a flexible health spending account?

You'll simply need to complete an enrollment form during your company's benefit election period. To learn the details of the enrollment process, check with your human resources department or your employee benefits manual.

How do I access the money in my account?

After you pay a medical or dental bill, complete a reimbursement form and give it and the receipt to your employer or benefits administrator, who will reimburse you.

You may also need to provide a written statement that the health care expense has not been and will not be reimbursed by your health insurance plan. Consult your employee benefits manual or check with your benefits administrator for more information on your company's reimbursement policy.

What happens if I don't spend all of the money in my flexible health spending account by the end of the year?

You forfeit it to your employer.

Plan your contributions carefully. It's better to underestimate your health care expenses than overestimate them when deciding how much to contribute to your flexible health spending account. Otherwise, you could lose your hard-earned contributions—or be forced to spend the money somewhat frivolously at year's end.

ADDITIONAL
RESOURCES

For more information on flexible spending accounts. You'll get the most information on your employer-provided flexible health spending account from your employee benefits manual or your human resources department. But another good resource is IRS Publication 969, *Health Savings Accounts and Other Tax-Favored Health Plans.*

Health Savings Accounts

If you work for a small employer or if you're self-employed, your only health insurance coverage may be a high-deductible health plan—one where you have to pay at least $1,000 (if you are single) or $2,000 (if you have a family) out of pocket before you begin receiving health insurance benefits. Fortunately, there is some tax relief designed especially for people like you. Health savings accounts allow you to sock away pre-tax dollars into an investment account to cover your out-of-pocket health care costs. The money in the account grows tax free, and you won't owe any taxes on your withdrawals provided you use the cash to pay for health care expenses.

How will a health savings account affect my bottom line?

You will get an immediate tax deduction on the amount you contribute to the account for the year. Your investment will grow free of taxes, and your withdrawals will be tax free as well.

> **EXAMPLE:** *Marvin invested $2,000 each year for three years into his health savings account. His contributions were exempt from federal taxes. Marvin's account grew by $500 each year, thanks to dividends. He did not have to pay any federal taxes on the dividends. Several years later, Marvin had a very expensive liver transplant. Marvin owed $20,000 in out-of-pocket health care costs. He withdrew all of the money in his health savings account—which had doubled in value—to cover those expenses. Marvin did*

not owe any taxes on the money he withdrew because he used the funds to pay for a qualifying health care expense.

How do I know if I am eligible to contribute to a health savings account?

You are eligible if your only health care coverage is a high-deductible plan—meaning one with an annual deductible of at least $2,000 for family coverage. If you have comprehensive group health insurance coverage through an employer-sponsored plan, you are not eligible. For detailed eligibility information, check IRS Publication 969, *Health Savings Accounts and Other Tax-Favored Health Plans.*

How much can I contribute to a health savings account?

Each year, you can contribute the smallest of the following:

- your annual health insurance deductible, or
- $2,650 for single coverage or $5,250 for family coverage.

What types of expenses does a flexible health spending account cover?

The money in the account covers just about all of your family's medical and dental expenses, including eye care.

ADDITIONAL RESOURCES

If you'd like a list of approved expenditures. The qualifying expenses are the same as those described below for the medical and dental expenses deduction. In addition, you can find a list in IRS Publication 502, *Medical and Dental Expenses.*

How do I enroll in a health savings account?

Contact a financial institution that offers this type of account.

ADDITIONAL RESOURCES

For a list of participating financial institutions. The HSA Insider provides a wealth of information about health savings accounts and how to open one. To find a financial institution, log on to www.hsainsider.com and click on the link marked "Who can open my Health Savings Account."

How do I use the money in my account to pay for a health care expense?

A health savings account works much like a regular bank or brokerage account. When you need funds for a health care expense, you can just withdraw the money directly from your account.

What happens if I don't spend all of the money in my health savings account by the end of the year?

Your contributions will accumulate from year to year, so you won't lose a penny if you don't make any withdrawals during the year.

What if I use the money in my health savings account for something other than a health care expense?

You'll owe income taxes on the funds. You may also owe a 10% penalty on your withdrawal.

How do I claim the health savings account tax break?

Complete Form 8889, *Health Savings Accounts.* To claim the deduction, enter the amount in line 11 on Form 8889 and line 28 of Form 1040. To claim a tax exemption for distributions from your health savings account, complete Part II of Form 8889.

Medical/Dental Expense Deduction

If you face unusually high medical bills, you may qualify for a (very) modest amount of tax relief. You can deduct your out-of-pocket health care expenses, but only to the extent that these expenses exceed 7.5% of your adjusted gross income. As a practical matter, most parents cannot benefit from this deduction unless they are uninsured or incur extraordinary medical bills for an unexpected health crisis.

How will the medical/dental expense deduction affect my bottom line?

You probably won't save too much, because you can deduct only expenses that exceed 7.5% of your adjusted income.

> **EXAMPLE:** *Maria had some childbirth complications that required her to remain in the hospital for nearly two weeks after her baby was born. Although Maria's insurance covered a good portion of the tab, she still spent $10,000 out of her own pocket. Her adjusted gross income for the year was $100,000. She was therefore able to deduct only $2,500 of her health care costs ($10,000 in health care bills minus 7.5% of $100,000). Because Maria was in the 28% tax bracket, this amounted to only $700 of savings on $10,000 worth of health care costs.*

How do I know if I am eligible to claim the medical/dental expense deduction?

You can claim the medical/dental expense deduction if your out-of-pocket health care costs are more than 7.5% of your adjusted gross income and you itemize your deductions.

What types of expenses qualify for the medical/dental expense deduction?

Just about all of your family's out-of-pocket medical and dental expenses—from hospital bills to birth control pills—qualify for this deduction.

I've had to pay some health care expenses for a child who I'm about to adopt, but the adoption is not yet final. Can I claim the deduction for those expenses?

Probably. If you pay for health care expenses for a soon-to-be-adopted child, you can deduct these costs so long as your child qualified as your dependent when the medical services were provided or when the expenses were paid. You can also claim the deduction for payments you make to reimburse your adoption agency for your child's health care expenses, as long as the agency paid the health care costs pursuant to an agreement with you.

> EXAMPLE: *Paul and Gabby agreed to adopt little Josephine, who required a kidney transplant before she could make the long trip to the United States from her native Uzbekistan. The couple asked the adoption agency to arrange for Josephine to have the operation and promised to repay all expenses. When Josephine's adoption was*

finalized, Paul and Gabby repaid the agency $20,000—the cost of the procedure. Josephine qualified as the couple's dependent at the time they paid this bill. Paul and Gabby could therefore deduct this expense to the extent it exceeded 7.5% of their adjusted gross income.

ADDITIONAL RESOURCES

For a complete list of qualifying health care expenses. To learn what medical/dental costs you can (and cannot) deduct, consult IRS Publication 502, *Medical and Dental Expenses.*

TIPS

If you are divorced. Both you and your child's other parent can claim this deduction for the health care costs that you pay out-of-pocket for your child, even though only one of you can claim your child as a dependent.

How do I claim the medical/dental expense deduction?

Complete items 1 through 4 of Schedule A of Form 1040, and attach Schedule A to your tax return. Include the amount of your medical/dental expense deduction as reflected on your Schedule A in the total itemized deductions you list on line 39 of Form 1040. You cannot claim the medical/dental expense deduction if you use Form 1040A. You do not have to send in any health care invoices or other proof of your health care expenses along with your tax return. However, the IRS recommends that you keep a record of the following:

- the name and address of each person/ entity to whom you paid health care expenses
- the amount and date of each payment, and
- invoices or receipts showing what health care was received, who received the care, and any other relevant details.

Having this information in your files will be critical if you are ever audited. ■

Chapter 31

Special Tax Breaks for Single Parents

The federal government recognizes it's tough for most single parents to raise a child on one income. To help, the tax code has two preferential filing statuses—head of household and qualifying widow(er) with dependent child—that enable qualifying single parents to enjoy better tax rates and higher standard deductions. If you are a single parent, you may be able to lower your tax bill—and put more money in your pocket—by using one of these filing statuses.

How will these preferential filing statuses affect my bottom line?

If you qualify to file as head of household or qualifying widow(er) with dependent child, you'll save a great deal in taxes. This is because more of your income will be taxed at lower tax rates. For example, if your filing status is single in 2005, you'll hit the 25% tax bracket once you earn more than $29,700. But if you file as head of household, you won't reach the 25% tax bracket until your income exceeds $39,800. And if you file as qualifying widow(er) with dependent child, you won't get into the 25%

tax bracket until you've earned more than $59,400.

The standard deduction—the tax deduction you automatically get if you don't itemize your deductions—is also much higher for these preferential filing statuses. For the 2005 tax year, for example, the standard deduction is $5,000 for a single person, $7,300 for head of household, and $10,000 for a qualifying widower with a dependent child.

What are the requirements for filing as head of household?

To file as head of household, you must be supporting your child on your own. This means that you must be either unmarried or, if you are married, living apart from your spouse and filing a separate tax return from your spouse. In addition, you and your child must meet the following requirements:

- your child must be your biological, adopted, step, or foster child
- your child must live with you for more than half the year (if your child is gone for school or travel, that time away doesn't count against you)
- your child cannot provide more than

half of his or her income (through a job, for example, or a trust fund)

- your child must be younger than 19 (or if older than 19, must be either a full-time student younger than 24 or permanently and totally disabled), and
- you must pay more than half the cost of keeping up a home for yourself and your child for the year.

If your spouse lives apart from you for reasons having nothing to do with the relationship—for example, your wife took a temporary job in another state but plans to return when the job is over—you cannot file as head of household.

TIPS

If your child does not meet the requirements listed above. You may still be able to file as head of household if you can claim the dependent exemption for your child. See IRS Publication 501, *Exemptions, Standard Deduction, and Filing Information.*

CAUTION

If you are a foster parent. Although foster parents are eligible to file as head of household, they often can't because of the amount of financial assistance they receive from the government and nonprofit agencies. Be sure to calculate in this assistance when determining whether you meet the requirements of paying more than half the cost of keeping up a home for yourself and your child. Chapter 33 covers special tax breaks for foster parents.

What are the requirements for filing as a qualifying widow(er) with dependent child? If your spouse died within the past two years, you can claim this filing status if the following are true:

- you can claim the dependent exemption for your child (see Chapter 28 for information about the dependent exemption)
- you were entitled to file a joint return with your spouse in the tax year that your spouse died (even if you did not actually file a joint tax return that year)
- you did not remarry before the end of the tax year, and
- you paid more than half of the cost of keeping up a home that is the main home for you and your child for the entire tax year.

My wife died just a few months ago. Can I use the qualifying widower exemption this year?

No. You must file a joint tax return for this year. Practically speaking, this won't make a difference, because filing a joint return entitles you to the same tax rates and standard deduction as a qualifying widow(er) with dependent child. For the next two tax years after this one, you can file as a qualifying widower.

I qualify for both filing statuses—head of household and qualifying widow(er). Which one should I use?

Qualifying widow(er) with dependent child, because your tax rates will be lowest this way.

If I want to use one of these special filing statuses, how do I do it?

Electing to use one of these filing statuses is simple. On either Form 1040 or 1040A, check box 4 to file as head of household and box 5 to file as qualifying widow(er) with dependent child.

ADDITIONAL RESOURCES

If you want to know more about your filing status. To see how your filing status can affect your tax rate and your standard deduction, check the IRS Tax Rate Schedules, available at www.irs.gov, and the standard deduction tables contained in IRS Publication 501, *Exemptions, Standard Deduction, and Filing Information.* This publication also has detailed information on the eligibility rules and associated tax benefits for the different filing statuses. ■

Chapter 32

Special Tax Breaks for Adoptive Parents

Adopting a child can be an expensive labor of love: With agency fees, attorney's fees, birth parent expenses, and travel and other incidental expenses, an adoption can cost $25,000 or more. To help ensure that adoption is a realistic option for moderate income families, the federal government offers some very generous tax breaks to adoptive parents.

 TIPS

Don't forget the standard tax breaks. This chapter describes tax breaks that are special for adoptive parents, but you aren't limited to these. You are also eligible for all of the other tax breaks that parents get—from the dependent exemption to the child care tax breaks—so long as you meet the requirements.

You'll Need Some Numbers

Your child will need either a Social Security number or an Adoption Taxpayer Identification Number for you to claim the tax benefits described in this and other chapters.

If the child you are adopting is a United States citizen, your child probably has a Social Security number already. But if you are adopting domestically and your child does not have one, you can obtain an Adoption Taxpayer Identification Number (ATIN) to claim child-related tax breaks while your child's adoption is pending. To apply for one, complete IRS Form W-7A, *Application for Taxpayer Identification Number for Pending U.S. Adoptions*. The ATIN will be valid for only two years, at which point you can extend it if your child's adoption is still not final. Once the adoption is final, you must stop using the ATIN and get a Social Security number for your child.

If you are adopting a child from another country, you will have to wait until the adoption is final and your child has entered the United States to obtain a Social Security number for your child. You will not be able to claim child-related tax breaks until then.

No matter where your child was born, once your child's adoption is final, you can apply for a Social Security number for your child by completing Form SS-5, which you can download at www.ssa.gov.

The Adoption Tax Credit

Through this credit, the federal government in essence reimburses adoptive parents for the expenses they incur to legally adopt a child—up to a limit. This credit applies to both international and domestic adoptions.

How will the adoption tax credit affect my bottom line?

The credit allows you to subtract your adoption expenses from your tax liability for the year. In 2004, the maximum credit you could claim for qualifying adoption expenses was $10,390 per adoption. The credit is adjusted each year for inflation.

> **EXAMPLE:** *Emily spent $15,000 in 2004 to adopt Miles, a rambunctious two-year-old who loved trucks, trucks, and trucks. Emily's total tax liability for the year came to $30,000. Because of the adoption tax credit, Emily's tax bill was reduced by $10,390— the maximum adoption tax credit for 2004. She therefore only owed the government $19,610 in taxes for the year.*

I spent money two years in a row in the process of adopting my son. Can I claim the credit for both years?

No. You can claim the credit only once per adoption.

What are the eligibility requirements for claiming the adoption tax credit?

To claim the credit, your child must be younger than 18 (or, if older than 18, must be incapable of caring for himself or herself because of a disability), you must have out-of-pocket costs related to the adoption, and your income must be within certain limits (see below).

I am formally adopting my wife's son. Can I claim the credit for this process?

No. Stepparent adoptions—which is what you are doing—do not qualify for the credit.

What costs qualify for the credit?

You can claim the adoption credit for adoption fees, court costs, attorney's fees, travel expenses, and other expenses directly related to the adoption. For example, if you travel to another country to attend a mandatory interview with your adoption agency, the cost of your plane ticket, your hotel stay, and your meals all qualify for the credit.

CAUTION

No double dipping. If you pay for the expenses using money from a government program, or if your employer or someone else gives you the money for the adoption, then you don't get to claim the credit for those expenses. The same holds true if you use money that you've already claimed some other tax credit or deduction for.

No credit for illegal adoptions. If you spend money on an adoption that is outside of the law—for example, you purchased a child in a foreign country or on the black market—you cannot claim the credit for those expenses.

My wife and I are paying a surrogate to have our baby for us. Can we use the credit for those expenses?

No. Expenses associated with surrogate parenting arrangements are not covered.

ADDITIONAL RESOURCES

To learn more about the adoption laws. A good resource is the National Adoption Information Clearinghouse, a website maintained by the United States Department of Health and Human Services Administration for Children and Families. Log on to http://naic.acf.hhs.gov and click on the link marked "Legal Issues and Laws."

I have a high income. Can I claim the credit? Maybe not. When your adjusted gross income exceeds certain specified limits, the amount of the adoption tax credit starts to phase out. For the 2004 tax year, for example, you would have lost a portion of your adoption tax credit if your adjusted gross income exceeded $155,861. You could not have claimed the adoption tax credit at all if that figure exceeded $195,860. You can find out more about the income limits for the adoption tax credit in IRS Publication 968, *Tax Benefits for Adoption.*

CAUTION

If you have foreign earned income. You'll need to add back your foreign income to your adjusted gross income when figuring your eligibility for the adoption tax credit.

When can I claim the adoption tax credit? The timing of when you can take the adoption tax credit depends on the citizenship status of the child you are adopting.

If the child you are adopting is a United States citizen or a legal resident of the United States and the adoption is not yet final, claim the credit in the year after you actually incur the expense. Once the adoption is final, you can take the adoption credit in the same year that you incur the expenses.

If you are adopting a foreign child, the rules are different. You cannot claim the adoption tax credit for any expenses until the adoption has actually become final.

ADDITIONAL RESOURCES

Is your child's adoption final? The rules on when an international adoption is considered final for purposes of the adoption tax credit are complicated. Check IRS Publication 968, *Tax Benefits for Adoption,* to learn more.

My husband and I are adopting two children. Can we claim a full adoption credit for each child?
Yes.

My wife and I spent a lot of money trying to adopt a little boy, but the adoption was unsuccessful. Can we still claim the credit?
If the attempt was for a domestic adoption, yes. But if you were trying to adopt internationally, then no.

CAUTION

If you later successfully adopt a child. If you claimed the adoption credit for an unsuccessful domestic adoption, and then later successfully adopt another child, the amount of the first credit will be subtracted from the amount you can claim the second time around.

ADDITIONAL RESOURCES

To learn more about the adoption tax credit. *Tax Benefits for Adoption,* and the instructions for completing IRS Form 8839, *Qualified Adoption Expenses,* provide helpful examples of how the adoption tax credit works, detailed instructions on claiming the credit, and useful worksheets on computing the amount of the tax credit you can claim.

Tax-Free Employer Assistance

Some employers give employees financial assistance to adopt a child. Usually, these employers will reimburse a certain percentage of specific adoption-related expenses, up to a certain dollar limit. For example, the International Data Group (IDG), a leading publisher of computer magazines, will reimburse up to $4,000 of eligible expenses for each adoption (up to a lifetime maximum of $10,000). If you're lucky enough to work for an employer that offers this kind of financial aid, you won't have to pay any federal income taxes on the adoption assistance you receive.

ADDITIONAL RESOURCES

To obtain a list of employers who offer some form of adoption assistance. The Adoption Friendly Workplace is a nonprofit organization that provides information on workplace benefits for adoptive parents. Log on to the organization's website at www .adoptionfriendlyworkplace.org to see whether your company or another company you're considering offers adoption assistance.

How will the tax break on employer adoption assistance affect my bottom line?
Normally, you have to pay taxes on all money you receive from your employer. But you may be exempt from paying income taxes on the money your employer gives you to cover adoption expenses—up to a maximum of about $10,000. (For 2004, the exclusion limit was $10,390; this amount is adjusted every year for inflation.)

The tax savings you'll enjoy as a result of this break will depend on your tax bracket. For example, if you receive $5,000 in adoption assistance from your employer and you are in the 25% tax bracket, you could save $1,250 in taxes. But if you are in the 15% tax bracket, the exclusion may shave only $750 off your tax bill.

CAUTION

If your employer offers more than $10,000 in adoption assistance. The total amount of the exclusion for adoption assistance from your employer is a little more than $10,000 per adoption. So if your employer gave you $10,390 in 2004 and then gave you an additional $5,000 in adoption assistance in 2005, both for the same adoption, you wouldn't have to pay any taxes on the $10,390 you receive in 2004. But you would have to pay taxes on the $5,000 of adoption assistance you receive in 2005, because you would have already used the maximum exclusion to which you are entitled.

What are the requirements for using the tax break?
The qualification requirements are generally the same as those for the adoption tax credit (see above), with one notable exception: what money counts as income. To figure out what your income is for using this particular tax break, you'll need to add the following to your adjusted gross income:

- the amount of your student loan interest deduction
- your tuition and fees deduction
- any foreign income you have, and
- the payments from your employer's adoption assistance program.

ADDITIONAL RESOURCES

For help calculating your income for purposes of this tax break. The instructions to IRS Form 8839, *Qualified Adoption Expenses,* contain a handy worksheet you can use.

When can I claim the exclusion?
If the child you are adopting is a United States citizen or a legal resident of the United States, you can claim the exclusion in the same year that you get the money from your employer, regardless of when the adoption becomes final.

If, on the other hand, you are adopting internationally, you cannot claim the exclusion until the adoption becomes final. So if your employer paid you money in a year before the adoption became final, for example, you will have to pay taxes on the money in the year you received it and then make an adjustment for the exclusion in the year when your adoption is final.

> EXAMPLE: *Steven received $4,000 from his employer in 2004 to reimburse him for some of the expenses he incurred in his efforts to adopt Lee, a young boy from China. Lee's adoption became final in 2005. Because Lee was not a United States citizen or legal resident of the United States, Steven had to pay taxes on the $4,000 in 2004. On his 2005 tax return, however, Steven made an adjustment to claim the exclusion for the $4,000 reimbursement.*

This tricky rule can result in greater than expected tax liability for the year in which you receive the money. Check with your human resources administrator about adjusting your withholdings, or talk to a tax professional about making estimated tax payments.

My employer has given me money to help with an adoption. I have also spent some of my own money on the adoption. Can I claim both the exclusion and the adoption tax credit?

Yes. You can claim the exclusion for the money that your employer gave you and the credit for the money of your own that you spent.

> EXAMPLE: *Keith and Genevieve spent $15,000 when they adopted their daughter, Nicky. Keith's company gave them $5,000. The couple claimed the exclusion for the $5,000—and so did not owe any taxes on the money. They claimed a tax credit for the remaining $10,000 of adoption-related expenses.*

ADDITIONAL RESOURCES

For more information about this exclusion. Check out IRS Publication 968, *Tax Benefits for Adoption,* and the instructions for completing Form 8839, *Qualified Adoption Expenses.* ∎

Chapter 33

Special Tax Breaks for Foster Parents

As a foster parent, you probably receive one or more forms of financial assistance from government agencies or government-affiliated nonprofit organizations to help you cover the costs of raising your foster child. Virtually all of the payments you receive are exempt from federal income taxes. This means that you do not have to report those payments when you file your annual tax return.

For example, you will not have to pay federal income taxes on:

- money that you receive to pay for food, clothing, medical care, housing, and other necessities for your foster child (these payments are often called cost-of-care reimbursements)
- payments to help you cover the extra expenses of raising a foster child with a disability or other health problem (these payments are often called difficulty-of-care payments or specialized-care payments)
- food stamps you receive to help cover your child's grocery expenses, or

- government-provided child-only cash assistance, such as Temporary Assistance to Needy Families payments.

Check with the agency providing you with payments to make sure that the funds you receive are tax-exempt.

TIPS

Foster care payments are usually also exempt from state taxes. But check with your state department of taxation or the agency providing you with payments to be sure.

No matter how much financial assistance you receive, however, it probably won't cover everything that you spend caring for and nurturing your foster child. Fortunately, you can claim a federal charitable tax deduction for these extra expenses.

If you spend money on things such as food, clothing, dance classes, tutoring, and child care, and you don't get reimbursed from a government or nonprofit agency, you can add up your total out-of-pocket costs and claim that amount as a charitable contribution on your federal income tax return. Just complete Schedule A of Form 1040 and enter the total amount of your itemized deductions on line 39. (You cannot use Form 1040A if you wish to claim the charitable contribution deduction.)

 CAUTION

If you adopt your foster child. You will not be able to claim a charitable contribution for any expenses associated with your child's care if you adopt your foster child. This is because a child's natural or adoptive parents are legally obligated to provide for a child's care.

 TIPS

Don't forget all the other parental tax breaks. As a foster parent, you are eligible to take all of the other tax breaks discussed in this part of the book, so long as you meet the eligibility requirements. Those breaks include the dependent exemption and the child tax credit. They also include preferential filing statuses such as head of household.

 ADDITIONAL RESOURCES

For more information about tax breaks for foster parents. Casey Family Programs, a nonprofit organization dedicated to improving foster care, has a terrific publication that can help. Download "Federal Tax Benefits for Foster and Adoptive Parents and Kinship Caregivers" for free from the organization's website at www .casey.org. ■

7. Guardians, Wills, and Other Things to Do Just in Case

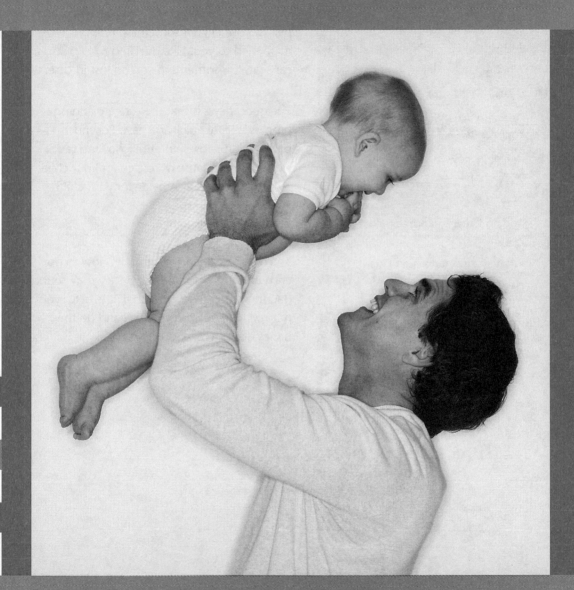

7

Contents

*I*n all likelihood, you will be around to care for your child through high school graduation and beyond. But it's still a good idea to write a will, name a guardian, and make other decisions about what would happen to your child if something unexpected happened to you. Like buckling a child into a car seat, it is something you do just in case.

The good news is that the estate planning process is fairly quick and easy. For most parents, it means doing the following tasks:
- choosing guardians to care for your child
- leaving assets to provide for your child
- writing a will, and
- buying life insurance.

The chapters that follow explain how to do each of these tasks. Although they may sound daunting, don't worry. With a little help, you may be able to write your will and do the basics in just a few hours.

In this part of the book, you will find the minimum that you need to do to protect your family. Eventually, you should do a few other things:

- think about avoiding probate (with a living trust, for example)
- consider ways to reduce estate taxes (but only if your estate will exceed a million or two dollars)
- plan for your own incapacity (with a living will and durable power of attorney, for example), and
- update your beneficiary designations (in your 401(k), for example).

But those issues aren't as pressing as wills and guardians and can wait until you have more time.

If you have a child with special needs, then you have some special issues to consider when planning your estate. *Special Needs Trusts: Protect Your Child's Financial Future,* written by Stephen Elias and published by Nolo, explains how you can leave money to a child with a disability without interfering with his or her eligibility for Social Security or Medicaid benefits. ■

Chapter 34

Choosing Guardians

Aguardian is someone who cares for your child in the unlikely event that neither you nor your child's other parent is able to do so. Deciding whom to name as guardian can be a tough task, to be sure, but it is also a doable one. This chapter provides the information and advice you need to make the right choices for your family.

ADDITIONAL RESOURCES

Everyone struggles with this issue. For a comforting article about the difficulty of dealing with guardianship—and for some excellent advice on how to make the right choice—see "Choosing Wisely: Nominating Guardians for Your Kids," by Liza Hanks, a Northern California estate planning attorney. Go to www.family works-law.com/basics_guardian. htm and scroll down to the end of the page, where you will find a link to a PDF version of the article.

Basic Information About Guardianship

This section lays out some basic information about guardianship so that you can have a good understanding of the legal and practical issues involved before you choose someone to fill this important role.

How does guardianship work?

When a child is left with no living parents, a judge steps in to name someone to take care of the child until age 18. This person is the child's "guardian of the person" or "personal guardian." (The personal guardian may or may not control the property the child inherits. It depends on the circumstances. See Chapter 35 for more about property management for children.) If the parents left a will or other document identifying a person to serve as the guardian, the judge will most likely follow the parents' choice, unless there is a compelling reason not to do so—for example, the parents' choice is very ill or is unwilling to serve as guardian.

What happens if I don't name a guardian for my child?

If both parents die without specifying who should be the guardian, a judge will have to make the call. Although the judge will try to act in the child's best interests, it may be difficult for a stranger to make the best choice. Family members from different sides of the family might clash over who should raise the child—leading to potentially bitter disputes that could further disrupt the child's life. That's why it's important for you to nominate a guardian.

I've chosen a guardian for my child. What do I have to do to make sure a judge knows of my decision if something happens to me?

Although you can communicate your choice in any type of document that you sign, the most common—and safest—way to name a guardian is through a valid will. Read Chapter 36 for guidance on writing a will.

Should I name an alternate guardian for my child, just in case?

Yes. Because of the possibility that your first choice might not work out, it's important to pick at least one alternate.

Once I name a guardian, can I change my mind?

Yes. Your decision is not set in stone. In fact, you should revisit this issue every so often, in case circumstances change. Pay attention to any changes in the guardian's life that might affect that person's ability and willingness to raise your child if you die. For example,

if your child's guardian is diagnosed with breast cancer, you might consider naming someone else so that the guardian wouldn't be faced with the possibility of raising a child while she battled her illness.

Should I ask for permission before naming someone as my child's guardian?

You are not legally required to ask permission before naming someone as your child's guardian. Still, it's a good idea to make sure that the person you have in mind is willing to take on the responsibility of caring for and raising your child if it becomes necessary.

My husband and I are raising our child together. Should I name him as the guardian in case I die?

There is no need to. Your husband will automatically get custody. You should, instead, name a third person, who will be called to duty if you and your spouse are both unavailable.

I am not married to my child's father. If I die, would he get custody even if I name someone else as guardian?

If the father is a legal parent, he would most likely get custody. (For information on when fathers are considered legal parents, see **Divorce, Same-Sex Partnerships, and Other Tricky Issues**, below.) This is not the news many divorced parents want to hear, but it is true. If you die but your child's other parent remains alive, your child's other parent—and not the person you named as your child's guardian—will almost always get sole custody of your child. Custody is the right to raise a child and make all important decisions affecting a child.

The exception to this rule can occur if the other parent is completely uninvolved in the child's life, while the person named as guardian is a caretaker for the child. In this case, the guardian you've named could fight for custody, and a judge would decide what would be in the child's best interests.

 CROSS REFERENCE

If yours is a nontraditional family. Not all people who parent a child are considered legal parents with an automatic right to custody. See **Divorce, Same-Sex Partnerships**, and Other Tricky Issues, below.

☑ CHECKLIST

What to Ask Yourself When Picking a Guardian

Choosing a guardian can be difficult. Start the process by asking yourself the following questions:

❑ Whom does my child know and love?
❑ Who knows and loves my child?
❑ Who has the best relationship with my child?
❑ Who has the time and emotional and physical energy to care for my child—and will still have it when my child is a teenager?
❑ Whose parenting style do I most respect?
❑ Whose values on important issues such as religion, education, and money are in sync with my own?
❑ Whose family would my child fit into best?
❑ Would my child have to move far away? How do I feel about the place where my child would live?
❑ Who would want the responsibility of raising my child in my place?
❑ How do I want my child to be raised? Who fits that mold?

Picking the Right Person

A good way to start the process is to create a list of potential guardians by asking yourself the questions listed in "What to Ask Yourself When Picking a Guardian," above. Then take a good hard look at each person on the list. No matter how much you love and respect these people, it may be difficult to envision some of them actually raising your child. For example, you may have always admired you sister's work ethic, but on more reflection you may view her as a workaholic who won't spend enough time with your child.

Place yourself in your child's shoes. Where would your child be happiest and most nurtured?

Try to spend a chunk of time with the people you are considering—a long weekend away or a day at the beach. Sometimes when you take the time to focus on them as potential parents to your own child, you may see things you hadn't noticed before, such as their discipline style (or lack thereof).

Do I have to name a relative as my child's guardian?

No, though many people do. Still, for some parents, a friend or neighbor is a better fit.

If you choose a friend as your child's guardian, family members may be offended by your decision. They may even attempt to contest your choice in court or distance themselves from your child after you have passed away. For these reasons, consider explaining your choice to the family members who might be unhappily surprised by your decision. You can do this face to face, or you can prepare a letter to each of them. Explain—in as positive and kind a way as possible—why you've chosen a particular friend for your child's guardian, rather than criticize the family member as a bad choice as guardian. Keep copies of these letters to relatives with your will. This way, your family members—and a judge, if it comes to that—will be able to understand your choice and respect it.

Should I choose a grandparent as my child's guardian?

Many experts caution against naming a grandparent because of the age and generation gap. For example, your mother may be a doting and devoted grandma, but not have the stamina to care for your child full time.

Nevertheless, a grandparent may be still be the best choice in your particular case—perhaps because the grandparent is young and healthy or because there's simply no one else whom you trust to do the job well.

Remember: You are picking someone that makes the most sense right now. You can always change your choice later.

I'd like to name a couple as my child's guardian. Is that possible?

It's possible, but not necessarily a good idea. If you name a couple and they divorce after they become guardians, the guardianship of your child will be an issue in their divorce settlement because they share legal responsibility for your child. Sometimes, that's a chance you might want to take, but if you prefer one of the members of the couple, it's best to name that person alone.

What if my chosen guardian is not a good money manager?

That's fine. Just be sure to name someone else to manage the property. (See Chapter 35 for more about leaving property to your children and naming someone to manage it.)

What if my chosen guardian lives in another state or country?

As long as you are comfortable with the idea of your child moving from home, it's fine. Make sure that your will says that the guardian can take your child to the state or country where the guardian lives. If your guardian lives outside the country, get a valid passport for your child and keep it current.

What if my child's other parent and I cannot agree on a guardian?

It's not uncommon for parents to have a difficult time agreeing on whom they should name as guardian. Things that are important to one parent may not be important to the other. A person whom one parent really wants to name may not satisfy the other. Remember: There is no perfect choice. As with all other areas of a relationship, this choice will be about compromise—something that is difficult, but necessary to do.

One thing you and your child's other parent should not do is name different guardians in your individual wills. If you do so and you both die at the same time, a judge will make the decision for you. This is precisely the scenario you are attempting to avoid by naming a guardian in the first place. So do your best to come up with someone right now with whom you both feel comfortable.

Can I name different guardians for different children?

Most parents want to keep siblings together, so that the children can grow up with each other's friendship and companionship. Still, you are not obligated to name the same personal guardian for all of your children. For example, if you have children from different marriages, or if there are large age gaps between your children, they may be best served by living with different guardians.

If you decide to name different guardians for different children, be aware that a judge might be reluctant to separate your children without a good reason. To avoid problems, write a letter explaining why you feel it would be best for your children to have different guardians. Keep a copy of this letter with your will.

Can I provide for a change in guardianship after a certain number of years?

Sometimes, people name a grandparent as a child's personal guardian only for a certain number of years—say, until the grandparent reaches age 70—and then provide for someone younger (such as the child's uncle or aunt) to take over the reins. This is certainly legal, but may not be in your child's best interests. Once your child has grown accustomed to one person's care, it would be a major upheaval for your child to then have to change homes and caregivers.

Divorce, Same-Sex Partnerships, and Other Tricky Issues

Having nontraditional family relationships makes the tough issue of guardianship even tougher. You may be divorced and not want your child's other parent to get custody. Or you may be raising a child in a loving and committed same-sex partnership and want to ensure that your partner gets custody. Whatever the issue, if you are not legally married to your child's other parent—or if you want someone other than your child's other parent to get custody—things get complicated fast. In this section, we sort out the legal twists and turns.

The big issue in all of this is the word "parent." Although that word means different things to different people, the law has very specific views on who is—and who is not—a parent. No matter what kind of relationship your child has with someone else (a loving stepparent, for example, or a grandmother), it is your child's other legal parent who will almost certainly get custody in the event of your death.

Legal Parents

Who are my child's legal parents?

The following are legal parents of a child so long as there has not been a court order terminating their rights:

- the woman who gave birth to the child
- if the mother was married at the time of the birth, the mother's husband
- if the mother was in a same-sex marriage in Massachusetts, domestic partnership in California, or civil union in Vermont at the time of birth, the mother's partner
- if the mother was not married at the time of the birth but named a father on the birth certificate, the named father so long as he has signed an acknowledgment of paternity or otherwise claimed to be the father
- if the child is adopted, the adoptive parent(s).

Common examples of people who might have a parent-type relationship with a child, but who are not legal parents of a child, include:

- stepparents
- a man whose child was born out of wedlock and who hasn't acknowledged paternity
- an individual with whom the legal parent lives but who is neither married to or in a registered domestic partnership with the legal parent.

Confused? Let's look at a few examples:

> **EXAMPLE 1:** *Lois and Carlos are married. Lois gives birth to a baby boy she names Milo and completes the paperwork for a birth certificate in which she names herself and Carlos as the parents. Lois and Carlos are Milo's legal parents.*
>
> *Lois and Carlos divorce when Milo is three. Lois marries a man named Luigi. Lois and Carlos are still Milo's legal parents. Luigi is a stepparent, not a legal parent.*

Several years go by in which Carlos has little contact with Milo. Eventually, Lois asks Carlos to agree to allow Luigi to adopt Milo. Carlos agrees, and the adoption takes place (this type of adoption is often called a step-parent adoption). Now Lois and Luigi are Milo's legal parents. Carlos is no longer a legal parent because of the adoption.

EXAMPLE 2: Jane gets pregnant and has a baby whom she names Tony. The father is Kyle, but the couple is not married. Jane puts Kyle's name on the birth certificate as Tony's father, and Kyle signs an acknowledgment of paternity. Kyle is Tony's legal parent.

Let's change the example a little bit and say that Jane does not put Kyle's name on the birth certificate. If Kyle does not sign a paternity statement or otherwise have a court legally declare him to be the father, he is not Tony's legal parent.

EXAMPLE 3: Lisa and Jessica are in a committed same-sex partnership and decide that they want to have a baby together. They are not registered domestic partners. Lisa uses a sperm bank to become pregnant. She eventually gives birth to Jack. Lisa is Jack's legal parent. Jessica is not.

When Jack is two, Lisa and Jessica break up. Lisa keeps custody of Jack. Jessica loves Jack and maintains close contact with him, something that Lisa allows and encourages. Still, Jessica has no legal rights to Jack. If Lisa were to die, anyone else could petition the court for custody of Jack.

Let's change the example and say that instead of breaking up when Jack is two, Lisa and Jessica, who live in California, decide to register as domestic partners. Shortly thereafter, Jessica adopts Jack. Now Jack has two legal parents—Lisa and Jessica. If Lisa were to die, Jessica would automatically get custody.

Divorce

I'm divorced from my daughter's father, who has had almost no involvement with her for years. I would like for my current husband to get custody of her if anything happens to me. What can I do?
The quickest and easiest thing to do is to name your current husband as guardian in your will and attach a letter explaining your choice. There's no guarantee that a judge will honor your wishes if your former husband contests, but at least you will have laid the groundwork for your current husband to fight for custody.

A potentially more difficult, but certain, route is to ask your former husband to consent to your current husband adopting your daughter. If he does so, this would make it almost certain that your current husband would get custody.

If your former husband does not consent, but you still want to pursue adoption, consult with an attorney.

I'm divorced from my son's mother, who has serious problems that make her, in my opinion, a potential danger to my son and me. I can't stand the thought of her getting custody if I weren't around. What can I do?

If your former wife is truly dangerous (she has a chronic drug or alcohol problem, mental illness, or a history of child abuse, for example) then consider having her parental rights terminated and then name someone else—perhaps your current spouse or a grandparent—as guardian. Consult with an attorney for help on doing this.

TIPS

If you have a terminal illness. In some states, if you have a terminal illness, there are laws that allow you to name a coguardian who can parent with you until your death and then take responsibility for your child after your death. In this situation, you might have the chance to persuade the judge in person, rather than by letter, of why your choice of guardian would be better than the child's other parents. Consult with an attorney for more information about this.

I'm in the middle of a divorce. Is there anything that I can do now to control whom my husband names as guardian in his will?

Yes. Talk to your husband about this issue now. Reach a consensus on who would be the best guardian for your child and make that agreement part of your divorce settlement.

Same-Sex Partnerships

I'm in a committed same-sex relationship. I gave birth to our son, but my partner and I are raising him together and consider ourselves his moms. How can I make sure that my partner would continue to raise him if something happened to me?

In a few states, your partner might be considered your son's legal parent, but in most places she would have no legal relationship with him. So you'd be wise to take some action now. Name your partner as your son's guardian. If you live in a state that allows it, have your partner adopt your son legally (this is often called a second-parent adoption).

ADDITIONAL RESOURCES

If you live in California. Nolo's *Do Your Own California Adoption,* by Frank Zagone and Emily Doskow, provides step-by-step instructions and all of the forms you need for a second-parent or stepparent adoption.

If you are in a same-sex partner-ship. There are some excellent organizations that can help you sort out these parenting and guardianship issues. Lambda Legal (on the Web at www.lambdalegal.org) is a national organization committed to achieving full recognition of the civil rights of lesbians, gay men, bisexuals, transgender people, and those with HIV. The National Center for Lesbian Rights (on the Web at www.nclrights.org) is a national legal resource center with a primary commitment to advancing the rights and safety of lesbians and their families. In addition, NCLR provides representation and resources to gay men and bisexual and transgender individuals on key issues that also significantly advance lesbian rights.

I live in a state that has a constitutional amendment defining marriage as being between a man and a woman. I'm in a same-sex relationship. Can my partner and I both be legal parents of a child?

Probably. Parentage and marriage are no longer completely bound together. However, some states that have constitutional amendments that prohibit same-sex marriage also have laws that won't allow two people of the same sex to be parents. Check with a knowledgeable lawyer in your state to find out more.

Can a child ever have more than two legal parents?

It's very rare, but it does happen. Most kids with three legal parents are in families with two lesbian parents and a man who served as sperm donor and acts as a father to the child. But these are unusual situations. Usually, the courts are reluctant to allow a child to have more than two legal parents, because of the increased likelihood of custody litigation if the relationship among the parents sours.

What to Do Next

If you've chosen a guardian for your child, congratulations—the hard part is over. Still, there are a few loose ends for you to tie up.

I have named a guardian in my will. Is there anything else I should do?

Explain your decision to the other important people in your child's life—for example, grandparents. This will minimize the possibility of hurt feelings or custody challenges down the line.

If your child is old enough to understand and deal with this issue, consider discussing your choice with your child. Although it will be difficult for your child to think about the possibility of your dying, it can be comforting for your child to know that someone would be there to provide care and guidance if something happened to you.

Should I discuss anything with my chosen guardian?

Yes. First, you need to find out if this person is willing to take on the responsibility of being a guardian. Second, though it can be awkward, it is a good idea to discuss the financial and practical reality of taking in a child. You need to make sure that whatever property you will be leaving to your children is sufficient. If it isn't, consider buying life insurance. (Chapter 37 provides guidance on doing this.) Talk to the guardian about what arrangements you are making and whether they will be enough to provide for your child. Third, you should talk with your guardian about your childrearing preferences on issues such as education and religion.

How can I ensure that my child's guardian will follow my wishes?

There is no way to ensure that the person you select as your child's guardian will raise and care for your child exactly as you would have done. But if you select someone whose values and parenting style are similar to your own, and give that person some concrete guidance in a letter, you are increasing the odds that your child will be raised in a way that you would like. The "Sample Letter to Guardian," below is an example of such a letter. If you choose to write one, keep a copy of it with your will.

Sample Letter to Guardian

Dear Ping,

If you are reading this letter, then we have passed away. There are not enough words to express to you our gratitude for taking over the care of Isabella. You are kind, generous, and nurturing. There is no one else we would trust to raise our daughter.

We are writing this letter to help you understand some of our hopes and dreams for our little girl. We hope that you will take our views into consideration as you raise and nurture her.

Family. If we could ask only one thing of you, it would be to help Isabella develop strong bonds with each and every member of our families on both sides. Please make sure that Isabella sees her grandparents, uncles, aunts, and cousins as often as possible—so that she can build a bond with each of them. In our view, nothing is more important than family to help a child understand her place in the world.

Education. Although we dream that Isabella will be high-achieving, we hope that you will be careful of overemphasizing academic success and competitiveness. We ask that you please take a balanced attitude with respect to Isabella's education. Please encourage Isabella and support her in her endeavors—be they academic, artistic, or athletic. Don't put unnecessary pressure on her. More than anything, we want to instill in Isabella a love of learning—a gift that will last a lifetime.

Discipline. We feel a child learns best through example, guidance, and encouragement. Please take care not to shout at Isabella or punish her harshly. Instead, please sit down and talk to her when she misbehaves. Please use gentle discipline tactics—such as time-outs if Isabella is still young or groundings and privilege suspensions if Isabella is older.

Religion. Though we value the tenets of our own religion, we have a tremendous respect for all religions. We're also quite skeptical of organized religion in all of its forms. For this reason, we ask that you do not force Isabella to attend church or Sunday school each week. Instead, please just help her grow up to be a spiritual and tolerant person as best you can.

Once again, we thank you for taking on this truly enormous responsibility.

Yours,

Joe and Melinda

Consider a video instead of a letter. If you hate letter writing and want to send a more personal message to your child's guardian, consider making a videotape on which you discuss your wishes for your child's future and childrearing preferences.

What happens if I have another child, but I die before I get the chance to update my will? Will my new child automatically get the same guardian that I named for my other child?

A judge would almost certainly award custody of your new child to the same guardian you named for your other child because judges don't like to separate siblings. Still, leaving a guardianship decision in the hands of a judge is never a good idea. It's best to update your will whenever you have a new baby, so that you can specifically name a guardian for your new child and make any other necessary changes to your estate plan. ■

Chapter 35

Dealing With Your Assets

A big part of making sure your family is cared for in the event of your death is figuring out what to do with your assets. First and foremost, you must decide: Who will get your money, house, and other assets? Your answer to this question will depend a lot on your family's structure—if you are married to your child's other parent, for example, or if you are single.

If there is any scenario in which your child would inherit either money or property from you, then you must make some more decisions, because unless your child is older than 18, he or she won't be able to own property worth more than a few thousand dollars. So you need to decide: Who will manage these assets for my child? And how will these assets be managed (for example, in a trust or custodial account)?

This chapter looks at all of these questions, and more, and leads you to some answers.

Deciding Who Will Get Your Assets

To whom do you want to leave your assets? Your spouse? Your child? Your parents? Although this is a very personal decision, there are some issues, both legal and practical, for you to consider. This section looks at those issues.

Should I leave everything to my spouse or divvy up my property between my spouse and our child?

Most couples who have a child together leave everything to each other. This way, the surviving spouse will have access to the money to take care of the family. They then name their child as a contingent, or alternative, beneficiary, just in case they and their spouse die together. (If they have more than one child, they name both as contingent beneficiaries.) If this is what you want to do, you can accomplish it quite easily through a simple will that you write yourself. (See Chapter 36 for more about writing your will yourself).

If your child is a minor. Children younger than 18 cannot own more than a few thousand dollars worth of property, so if you name a minor child as either a primary or contingent beneficiary, you must also choose a management structure for the assets. See *Choosing a Management Structure: Custodial Accounts and Trusts,* below, for guidance on this issue.

There may be reasons why you might not want to leave all of your assets to your spouse, however. Perhaps your husband or wife is incapacitated and can't manage assets. Or perhaps you have reasons for not trusting your spouse to take adequate care of your child. Or you might simply want to leave some assets to other people or organizations. If there is a reason that you are reluctant to leave all of your assets to your spouse, there are ways to deal with your concerns. Just be aware that your spouse will have the right to claim some share of your property—usually no more than a third, though it depends on your state's law. For this reason, it's best to consult with an estate planning attorney if you don't want to leave a significant portion of your assets to your spouse.

I am in a committed relationship with my child's other parent, but we are not married. Can I leave everything to my partner?

Yes. In fact, that is what most people in your position do. They make their partner their primary beneficiary, and they make their child their contingent beneficiary.

I am married, and I have children from a previous relationship. How can I make sure everyone is cared for?
There are a number of ways to deal with your situation. For example, you could divide your property between your children and your spouse, or you could set up more complicated arrangements involving trusts. There's no one-size-fits-all solution—it depends on your family and your needs. Consult an estate planning attorney.

I am a single parent. Can I leave all of my assets to my child, even though he is just a baby?
Yes. In fact, that is what many single parents do. They then choose a trusted adult to manage their child's assets until the child is old enough to do so. Be sure to read the sections below on how you can set up such an arrangement for your child.

I have two children. Do I have to leave the same amount of property to each of them?
No. Just as there is no law that requires you to spend the same amount of money on each child during your lifetime, there is no law that requires you to leave the same amount to each child at your death. For example, if you think that one child has more needs than the other, then you can certainly leave that child more.

Deciding How the Assets Will Be Managed

If there is any possibility that your child will inherit assets from you—say as a primary beneficiary or a contingent beneficiary of your will, life insurance policy, or 401(k) plan—then it's a good idea to choose both a legal structure (for example, a trust) to hold those assets and a person (for example, a trustee) to manage those assets. First, this section takes a look at management structures. Then, it helps you pick a person to do the managing.

CAUTION

If you do nothing. If you don't arrange for property management for children younger than 18 and the assets are worth more than a few thousand dollars, the probate court will do it for you by appointing a property guardian. This arrangement comes with some headaches: Usually, a court-appointed guardian must make frequent reports to the court and has limited authority to decide how the property should be managed. To avoid those headaches, it's best for you to make decisions about property management for your child.

Choosing a Management Structure: Custodial Accounts and Trusts

Does it really matter which management structure I choose, so long as I choose something?

Yes. The structure you choose will determine such things as your child's age when he or she gets control of the money, the ways in which the money can be used, and whether a court will have oversight.

What are my options?

There are two main types of arrangements you can make for your child's assets: Custodial accounts and trusts.

Custodial accounts are a popular option because they cost virtually nothing to establish—you can just open one up at a bank or brokerage company or state in your will that you are leaving the assets to your child in a custodial account. These accounts get established under the rules of the Uniform Transfers to Minors Act (UTMA)—something that every state except Vermont and South Carolina has adopted. The custodian manages the assets until the child is a certain age (21 in most states—see "The Uniform Transfers to Minors Act: When Will Your Child Gain Control of the Assets in a Custodial Account?" in the appendix to find out at what age your child would gain control in your state), and the custodian is free to spend the money for the child's benefit in any way he or she pleases—without court supervision. Custodial accounts can have either benefits or drawbacks, depending on your perspective. If you want the money to be managed until your child is older, or if you want more control over how the manager spends the money, then a trust might be a better choice for you.

A **trust** gives you more control over your child's inheritance than does a custodial account. You can place restrictions on how and when the trustee may spend your child's assets, and you can decide how old your child must be to receive his or her inheritance outright, if ever. A trust comes with more tax and administrative hassles than a custodial account. For example, income from a trust may be taxed at a higher rate, and the trustee will have to file a separate tax return for the trust each year. At the time your child gains control of the trust assets, the trustee will have to give your child an accounting of how the money was spent. You can create a trust on your own through your will so long as you include the terms of the trust (if you are using a software program or a book to write your own will, either should include terms for you to use). If you don't include terms, your state's law will provide them.

TIPS

If you have more than one child. People with more than one child usually leave all of their assets to their children collectively in trust (often called a "family pot trust") instead of dividing their assets among their children, something that could pose problems if one child needs more assets than the other. As with trusts for one child, a family pot trust can be created through your will.

TIPS

Life insurance proceeds. You can name a custodial account or trust to hold life insurance proceeds that you leave to a minor child. That way, the custodian or trustee will manage the money until the child is old enough to do so. See Chapter 37 for more about life insurance.

What should be my considerations in choosing a management structure? If simplicity and low cost are the most important issues to you—and if you don't mind your child inheriting money at 21 or 25 (depending on your state's law)—then use a custodial account. But if you want control and flexibility in planning, your best bet is a trust.

Can I set up more than one property management structure for my child's inheritance?
Yes. There are some cases when multiple management structures make sense. For example, you might want to place some assets—such as your family's home—in a family pot trust, while creating individual child's trusts funded with cash for each of your children.

Do I have to choose the same management structure for each of my children?
No. Unless you combine your children's assets in a family pot trust, you don't have to use the same property management structure for each of your children's inheritances (although most people do). People sometimes choose different property management structures when children are of different ages or if the children are from different marriages.

> **EXAMPLE:** *Sally decided to establish a family pot trust for her two youngest children, aged 2 and 4. Sally didn't want her 12-year-old daughter from a previous marriage to have to wait until her younger two children grew up in order to access her inheritance. So Sally set up a separate custodial account for her.*

Choosing a Manager of Your Assets

I have chosen a personal guardian for my child. Should the same person manage the property my child may inherit from me?
The least complicated way to go is to make the same person the personal guardian and the money manager. But you don't have to. Different people have different strengths, and a person who has excellent parenting skills might not have excellent money skills. If you decide to choose two different people, be sure that the personal guardian and the person who is managing the property communicate well and agree on important issues.

I have decided that I do not want my child's personal guardian to manage the money. Should I choose a lawyer or accountant to manage the property?
There is no need to find a legal or financial whiz to supervise your child's inheritance. In fact, for most families, finding someone who knows and cares about their children is more important than trusting a stranger with your funds. Just be sure that whomever you name is reasonably good at managing money. If a financial, legal, or tax issue arises, that person can seek professional help—and pay for it with the property you've left. ■

Chapter 36

Writing a Will

Every parent should have a will. It can accomplish a number of important tasks, including naming a personal guardian to care for minor children, leaving assets to provide for those children, and creating a management structure for those assets. Choosing guardians and leaving assets involve tough decisions. (Chapters 34 and 35 respectively, help you make these decisions.) But writing a will is pretty straightforward. You can hire a lawyer to write your will, or you can write it yourself.

BABYCENTER POLL

Haven't prepared a will yet? You are not alone. More than 72% of the 49,100 respondents to a recent BabyCenter.com poll had not yet written their wills.

What is a will?

Although it sounds formal, a will is just a few pieces of paper that you sign in front of witnesses and that say what you want to happen after you die. A basic will can do all of the following:

- leave your property to the people and organizations you choose
- name someone to care for your minor children
- name someone to manage property you leave to minor children, and
- name your executor (who is the person with authority to make sure that the terms of your will are carried out).

Choosing the Executor

The executor (called a personal representative in some states) is the person named in a will to be in charge of winding up the person's financial affairs after death. Basically, that means taking care of property, paying bills and taxes, and seeing to it that assets are transferred to their new rightful owners. If probate court proceedings are required, as they often are, the executor must handle them or hire a lawyer to do so.

The person you choose should be honest, organized, and good at communicating with people. If possible, name someone who lives nearby and who is familiar with your financial matters; that will make it easier to do chores such as collecting mail and finding important records and papers.

No matter whom you pick, make sure the person is willing to do the job. Discuss it together before you finalize your will.

When it comes time, an executor can accept or decline this responsibility. And someone who agrees to serve can resign at any time. That's why you should name an alternate executor in your will—a person who can take over from the executor if necessary. If no one is available, the court will appoint someone to step in. For ideas about planning ahead to make an executor's job easier, see *The Executor's Guide,* by Mary Randolph (Nolo).

What happens if I die without a will?
If you don't make a will before your death, state law will determine who gets your property (if you are married, everything will go to your spouse and children; if you are not married, everything will go to your children in equal shares), and a judge will decide who will raise your children if the other legal parent is unfit or unavailable.

If you are part of an unmarried same-sex couple, the survivor will not inherit anything unless you live in one of the few states that allows registered domestic partners to inherit like spouses: California, Maine, and Vermont.

Should my spouse and I have separate wills?
Yes. Although it is possible for you and your spouse to have a joint will, estate planners recommend against it. Instead, most married people have individual wills that are mirror images of one another's.

Does all of my property pass through my will?
No. The following property does not pass through your will (so be sure to review and update these beneficiary designations periodically, especially when you have a child):

- property you hold in joint tenancy with someone else (or in "tenancy by the entirety" or "community property with right of survivorship" with your spouse)
- property you've transferred to a living trust
- proceeds of a life insurance policy
- money in a pension plan, individual retirement account (IRA), 401(k) plan, or other retirement plan

- stocks or bonds held in beneficiary (transfer-on-death or TOD) form, and
- money in a payable-on-death bank account.

Do I have to hire a lawyer to write my will?

No. Most new parents do not need a lawyer to prepare a clear, valid, and binding will. You just need to know what you own and who will care for your children and have a good resource to guide you (see our suggestions below). You can probably prepare your own will in less than an hour.

You Can Write Your Will Yourself

If you want to write your will yourself, a terrific Nolo product you can use is *Quicken WillMaker Plus*, a software program that helps you create a customized will by first taking you through a step-by-step interview. The program prepares your will for you based on your answers to the interview questions and automatically conforms your will to the laws of your state. In addition, the program can help you prepare an advanced health care directive (sometimes called a living will) and a durable power of attorney—two documents that would be critical if you were to become incapacitated. If you're more of a book person, then take a look at *Nolo's Simple Will Book*, by Denis Clifford (Nolo).

Under what circumstances should I hire a lawyer to prepare my will?

Although most people don't need a lawyer, some circumstances make getting expert help a good idea. Call a lawyer if:

- you feel uncomfortable preparing a will on your own
- you have questions that aren't answered by this book or other estate planning resources
- you have a great deal of assets (say, $1.5 million or more), and you want to take steps to minimize your potential estate tax bill
- you want to make complex arrangements with respect to your property after you die—for example, you want to leave your house in trust to your spouse until he or she dies, and then have the house go to your child from a previous marriage
- you don't want your child's other parent to have custody of your child if you die
- you want to set up a trust for the long-term care of a child with special needs
- you want to leave all (or even most) of your assets to someone other than your spouse, or
- you're afraid someone will contest your will or some of its provisions—for example, you're concerned that family members will challenge your choice of guardian for your child.

How much will a lawyer charge to prepare my will?

If all you need is a simple will, a lawyer will probably charge you a flat fee of $500 to $1,000 to prepare it. (Most lawyers will also charge a flat fee for doing both spouse's wills.) Most lawyers will include in this fee two other documents that would be important in the unlikely event that you become incapacitated: A durable power of attorney for property management and an advanced health directive (sometimes called a living will).

If you require more assistance—for example, you need your lawyer to set up a living trust for you as well—then a lawyer may charge you by the hour (anywhere from $150 to $350 per hour). Be sure to find out the lawyer's fee, and how this fee will be calculated, in advance.

How do I find a good lawyer to prepare my will?

A lawyer's reputation in the community is usually a good mark of the lawyer's skill and attention to clients. So begin your search by asking friends and family members for recommendations. Other good resources include churches, accountants, and financial advisors.

 TIPS

If you need serious help with a complicated estate plan, then only the very best will do. Look for a fellow of the American College of Trust and Estate Counsel (ACTEC)—a nonprofit organization whose members are the best estate planning attorneys in the country. To become an ACTEC fellow, a lawyer must be nominated by a current ACTEC fellow, show substantial contributions to the field of estate planning, and be elected by the ACTEC membership at large. You can find an ACTEC fellow in your area by logging on to ACTEC's website at www.actec.org.

I've set up an initial consultation with a lawyer. What questions should I ask?

The purpose of an initial consultation is to find out if the lawyer is a good fit for you. So don't feel compelled to hire the first lawyer you meet. You might need to talk to two or three lawyers before you find someone who makes you feel comfortable and whose opinion you respect. Here are a few questions to ask before hiring someone:

- "What percentage of your practice consists of estate planning?" A lawyer who specializes in wills and other estate planning matters will be more knowledgeable (but may be more expensive) than a generalist who also practices other types of law.

- "How long have you been an estate planning lawyer?" Experience counts.
- "What are your fees?" You don't want to break the bank by hiring a lawyer who's far outside your price range. Ask your lawyer whether you'll be charged a flat fee or an hourly rate. If you'll be charged by the hour, ask for an estimate of the number of hours the work will take. Will you also be charged for incidental expenses such as photocopies and faxes?
- "Where and when did you graduate from law school?" Although credentials matter, it's far more important to find a lawyer with experience in estate planning than a Harvard Law graduate who's new to the field.
- "What experience do you have in handling situations like mine?"
- "If I need to change my will, how much will you charge?" The fee should be substantially less than the cost of preparing the original will.

This attorney will be helping you make some very personal and important decisions for your child and your family, so the lawyer's personal style is as important as his or her resume. Does the lawyer's attitude and approach put you at ease? Does the lawyer seem to be paying attention to your concerns? Is the lawyer trying to rush you out the door, so that the next client can be ushered in? Look for a lawyer with whom you can communicate well.

☑ CHECKLIST

Interviewing a Lawyer

When interviewing prospective lawyers, be sure to ask the following questions:
- ❑ What percentage of your practice is estate planning?
- ❑ How long have you been an estate planning lawyer?
- ❑ Where did you attend law school, and when did you graduate?
- ❑ What are your fees?
- ❑ How will your fees be calculated?
- ❑ What is included in your fees?
- ❑ What kind of experience do you have with situations like mine?
- ❑ How much will you charge me to change my will?

If I hire a lawyer to prepare my will, what will the process be like?

After the initial meeting, you'll probably meet with the lawyer one more time—or at least speak on the phone—so that the lawyer completely understands your wishes. The lawyer will then prepare your will and send it to you for review. Read the will carefully to make sure that it accurately reflects your wishes. If you don't understand some of the legal jargon, make a note so that you can get your lawyer to explain it to you. You'll then have the opportunity to ask your lawyer questions and make comments. Your lawyer will make any needed changes and send you a revised will to review.

Once you are happy with the language and structure of your will, your lawyer will schedule a signing to finalize your will. All you'll then need to do is sign your will in the presence of two witnesses (three if you live in Vermont). The lawyer will give you the signed original.

Do I need to file my will with a court or in public records somewhere?

No. A will doesn't need to be recorded or filed with any government agency, although it can be in a few states. Just keep your will in a safe, accessible place and be sure the person in charge of winding up your affairs (your executor) knows where it is.

 TIPS

Finding a safe place for your will and other estate planning documents. Most people put their will in a waterproof, fireproof box that they keep at home. Safety deposit boxes aren't a good idea unless your executor has the authority to open the box. Along with your will, include copies of other important documents, such as any letters you write to your child, your child's guardian, or family members; details on any insurance policies and retirement plans you own; and a list of your bank or brokerage accounts. Take a look at these documents every few years and make sure they're up to date. ■

Chapter 37

Adding Life Insurance to Your Plan

For almost all young families, life insurance is critical. This chapter explains the benefits of life insurance, helps you decide what type to purchase, and guides you through figuring out how much to purchase.

What Life Insurance Can Do

Although life insurance does not need to be a part of every person's estate plan, it is essential for most families. Life insurance can help solve several common problems by:

- **Providing financial security to dependents.** Life insurance can be a good way to make sure survivors have enough cash to invest for long-term needs and for current living expenses if a parent dies unexpectedly.
- **Providing immediate cash at death.** Insurance proceeds are a handy source of cash to pay debts, funeral expenses, and taxes.
- **Avoiding probate.** The proceeds of a life insurance policy do not have to go through probate, unless you name your estate as the beneficiary of the policy

(and there is little reason to do so). No probate means the proceeds can be transferred to survivors with little red tape, cost, or delay.

Deciding Whether to Buy a Policy

Although not every parent needs life insurance, most do. For some parents, the choice is obvious: If you live paycheck to paycheck with very little left over at the end of the month, you need life insurance to ensure your dependants' financial well-being if you die. For wealthy parents, it might be a closer call.

I work full time to support my family. Although we don't live paycheck to paycheck, we aren't wealthy. Do I need life insurance?

Yes. For young parents, life insurance is such a bargain that there is little reason not to have it. And the protection that it provides to your family is priceless.

I'm a stay-at-home parent. Do I need life insurance if my spouse is covered?

It depends. Ask yourself: If I weren't around to provide child care, how much would it cost to buy that for as long as it was needed? If your spouse would not be able to comfortably afford child care, taking into account assets such as Social Security survivor's benefits, then it is wise to purchase life insurance. Even if your spouse could afford it, you might want to purchase some life insurance so that your spouse could switch to part-time work, thereby continuing the benefit to your children of having a parent care for them.

I already have life insurance coverage through my job. Do I need to buy my own life insurance policy?

Maybe. This is because you may lose employer-provided life insurance if you leave or lose your job. If that happens, you may have difficulty purchasing a policy at that time, because policies are more expensive and more difficult to get as you get older.

Should I buy life insurance for my child?

As a new parent, you'll probably receive plenty of fliers in the mail offering life insurance coverage for your child at just pennies a day. Though these policies may seem like a bargain, there's really no reason to purchase life insurance for your child. People need life insurance coverage only if they help support a family—something your baby probably does not do.

Choosing a Type of Policy: Term and Permanent Life Insurance

The type of policy you choose will determine the amount of your premiums and the length of coverage. This section helps you choose between the two main types of policies: term and permanent.

What is the difference between term and permanent insurance?

Term life insurance provides insurance protection for a fixed term, anywhere from one to 30 years. If you die while the policy is in effect, the insurance company will pay the proceeds of your policy to the beneficiary you named. If, however, you die after the term of your policy has ended, your family will get nothing at all.

Permanent life insurance is a both an insurance policy and an investment vehicle. Each year, you invest a certain sum of money in your permanent life policy. Part of the money goes toward the premiums for your life insurance coverage, and the rest goes into a tax-deferred savings account. Unlike term life insurance, which lasts for only a set period of time, a permanent life insurance policy remains in effect for your entire life, as long as you pay the premiums. Permanent insurance is anywhere from four to 15 times more expensive than term.

What type should I buy?

For most young families, term life insurance is the best and least expensive way to provide financial security for your children in the unlikely event that tragedy strikes. Here's why:

- Term life insurance is downright cheap compared to permanent life insurance. This is especially true if you buy term insurance when you are in your 20s or early 30s. A healthy 30-year-old father, for example, could purchase half a million dollars worth of term life insurance for as little as $500 per year.

- Most parents need life insurance only when their children are young or in school. Paying extra to extend life insurance coverage until well into your child's adulthood—even middle age—makes little financial sense for the average family.

- Term life insurance is easy to cancel if your needs change or you decide to switch insurance carriers. All you have to do is stop paying the premiums, and your coverage will end.

Permanent life insurance, on the other hand, is best for the wealthy or for older individuals who would have to pay sizable term life premiums anyway. For the rest of us, permanent life insurance provides far too little bang for our precious buck. Here are some drawbacks:

- Permanent life insurance is expensive. Why spend so much when you can get adequate coverage for much less with a simple term life policy?

- Permanent life insurance comes weighted down with hefty maintenance fees and commissions. These costs will eat into the investment portion of your premiums.

- It's difficult to cancel a permanent life policy. To get out of the contract, you'll have to pay a surrender charge, which can be as much as 10% of your policy's payoff value.

Insurance agents get hefty commissions when they sell permanent life policies. Your insurance agent may make a big plug for permanent life insurance—touting it as a retirement plan or a tax-free savings plan. Don't take your agent's advice at face value on this issue, because your agent stands to make much more selling a permanent life policy than a term life one.

TIPS

Get help sizing up a permanent life policy. If you're still intrigued by the idea of permanent life insurance, then at least get an expert opinion on the policy's investment returns before taking the plunge. The Consumer Federation of America (CFA) will do exactly that for you for the bargain sum of $60 for the first policy and $45 for each additional policy. Check out their Life Insurance Rate of Return Service on the CFA website at www.consumerfed.org or call 603-224-2805 for details.

Buying a Policy

Once you've decided that life insurance is necessary for your family, you have to decide how much to buy and from whom. You'll also have to reveal a lot about your physical and mental health during the application process.

How much life insurance should I buy?
A rule of thumb is to purchase life insurance in the amount of six to ten times your annual income. For example, if you earn $100,000 each year, you should purchase somewhere between $600,000 and $1 million worth of life insurance coverage. Having said that, your family could require much more or less coverage, depending on your needs and assets. If your family has managed to save enough to pay for college education and a comfortable retirement, for example, you'll need a smaller policy than a family that has no savings.

TIPS

Cut out the guesswork. To get some help calculating the right amount of life insurance to buy, check out *Smart Money's* handy online worksheet at http://smartmoney.com/insurance/life/#worksheet.

How much does life insurance cost?

Life insurance costs different amounts for different people. Premiums will depend on a number of risk factors, including your age and health. For example, a 40-year-old asthmatic who recently kicked a long-time smoking habit will pay more than a 30-year-old in good health who never smoked. We explain more about risk factors, below.

I know the type and amount of insurance I want. Now I am ready to buy. Where should I start?

You can get life insurance directly through a life insurance company or by using an insurance agent or online insurance broker. If you're Web-savvy, two good places to begin the process are www.insure.com and www.accuquote.com. Both will give you a ballpark insurance quote with just a few clicks of your mouse and will enable you to compare quotes from different companies. You can then go directly to the insurance company to complete the application process, if you like, or purchase a policy through the site.

How should I choose an insurance company?

There are more life insurance companies than you can possibly keep track of, so choosing among them can be tricky. Price is important, as is a history of treating customers well and paying claims fairly and on time. You also want a company that is financially sound.

The best way to check up on your insurance company is by requesting a rating from Weiss Ratings, Inc.—the most accurate of the various insurance rating services (www.weissratings.com). You can buy a Weiss rating on an individual insurance company for $14.99 or a comprehensive rating analysis report for $49.

If you'd prefer to do your homework free of charge, you can look up Standard & Poor's ratings on insurance companies at www.insure.com. Insurance companies that are rated AA or better by Standard & Poor's are a safe bet. You might also want to check A.M. Best's website (www.ambest.com) to make sure that your company has an A.M. Best rating of at least A–.

You can also compare insurance companies on the basis of their consumer complaint records. Check with your state's insurance department for complaint-related information. The National Association of Insurance Commissioners website at www.naic.org is also a useful resource. It provides easy-to-find links to each state's insurance department websites and contains plenty of data on consumer complaints against insurance companies.

Choose your insurance company wisely. If your insurance company goes under, your state's insurance guarantee fund will be responsible for making sure your claim gets paid. However, state guarantee funds usually have relatively low caps on how much they will pay per claim—which means that you could get paid only $300,000 on a $1 million policy. What's more, obtaining payment from a state guarantee fund usually involves delays and disputes.

What will the application process be like? Before an insurance company will agree to insure your life—and on what terms—it will assess your health and your lifestyle, including your age, weight, health history, family's health history, whether you are or ever were a smoker, mental health, activities, credit history, and driving record. You'll have to allow access to your medical records and submit to a physical examination, usually in your home or office.

Once the evaluation is complete, the company will assign you to a risk category and price your policy accordingly.

My insurance quote is higher than I expected. Is there anything I can do?
The insurance company has probably identified a risk factor, such as high blood pressure, that puts you into a higher rate category. Ask whether this is the case. If so and if you have a good explanation, you may be able to talk your way into a lower rate by writing a letter to your insurance company explaining the situation.

EXAMPLE: *When Simone's insurance agent presented her with her life insurance quote, she was surprised to discover that she didn't qualify for preferred status and the low rates that come with it. Her agent explained that the fact that Simone had recently been taking antidepressants may have caused the bump in her rates.*

Simone wrote a letter to the insurance company explaining the cause for her six-month depression: a divorce. Simone also informed the company that she had since recovered and was no longer taking antidepressants, and she included a note from her doctor confirming that she had not taken antidepressants in three months. These efforts paid off: Simone qualified for a lower risk category and lower premiums.

If a long-term health issue such as diabetes is standing between you and affordable life insurance coverage, check with the national insurance carriers that specialize in providing life insurance to individuals with serious health issues. The list includes: CNA (www.cna.com or 800-262-0348), Empire General (www.empiregeneral.com or 800-688-3518), Banner Life (www.bannerlife.com or 800-638-8428), and Guarantee Trust Life (www.gtlic.com or 888-898-3279). Because these companies have experience with people dealing with chronic health problems, they know better than to lump all people with the same health issue into the same risk category. What this means is that you may have to pay only about 5% to 25% more than someone who does not suffer from your health problems for the same level of life insurance coverage.

If circumstances may change in the future, consider settling for a pricey life insurance policy now and reapplying later when your health has improved.

> **EXAMPLE:** *Steven gained nearly 100 pounds after he stopped running marathons and began working as a day trader. He knew that he would be able to lose the weight if someone just gave him the right push, and his life insurance quote turned out to be exactly that. Steven purchased the expensive policy and promised himself that he would bring down his rates next year once he had slimmed down.*
>
> *For the next year, Steven ran on his treadmill for an hour each day and adhered closely to a sensible diet. He lost weight, reapplied for life insurance, and was delighted to learn that he had knocked several hundred dollars off his annual premium.*

Postponing the purchase of life insurance until you qualify for a lower risk category is not a good idea. If tragedy strikes between now and then, your family could be left without enough money—a possibility that's hardly worth the savings.

CAUTION

Don't lie on your insurance application. If your insurance company learns of any misrepresentations in your application (for example, if you failed to report a long history of smoking or heart disease) the company could refuse to pay the proceeds of the policy to your beneficiary when you die.

Naming a Beneficiary

The purpose of life insurance is to provide for loved ones in the unlikely event of your death. So deciding whom to name as the beneficiary is an important part of the process.

If you are married, the most sensible thing to do is to name your spouse, who would manage the money for the benefit of your family if you died unexpectedly, as the primary beneficiary. You can name your child as the contingent beneficiary. Single people can name their child as the primary beneficiary.

Because minor children cannot own property, if you name a child as either the primary or contingent beneficiary, you must name a custodian to manage and spend the money on your child's behalf. Your insurance company should be able to provide you with the forms to do this. ■

8

Contents

Safety is a parent's most basic task, and it touches on almost every aspect of your life—from baby-proofing your home to holding your toddler's hand as you cross the street. A great deal of keeping your child safe depends on your individual taste and your tolerance for risk. And it depends on your child as well—how adventurous he or she is, or how cautious. Some parents have to put a latch on every drawer and a baby monitor in every room; other parents do not. It's up to you.

There are some things, however, that all parents must do—and they must do them in essentially the same way. All parents must make sure that the baby products they buy are safe, and they must eliminate home health hazards—such as lead paint and poisons. In addition, they must make sure that their child is properly restrained when traveling by car or by plane. The chapters that follow look at these areas and help you get the job done.

Chapter 38

Buying Safe Products

As a parent, you want to give your child the best of everything. You'll probably spend weeks setting up your child's nursery, selecting the perfect crib, the cutest bedding, and the most adorable mobile. And the nursery is just the beginning: You might also buy a high chair, an infant swing, and some toys—just to name a few of the thousands of products available to new parents for their little ones.

Of course, cute and adorable should not be your only considerations when buying something for your child: You must also make sure that everything you buy is safe. This can be easier said than done. Manufacturers are not required to test products for safety before selling them, and many unsafe products make it onto store shelves every year. So it behooves you, the parent, to take some care when choosing a product for your child. Fortunately, resources exist to help you weed out the safe from the unsafe, and you can learn all about them in this chapter.

CROSS REFERENCE

Read Chapter 40, *Safety in the Car.* There, you'll find important information about choosing a safe car seat for your child—and using it properly.

FAST FACTS

Baby products injure tens of thousands of children each year. In 2003, more than 60,000 children younger than five were treated in emergency rooms for injuries involving all kinds of nursery products—from car seats to cribs to strollers to high chairs. And more than 70,000 children were treated for injuries involving toys.

Picking Safe Products

No matter what kind of product you are buying, do the following homework to ensure that the product is safe:

❑ Look for the Juvenile Products Manufacturers Association seal of approval.

❑ Read *Consumer Reports* reviews of the product.

❑ Read the packaging to make sure the product is designed for your child's age group.

❑ Find out whether the product has been recalled.

If a product is sold new in a store, can I assume that it is safe?

No. Although the government does set safety standards for many children's products, and quality manufacturers do safety-test products before they hit the stores, dozens of children's products are recalled each year because of safety problems that are discovered after parents begin using these products. (See "Recent Recalls Involve Trusted Brands," below, for some examples.) What's more, a number of widely available children's products—such as baby bath seats—are considered dangerous by safety experts but are sold nonetheless. You can find a list of popular children's products with unsafe track records at the website of Kids in Danger, a nonprofit organization dedicated to protecting children from defective products. Log on to www.kidsindanger.org and click on "Product Hazards" in the left-hand menu bar.

How do I choose safe products for my child?

First, look for a seal from the Juvenile Products Manufacturers Association (JPMA), a trade organization whose safety standards are much higher than those issued by the federal government. The JPMA currently certifies a wide variety of products, from bassinets and cradles to infant carriers and walkers. For a complete list of products, log on to www.jpma.org, click on "Consumer" in the top menu bar, and then click on "Certification Program." in the pull-down menu.

Second, find out what *Consumer Reports* has to say about the product. The easiest way is to log onto www.consumerreports.org, where you will find free and for-fee information about baby products and gear. You can also find the group's reviews and ratings compiled in the book *Consumer Reports Best Baby Products,* by Sandra Gordon.

Third, read the packaging to make sure that the toy or product is age-appropriate for your child. The age you see on the label reflects important characteristics about the product—such as whether it has small parts that could choke or sharp edges and points that could scratch.

Fourth, find out if the product has been recalled (see below).

The federal government has lots of information for you. The Consumer Product Safety Commission (CPSC), which is the federal agency that regulates many baby products, has tons of helpful (and free) child safety publications. Log onto the agency's website at www.cpsc.gov, click on the "CPSC Publications" link, and then click on the "Child Safety" link. Among the publications you'll find there are "The Safe Nursery: A Booklet to Help Avoid Injuries From Nursery Furniture and Equipment," "Baby Safety Checklist," and "Baby Products Safety Alert."

The Skinny on Regulation

Not every product is government regulated, but many are. Three main agencies create safety standards.

- The U.S. Consumer Product Safety Commission (CPSC) issues mandatory safety standards for many children's products, including cribs, pacifiers, baby bouncers and walkers, toys, sleepwear, and bicycles. The CPSC also issues mandatory standards for many other products that could affect your child's safety, including child-resistant packaging (for medicines and poisons), lead paint, and asbestos. To find out more, log onto www.cpsc.gov.
- The National Highway Traffic Safety Administration (NHTSA) sets safety standards for car seats. The NHTSA's car seat safety standard—Federal Motor Vehicle Safety Standard 213 ("Child Restraint Systems")—has been in place and updated regularly since 1981. The NHTSA also crash tests all car seats to make sure that they are safe for children. To find out more, log onto www.nhtsa.gov.
- Finally, the federal Food and Drug Administration (FDA) regulates food and drug products for children—everything from infant formula to children's Tylenol to infant vaccines. For more information, log onto the "Parents' Corner" portion of the FDA website at www.fda.gov/oc/opacom/kids/html/parents__corner.htm.

In addition, some states have additional safety regulations. For example, a number of states—such as California and Pennsylvania—set standards for crib safety that are higher than the federal standard. Check with your state's department of consumer affairs to learn about child safety laws in your state. To find yours, check out State and Local Government on the Net at www.statelocalgov.net.

How can I find out if a product I am considering has been recalled?

The CPSC maintains a complete list of recalled product alerts on its website. These recall alerts contain important information such as:

- a description of the product being recalled, including product numbers and when and where the product was sold
- possible injuries that could result from using the product
- steps the manufacturer is taking to remedy the situation, and
- contact information for the manufacturer.

Just log on to www.cpsc.gov, click on "Recalls and Product Safety News," and then click on "Child products (not including toys)" or "Toys" to get started.

 TIPS

Sign up for free recall alert emails. Instead of checking the CPSC's website periodically, you could just look in your email inbox for up-to-the-minute recall information for children's products. To sign up for the CPSC's email alert service, log on to www.cpsc.gov and click on "Sign Up for Email Announcements."

 BABYCENTER RESOURCES

Customized recall alerts for BabyCenter.com Plus members. If you're a BabyCenter.com Plus subscriber, you can register the major baby products that you own—such as your high chair or stroller—and let BabyCenter.com email you if any of the products you register get recalled. Sign up on BabyCenter.com's *Parent Savvy* page (www.babycenter.com/parent savvy).

Recent Recalls Involve Trusted Brands

The CPSC recalls dozens of children's products each year. You might be surprised to learn that many of these recalled products are made by major children's manufacturers that parents have grown to trust. For example:

- In March of 2005, Graco recalled 1.2 million toddler beds because it received reports that children's arms and legs were getting caught in the slats in the guard rails and footboard.
- In February of 2005, Playtex recalled more than 30,000 Hip Hammock infant carriers because it discovered that the shoulder strap could detach and an infant could fall out.
- In June of 2003, Fisher-Price recalled more than 200,000 crib mobiles because the battery compartment could not contain battery leaks, putting children at risk of burns.

What should I do if a product I buy turns out to be unsafe for my child?

Contact the manufacturer immediately to let the company know of the problem. You should also file a report with the CPSC. (You can do this on the Internet by logging on to www.cpsc.gov and clicking on the link marked "Report an Unsafe Product." Or you can call the CPSC's hotline number at 800-638-2772.)

Even if your child is not actually injured by the product, you can help prevent injuries to other children by reporting dangerous conditions, such as a sharp edge on a high-chair tray or a small detachable part on a toy for toddlers.

Is it safe to purchase used children's products or take hand-me-downs from family or friends?

Yes—so long as the product isn't too old and worn out—and so long as you make sure that the product is still safe. This means you should:

- copy the manufacturer name and product number off of the label and then check to see whether the product has been recalled
- check to see whether safety standards have changed since the year the product was produced (this is especially important with car seats, playpens, safety gates, and cribs—because safety standards for these products have improved quite a bit in recent years)

- carefully inspect the product to make sure it isn't damaged or worn out (for example, look to see that belts and buckles work properly on high chairs, strollers, and baby swings, and check to see whether toys have loose parts), and
- make sure the product meets the safety specifications in the CPSC publication "The Safe Nursery."

 TIPS

Hang on to your receipts and warranties. The products you buy for your child will invariably break from time to time—whether it's a stroller wheel that pops off as you make your way through the park or an unzippable zipper on your child's crib tent. You'll have an easier time getting the manufacturer to fix the product for you free of charge (or send you a brand new one) if you can produce your receipt and a copy of the product warranty You may even want to make most of your purchases at well-established superstores—such as Buy Buy Baby on the East Coast (see www.buybuybaby.com)—to take advantage of generous return policies on broken items. (Buy Buy Baby will often let you exchange a broken item months after the manufacturer's warranty has run out, as long as you've kept a copy of your original receipt.)

Save money on new baby products. If you need to keep costs down, you'll be happy to know that some of the safest baby products on the market are also the most reasonably priced. For example, the highly rated Delta Luv crib is only $110. And the highly rated J. Mason Safe Surround Sport play yard is only $40. To learn more about buying new baby products that won't break the bank, check out *Baby Bargains: Secrets to Saving 20% to 50% on Baby Furniture, Equipment, Clothes, Toys, Maternity Wear, and Much, Much More!*, by Denise and Alan Fields (Windsor Peak Press). ■

Chapter 39

Eliminating Home Health Hazards

For most young children, their home is their haven, the place where they feel most comfortable and secure. But it can also be a dangerous place, unless parents take steps to ensure that it is hazard free. At a most basic level, this involves doing things such as putting baby gates on stairs and covers on outlets. Indeed, baby-proofing is as fundamental a part of being a parent as changing diapers and giving baths.

This chapter takes a look at two hazards that many parents don't even realize exist in their home: lead hazards (in paint, drinking water, and soil) and poisonous household products, such as pesticides.

Protecting Your Child From Lead

Lead is a highly toxic element that can cause serious health problems in both children and adults. But for many years, the health hazards were not recognized, and lead was widely used in everything from household paint and water pipes to gasoline.

The federal government banned the use of lead in these common consumer products in 1978, but children continue to suffer lead poisoning through exposure to lead dust from leaded household paint, lead-contaminated drinking water, and soil tainted with lead from gasoline or exterior paint.

If you live in a home that predates 1978, it's important to find out whether your home contains lead-based paint. If it does, and if that paint has begun to deteriorate and release lead dust into the air, it may pose a hazard to your family. You should also determine whether your drinking water and the soil in your backyard is contaminated with lead.

If it turns out that lead is a problem in your home, don't worry. There are a number of easy and relatively inexpensive steps that you can take to make your home safe for your child.

For more information. One of the best resources on creating a safe home for your child is BabyCenter .com's "Keeping Your Baby Safe" section. You can find a link to it on BabyCenter.com's *Parent Savvy* page at www.babycenter.com/parentsavvy. There you will find an extensive collection of articles—including room-by-room guides to childproofing your home, preparing for an emergency, infant first aid, and the safety of food, medicine, chemicals, household plants, and pets. You'll also find plenty of advice on child safety away from home (hotels, other people's houses, zoos, restaurants, beaches and pools, amusement parks, shopping centers, playgrounds, and so on).

To learn more about lead-based paint and other lead hazards. This chapter provides a good overview of the issues, but if you want more information, check out the U.S. Environmental Protection Agency's (EPA's) pamphlet entitled "Protect Your Family From Lead in Your Home," which you can download free at www.epa.gov/opptintr/ lead/leadpdfe.pdf. The National Safety Council's (NSC's) website at www.nsc.org/issues/lead also has plenty of information on lead poisoning and prevention. Finally, check out the National Lead Information Center (NLIC), a joint project of the EPA, the Centers for Disease Control and Prevention, and the Department of Housing and Urban Development. See www.epa.gov/lead/nlic.htm. The NLIC provides information about lead hazards and their prevention and can refer to you state and local agencies in charge of lead hazards. It also includes lots of useful links and free publications such as "Lead in Your Home: A Parent's Reference Guide."

 FAST FACTS

Lead-based paint hazards affect millions of homes. The U.S. Department of Housing and Urban Development estimates that about 38 million American homes still contain some lead-based paint. And about 24 million homes—a quarter of the country's housing stock—have significant lead-based paint hazards (from peeling lead paint, for example).

Children younger than six are most at risk
for lead-related damage because their
brains and nervous systems are still developing and because their bodies absorb
more lead than adult bodies.

Some of the health problems that lead can
cause in children include: anemia; learning disabilities; attention deficit disorder;
lowered intelligence; speech, language, and
behavioral problems; poor muscle coordination; impaired muscle and bone growth;
hearing problems; and nervous system and
kidney damage. In cases of extremely high
exposure to lead, children can suffer seizures
and even death.

Children are not the only victims of lead
exposure. Pregnant women are particularly
at risk, because the lead can easily be transferred to their growing babies. And adults
can suffer everything from high blood
pressure and digestive difficulties to fertility
problems and nerve disorders as a result of
lead poisoning.

Lead Hazards in the Home

How could my child be exposed to lead in
my home?

By far the most common source of lead
exposure is through breathing or swallowing
lead dust, which is created when lead-based
paint deteriorates (by peeling or chipping,
for example), releasing tiny particles of lead
into the air. Lead dust can also be created
when lead-based paint is disturbed through
wear and tear (for example, when a painted
door or window is opened and shut frequently) or during home renovation.

Young children are far more likely to
ingest lead dust than are grownups, simply because they put so many more things
into their mouths. A ten-month-old girl
might drop her pacifier on the floor and
then promptly pick it up and put it into her
mouth. Or a two-year-old boy might leave
his cracker on a painted windowsill and then
return to eat it a few minutes later.

For very young children, eating or chewing on lead paint is also a problem. If paint
is peeling in a corner of your living room, for
example, your curious six-month-old daughter might pick up stray paint chips and pop
them straight into her mouth.

Lead-contaminated water is another common source of lead exposure. If your pipes
are made of lead or held together using
lead solder, the lead could leach out into
your drinking water. Lead is tasteless, so you
wouldn't even notice. Formula-fed infants
whose formula is made using tap water
are particularly at risk of water-based lead
poisoning.

The soil in your yard may have become
tainted with lead from the exterior paint
on your home or from leaded gasoline
(exhaust fumes contain lead, which settles
on the ground). You should be especially
concerned about lead contamination in your
soil if you live near a well-traveled highway or road that has been used since the
1970s—before the Environmental Protection
Agency's reduction of lead in gasoline.

Your family can also track lead contaminated soil into your home on your shoes—
and your child could accidentally ingest the

soil just by dropping toys or bottles on the floor and then putting those items into his or her mouth. Babies and toddlers playing outside might also eat the soil directly, as part of their exploration of the world around them.

Testing Your Child for Lead

How can I tell if my child is in danger because of exposure to lead in my home? Children suffering from lead poisoning often have no obvious symptoms. So the only way to find out is through a blood test, which your child's pediatrician can easily administer. If your child's blood lead level is below a certain number (ten micrograms of lead per deciliter of blood), then you won't have anything to worry about. But if your child's blood level is above that, your child has suffered lead poisoning and may need special medical treatment.

FAST FACTS

Too many children suffer from lead poisoning. According to the Centers for Disease Control, nearly half a million American children in the United States have blood lead levels high enough to cause irreversible health damage.

When and how often should I have my child tested for lead?
The Children's Health Environmental Coalition (www.checnet.org), a national nonprofit group dedicated to educating parents and the public about environmental toxins affecting children's health, recommends testing children for lead when they reach one year of

age and every year thereafter until age five. You should also have older children tested for lead if your home has peeling or deteriorating paint.

Advice for Homeowners

I live in an older home. How can I make sure it is safe for my child?

The best thing to do is to arrange for a certified lead inspector to examine your home and to test paint, dust, soil, and water samples. An inspector will be able to tell you whether your home has lead-based paint, where it is located, whether there is a lead dust problem in your home, whether the soil around your home is contaminated with lead, and whether your drinking water is contaminated with lead. In addition, the inspector can advise you on how best to reduce the risks of lead exposure in your home. A comprehensive lead inspection costs several hundred dollars, depending on the size of your home.

How can I find a lead professional to inspect my home?

To find a lead testing professional in your area, contact your state's department of health. You can find yours at State and Local Government on the Net at www.statelocalgov.net. Many states have certification programs for lead professionals, and you may be able to get a list of state-certified lead professionals in your area. If your state's department of health can't help you, then look in your local Yellow Pages under the headings "Environmental Consultants" or

"Environmental Services." Before selecting someone, check the person's qualifications and understand what you will be getting for your money. Here are some tips:

- Make sure the professional is certified by your state, if your state has a certification program. Ask to see a copy of the professional's certification.
- If your state has no certification program for lead professionals, then try to hire a person who has completed a course in lead risk assessment approved by the Environmental Protection Agency. Ask to see a copy of the person's certificate of course completion.
- Get the names and telephone numbers of three references. Call each one and ask whether the inspector was able to answer the customer's questions and supply guidance on how to resolve any problems.
- Find out what will be included in the inspector's lead risk assessment. Will the inspector test paint, dust, soil, and water samples? Will you get recommendations on how to reduce the risk of lead exposure in your home?
- Ask for a written cost estimate, as well as a written description of the services the inspector will provide.

My local hardware store has a kit that I can use to test for lead paint. Why should I pay to have a professional inspect my house when I can buy a kit for less than $30?

There are a couple of reasons why a lead paint test kit isn't a good substitute for a lead inspection. First, these kits are unreliable about 30% of the time—so you might think that your home is safe when in fact there's lead paint throughout. Second, a lead paint test will tell you only whether your home has lead paint. You won't find out whether your home has lead dust, or whether your soil and water are contaminated with lead.

If lead-based paint is present in my home, does that necessarily mean that it poses a hazard?

No. Lead paint in good condition (or completely covered up by another coat of paint) is generally not hazardous. Problems arise only when the paint begins to deteriorate or when the paint is disturbed through wear and tear or renovations. This is when chips fall on the floor or lead is released into the air, forming lead dust. Check the National Lead Information Center website at www .epa.gov/lead/nlic.htm for useful publications on home renovations and painting.

I own my house. An inspector told me that it has deteriorating lead-based paint. What should I do?

One relatively easy and economical option is to repaint your home using lead encapsulating paint. Unlike regular paint, encapsulating paint is specially formulated to seal in the old lead paint and keep lead from escaping and creating lead dust. Encapsulating paint must adhere to federal standards and comes with a 20-year warranty. It costs about 50 cents per square foot. The National Lead Information Center recommends that you hire a lead professional to apply encapsulating paint. If you decide to do the work yourself, just make sure that you can do so legally in your state (some states require that lead abatement work, such as encapsulation, be performed by a certified lead professional). Follow the instructions carefully and apply the correct thickness of paint. Otherwise, you will void the warranty, and the encapsulation treatment may not work. Finally, it's a smart idea to hire a lead inspector to oversee the work and document the results. Be sure to keep careful records of the lead inspection report and your encapsulation treatment. You'll need to show these records to a buyer if you sell your home later (see below).

TIPS

Consider ChildGuard paint. Although there are many encapsulating paints on the market that meet federal standards, Fiberlock's ChildGuard paint stands out from the crowd. This safe, nontoxic paint includes a special ingredient that makes the paint taste bitter (to discourage children from chewing on the paint). You can buy the paint online at www.fiberlock.com.

Encapsulation won't work for areas with heavy wear and tear. Applying a coat of encapsulating paint works well for relatively undisturbed areas, such as walls and ceilings. But for window jambs, door jambs, and banisters, encapsulation isn't a good solution. You'll need to remove the painted item or, if you want to keep the item, hire a lead abatement contractor to remove the lead paint from the item's surface. To find a lead abatement specialist, contact the National Lead Information Center at 800-424-LEAD, www.epa.gov/lead/nlic.htm. The National Lead Information Center will put you in touch with your state or local agency in charge of lead hazards, and that agency will give you the names of qualified lead abatement contractors in your area.

I've learned that the soil in my backyard is contaminated with lead. What should I do? You can remove and replace the soil or, more reasonably, cover it with sand, wood chips, stone, or sod. You can also plant grass. Don't let your children play in the lead-contaminated soil until you've had a chance to cover it up.

Simple Steps to Minimize Your Family's Lead Exposure

If you live in an older home, your child may be at risk of lead exposure from a variety of sources—from lead dust in your air to lead in your drinking water. Fortunately, there are a few simple things you can do to reduce the risk of lead poisoning:

Clean your house meticulously. Vacuum your house at least once a week using a vacuum cleaner with a HEPA dust filter. (HEPA vacuums aren't too pricey: The Shark Bagless Canister Vacuum with a HEPA filter, for example, runs for less than $100.) Follow up with a wet mopping of your floors.

Have your child tested for lead. Let your child's doctor know about the potential lead exposure in your home and make sure that your child is tested annually for lead.

Feed your child a healthy diet. Children who eat a nutritious diet, with plenty of foods high in calcium and iron, absorb less lead than children with inadequate diets.

Wash your child's hands and toys often. Especially before eating and sleeping, be sure to give your child's hands a good scrub with soap and water. And clean bottles, pacifiers, and toys on a regular basis.

Use only cold water for drinking and cooking. Let your water run for at least 30 seconds before drinking it, to flush out water that has been sitting in your pipes for a while. And if you're at all concerned about the quality of your tap water, use bottled water to make your baby's formula.

Take off your shoes before you enter your home. This way, you won't track in lead-contaminated soil from the outside.

Advice for Renters

I rent my home, which was built in 1912. Does the law require my landlord to inspect my home for lead-based paint hazards? Although landlords must disclose any lead hazards that they know about before you move into an apartment or rental (see **Federal Lead-Based Paint Disclosures,** below), there is no federal law that requires your landlord to inspect your home for lead-based paint hazards. However, a state or local law may impose this inspection obligation on your landlord. For example, New York City landlords must visually inspect apartments where children younger than six live for peeling or deteriorating paint every year.

If there is no state or local law that requires your landlord to inspect your home for lead-based paint hazards, you may want to arrange for a lead inspection on your own.

I rent my home. Does the law require my landlord to fix lead-based paint hazards? There is no federal law that requires private landlords to repair chipped and peeling paint or to seal off lead paint using special encapsulating paint. However, laws in practically all states require that landlords provide tenants with a safe place to live—this requirement is known as the "warranty of habitability." A home that is laced with lead hazards is not habitable. Your state law may require your landlord to repair lead-based paint hazards, by covering areas of peeling paint, for example. Check with the agency in charge of lead hazards in your state to learn about your rights. You can find a list of state agencies by contacting the National Lead Information Center online at www.epa.gov/lead/nlic.htm or by phone at 800-424-LEAD. Or check with your state environmental agency. You can find yours by searching your state agencies on State and Local Government on the Net at www .statelocalgov.net.

TIPS

If you live in federally-subsidized housing. The federal Lead Safe Housing Rule requires that housing financially assisted by the federal government or sold by the federal government be free of lead-based paint hazards. You can find more information about the Lead Safe Housing Rule at the U.S. Department of Housing and Urban Development website. Log on to www .hud.gov/offices/lead/leadtips.cfm and click on "Lead Paint Regulations (Lead Safe Housing Rule)."

I live in an old rental apartment, and the paint is peeling and chipped. What should I do?
Tell your landlord immediately. Send your notice in writing and keep a copy for yourself. If your landlord does not respond within a few days, check with the state agency in charge of lead hazards to learn about your rights.

Even if your state law does not require your landlord to repair lead-based paint hazards, you may be able to convince your landlord to do so voluntarily. In cases where children have suffered serious lead poisoning, landlords have had to fork over enormous amounts of money in lawsuits.

My landlord refuses to do anything about the deteriorating lead-based paint in my home. What are my options?

You could continue to live in your home and deal with the lead paint problem on your own (see "Simple Steps to Minimize Your Family's Lead Exposure," above). You may even want to repaint your apartment. But be warned that painting with standard paint—rather than special encapsulating paint—is only a temporary solution. This is because the lead paint can continue to loosen from the surface below to create lead dust.

Another option is to move out. If you are locked into a long lease, you may be legally justified in breaking your lease on the grounds that your home is unsafe to live in. If you do this, be sure to keep careful records of the lead paint problem. For example, take photographs of the areas of peeling paint. And if you've had your home inspected for lead hazards, keep a copy of the report in your files.

Your Rights as a Tenant

If you rent your home, your landlord has obligations under state law to provide a safe environment for you and your child. Your state probably has laws requiring your landlord to install and maintain smoke alarms, door locks, and window guards. Your landlord may also be required to take steps to remove rodent or cockroach infestation in your home.

Fortunately, landlords cannot avoid safety obligations that primarily benefit children (such as swimming pool fences and gates) simply by refusing to rent to families with children (or charging families more for the same rental unit). The federal Fair Housing Act prohibits landlords from discriminating against families with children or pregnant women. When it comes to lead, landlords who know of the presence of lead paint hazards in their rentals cannot avoid dealing with the problem by not renting to families.

You can learn more about the federal Fair Housing Act at the U.S. Department of Housing and Urban Development's website (www.hud.gov). Just log on to www.hud.gov and click on the link marked "Fair Housing" in the left-hand menu bar.

In addition, a wonderful resource on tenant rights (leases and rental agreement, rent and security deposits, discrimination, repairs and injuries, environmental health hazards such as lead, and more) is *Every Tenant's Legal Guide,* by Janet Portman and Marcia Stewart (Nolo). This book covers federal and state laws on a wide variety of issues that affect tenants.

Federal Lead-Based Paint Disclosures

I'm moving into a new home. How can I find out about potential lead-based paint hazards?

Under the federal Residential Lead-Based Paint Hazard Reduction Act, sellers and landlords must disclose known lead hazards and provide an EPA pamphlet ("Protecting Your Family From Lead in Your Home") to buyers or renters before selling or leasing a home built before 1978. This means that if the seller or landlord of your new home is aware of the presence of lead-based paint, or lead hazards (such as lead-contaminated soil), the seller or landlord must tell you about these potential dangers in a written disclosure sheet before you sign your lease or contract. If you are buying a home, the seller must give you a ten-day window to conduct a lead hazard risk assessment before signing the contract.

Does the law require the seller of a home to remove lead-based paint hazards?

No. All the federal law requires is that the seller disclose known lead-based paint and lead-based paint hazards to you before you purchase the home or move into the rental.

CAUTION

Not all homes are covered. The Lead Based Paint Hazard Reduction Act does not apply to foreclosure sales, studio apartments, efficiencies, lofts, dormitories, rental housing that has been inspected by a certified lead inspector and found to be free of lead-based paint, rentals of individual rooms, leases for less than 100 days, or housing set aside for the elderly and people with disabilities (provided no children younger than six live there or are expected to live there).

My landlord is doing a lot of remodeling work around my apartment building. Do I have any rights in this kind of situation?

Under the federal Toxic Substances Control Act, a landlord or contractor who performs renovation work that disturbs painted surfaces on rental property must provide tenants with lead hazard information before the renovation work begins, including the EPA pamphlet "Protect Your Family From Lead in Your Home." Not every renovation triggers the federal law, though. There are four big exceptions:

- emergency renovations required as a result of a fire or other event
- minor repairs or maintenance affecting two square feet or less of a painted surface

- renovations in certified lead-free properties, and
- common area renovations in buildings with three or fewer units.

Landlords or contractors who fail to give tenants the required information about renovation lead hazards face harsh penalties—up to $27,500 per day for willful violations.

Lead in Tap Water

Should I worry about lead in my tap water? Water pipes in older homes were commonly made of lead or bonded together by lead solder. Lead from the pipes can leach out to your tap water. You can visually confirm whether the pipe and solder are leaded, but you cannot see, smell, or taste lead contamination in water.

If you're concerned about lead in your tap water, the best thing to do is to test your water for lead. You can purchase an easy do-it-yourself test kit for about $20. You can buy a test kit from Clean Water Lead Testing, Inc. (www.leadtesting.org), a nonprofit organization that researches lead pollution and other environmental problems.

What can I do to reduce the risk of lead poisoning from my tap water? Run your tap water for at least 30 seconds, until the water becomes very cold. This will flush out any water that has been sitting in the pipes. Also, never use hot tap water for cooking, because hot water tends to absorb more lead.

Protecting Your Child From Poisons

One of the most serious risks your child faces in your home is the possibility of accidental ingestion of poisonous household products, such as cleaning supplies or pesticides. Here you'll get answers to your basic questions on household poisoning.

 FAST FACTS

More than a million children are exposed to poisons each year. If you think household poisoning is a rare event, think again. In 2003, there were 2,395,582 human toxic exposures reported to poison control centers. 52% of these cases involved children younger than six, and 93% of the poisonings took place in a home environment.

What steps can I take to prevent my child from getting poisoned in my home?
It's easy to keep even the most inquisitive toddler safe from household poisoning if you just take a few commonsense steps to make your home safe for your child:

- **Read all labels carefully.** You might not realize that many everyday household products—such as mouthwash and perfume—are dangerous to children. So read all labels carefully to find out which of your household products pose a danger to your child. Labels also contain other important information, like usage and storage instructions. Follow these instructions to the letter. For example, if the label of a household cleaner says that you should open a window or wear gloves before use, then do so.

- **Keep all dangerous products out of the reach of your child.** Be sure to use child safety locks on all cabinets that contain poisonous products. If you store products in cabinets that are high up off the ground, you still may need child locks. After all, your enterprising toddler might use a stool or chair to reach the cabinet—and all of its tempting contents.

- **Don't trust childproof packages.** Childproof containers aren't nearly as foolproof as you might imagine. A determined child might be able to open the container, especially if you didn't shut the container properly the last time you used it. So treat medicines in childproof containers with the same caution as other dangerous poisons, keeping them well out of your child's reach.

- **Keep poisonous products in their original containers.** The last thing you want is to mistake a toxic liquid for apple juice (a horror story heard by many poison control centers). Also, it's important to have the product label handy at all times, for usage instructions and in case there is ever a poisoning incident.

- **Never, ever refer to medicine as "candy."** A curious child may want to try your tasty "candy" when you are not looking.

- **Don't let your child chew on household plants.** Some plants, such as a philodendron, are poisonous.
- **Be especially careful when routines are disrupted or you are away from home.** When relatives are visiting or you are in the middle of a move, it can be easy to become a little careless with household poisons. And when you're away from home, poisonous substances may be in easy reach of your child—particularly if Grandma hasn't done a good job of baby-proofing.
- **Post the nationwide poison control center's number (800-222-1222) and your doctor's phone number on your fridge.** Your child might ingest, inhale, or come into contact with a toxic substance at some point in the next couple of years—even if you are scrupulously careful about poison prevention. So keep these important numbers handy, just in case.

Are there any laws designed to prevent child poisoning by household products?

It would be next to impossible to outlaw the use of poisonous substances in household products because an enormous number of useful everyday items—such as sunscreen and Tylenol—can be poisonous when ingested by children. But the federal government has taken steps to reduce the risk of poisoning. Thanks to the federal Poison Prevention Packaging Act of 1970, child-resistant packaging is required for any household product that can cause serious injury to children if handled, used, or ingested. The packaging must be difficult for a child younger than five to open (but child-resistant packaging often confounds adults as well!).

The federal government also has labeling standards for hazardous substances. For example, the U.S. Environmental Protection Agency has a three-level label system for pesticides (such as Raid) and toxic substances (such as oven cleaner):

- **"Caution" for products that are somewhat harmful.** These products may cause minor health problems—such as dizziness or stomach upset—but your child is unlikely to suffer permanent damage from coming into contact with these products.
- **"Warning" for products that are very harmful.** Your child could be seriously harmed by these products, and the product might also easily catch on fire. By law, these products must be in child-resistant packaging; and
- **"Danger" for products that are extremely harmful.** These products can cause severe harm to your child, ranging from tissue damage to death. Of course, these products must be in child-resistant packaging.

Be sure to read the product labels carefully on all of your household products, and keep dangerous products out of the reach of your child.

What should I do if my child swallows a poisonous household product?

First, save the container so you know exactly what your child ingested. Then, call your local poison control center immediately—even if your child seems perfectly fine or you're not sure if something is really a hazard. Dial 800-222-1222 to be connected to a poison control specialist in your area. The poison control hotlines are open 24 hours a day, seven days a week, and all calls are toll-free.

CAUTION

Don't induce vomiting first. Different household substances pose different levels of risk, and the instructions for resolving the problem will vary depending on what your child ingested. So don't take any action on your own without first speaking to a poison control specialist.

CAUTION

If your child appears to be ill. Some symptoms should be taken very, very seriously. If your child appears to have difficulty breathing, seems unusually sleepy, complains of severe throat pain, has burns on the lips or mouth, begins convulsing. or becomes unconscious, call 911 immediately. Be sure to take the container of the substance your child has ingested with you, so you can show it to the emergency room doctors.

What should I do if my child gets a poisonous substance on his skin?
Take off your child's clothes and rinse the skin with warm water. If the skin appears to be burned (for example, if the affected area is red or raised), then keep rinsing the skin for 15 minutes. Check with your local poison control center for additional instructions.

What should I do if my child gets a poisonous substance in her eye?
Rinse out your child's eye, by pouring lukewarm water into the inner corner of your child's eye, while holding your child's eyelids open. This is, of course, easier said than done. You may need someone else's help, so that one of you can hold the child while the other rinses the eye. But if you're alone, wrap your child in a towel or blanket (to keep arms from flailing), carry your child under one arm, and then try to rinse out the eye. Contact your local poison control center for additional instructions.

What should I do if my child inhales toxic fumes—such as roach spray?
Take your child out for some fresh air immediately, and call your local poison control center for additional instructions. If your child appears have difficulty breathing, call 911 immediately.

To learn more about poison prevention. The National Safety Council has plenty of useful information on its website. Log on to www.nsc.org, click on "Resources" in the top menu bar, and then select "Poison Prevention." Another useful resource is the National Poison Prevention Week Council, which will supply you with free booklets on child safety. Log on to www.poisonprevention.org and click on "Products" for more information. ■

Chapter 40

Safety in the Car

Unless you live in a very urban area like New York City, chances are your child will spend some part of every day in a car—riding to day care, to school, or to your local shopping mall. Although car travel can be dangerous (car accidents are the leading cause of death for children aged two to 14), it doesn't have to be. In fact, you can make car travel dramatically safer for your child just by using a proper car seat.

 FAST FACTS

Car seats save lives. Research shows that car seat use reduces the risk of fatal injury from car accidents by 71% for infants and 54% for children aged one to four.

Car seats are so bulky. Do I have to use one? Absolutely. Not only could it mean the difference between life and death for your child, it's the law. All 50 states require parents to keep children younger than four in a car seat. And some states require booster seats for older children.

How can I find out about my state's car seat laws?
For a quick summary of your state's laws on car seat use, check the chart put together by the National Highway Transportation Safety Administration (NHTSA), available at www .nhtsa.dot.gov/people/injury/airbags/Occu-pantProtectionFacts/appendixc.htm. If you want more detailed information, contact your state department of transportation. To find yours, log on to www.statelocalgov.net.

Many state car seat laws are too lax. Depending on the state in which you live, your state's car seat law may not go far enough to protect your child. The best thing to do is to follow the NHTSA's recommendations when it comes to child safety seats, which you can find below.

What is the safest way for my infant to ride in a car?

If your child is younger than one, he or she should be in a rear-facing car seat in the back seat of your car. Check the weight limit on your car seat. Some rear-facing car seats are designed for use only until your child reaches 20-22 pounds; other rear-facing car seats can be used until your child reaches 35 pounds.

I drive a pickup truck, so there is no back-seat. Can my child ride in front with me?

Yes (the same is true for small cars with no rear seats). To reduce the risk to your child, however, it is essential that you take the following steps:

- move the front passenger seat as far back as possible
- ensure that your child is properly restrained in an age appropriate car seat, and
- disable the passenger air bag (see "Disabling Air Bags," below).

Disabling Air Bags

If your child must ride in the front seat of your car or truck, it is vitally important that you disable the air bag. To do so, look for the air bag on/off switch and put it in the "off" position. (Consult your automobile owner's manual or contact your vehicle manufacturer if you need help finding or operating this switch.)

If your air bag does not have an on/off switch, check with your vehicle's manufacturer to see whether a switch is available for your model. Even if the manufacturer does not make a switch, there may be one on the market that is compatible with your vehicle. Ask your auto dealer or repair shop about this. When you've confirmed that a switch is available for your car, obtain authorization from the NHTSA before installing the switch. To do so, complete and submit a "Request for Air Bag On-Off Switch" form (available online at www .safercar.gov/airbags/Brochure/Switch-Request.PDF). The NHTSA will send you a formal authorization letter that you can then present to your auto dealer or repair shop.

If you have an older vehicle, you may not be able to find a switch. In that case, you'll need to apply to the NHTSA for permission to deactivate your passenger air bags. Your auto dealer or repair shop will deactivate your pass 0enger air bags only upon seeing written permission from the NHTSA. To learn about the air bag deactivation request and approval process, log on to www.safercar.gov, click on "Air Bags," and then click on "Air Bag Deactivation" in the left-hand menu bar.

My car has side-impact air bags in the back seat. Should I be worried about my child's safety?

If your vehicle is equipped with side-impact air bags, you need to learn whether the manufacturer has complied with voluntary testing procedures—known as "out-of-position testing"—to minimize the risk to children seated close to a side-impact air bag. (The federal government does not regulate side-impact air bags, so safety testing procedures for these air bags are optional.) To do so, check your owner's manual or ask your auto dealer or vehicle manufacturer. If your car was manufactured in 2004 or 2005, you can also find the answer at www.safercar. gov. Just click on "2004 & 2005 Vehicles with Side Air Bags," then click on your particular make and model number, and then scroll down until you see the column marked "SAB Out of Position Testing." (The NHTSA is planning on expanding its database to include side air bag testing information for 1997-2003 models in the near future.)

You won't have to worry if your car's side-impact air bags meet out-of-position testing specifications. But if you're not sure or if your car does not meet these specifications, then contact your vehicle's manufacturer to find out the safest place for your child to be seated in the back seat of your car. You can find contact numbers for major vehicle manufacturers at www.safercar.gov. Just click on "Air Bags," and then click on "Side-impact Air Bags" in the FAQs section in the left-hand menu bar.

My baby is off the charts, he is so big. What kind of car seat should I buy?

Because your baby is so big, he may outgrow an infant car seat long before he reaches age one. Instead, purchase a convertible car seat—one that can be used rear-facing at first and then forward-facing when your child is a toddler.

My baby was born premature, and she just swims around in even the smallest car seat. What can I do?

You may need a car bed instead of an infant car seat if your baby is extremely small. Check with your pediatrician for recommendations.

What is the safest way for my toddler to ride in a car?

Once your child is older than one and weighs more than 20 pounds, your child is ready for a forward-facing car seat in the back seat of your car. If you purchased a convertible car seat, you can use the same car seat that you used when your child was an infant—just facing forward instead of backward. But if your child's first car seat was an infant-only car seat, you'll need to purchase a new forward-facing toddler car seat for your child.

What is the safest way for my older child to ride in a car?

When your child weighs 40 pounds or so and reaches age four, your child will no longer be able to ride in a toddler seat. At that point, your child will be ready to sit in a booster seat in the back seat of your car. Your child should continue using a booster seat until your child is 4'9" or taller.

CAUTION

A seat belt is not enough. A child shorter than 4'9" is not ready to use an adult shoulder belt or lap belt without a booster seat, because the belt will not fit properly. In fact, using an adult safety belt without a booster seat is dangerous. The belt could cut into your child and injure your child's abdomen if an accident occurs.

ADDITIONAL RESOURCES

To see if your child needs a booster seat. For an older child, you might be unsure whether to use a booster seat. A terrific resource is www.boosterseat. gov, a website sponsored by the National Highway Transportation Safety Administration Just type in your child's age, weight, and height, and the site will tell you whether your child should ride in a booster seat.

My child no longer needs a booster seat. Can my child sit in the front seat now?

It depends on the age of your child. The safest place for a child younger than 12 is still the back seat.

How do I choose a safe car seat for my child?

All car seats must meet safety standards set by the National Highway Transportation Safety Administration (NHTSA) and must pass the agency's crash tests. Although every car seat on the market today is safe for your child to use, some car seats are safer than others. *Consumer Reports* conducts even more rigorous car seat crash testing than does the NHTSA, so it's a good idea to check *Consumer Reports* for its latest car seat recommendations.

Ease of use is also an important feature in a car seat. The easier it is to snap your child into a car seat, the less tempted you may be to keep your child in your lap for short rides. And the easier a car seat is to install in your car, the more likely you are to take your car seat with you when you travel in someone else's car. To find out which car seats get the highest marks for being easy to use, check out the NHTSA's "Child Safety Seat Ease of Use Ratings" at www.nhtsa.dot.gov/CPS/CSSRating/Index.cfm.

My car seat came with a registration card. Should I fill this out?

Yes, because the manufacturer needs to have your contact information on file so that it can get in touch with you if it ever recalls the seat. If you have a used car seat, complete the NHTSA's Child Safety Seat Registration Form. The NHTSA will then forward your contact information to the car seat's manufacturer. To find this registration form, log on to www.nhtsa.gov, click on "Child Safety Seat Information" in the Quick Links pull-down menu, and then click on the link marked "Child Safety Seat Registration for Your Child's Continued Safety."

How can I find out about car seat recalls?

Once you've purchased a car seat, the manufacturer should get in touch with you if the car seat you purchased is recalled for any reason (see above). But if you'd like to learn about a manufacturer's recall history before you choose a car seat for your child, the website of the NHTSA's Office of Defects Investigation has detailed recall information for each manufacturer. Just log on to www-odi.nhtsa.dot.gov/cars/problems/recalls/childseat.cfm to get started.

I'm not sure whether I've installed my car seat correctly. Is there a place I can go to have my car seat checked?

Many communities have child passenger safety inspection stations where you can go to have your car seat installation checked. To find the inspection station closest to you, log on to the NHTSA's website at www.nhtsa.dot.gov/CPS/CPSFitting/Index.cfm and enter your zip code.

ADDITIONAL RESOURCES

To learn more about using a car seat. The NHTSA's website at www.nhtsa.dot.gov/people/injury/childps/csr2001/csrhtml contains tips for the proper installation and use of your child's car seat.

My car was recently involved in an accident. Should I replace my child's car seat?

The NHTSA recommends that you replace your child's car seat after a moderate or severe crash—even if there is no obvious damage to the car seat. But you do not have to replace your child's car seat after a minor crash if all of the following requirements are met:

- you could drive the car away from the crash site
- the door nearest the car seat was not damaged
- there were no injuries to anyone in the car
- the air bags did not deploy, and
- there is no visible damage to the child's car seat.

I'm thinking about buying a used car seat. Do you have any advice?

It's best to buy a brand new car seat, if you can. But if you need to save a little money by purchasing a car seat second-hand, here are some important tips:

- Make sure the car seat has a label listing its manufacturing date. Don't buy a car seat more than six years old.
- Make sure that the label states that the car seat meets all federal motor vehicle safety standards.
- Ask the owner about previous car accidents. A car seat that has been in a car accident may no longer be safe.

- Inspect the car seat carefully. Check that the belts and buckles work correctly and that the car seat can be easily installed in your car. Also take a close look to make sure that there are no missing or broken parts.
- Confirm that the car seat has not been recalled (see above).

Do I have to use a car seat when I travel by cab?

It depends on where you live. Some states require you to use a car seat even if you are traveling by taxicab. Check with your state's department of transportation to find out about the law in your state. In New York City, for example, seatbelt and car seat laws do not apply to taxicabs, but if you bring your own car seat, the cab driver must allow you to install it and cannot refuse to give you a ride just because you wish to use it.

TIPS

Some car companies offer car seats. Instead of hailing a taxi, you might want to call a car company instead. Many companies have car seats in stock and (for a small additional fee) can send a car with an age-appropriate safety seat already installed.

Making do on trains and buses.
If you travel with your child on public transportation—such as buses and subways—you already know that installing a car seat is not an option. But the good news is that trains and buses are generally quite safe. Just use good sense: Keep your child away from closing doors and hold your child firmly while the bus or train is in motion.

Car safety is more than just buckling up. Never leave your child in an unlocked car, especially with the keys in the ignition, even if it's just for a minute while you run into the convenience store. And don't risk your child's safety by leaving your child in a locked car on a hot day. ■

I'm going on vacation, and I'll be renting a car. Can I rent a car seat as well?
If you are traveling within the United States, most major car rental companies will rent you a good quality, age-appropriate car seat along with your car. But you will have to pay a few extra dollars a day for the privilege of not having to lug your own car seat from home when you go on vacation.

Car rental companies in some international destinations, such as the South Pacific, may not rent out car seats (or they might be in bad shape and not age-appropriate).

Chapter 41

Safety While Traveling by Plane

Taking a baby on a plane can be a nerve-wracking experience, but with a little planning on your part, it is certainly doable. You must be aware of certain issues, however, such as whether your child can travel on your lap and whether your child needs a passport.

How long into my pregnancy can I continue flying?

The answer depends on your health and on airline policy. To learn about the former, talk to your doctor.

For the latter, it depends on the airline that you are flying. Some airlines—such as Continental Airlines—will let you fly up to seven days before your due date. (And if you want to fly within seven days of your due date, you just have to provide the airline with a doctor's note stating that you are fit to travel by plane.) Many airlines—such as United Airlines—require a doctor's note if you wish to travel in your ninth month of pregnancy. Finally, a few airlines—such as Virgin Atlantic—require a doctor's note once you've passed your 28th week of pregnancy. Be sure to check with your airline well in advance about their rules regarding pregnant travelers.

TIPS

Carry a doctor's note when you fly. Once you begin showing, it's a smart idea to tuck a doctor's note into your wallet confirming your due date and stating that you are fit to fly—even if your airline does not require it until much later in your pregnancy. This way, you won't run into trouble if, for example, an airline agent thinks you're in your ninth month when you're really in your seventh.

How soon can I travel with my baby?

Many airlines will not let you travel with a baby younger than seven days (although you probably won't want to fly with such a young baby, anyway). Check with your airline if you plan on traveling in the first few days after your baby's birth.

Will I have to purchase a separate airline ticket for my baby?

Under the Federal Aviation Administration (FAA) guidelines, you do not have to purchase an airline ticket for a child younger than two if you are flying within the United States. But be warned: If you don't buy a separate ticket, your child is not guaranteed a separate seat. This means that your baby may have to sit on your lap during the flight—but you won't have to pay a penny in airfare for your baby. If you're traveling internationally, however, you may have to pay 10% of the cost of an adult ticket just to have your little one share your seat.

Is it safe to travel with my baby on my lap during a flight?

No. If there is heavy turbulence, you may not be able to keep your grip on your child, and your child could be thrown against the ceiling or the back of the plane. For this reason, the American Academy of Pediatrics recommends that you pay for a separate seat for your child and keep your child in a car seat during the flight.

CAUTION

A safety harness isn't safe enough. You might be tempted to solve the problem with a so-called safety harness or vest that attaches your child to your seat belt while your child sits in your lap. But these safety harnesses do little to prevent injuries. The FAA does not certify or approve of these devices and has even banned their use during takeoff, landing, or taxiing. And many airlines will not permit the use of safety harnesses or vests at all.

TIPS

If you'd rather not pay for a separate seat. Your best bet is to travel during off-peak hours, when the flight is likely to be under-booked. This way, you may get a seat for your child without having to pay for it. And if you are traveling with a spouse or partner, ask for a window seat and an aisle seat (instead of two seats next to each other). Other passengers tend to avoid booking middle seats, so you'll have a better chance of having an empty seat in your row.

Do airlines offer any discounts for infant tickets?

For domestic travel, most airlines will offer a 50% discount off the regular rate for a child younger than two. But you may only save 25% on an international ticket for your child. To purchase a ticket at the infant rate, you often have to contact the airline directly (instead of booking your ticket online).

CAUTION

You may not get half off a promotional fare. The child discount usually applies to the published adult fare for your child. This means that if an airline is offering a special fare of $250 round trip from New York to San Francisco, for example, but the regular fare is $500, you'll probably have to pay $250 (not $125) for your child's ticket.

Once your child turns two, you may have to pay full price for airfare. But check with your airline.

Should I keep my child in a car seat during the flight?

The American Academy of Pediatrics recommends that a child weighing less than 40 pounds be kept in a car seat during air travel.

How do I know if my car seat is safe for airplane use?

First, check the label. It should say something like: "This restraint is certified for use in motor vehicles and aircraft."

Second, measure your car seat. If it is wider than 16", it probably won't fit in a coach (or economy) seat. Also, most airlines require that you keep your child in a window seat in a nonexit row. A family traveling with more than one child may have to sit in separate rows, so that each child can sit in a window seat.

CAUTION

Booster seats are not allowed. Most booster seats cannot be used during takeoff and landing, because crash tests have shown that booster seats do not provide enough protection for a child in an airplane seat.

Will my child's stroller count against my baggage allowance?

Many airlines do not count a stroller as a piece of baggage for purposes of the baggage allowance rules. If your airline lets you check two pieces of baggage, for example, you probably won't have to pay extra to check two suitcases plus a stroller. But baggage policies differ from airline to airline, so check to make sure.

To learn more about flying safely with a child. Check the Federal Aviation Administration's website at www.faa.gov/passengers/childtips. cfm to learn more about safe air travel with your child. Another useful resource is CPSafety, a nonprofit organization dedicated to safe travel for children. Log on to the organization's website at www .cpsafety.com and click on the link marked "Air Travel" in the left-hand menu bar.

TIPS

If you buy a seat for your child. Your child will qualify for a baggage allowance—which means that you can check additional baggage for free. For example, Delta Airlines will let you check two additional pieces of baggage if you buy a seat for your child on a domestic flight, so you can take your infant swing and your ExerSaucer, if you'd like.

How old must my child be to travel alone? If you have family members who live far away, you may want to send your little one to visit a grandma or an uncle—while you stay home. Of course, a big part of the answer to this question depends on your child. But as far as airline regulations are concerned, most will not allow a child younger than five to fly alone. If your child is between the ages of five and 14, most airlines will let your child travel alone on nonstop flights. Some airlines have higher age limits for connecting flights.

When your child is old enough to travel alone, the airline will provide supervision and assistance to your child during the flight. You'll have to pay extra for these unaccompanied minor services (even if you feel your child is perfectly capable of handling the journey without supervision). For domestic flights, expect to pay in the range of $40 to $50 each way for a nonstop flight and $75 each way for a connecting flight. The rates are usually higher for international flights.

I'm nervous about my eight-year-old son traveling alone. What should I do to prepare? Talk to the airline in advance about its unaccompanied minor services and ask what you can do to ensure a smooth trip for your child. Give your child a cellular phone, so that you can talk with your child once your child has passed security (if you cannot accompany your child to the gate) and before the plane takes off. Make sure your child has emergency contact information and a supply of cash to cover unexpected expenses.

Travel Identification for Your Child

If you're a seasoned traveler, you're used to whipping out your driver's license or passport when checking in at the airport. But you may not have given much thought to travel identification for your child.

If you are traveling domestically and you haven't purchased a ticket for your child because your child is younger than two, you'll need a birth certificate to prove your child's age. Similarly, you will need a birth certificate to prove your child's age if you purchased a special youth fare for your child.

If you are traveling abroad, your child will need a passport. The passport application process is a bit different for children than for grownups. You and your child's other parent must take your child and apply in person at a passport acceptance facility—usually a post office or public library specially designated to accept passport applications. (You cannot use a passport processing service to apply for a child's passport.) For the location of the passport acceptance facility nearest you, log on to the U.S. Department of State's website at http://iafdb.travel.state.gov and enter your zip code.

To apply, you'll need to complete a number of forms, provide identification for you and your child, and pay a fee. To find out more, check the U.S. Department of State's website. Just log on to http://travel.state.gov/passport/passport and click on "Minors Under Age 14" in the left-hand menu bar.

BABYCENTER RESOURCES

For some tips on traveling with your child. Traveling with your child can be an adventure unto itself. But with a little advance planning and advice from other well-traveled parents, it can be a pleasure. Go to the *Parent Savvy* page on BabyCenter.com (www .babycenter.com/parentsavvy) and look for the links to the "Travel with a Baby" or "Travel with a Toddler" sections. ■

Appendix

A

Contents

Resources for Parents

Adoptive and Foster Parents

- American Academy of Adoption Attorneys *www.adoptionattorneys.org*
- Casey Family Programs *www.casey.org*
- The Adoption Friendly Workplace *www.adoptionfriendlyworkplace.org*
- National Adoption Information Clearinghouse *www.naic.acf.hhs.gov*

Au Pairs

- Au Pair Association *www.iapa.org*
- Au Pair in America *www.aupairinamerica.com*
- InterExchange *www.interexchange.org*
- The U.S. State Department *www.exchanges.state.gov*

Breastfeeding

- La Leche League *www.lalecheleague.org*
- Medela *www.medela.com*

Day Care

- The Child Care Law Center *www.childcarelaw.org*
- Child Care Resource and Referral Agency *www.childcareaware.org*
- National Resource Center for Health and Safety in Child Care *www.nrc.uchsc.edu*
- National Association for the Education of Young Children *www.naeyc.org*
- National Association of Family Child Care *www.nafccc.org*

Doulas

- Doulas of North America website *www.dona.org*

Estate Planning

- American College Trust and Estate Counsel *www.actec.org*
- Nolo *www.nolo.com*

Family-Friendly Work Arrangements

- American Staffing Association *www.staffingday.net*
- Families and Work Institute *www.whenworkworks.org*
- Work Options *www.workoptions.com*

Family Physicians and Pediatricians

- Academy of Family Physicians *www.aafp.org*
- American Academy of Family Practice *www.familydoctor.org*
- The American Academy of Pediatrics *www.aap.org*
- The American Board of Family Medicine *www.theabfm.org*
- The American Board of Pediatrics *www.abp.org*
- Federation of State Medical Boards *www.fsmb.org*

Health Insurance

- The Agency for Healthcare Research and Quality *www.ahrq.com*
- National Association of Insurance Commissioners *www.naic.org*
- Insure.com's Health Insurance Law and Benefits Tool *http://info.insure.com/health/lawtool.cfm*
- The National Committee for Quality Assurance *www.hprc.ncqa.org*
- Insure Kids Now!, a division of the U.S. Department of Health and Human Services *www.insurekidsnow.gov*

Hospitals and Birth Centers

- Joint Commission on Accreditation of Healthcare Organizations *www.jcaho.org*
- The Commission for the Accreditation of Birth Centers *www.birthcenters.org*
- U.S. News/American Hospital Association National Directory *www.usnews.com/usnews/health/hospitals/hosp_home.htm*

Lesbian/Gay Parenting and Guardianship

- Lambda Legal *www.lambdalegal.org*
- National Center for Lesbian Rights *www.nclrights.org*

Life Insurance

- Accuqote *www.accuquote.com*
- A.M. Best's website *www.ambest.com*
- Consumer Federation of America *www.consumerfed.org*
- Insure.com *www.insure.com*
- The National Association of Insurance Commissioners *www.naic.com*
- *Smart Money's* online worksheet *http://smartmoney.com/insurance/life/#worksheet*
- Weiss Ratings Inc. *www.weissratings.com*

Medical Tests for Newborns

- The March of Dimes *www.marchofdimes.com*
- The National Newborn Screening and Genetics Resource Center
  http://genes-r-us.uthscsa.edu/index.htm

Midwives

- American College of Nurse Midwives Certification Council *www.accmidwife.org*
- Citizens for Midwifery *www.cfmidwifery.org*
- College of Nurse-Midwives *www.midwife.org*
- Midwifery Education Accreditation Council *www.meacschools.org*
- The North American Registry of Midwives *www.narm.org*

Nannies

- The Alliance of Professional Nanny Agencies *www.theapna.org*
- Citizenship and Immigration Services *www.uscis.gov*
- Driving Record.org *www.drivingrecord.org*
- The International Nanny Association *www.nanny.org*
- Nanny Check *www.nannycheck.com*
- Nanny Network *www.nannynetwork.com*
- The Parents for Megan's Law *www.parentsformeganslaw.com*
- US Search *www.ussearch.com*

- Breedlove & Associates *www.breedlove-online.com*
- Care Entrée *www.nannyinsurance.com*
- Eisenberg Associates *www.eisenbergassociates.com*
- Legally Nanny *www.legallynanny.com*
- The Insurance Information Institute *www.iii.org*
- Nanny Tax, Inc. *www.nannytax.com*
- PayCycle *www.paycycle.com*
- ProCare Benefit Card *www.procarecard.com*

Obstetricians

- American Board of Medical Specialties *www.abms.org*
- American Board of Obstetrics and Gynecology *www.abog.org*
- ChoiceTrust *www.choicetrust.com*
- HealthGrades *www.healthgrades.com*
- The Society for Maternal-Fetal Medicine *www.smfm.org*

Parental Leave

- National Partnership for Women & Families *www.nationalpartnership.org*
- The U.S. Department of Labor's Family and Medical Leave Act Advisor *www.dol.gov/elaws/esa/fmla/s1.asp*

Personal Finance

- Kiplinger *www.kiplinger.com*
- IRS *www.irs.gov*
- MSN Money *www.moneycentral.msn.com*
- *Smart Money www.smartmoney.com*

Rights in the Workplace

- Equal Employment Opportunity Commission *www.eeoc.gov*
- Equal Rights Advocates *www.equalrights.org*
- National Institute for Occupational Safety and Health *www.cdc.gov/niosh*
- Occupational Safety and Health Administration *www.osha.gov*
- Workplace Fairness *www.workplacefairness.org*

Safety

- CPSafety *www.cpsafety.com*
- Federal Aviation Administration *www.faa.gov*
- Booster Seat.gov *www.boosterseat.gov*
- National Highway Transportation Safety Administration *www.nhtsa.dot.gov*
- The Children's Health Environmental Coalition *www.checnet.org*
- National Lead Information Center *www.epa.gov/lead/nlic.htm*
- National Safety Council *www.nsc.org/issues/lead*
- Safe Housing Rule *www.hud.gov/offices/lead/leadtips.cfm*
- The U.S. Environmental Protection Agency's safe water section *www.epa.gov/safewater*
- Consumer Product Safety Commission *www.cpsc.org*
- *Consumer Reports www.consumerreports.org*
- The Federal Food and Drug Administration, "Parents Corner" *www.fda.gov/oc/opacom/kids/html/parents__corner.htm*
- Juvenile Products Manufacturers Association *www.jpma.org*
- Kids in Danger *www.kidsindanger.org*

Saving for Education

- Bonds Online *www.bondsonline.com*
- FMS Bonds.com *www.fmsbonds.com*
- College Board *www.collegeboard.com*
- Federal Student Aid *www.studentaid.ed.gov*
- Finaid *www.finaid.org*
- Independent 529 Plan *www.independent529plan.org*
- Saving For College.com *www.savingforcollege.com*

Tax Breaks

- The HSA Insider *www.hsainsider.com*
- IRS *www.irs.gov*
- Yahoo's Finance Tax Center *http://taxes.yahoo.com/stateforms.html*

The Uniform Transfers to Minors Act:

When Will Your Child Gain Control of the Assets in a Custodial Account?

STATE	Age at which your child will gain control	STATE	Age at which your child will gain control
Alabama	21	Montana	21
Alaska	18 (can be extended up to age 25)	Nebraska	21
Arizona	21	Nevada	18 (can be extended up to age 25)
Arkansas	21 (can be reduced to no lower than age 18)	New Hampshire	21
California	18 (can be extended up to age 25)	New Jersey	21 (can be reduced to no lower than age 18)
Colorado	21	New Mexico	21
Connecticut	21	New York	21
Delaware	21	North Carolina	21 (can be reduced to no lower than age 18)
District of Columbia	18	North Dakota	21
Florida	21	Ohio	21
Georgia	21	Oklahoma	18
Hawaii	21	Oregon	21 (can be extended up to age 25)
Idaho	21	Pennsylvania	21
Illinois	21	Rhode Island	18
Indiana	21	South Carolina	UTMA not adopted
Iowa	21	South Dakota	18
Kansas	21	Tennessee	21
Kentucky	18	Texas	21
Louisiana	18	Utah	21
Maine	18 (can be extended up to age 21)	Vermont	UTMA not adopted
Maryland	21	Virginia	18 (can be extended up to age 21)
Mass.	21	Washington	21
Michigan	18 (can be extended up to age 21)	West Virginia	21
Minnesota	21	Wisconsin	21
Mississippi	21	Wyoming	21
Missouri	21	■	

Index

Medical tests
  lead exposure testing, 362–63, 365
  for newborns, 43–45
  prenatal testing, 114
Medical treatment authorization, 183, 184, 188, 212
Medicines, as poison hazards, 370
Megan's Law database checks, 162
Midwives
  certified nurse midwives, 5–6, 19–22, 37, 114
  checking licenses/certification, 3
  direct entry midwives, 6, 22–24, 37
  health insurance coverage, 20, 114
Minimum wage law, nanny compensation and, 171, 172, 174
Mortgages. See Home mortgages
Municipal bonds, 240
Mutual funds accounts, in parent's name, 239–40

N

Naming children, 47, 48
Nannies, 141–88
  advantages and disadvantages, 141–42
  background checks, 147, 161–63, 165
  for backup care, 136
  basics, 132, 139
  benefits and perks, 147, 172, 177–78, 193
  cars and driver's licenses, 147, 148–49, 158
  checklist for finding/hiring, 149
  considerations before hiring, 142–49
  emergency preparedness/handling, 148, 155–56, 158, 182–83
  employers' legal obligations, 166, 168–70, 172, 174–75, 176
  employers' tax obligations, 147, 168, 174–76, 197
  employment agreements, 166, 175, 179–80, 181, 185–87, 194
  English ability, 148
  experience and training, 144–45, 157
  firing, 183–84
  getting a new nanny started, 181, 184

  health insurance for, 177–78
  immigration status, 147–48, 163, 169, 174, 179
  in-person interviews, 155–59
  interview follow-up, 160
  licensing requirements, 194
  live-in vs. live-out, 145–46
  paying, how and how much, 145, 146–47, 151, 165, 171–76
  paying, typical amounts, 135, 146
  paying under the table, 147, 175–76, 179, 287
  recordkeeping, 175
  reference checks, 147, 151, 152–53, 166, 168
  relatives as, 133
  searching for, 149, 150–51, 193
  sharing a nanny with another family, 132, 135, 139, 189–95
  telephone prescreening, 151–52
  time off/vacation/holidays, 173, 176–77, 180
  trial periods, 160
  work-at-home parents, 149
  working with an agency, 163–68
  work responsibilities, 141–42, 144
  work schedule, 143–44
  See also Au pairs
Nanny placement agencies, 163–68
National Adoption Information Clearinghouse, 307
National Center for Lesbian Rights (NCLR), 327
National Committee for Quality Assurance (NCQA), 112
National Highway Traffic Safety Administration (NHTSA), 355, 375–80
National Institute for Occupational Safety and Health, 75
National Lead Information Center (NLIC), 360, 364, 366
National Lead Safety Council (NSC), 360
National Newborn Screening and Genetics Resource Center, 43
National Partnership for Women & Families, 78, 84, 105

head-of-household filing status, 301–2

health insurance issues, 122–23, 125

legal guides for, 48

naming your child, 47

See also Same-sex couples

UPromise education rewards program, 273

UTMA (Uniform Transfers to Minors Act), 261, 333, 396–97

V

Vacation time

accrual, FMLA leave and, 79–80, 82

for nannies, 176, 180

using for doctor's appointments, 82

using for parental leave, 76, 77, 89

W

Water, lead contamination, 361, 365, 369

WebMD, 25

Websites. *See* BabyCenter.com; Online resources

Widow(er)s, special tax filing status for, 301, 302

Wills, 334, 337–42. *See also* Estate planning

Women for Hire, 91

Workers' compensation insurance, for nannies, 169–70

Working at home. *See* Telecommuting

Working Mother, 104

WorkLife Law, 108

Workplace Fairness, 73

Workplace issues, 65, 67

announcing pregnancy to employer, 68–70

breast milk expression/storage, 59–62

family-friendly work schedules, 93–104

hazardous/strenuous work while pregnant, 73–75, 76

job searches while pregnant, 75–76

switching jobs during pregnancy, 76, 117

time off during pregnancy, 68

time off for child-related issues, 105–6, 124

unfair treatment of parents, 107–8

unfair treatment while pregnant, 70–73

See also Child care; Health insurance; Parental leave; Work schedules

Work-related expenses, 88

Work schedules, 93–104, 392

basics, 93–96

best companies for family-friendly schedules, 104

child care options and, 100, 135, 145–46

compressed workweek schedules, 94, 100–101

flextime, 93, 94, 99–100

job sharing, 94–95, 96, 101–3

part-time schedules, 95, 103–4, 111, 124, 125

telecommuting, 94, 96, 98–99, 136

temping as alternative to full-time work, 98 ■

Remember:

Little publishers have big ears.
We really listen to you.

Take 2 Minutes & Give Us Your 2 cents

Your comments make a big difference in the development and revision of Nolo books and software. Please take a few minutes and register your Nolo product—and your comments—with us. Not only will your input make a difference, you'll receive special offers available only to registered owners of Nolo products on our newest books and software. Register now by:

PHONE
1-800-728-3555

FAX
1-800-645-0895

EMAIL
cs@nolo.com

or **MAIL** us
this registration card

fold here

Registration Card

NAME _____ DATE _____

ADDRESS _____

CITY _____ STATE _____ ZIP _____

PHONE _____ EMAIL _____

WHERE DID YOU HEAR ABOUT THIS PRODUCT? _____

WHERE DID YOU PURCHASE THIS PRODUCT? _____

DID YOU CONSULT A LAWYER? (PLEASE CIRCLE ONE)   YES   NO   NOT APPLICABLE

DID YOU FIND THIS BOOK HELPFUL?   (VERY)   5   4   3   2   1   (NOT AT ALL)

COMMENTS _____

_____

_____

WAS IT EASY TO USE?   (VERY EASY)   5   4   3   2   1   (VERY DIFFICULT)

We occasionally make our mailing list available to carefully selected companies whose products may be of interest to you.

☐ If you do not wish to receive mailings from these companies, please check this box.

☐ You can quote me in future Nolo promotional materials.
   Daytime phone number _____ .

PRNT 1.0

"Nolo helps lay people perform legal tasks without the aid—or fees—of lawyers."

—USA TODAY

Nolo books are ..."written in plain language, free of legal mumbo jumbo, and spiced with witty personal observations."

—ASSOCIATED PRESS

"...Nolo publications...guide people simply through the how, when, where and why of law."

—WASHINGTON POST

"Increasingly, people who are not lawyers are performing tasks usually regarded as legal work... And consumers, using books like Nolo's, do routine legal work themselves."

—NEW YORK TIMES

"...All of [Nolo's] books are easy-to-understand, are updated regularly, provide pull-out forms...and are often quite moving in their sense of compassion for the struggles of the lay reader."

—SAN FRANCISCO CHRONICLE

fold here

- -

Place
stamp here

ASHE COUNTY PUBLIC LIBRARY
148 Library Drive
West Jefferson, NC 28694-9793

Nolo
950 Parker Street
Berkeley, CA 94710-9867

Attn: PRNT 1.0